COLLECTION LATOMUS
VOL. 350

STRUCTURE AND PERFORMANCE IN THE ROMAN ECONOMY

MODELS, METHODS AND CASE STUDIES

LATOMUS

www.latomus.be

La Revue *Latomus*, fondée en 1937 par M.-A. KUGENER, L. HERRMANN et M. RENARD, ainsi que la « Collection Latomus », fondée en 1939 par M. RENARD, sont publiées par la « Société d'études latines de Bruxelles - Latomus », A.S.B.L. La revue paraît quatre fois par an. Elle forme annuellement un tome de 500 à 1.200 pages. Chaque article est signé et l'auteur en est seul responsable. Tout ouvrage intéressant les études latines adressé à la revue fera l'objet d'un compte rendu dans la mesure du possible, mais aucune réplique ne pourra être insérée.

Présentation des manuscrits : voir le site électronique <www.latomus.be>.

Contact : Prof. David ENGELS, directeur général de *Latomus*, Boîte Postale 54, B-1170 Bruxelles (Belgique), info@latomus.be.

Abonnements et commandes : Éditions Peeters, Bondgenotenlaan 153, B-3000 Leuven, Belgique. <peeters@peeters-leuven.be> ; site internet : <http://www.peeters-leuven.be>.

Pour l'achat des tomes I à XXI: Schmidt Periodicals GmbH, Dettendorf, D-83075 Bad Feilnbach <schmidt@periodicals.com> ; site internet : <http://www.periodicals.com>

COLLECTION LATOMUS
Fondée par M. Renard en 1939
Continuée par J. Dumortier-Bibauw et C. Deroux
Dirigée par D. Engels
VOLUME 350

Paul ERDKAMP and Koenraad VERBOVEN (eds.)

Structure and Performance in the Roman Economy

Models, Methods and Case Studies

ÉDITIONS LATOMUS
BRUXELLES
2015

ISBN 978-90-429-3280-7
D/2015/0602/53

Table of Contents

Preface

This is the first book published by the research network 'structural Determinants of Economic Performance in the Roman World' (2012-2016), funded by the Research Foundation Flanders (FWO) to stimulate research on Roman economic development. The network's aim is to identify the causes and constraints of economic growth and development in the Roman world. The eight papers we present here explore theories, models and methods that enhance our ability to explain Roman economic performance and offer relevant and original case studies. Seven were discussed at a meeting in Brussels in 2012, generously sponsored as a 'Contactforum' by the Royal Flemish Academy of Belgium for Science and the Arts. The paper by George Grantham was originally discussed at an authors' meeting in Ghent in 2013 for a book on 'Work, Labour and Professions in the Roman World'. The close ties it showed with the papers by Jeroen Poblome and Koenraad Verboven made us suggest the author to publish it here. We are grateful to him for generously accepting this suggestion. The paper by Wim Broekaert was written on invitation to complete the book with a contribution on Social Network Analysis.

Thanks are due to the Research Foundation Flanders (FWO) and the Royal Flemish Academy of Belgium for Science and the Arts for making this project financially feasible, and to Latomus for accepting to publish this volume in their 'Collection'. Last but not least we wish to thank our editorial assistants Kasey Reed, Luka Tjampens and Nicolas Solonakis for their help in preparing the manuscript.

Gent, March 2015

Koenraad VERBOVEN

Models or Muddles? What are Theories Good for in Ancient Economic History?

Explaining economic data is never straightforward. Common sense and intuition sometimes allow us to narrate what happened, and arrange historical and archaeological data in their chronological sequence and geographic location. This, however, tells us little about the interplay of forces beyond the agents' control, of structural constraints imposed on them, of the unintended effects of their actions, or of the institutional and physical constraints imposed on what they could and would do.

On the other hand, merely to avoid narratives is no solution either. Describing economic realities, with or without maps and graphs (where Rome's food came from, how much gold and silver was minted ...) is bound to give us a better sense of the scale and direction of output, distribution, and technological potential. But however sophisticated the means used to find and visualise them, data never in themselves explain the processes from which they are the outcomes. The graphs derived from lead isotope analyses of ice-core samples, for instance, show that lead and silver output increased from the late 6th c. BCE to peak in the 1st c. CE before going down again to reach an all-time low in the 9th c. CE, after which it took another eight centuries to get back to the Roman levels. But what made this increased output possible? Why did it decline—given that the known mining areas were not exhausted?[1]

To answer questions like these we need models—simplified versions of reality—and theories—sets of logical propositions tying the bits and pieces of a model together. Historians are no great model builders. We are trained to think bottom-up, to process data inductively. There is no need to be ashamed of this (if you are an historian), or to be smug and superior about it (if you're an economist). It is true that historians sometimes do their work merely by generalising through rule of thumb, recognising patterns from broken bits and pieces. But more rigid ways to process primary historical data are equally well established: prosopography, social network analysis, historical statistics,

[1] Cf. W. SCHEIDEL, *In Search of Roman Economic Growth* in *JRA* 22, 2009, p. 46-70.

Geographic Information Systems, and many more techniques have long become standard instruments in the historian's toolbox. Sometimes, however, a 'fuzzy-pattern-recognizing-approach' is the only sensible way to progress. Using inferential statistics to process poorly preserved primary data, scattered through time and space, might look awesome to the blushing historian and comfortably familiar to the cool economist, but does not produce reliable derived data.

Historians are experts in interpreting the damage done to a body of evidence by time or by human preferences and schemes. It is their job to deliver data that are sound, or at least to identify those that are not. Economists, on the other hand, are trained model builders and users. They are wont to pick up 'signals' through the noise of real-life data that confirm, contradict or improve their models. But they are abysmally bad at picking up signals that aren't broadcasted on the frequency their models are attuned to. Economic historians (why isn't there a word to describe historical economists?) should ideally be good at both.

Social life is infinitely complex. Society is made up of unique individuals that are all autonomous agents. The interactions in which they engage are infinitely varied. Yet not all events have the same impact. Not all that happens shapes the course of history to the same extent. Theoretical models are useful because they help to identify which events matter more and how they possibly and logically relate to each other.

There are, however, risks involved for historians using theoretical models designed by social scientists. A familiar critique by colleagues who reject model based approaches runs like this: "You find only what you set out to find, you see only what your model allows you to label." That may be true if you lock yourself up in your room and stop reading your colleagues' work. I doubt, however, that any professional historian who actively participates in academic debates, has the luxury or audacity to ignore what does not fit into his or her preferred model. Models and theories certainly have their limits. We should rightly be aware of the limitations of the models we apply, but that is equally true of the informal mental models with which even the most persistent positivist tries to make sense of his sources—"die reinen, unverfälschten Zeugen der Vergangenheit".[2] Setting out to answer research questions always limits the scope of what we aim to do. Every answer needs a question. Every question allows only a limited number of answers.

Potentially more problematic is the enthusiasm with which some of us (I plead guilty) embrace flashy theoretical models that promise a new approach to dusty old reality. Such 'catwalk models' come and go. They brighten up the show, but what is left when they have gone? A good question, but hardly a reason not to try out new models. Even the most evanescent catwalk models matter over time. How many of us still dress the way our parents did? Where

[2] H. BENGTSON, *Einführung in die Alte Geschichte*, 2. Ausgabe, München, 1962, p. 61-62.

have all the flowery wall-papers gone that dressed our grandparents' houses? The bell-bottom trousers and tie-dye shirts of the hippie '60s? Some social-science models applied in historical research will no doubt turn out to be less useful or robust than hoped for. But that does not necessarily mean that they will not have a positive impact on how debates evolve.

The critique does alert us, however, to a property of theoretical models that is often overlooked: they are never final. The truth is always out there. It is never contained in any model or theory. These are only means to explain a reality too complex for us to grasp intuitively. Theoretical models have greatly increased our understanding of reality, but they have done so by improving on previous ones and giving way to new ones. As Ptolemy's model was overtaken by Copernicus' and Kepler's, Newton's laws of gravitation and motion by Einstein's relativity theory and Quantum Mechanics, so too in social sciences theories and models are not made for eternity. Over the past decades, more than any other social science, economics has experienced major shifts and changes in its core theories. New Institutional Economics improved drastically on neo-classical equilibrium theory. Behavioural economics showed fundamental flaws in rational action theory. Complexity economics offers a way to tackle the out-of-equilibrium dynamics of real economies, beyond the grasp of neo-classical general equilibrium theory. Mainstream economics has become a bursting field of exciting, often conflicting new ideas and approaches.[3] Clearly, this poses a challenge to economic historians: which models should we use? What is their potential? What are their limitations? What imperfections of previous models do they address?

We hope that this book will help ancient historians to assess the possibilities of some of the theories and models that are currently available. Most of all, however, we hope that it will make them aware of the need to reflect on the models they wish to use.

The first part of this book discusses a number of models used or ready-to-use in economic history research of other periods. We haven't included a specific chapter on neo-classical economic theory. Partly because we felt that, being at the core of economic sciences, it is sufficiently (even though only indirectly) covered in the contributions that have been included. Partly also because we feel that we cannot improve on the excellent introduction to it given by Peter Temin in the recent Cambridge Companion to the Roman Economy.[4]

[3] A tenured professor at the MIT Department of Economics once told me that he aimed to "take the market out of economics" (it goes to show you never can tell).

[4] P. TEMIN, *The Contribution of Economics* in W. SCHEIDEL (ed.), *The Cambridge Companion to the Roman Economy*, Cambridge, 2012, p. 45-70. See also P. TEMIN, *The Roman Market Economy*, Princeton, N.J., 2013.

Ancient historians have to work with very few or highly problematic data (usually a combination of both) that make it hard to validate or disprove models, and thus to identify and assess their explanatory potential. By using comparative history, Erdkamp argues, ancient historians can find models that have been validated for other pre-industrial societies and then study whether the conditions under which such a model works are also present for the ancient world.

Verboven discusses the pros and cons of New Institutional Economics—very popular today among ancient historians, but under heavy criticism from medieval and early-modern historians. He points also to other promising theories in economics today, such as Behavioural Economics and Developments Economics that have hardly been tried yet in ancient economic history.

Grantham discusses an alternative to the 'general equilibrium model' of neoclassical theory: the 'search equilibrium model' (SEM) developed by Peter Diamond. Contrary to the neoclassical model, SEMs are dynamic systems with multiple equilibrium states between which they continuously hover in response to even minor stochastic shocks. SEMs explain changes in supply by the number of potential matches between agents selling and buying products, without imagining a price-setting mechanism to guide producers. The model allows huge and sudden swings without requiring changes in exogenous variables as technology or population levels. Its attraction for ancient historians is partly that it draws attention to the economic effects of urbanization and increased connectivity.

Poblome proposes an even more substantial paradigm shift by advocating Complex Adaptive Systems (CAS) as an analytical model. Complex systems theory studies the emergent properties of systems that consist of interacting autonomous sub-entities, such as economic agents. Each agent acts independently but in response to the actions of other agents. Change does not come (only) from outside the system—as it does in neoclassical equilibrium theory—but is a feature of the system itself. Overall growth is possible in CASystems, but it is typically non-linear. The system's constituent parts continuously shift and change—some going up, some going down. The system as a whole follows an 'adaptive cycle' characterized by growth, consolidation, collapse and reorganization. Consequently linear trends in archaeo-economic proxy-data cannot be read as signalling overall growth or decline. Instead the adaptive cycle of which they are part must be identified.

The second part of the book focuses on methodologies. Theoretical models alone are impotent. Being mere intellectual constructs designed to explain reality, the validity of theoretical models depends on how successful they are in explaining empirical observations. This is where methodology comes in, providing the tools to 'translate' raw data—textual or non-textual, human or natural—in formats that fit the vocabulary of the theories we wish to test.

Methodology itself may rely on empirical models that process empirical data in a mathematical format to reveal patterns in how the data are (or may be) related. The mathematical format allows further analysis and visualisation by means of a computer. Empirical models provide a link between reality and theory. They allow us to contradict or confirm propositions derived from theoretical models. Statistical models provide the most familiar example of this category of models, but they are far from being the only ones.[5] Social Network Analysis has been particularly popular the past years. Wim Broekaert shows its potential for ancient economic history by a case study of the Roman boards of *magistri* attested on Delos. The results are consistent with the view proposed by Hatzfeld and Flambard that these *magistri* were the officers of private associations of Roman businessmen, rather than representatives of the Roman community on island, as recently proposed by Hasenohr.

But there are limits to what is possible in ancient history. We rarely have the data to construct formal empirical models. Many questions inevitably can be tackled only through informal models. The methodology is qualitative and often looks more familiar to historians.

Dennis Kehoe gives us an example by analysing the distributional effects of the social and legal institutions documented in the Roman Empire. The existence of these institutions and the continuing central role they played in maintaining the imperial political system implies that peasants and lower-middle income urban groups were not destitute. The empire could only exist as long as it could rely on a substantial lower-middle-segment of the population living reliably—although probably not very much—above subsistence level. Hence imperial institutions offered protection to these groups and redistributed resources if necessary.

Annalisa Marzano's contribution shows the methodological potential of archaeology in addressing questions of economic development. The archaeology of Roman villas shows profound changes in the economic organization of a region. It evidences large capital investments, transfer of technological know-how, changes in management practice and labour organization, social networks of the owner providing access to information, capital, means of transportation and markets and so forth. Many of the relevant archaeological data can be quantified to show patterns of development. While it remains impossible to translate these proxy-data into macro-economic growth indicators (such as GDP), they make it very hard to argue for models that would exclude growth or expanding markets.

[5] A wonderful example of data-modelling is *ORBIS. The Stanford Geospatial Network Model of the Roman World*, orbis.stanford.edu, created by Walter Scheidel and Elijah Meeks.

The last contribution by Anne Kolb surveys the epigraphic evidence of technological know-how. The inscriptions are not very numerous, but they nevertheless show the self-confidence and pride of the commissioners or executioners of extraordinary technological feats.

PART I.
THEORIES AND MODELS

Paul ERDKAMP

Structural Determinants of Economic Performance in the Roman World and Early Modern Europe. A Comparative Approach

1 Introduction: evidence and models

Although archaeologists and historians have extracted a veritable mass of data on the economy of the Roman world from a wide range of sources, it is an understatement to say that the study of the Roman economy is hampered by a lack of data on some of the core issues in economic analysis, such as population, division of labour, and trends in wages and prices. Symptomatic of our ignorance are the extremely wide margins in the debate on the population size of such well-documented regions as Italy or Egypt. Market prices of grain in the entire Roman Empire over a period of centuries can be counted on the fingers of two hands, while division of labour has to be studied by counting the number of occupations mentioned on gravestones. When historians working on the economy of early modern Europe complain about the difficulties of their data on population sizes and densities, mortality and fertility, wages and living standards, they may expect little sympathy from ancient historians, whose response can merely be "if only…".

Archaeologists offer many proxy-data that partly help to circumvent this shortage, varying from shipwrecks to olive presses and pottery sherds, but sufficient clarity about the economic context of these data is often lacking. A basic problem in evaluating this kind of evidence is that each of these proxy-data can only be assessed relatively, not absolutely. In other words, each phenomenon is plotted on its own map, with its own, unknown scale, which hampers our attempt to integrate these individual figures into one map of Roman economic development. In his chapter, Jeroen Poblome discusses the problems in interpreting the scales and processes in the Roman economy on the basis of archaeological data, stressing the need for interpretative models.

The problems of the textual evidence hardly require elaboration: the written evidence on economic issues is not only sparse, but also one-sided, fragmented, and distorted. Again, context is lacking, though in a different way than regarding archaeological data. To give an example, if Pliny the Younger tells us about the shift on his estate from monetary rents into a sharecropping arrangement, we have some information on the characteristics and context of this particular case, but it remains a single case, which may be typical or not, and its general implications are difficult to ascertain.

The shortcomings of the evidence hamper quantification and causality. Both problems were at the heart of the controversy between primitivists and modernists, a debate that many of us are eager to declare settled. But while we can confidently state that much progress has been made in our understanding of the Roman economy since the days of Moses Finley, we are still confronted with some basic uncertainties. Sure, commerce was much more important than Finley allowed for, but it remains unclear how much of the income of the elites or other segments of society was based on trade. Increasing wealth seems likely, but how much did the urban or rural populace actually consume? Was the population of the Roman Empire, except for a tiny minority, living just slightly above subsistence level, as some assume, or were most people at the height of the empire more prosperous and healthy than most Europeans in the next 1500 years, as others postulate? In short, despite the wealth of data to study, it remains difficult to quantify the economic performance of the Roman world, and to establish its determining factors purely on the basis of the ancient evidence.

To overcome the shortcomings of the ancient evidence it is necessary to apply models that derive from the study of societies that offer sufficient empirical data to understand the causal relationships that underlie their economic development. It is not quantification that will profit most from this comparative method. The study of early-modern Europe or imperial China will not provide the missing statistics for the ancient world. However, the application of social and economic models and concepts is crucial for understanding the structural determinants of economic performance in the Roman world. Some archaeologists and historians remain sceptical regarding the application of 'external' ideas that are seen as imposed on the ancient data. They are right insofar as the model in itself does not constitute proof. That Europe or China went down a particular path of economic growth does not mean that the Roman Empire went down the same path, even if economic growth in the Roman world may be considered likely on the basis of the ancient evidence. But that should not be the purpose of the comparative exercise. Making sense of a myriad of historical data is always a question of imposing a pattern of causal relationships that do not stem from the data themselves but is the result of underlying assumptions—assumptions that can be adjusted in order to fit the evidence. Sometimes mere intuition based on common-sense knowledge about how the world works is sufficient to offer a valid interpretation of our data, but we should realize that intuition is influenced by our perception of patterns. Even stronger: data do not pop up by themselves, but are at least in part the result of the patterns that we impose. Hence, we tend to see what we expect to see, and thus it is better to be explicit and critical regarding the assumptions that underlie the patterns that we construct.

Because it is necessary for our discipline to use models and concepts derived from the study of other periods, the contribution that ancient history can make by itself to the evaluation and perfection of such models and analytical tools is inevitably limited. In his brilliant study of Greco-Roman Egypt, Andrew Monson not only makes excellent use of insights from the social sciences to clarify developments in Ptolemaic and Roman Egypt, he is also confident about "the ability of historical evidence and papyrological data in particular [...] to lend empirical support to theories whose implications extend beyond the study of Greco-Roman Egypt."[1] However, as we need the economic and social models derived from later times to interpret the ancient data and thus optimize our understanding of ancient developments, we would run the danger of circular reasoning to use these same results to confirm the validity of the models that we applied. It must be feared that ancient history will very much remain a consumer of other disciplines' theories, having little to return beyond the conclusion that one model fits the ancient data better than the other.

While the use of social and economic theory to provide the analytical tools for ancient history has become widespread, it is a different matter where to find the best comparison to the classical world. Influenced by Polanyi's emphasis on extra-economic aspects, it was for some time common to seek parallels in anthropological studies of contemporary pre-modern tribes and peoples, but while the value of some of these approaches cannot be denied, from an economic perspective the Roman world is better served by a comparison with more complex societies. Owing to its common roots in the Greco-Roman world, but also because of historiographical traditions and access to source-material and modern publications, ancient historians tended to seek comparisons in pre-industrial Europe.[2] Although the result has been a growing understanding of the factors underlying socio-economic and demographic developments in the ancient Mediterranean world, this tendency has caused a restriction and delimitation of research perspectives. Realizing that the a priori assumptions implicit in the focus on pre-industrial Europe restricts and delimits the outcomes of the comparative method, the outlook of ancient historians has rightly broadened to include Asian societies, in particular India (Peter Bang[3]) and China (Walter Scheidel). In some

[1] A. MONSON, *From the Ptolemies to the Romans. Political and Economic Change in Egypt*, Cambridge, 2012.

[2] W. SCHEIDEL, *Rome and China. Comparative Perspectives on Ancient World Empires*, Oxford, 2009, p. 3-10.

[3] P. BANG, *The Roman Bazaar. A Comparative Study of Trade and Markets in a Tributary Economy*, Cambridge, 2008. For a critique, see M. SILVER, *Historical Otherness, the Roman Bazaar, and Primitivism: P.F. Bang on the Roman Economy* in *JRA* 22, 2009, p. 421-440.

respects the resemblance between the Roman Empire and imperial China seems closer, as both empires were clearly not an agglomeration of emerging nation states, as early-modern Europe was. Moreover, both empires depended to a large extent on the functioning of largely self-governing cities, whose economic and political relations to the surrounding countryside was different from that of the cities of early Europe. Nevertheless, we should not dismiss the usefulness of the models that are derived from the study of early-modern Europe, in particular because the study of the economic development of Europe is less hampered by a dearth of quantifiable data than the Mediterranean or East-Asian ancient world. Moreover, the value of the comparative method is not directly based on the degree of resemblance, but on the ability to shed light on the factors underlying economic developments.

The remainder of this article will discuss the contribution that recent research on the economic history of pre-industrial Europe can make to our understanding of developments in the ancient world. Before discussing various key themes in recent economic history, we may start with a few general notions which may productively be applied in the research of ancient historians and archaeologists.

(1.) Realizing that world history cannot be divided into a post-industrial era of growth and a homogeneous pre-industrial era of inertia, economic historians are looking further and further back in history to find cases of significant growth. While the economic history studied by economic historians used to begin with the High Middle Ages, scholars like George Grantham and J. Goldstone have included the Roman world in their vision of long-term developments.[4] In other words, both ancient and modern historians agree that the economic history of classical antiquity is not significantly different from that of later times and can be studied in the same terms.

(2.) Nations like England and the Netherlands went down a certain path towards economic growth, in which agriculture modernized early, leading on the one hand to modern cultivation techniques and optimizing levels of labour input, on the other to a relatively low share of agriculture in the occupational structure of the population, resulting in high levels of specialization and productivity. However, other countries went down different paths, and the realization is that economic growth is not a fixed route from A to B. Hence, other countries should not be analysed in terms of resemblance to the 'ideal' situation of England and the Low Countries.

(3.) Recent studies emphasize that economic growth stems from the interplay of urbanization, division of labour, specialization, increasing labour productivity

[4] G. Grantham, *Contra Ricardo: on the Macroeconomics of Pre-Industrial Economies* in *European Review of Economic History* 3, 1999, p. 199-232; J. Goldstone, *Efflorescences and Economic Growth in World History: Rethinking the 'Rise of the West' and the Industrial Revolution* in *Journal of World History* 13, 2002, p. 323-389.

and market integration, taking place against the background of an increasingly productive agriculture. Wrigley rightly points out that this is a "unitary process", which means that there is no point in trying to identify a single factor that triggered growth, as all changes occur simultaneously in a mutually enforcing process.[5] Hence, 'chicken or egg'-debates on whether technological innovation or increasing urbanization were cause or effect are pointless in the sense that all variables were causes and effects at the same time.

(4.) A valuable concept is that of 'inefficiencies', referring to the inefficient allocation of production factors hampering economic growth.[6] The insight that the productive potential of past economies was not realized radically changes our approach to economic growth, as it implies that economic growth was the result of a more efficient allocation of production factors rather than being dependent on new technologies or innovations. It was not the backward nature of pre-industrial agriculture, trade, or manufacture that limited economic performance, it was rather that the productive potential of agriculture, trade, or manufacture could not be realized by the inefficient allocation of labour, capital and other means of production. Hence, changes in society that caused shifts in the allocation of production factors are crucial for our understanding of economic development.

(5.) Older models favoured supply-side factors, i.e. changes on the production-side of the equation, but more recently the importance of demand-side factors are emphasized: under the heading of 'industrious revolution', De Vries argued that as workers and producers encountered increasing opportunities to consume, they became more willing to work harder in order to consume more.[7] In other words, consumption patterns, living standards and social inequality have moved into the focus of the study of economic growth.[8]

[5] E. A. WRIGLEY, *The Transition to an Advanced Organic Economy: Half a Millennium of English Agriculture* in *Economic History Review* 59, 2006, p. 468-469.

[6] S. R. EPSTEIN, *The Rise of the West* in J.A. HALL / R. SCHROEDER, *An Anatomy of Power. The Social Theory of Michael Mann*, Cambridge, 2006, p. 253-255. Also B. J. P. VAN BAVEL, *Markets for Land, Labor, and Capital in Northern Italy and the Low Countries, Twelfth to Seventeenth Centuries* in *Journal of Interdisciplinary History* 41, 2011, p. 503-531.

[7] J. DE VRIES, *The Industrious Revolution. Consumer Behaviour and the Household Economy, 1650 to the Present*, Cambridge, 2008. Cf. R. C. ALLEN / J. L. WEISDORF, *Was there an 'Industrious Revolution' Before the Industrial Revolution? An Empirical Exercise for England, c. 1300-1830* in *Economic History Review* 64, 2011, p. 715-729.

[8] S. BROADBERRY / B. GUPTA, *The Early Modern Great Divergence: Wages, Prices and Economic Development in Europe and Asia, 1500-1800* in *Economic History Review* 599, 2006, p. 2-31; R.C. ALLEN *et al.*, *Wages, Prices, and Living Standards in China, 1738-1925: in Comparison with Europe, Japan, and India* in *Economic History Review* 64, 2011, p. 8-38; P. MALANIMA, *When Did England Overtake Italy? Medieval and Early Modern Divergence in Prices and Wages* in *European Review of Economic History* 17, 2013, p. 45-70. On the ancient world, see in particular W. SCHEIDEL, *Real Wages in Early Economies. Evidence for Living Standards from 1800 BCE to 1300 CE* in *Journal of the Economic and*

(6.) Finally we must mention New Institutional Economics, which for more than a decade has stimulated valuable new approaches to the economic history of the ancient world. Research from a NIE-perspective is not standing still, as is elaborated by Koen Verboven in this volume. There has been a tendency among ancient historians to approach NIE solely from an 'optimistic' angle and to focus on those elements in Roman society that lessened transactions costs and allowed the commercial sectors to perform better, such as Roman law, improved travel and communication, and institutions such as the *collegia*. Taking the lead from modern historians,[9] NIE-inspired research into the ancient world is now becoming more balanced, taking also into account those features of ancient society that hampered the full exploitation of economic opportunities.

It is clear that these trends in modern economic history, in particular the emphasis on the formal and informal institutions of NIE and the social and political context of the allocation of resources, have brought social, political and cultural aspects back into the study of the ancient economy. In his chapter, Kehoe combines both issues by arguing that legal and social institutions had an important effect on the distribution of wealth in the Roman Empire and on the performance of the economy in general. While the primitivist standpoints of Moses Finley must be rejected as incompatible with the empirical data on the ancient economy, his viewpoints remain very much part of the modern debate.

2 Population, land and agriculture

Ancient historians face an almost complete lack of figures that would allow us to estimate directly total production in the Roman world. In the absence of precise and reliable figures, economic historians of later periods regard population density and urbanization rate as good indicators of economic performance, which is based on the idea that a denser population inevitably reflects a more productive use of the land.[10] Moreover, urban populations are less involved in working the land, which means that a higher urbanization rate reflects the ability to sustain larger non-agricultural sectors. As urban populations generally tend to have higher living standards, a larger percentage of urban dwellers means a more than proportionate increase of total agricultural production. In the case of the Roman

Social History of the Orient 53, 2010, p. 425-462.

[9] In particular, S. OGILVIE, *'Whatever is, is Right'? Economic Institutions in Pre-Industrial Europe* in *Economic History Review* 60, 2007, p. 649-684.

[10] P. MALANIMA, *Urbanisation and the Italian Economy during the Last Millennium* in *European Review of Economic History* 9, 2005, p. 97-122; P. MALANIMA, *The Long Decline of a Leading Economy: GDP in Central and Northern Italy, 1300-1913* in *European Review of Economic History* 15, 2010, p. 169-219.

world, both indicators support the notion of economic growth, since both the population density and urbanization rate increased. According to the estimates of Walter Scheidel, the population of the region of the Roman Empire quadrupled between 1200 BC and AD 200, while cities had an increasing share in this growing population.[11] In that sense, economic growth is beyond doubt, even though direct figures on production or productivity are lacking for antiquity.

Ancient historians have often referred to the models of Thomas Malthus and Ester Boserup to stress the tension between demographic growth and available land. Land is a limited good, the Neo-Malthusian model emphasizes, and increased pressure on this limited production factor, which can only be made partly good by the clearance of marginal lands, inevitably leads to a fall in per capita production. Boserup, on the other hand, points out that agricultural societies respond to the increased demographic pressure by changing into more labour-intensive cultivation practices. However, without significant technological progress, it is often argued, investing more and more labour in the same amount of land leads to a drop in labour productivity. Neo-Malthusians are pessimistic about the progress in per capita production that can be made under conditions of population growth.[12] In particular, as they believe that up to the demographic transition of the 19th and 20th centuries, a rise in per capita income inevitably stimulated fertility levels. However, this aspect must remain outside our discussion. The Neo-Malthusian model also predicts that population decline would cause livings standards to rise, confirmation of which can be seen in precisely such a trend in western Europe in the post-Black Death era.

Recent publications, however, have questioned the general validity of the model. Persson points out that the countries that during the past millennium best conform to the Malthusian prediction are precisely those countries that had the lowest population densities and where room for population growth—quite literally—should have been greatest.[13] Equally contradicting the Neo-Malthusian prediction is the contraction of the per capita income in parts of Spain by one quarter between the 1340s and 1370s.[14] Also the Roman world does not quite fit the Malthusian model. The most densely populated parts of the Roman Empire have to be sought in the Mediterranean heartlands and in the Near East, and it is precisely in the regions with a long history of dense habitation and urbanization,

[11] W. SCHEIDEL, *Demography* in W. SCHEIDEL / I. MORRIS / R. P. SALLER (eds.), *The Cambridge Economic History of the Greco-Roman World*, Cambridge, 2007, p. 42.

[12] Boldly stated in G. CLARK, *A Farewell to Alms. A Brief Economic History of the World*, Princeton, 2007. Also G. CLARK, *In Defense of the Malthusian Interpretation of History* in *European Review of Economic History* 12, 2008, p. 175-199.

[13] K. G. PERSSON, *The Malthus Delusion* in *European Review of Economic History* 12, 2008, p. 165-173; G. GRANTHAM, *Explaining the Industrial Transition. A Non-Malthusian Perspective* in *European Review of Economic History* 12, 2008, p. 155-165.

[14] C. ALVAREZ-NOGAL / L. PRADOS DE LA ESCOSURA, *The Rise and Fall of Spain (1270-1850)* in *Economic History Review* 66, 2013, p. 3-19.

such as Egypt, Palestine and Syria, that the population continued to increase until the 5th and 6th centuries AD. In contrast, we see falling population and urbanization levels already from the 3rd century AD onwards in west and central Europe. Hence, the regions that show the earliest fall of population and urbanization levels are precisely those that should have least exhausted available land, while those regions that exploited the countryside most intensively show signs of continued population growth.

On a related note, economic historians of early modern Europe have argued that agricultural production was more elastic than the Neo-Malthusian model assumes. Improved methods of cultivation and higher yields were partly the result of increased levels of specialization in farming, partly of the increased scale of production.

In addition, shifts within the inefficient allocation of resources contributed to increases in output without concomitant increases in input. In the first place, a variable part of the agricultural surplus did not reach consumers. Pre-industrial producers were faced with permanent uncertainty about future production, while for various reasons the market in grains and other staple foods was unable to eliminate this uncertainty. If the harvest failed, smallholders could not simply buy what they needed, if only because they did not have sufficient reserves and buying power. Hence, the weaker the market integration, the stronger the incentive to overproduce, while the weakness of the market meant that the production over and above normal needs did not find its way to outside consumers. Hence, it was often a question of feasting on bread and feeding the rest to the household's animals in good years, slaughtering the animals and eating the fodder, including acorns, in bad years. The result of weak markets and risk-avoiding production strategies was that on average a large part of the arable land was not turned to optimal use. Improved market integration reduced the risk in bad years and provided the opportunity to sell local surplus in good years, thereby improving the allocation of resources. Another instance of 'inefficiency' is caused by the tendency among smallholders to employ too many workers on the land. This tendency is caused by the lack of adequate employment opportunities outside the family farm. All those household members who did not find employment elsewhere worked the land, resulting in inefficiently high levels of labour input. Insofar as changes in the wider economy opened up employment opportunities outside the farm, labour input was adjusted to more productive levels. The emergence of landed estates at the cost of smallholding farms that optimized their labour input by employing permanent servile workforces next to seasonal labourers had the same effect. In short, the inefficiencies in the distribution of agricultural surpluses and labour offered much scope for improving agricultural production.

3 Investment and technology

Archaeology reveals the scale of capital-intensive market-oriented agriculture in the Roman world, as may be seen in the contribution by Annalisa Marzano in this volume. To the extent that capital was invested in costly installations for such less essential crops as wine and olives, the investment was not so much a response to the increased demographic pressure on the land, as to the emergence of prosperous urban markets. Moreover, some of the costly installations aimed at reducing labour input, not at raising land productivity. On the other hand, investment in irrigation and drainage systems, which also benefited the cultivation of grains and other staple foods, may reflect a need to expand the available land for arable farming and to increase its productivity in order to feed an increasing population. However, this does not change the fact that investments were only economical when there was a sufficiently prosperous and stable market for the farm's products. European developments show that small and dispersed markets were too volatile and costly to sustain capital-intensive farming. In other words, the emergence of prosperous cities stimulated capital-intensive farming in their hinterlands and in those regions that had easy access to external markets and at the same time stimulated the utilization and further development of innovative technologies.[15] Moreover, the same emergence of urban markets increased the demand for manufactured goods, whose raw materials, including leather, wool, and flax, were often produced on the land as well, which further stimulated investments in agriculture.[16] Hence, technological innovation in agriculture did not so much trigger the increases in surplus production that allowed population growth and higher levels of urbanization, as it was a response to the changes in market conditions that accompanied larger cities and higher population densities.[17]

In the words of the economic historian Regina Grafe, there was a tremendous amount of 'slack' in the early-modern economy and this image seems also promising for the Roman economy, where growth should not be seen in terms of maximizing potential output but in terms of realizing the output that was already possible.[18] Technological progress in the Roman world offers some cases in point. For example, the technology to build large ships was already known in Hellenistic times, but it was only in Roman times that conditions encouraged more large vessels to be built and used on the structural transport routes across the

[15] GRANTHAM, *Explaining* [n. 13], p. 161.

[16] WRIGLEY, *Transition* [n. 5]; R. C. ALLEN, *Progress and Poverty in Early Modern Europe* in *Economic History Review* 56, 2003, p. 418.

[17] ALLEN, *Progress and Poverty* [n. 16], *loc.cit.*

[18] R. GRAFE, *Distant Tyranny. Markets, Power, and Backwardness in Spain, 1650-1800*, Princeton, 2012, p. 198.

Mediterranean. Likewise, as Andrew Wilson has shown, irrigation and drainage was applied on a larger scale in Roman times than ever before, but the technological know-how pre-dates Roman times. These developments realized already available increases in agricultural productivity and efficiency in shipment.[19]

4 Urbanization

In early-modern Europe, one crucial element in the process of removing slack consisted of the shift of labour within agriculture towards other economic sectors.[20] Rather than seeing the large proportion of the population working the land as the consequence of the unproductiveness of a backward economy, it is more accurate to see the high proportion in agriculture as restraining economic performance, including that of agriculture. This process is characterized by the interplay of factors that on the one hand stimulated a shift to non-agricultural sectors, on the other constrained further development.

Urbanization is as much a result of this development as it is a factor driving economic performance. Urbanization reflects a shift in the occupational structure, as the urban population was less involved in agricultural production. Increased urbanization thus indicates higher levels of agricultural labour productivity. As the case of cities like London or Madrid shows, the presence of large cities stimulated agricultural developments in their hinterland, which was caused not only by the higher demand, but also by the increased stability of demand, which lowered the risks involved in investments. As George Grantham (in this volume) explains, large-scale investments in production for small and volatile markets run the risk of oversupplying the market, leading to a fall in prices. Large markets do not have this effect, thereby also allowing further specialization, as the market for each specialized product is large enough to sustain increased production. Moreover, large markets reduce transactions costs, as the geographical size of the market decreases and the density increases, allowing cheaper transport and easier communication. In the case of Madrid it is observed that this market was a driving force behind the market integration in the region. The physical and institutional infrastructure that emerged in response to urban demand reduced transaction costs

[19] On Roman attitudes to technological skill, see Kolb in this volume.

[20] ALLEN, *Progress and Poverty* [n. 16]; G. FEDERICO / P. MALANIMA, *Progress, Decline, Growth. Product and Productivity in Italian Agriculture, 1000-2000* in *Economic History Review* 57, 2004, p. 437-464; BROADBERRY / GUPTA, *Great Divergence* [n. 8]; WRIGLEY, *Transition* [n. 5]; S. BROADBERRY / B. M. S. CAMPBELL / B. VAN LEEUWEN, *When Did Britain Industrialise? The Sectoral Distribution of the Labour Force and Labour Productivity in Britain, 1381-1851* in *Explorations in Economic History* 50, 2013, p. 16-27.

beyond the metropolitan market. While the idea that metropoleis stimulate agriculture in their hinterland is not new,[21] the detailed analysis of early-modern cases sheds light on similar developments in the hinterland of Roman cities and legionary camps throughout the Empire. Moreover, it offers a good model for understanding the reverse effects of de-urbanization in the western half of the empire in the late Roman Empire.

5 Market integration, division of labour and specialization

Increases in the exchange of goods and in occupational specialization were important elements in achieving economic growth, a notion that in economic literature is named after the first economist to point it out, Adam Smith. 'smithian' growth is based on the productivity gains that were the result of increased market integration and specialization, triggering a process of growth as the various determinants of economic performance spiralled upwards in a movement of mutually enforcing improvement. Market integration may be taken not as sole cause, but as the starting point in understanding these interlocking developments.[22] Improved market integration increased the scope for regional and individual specialization, as it lowered the threshold of risk and effort in connecting supply and demand. A higher degree of regional specialization allowed farmers to concentrate on those crops to which soil and climate were best suited, thus improving levels of soil and labour productivity in agriculture. Specialization in certain crops also lowered the threshold for investing capital in the installations and tools required for these activities. Improved market functioning allowed increasing specialization by individual workers in smaller segments of the market, resulting in more expertise in the tasks that were executed and thus higher labour productivity. Hence, in big cities one finds artisans who make the upper or lower halves of shoes, as Xenophon (*Cyropaedia* VIII, 2, 5) writes, while in the countryside the carpenter might make chairs, tables, and even build the house. Increased specialization also lowered the threshold for investing

[21] H. W. PLEKET, *Rome: a Pre-Industrial Megalopolis* in T. BARKER / A. SUTCLIFFE (eds.), *Megalopolis: the Giant City in History*, London, 1993, p. 14-35; N. MORLEY, *Metropolis and Hinterland. The City of Rome and the Italian Economy, 200 BC - AD 200*, Cambridge, 1996; P. ERDKAMP, *Urbanism* in W. SCHEIDEL (ed.), *The Cambridge Companion to the Roman Economy*, Cambridge, 2012, p. 241-265.

[22] S. R. EPSTEIN, *Freedom and Growth. The Rise of States and Markets in Europe, 1300-1750*, London 2000; V. BATEMAN, *The Evolution of Markets in Early Modern Europe, 1350-1800: a Study of Wheat Prices* in *Economic History Review* 64, 2011, p. 466; D. CHILOSI / T. E. MURPHY / R. STUDER / A. COŞKUN TUNÇER, *Europe's Many Integrations: Geography and Grain Markets, 1620-1913* in *Explorations in Economic History* 50, 2013, p. 46-68.

capital in those tools and equipment, as for instance fulleries in textile production, which eased the production process and/or improved labour productivity. Increased specialization itself creates better conditions for specialists, as George Grantham points out, as it lowers the extent of autarky and at the same time increases the number of people offering goods and services. As specialization increases, the artisan will find more customers, and at the same time more people that offer the services and goods that he requires, such as transportation, food, and tools.[23] In short, the essence of Smithian growth is that it raises total production and productivity levels of land and labour—and, undoubtedly, capital as well—by changing the conditions of economic activities without requiring any significant innovations.

However, the wider context of the above sketched processes can also provide constraints, as is clearly seen for instance in the wide divergence in urbanization rate or occupational structure within early-modern Europe. While in 1800 no more than 35 % of the population was working the land in England and 41% in The Netherlands, the agricultural sector still employed 58% of the population of Italy and 64% of Spain.[24] Hence, simply pointing out that there was 'smithian growth' in the Roman world does not add much to our understanding if we do not also pay attention to constraining factors.

A major brake on economic growth was the performance of the market, as the risks involved in specialization, which by definition meant dependence on the market, were inversely proportional to the extent of market integration. The much higher costs of overland transportation inevitably meant that inland regions were more constrained than coastal regions. However, market integration is not only a function of transportation costs. In the case of Spain, a strong case has been made for seeing the political and administrative fragmentation of the country as an obstacle to further integration of the internal markets, despite its image of a strongly bureaucratic and centralized absolutist state.[25] As a consequence, relying on the market was more costly and risky, hampering specialization and the development of an internal market for goods and services. If there was little demand for goods or services, few workers could find employment in these sectors, forcing them to remain on the land, resulting in underemployment and low agricultural labour productivity. Under these circumstances, smallholders welcomed any opportunity to use their spare labour for some subsidiary employment. The Spanish transport sector is a good case in point, as there was

[23] GRANTHAM, *Contra Ricardo* [n. 4], 217-222; PERSSON, *Economic History* [n. 13], p. 26-28.

[24] GOLDSTONE, *Efflorescences* [n. 4], p. 347; ALLEN, *Progress and Poverty* [n. 16], p. 408; WRIGLEY, *Transition* [n. 5], p. 453-454; ALVAREZ-NOGAL / PRADOS DE LA ESCOSURA, *The Rise and Fall of Spain* [n. 14], p, 12-16.

[25] GRAFE, *Distant Tyranny* [n. 18], p. 188.

only a very small sector of professional transport specialists. Most of overland transport was undertaken by seasonally employed peasant transporters and their oxen.[26] Hence, subsidiary employment, for instance in the form of proto-industrial manufacture of textiles by rural households, is nowadays not seen as a step towards modernization, but as an indication of economic stagnation.[27]

6 State and elite

Thirty years ago, and in the context of the then prevalent disapproval of empires and capitols as 'predatory' and 'parasitic', David Ringrose in his study of Madrid compared the Spanish capitol to ancient Rome, as both were "consuming the wealth of their empires without directly contributing to the creation of wealth".[28] In this traditional view, the early-modern absolutist state is seen as a force that strengthened the rent-seeking behaviour of officials, bureaucrats, and aristocracies to the detriment of more productive investments in the economy. The fast pace of economic growth in early-modern England was linked to the policies of the Parliament, stagnation in France to the supposedly absolutist monarchy. Such causality has come under scrutiny, as it is pointed out that the tax rate in England was actually higher than in France, while it was not taxation as such that held back French economic performance.[29] Scepticism regarding these views does not mean, however, that the determining role of the governmental structure is denied. As Regina Grafe writes in her recent study of the economic and political development of early-modern Spain, "institutions, chief among them the state, are the most likely source of differential growth paths across countries".[30] Her monograph, which offers a meticulous and wide-ranging analysis of the political and social constraints on the economic development in Spain, offers various viewpoints and conclusions that are also very useful for ancient historians in their analysis of the constraints on economic performance in the Roman world. Her approach also offers a welcome counterpoint to the tendency among ancient historians to use the perspectives of New Institutional Economics one-sidedly to demonstrate the beneficial impact of Roman rule. A middle course must be steered between the Scylla of the predatory state and too rosy a Charybdis.

[26] GRAFE, *Distant Tyranny* [n. 18], p. 105-106.
[27] ALLEN, *Progress and Poverty* [n. 16], p. 422-423; BROADBERRY / GUPTA, *Great Divergence* [n. 8], p. 10.
[28] D. R. RINGROSE, *Madrid and the Spanish Economy, 1560-1850*, Berkeley, 1983, p. 4.
[29] ALLEN, *Progress and Poverty* [n. 16], p. 429-433.
[30] GRAFE, *Distant Tyranny* [n. 18], p. 6.

In contrast to the emphasis on coercion in the older models of absolutist states, Grafe[31] points out that the Spanish rulers did not—or were not able to—play the cards of compulsion and oppression to achieve their goals, but obtained a more or less workable level of cooperation and order by allowing the local powers a large scope for self-determination. Leaving the responsibility for local affairs within their Iberian domains to local powers as long as these did not threaten the stability of the whole, the Spanish kingdom did not develop any meaningful trans-territorial institutions. Rather than a predatory state, we have a multipolar state with fragmented sovereignty that aimed at sufficing strategies rather than trying to maximize its power at all levels. Such a model of political power seems valid for the Roman Empire too, where the imperial authorities left local executive power to the urban elites, who ruled the urban communities and their hinterland almost like independent city-states. Political connectivity between cities was based more on social networks than on political institutions, as trans-territorial institutions, for instance on a provincial level, remained weak. In the case of Spain, decentralization went even further, as in many parts of this heterogeneous kingdom sovereignty was placed in the hands of—or contested by—such institutions as the Church, guilds, and other corporate institutions. The extent to which a similar model of fragmented local power applies in the case of Roman municipalities might be fruitfully explored. Grafe argues convincingly that the disintegration of political power, the fragmentation of legal authority, and the transfer of fiscal competence to local rulers and institutions hampered the development of the Spanish economy. Manufacturers and landowners, traders and consumers were subjected to a disintegrated tax regime of localized indirect dues and customs, which added even more to transactions costs than the inland position of much of Spain. It might be worthwhile to study the economic integration and market connections in the Roman world from the perspective of the fragmented authority of imperial rulers and local elites, local taxes and customs, and local policies on commerce and the consumer market.

Europe's early-modern states resembled the Roman Empire also in the sense that military spending consumed by far the largest part of the state budget. Early-modern estimates are very similar to those of imperial Rome, where most of the monetary taxes were spent on the legions. However, in both cases the estimates of state spending give a distorted view, as most of public expenses were paid on the city level in the early-modern states as well as in the Roman Empire. As far

[31] GRAFE, *Distant Tyranny* [n. 18], esp. Ch. 7. 'Market Growth and Governance in Early Modern Spain'. Contra D. C. NORTH / B. R. WEINGAST, *Constitutions and Commitment: the Evolution of Institutions Governing Public Choice in Seventeenth-Century England* in *Journal of Economic History* 49, 1989, p. 803-832. Cf. D. ACEMOGLU / S. JOHNSON / J. ROBINSON, *The Rise of Europe: Atlantic Trade, Institutional Change, and Economic Growth* in *American Economic Review* 95, 2005, p. 546-579: emphasis on institutional change in non-absolutist states.

as state finances are concerned, the major difference between Rome and the early-modern states is that the latter borrowed much of its capital from private institutions, in the case of Spain with local tax revenues as collateral. Again, what were the consequences of this fundamental difference in the development of economy and state?

We may end with the conclusion that the most crucial contribution that the comparative method makes to the study of the Roman world is that it frees us from the perspectives of our sources and leads us to questions and approaches that we might otherwise have missed.

Koenraad VERBOVEN

The Knights who Say NIE. Can Neo-Institutional Economics Live up to Its Expectation in Ancient History Research?

1 New Institutional Economics

1.1 Economic History

The editors of the *Cambridge Economic History of the Greco-Roman World* have proposed a research program inspired by what Douglass North saw as the task of economic history: "to explain the structure and performance of economies through time".[1] To achieve this, they have formulated three challenges for the 21st century: (1) to find ways to document performance more accurately (mainly by using archaeological data), (2) to clarify relationships between structures and performance by building on 20th c. advances in understanding institutions and ideology and (3) to pursue a comparative analysis of why the Greco-Roman economy broke down.[2]

When the *CEHGRW* was published, in 2007, this emphasis on NIE was not entirely new. Its use in ancient economic history had started in the 1990s with scholars like Alain Bresson, Dennis Kehoe or Elio Lo Cascio. Compared to the economic history of preindustrial Europe and the modern world, however, ancient economic history was a late convert. The dominance of the Finley model in the 1970s and 1980s was only partly responsible for this. A more fundamental reason was the limited scope for quantification in ancient economic history, before new technologies and user friendly computer programs changed heuristics and data analysis in the 1990s in archaeology, numismatics, papyrology and epigraphy.

[1] D. C. NORTH, *Structure and Change in Economic History*, New York, 1981, p. 3; see also ID., *Structure and Performance: The Task of Economic History* in *Journal of Economic Literature* 16, 1978, p. 963-978. North's thinking has changed through the years (see below), but this basic 'challenge' has stayed the same.

[2] W. SCHEIDEL / I. MORRIS / R. P. SALLER (eds.), *The Cambridge Economic History of the Greco-Roman World*, Cambridge, 2007, p. 7.

Neo-institutionalism was influential from the start in medieval and modern economic history. In tandem with cliometrics it shaped the 'New Economic History' in the 1960s and 1970s. Although this was never an undisputed school and always found its staunchest supporters more among economists than among historians, its influence steadily grew, familiarizing historians with economic theories and models. When North and Fogel received the 1993 Nobel Price "for having renewed research in economic history by applying economic theory and quantitative methods in order to explain economic and institutional change", NIE's impact on economic history peaked.[3]

Gunnar Persson's introduction to his celebrated economic history of Europe integrates neo-institutional economics into the definition itself of economic History: it "is concerned with how well mankind, over time, has used resources to create wealth, food and shelter, bread and roses". The efficiency with which this is done depends on technology and institutions, which implies that "Economic history traces the efficiency characteristics of institutions by studying the development of commodity and labour markets, financial intermediaries (banks), the legal framework of contract enforcement, property rights, openness to trade and international flows".[4]

Should we take over this mission statement for ancient economic history?

1.2 Criticism against NIE

The past decade or so, criticism of New Institutional Economics has grown. In economics, Polanyi-substantivists[5] and neo-Marxists[6] formulated objections that provided much of the lead for Francesco Boldizzoni's book *The Poverty of Clio* (2011). These heterodox economists generally criticize NIE not so much for projecting back the market exchange system into the dawn of man (something Polanyi himself did) but of treating the market as the only natural system capable in itself of realizing real economic development. Good institutions are assumed

[3] C. GOLDIN. *Cliometrics and the Nobel* in *Journal of Economic Perspectives* 9, 1995, p. 191-208.

[4] K. G. PERSSON, *An Economic History of Europe: Knowledge, Institutions and Growth, 600 to the Present*, Cambridge, 2010, p. 1.

[5] M. HARVEY / R. RAMLOGAN / S. RANDLES (eds.), *Karl Polanyi. New Perspectives on the Place of Economy in Society*, Manchester, 2008; see also K. HARRISS, *Institutions, Politics and Culture: A Polanyian Perspective on Economic Change* in *International Review of Sociology / Revue Internationale de Sociologie* 13, 2003, p. 343-355 and the other articles in the same volume of the *International Review of Sociology* 13, 2003.

[6] D. ANKARLOO / G. PALERMO, *Anti-Williamson: a Marxian Critique of New Institutional Economics* in *Cambridge Journal of Economics* 28, 2004, p. 413-429; D. ANKARLOO, *New Institutional Economics and Economic History* in *Capital & Class* 26, 2002, p. 9-36.

to develop teleologically to remedy market failures, bad institutions to cause market failures. Social and political structures are simply dead weight.

Particularly among neo-Marxist economists the tone is hostile. NIE is portrayed as an ideological construct intended (consciously or not) to justify capitalism, with a hidden agenda directed against social sciences not embracing neoclassical theory. To quote Boldizzoni: "with the new institutionalism, economics has entered the second phase of aggression toward the other social sciences that started in the 1970s and is defined by its own creators as 'economic imperialism'. It is an offensive aimed at demonstrating that economics can also explain noneconomic phenomena better than the social sciences that focus on doing just that."[7] Whether they are right or wrong, such politicized and often *ad hominem* critiques are intellectually neither stimulating, nor fruitful.

Other arguments against New Institutional Economics, however, are clearly to the point. A recurrent critique is that economists (whether neo-institutionalist or other) venturing in historical research have an insufficient grasp of historical skills to read and interpret sources correctly. They take a deductive approach and make the sources fit the model rather than adapt or reject it when contradictions become insurmountable.

This type of criticism was forcefully raised against Greif's influential studies of Mediterranean commerce by Genoese traders and the Jewish Maghribi merchant community. Greif argued that agency among the Maghribi relied on private contract enforcement based on the participants' reputation and the willingness of the Maghribi to punish transgressors by exclusion from their community. The formal legal system would not have played a significant role in contract enforcement. Genoese traders on the other hand relied primarily on formal legal contract enforcement. Private reputation based enforcement would have been of limited use because there was no comparably strong closed community to exclude transgressors. Ultimately, according to Greif, it was the 'collectivist beliefs' of the Maghribi versus the 'individualist beliefs' of the Christian Genoese that explain the difference.[8] Edwards and Ogilvie wrote a sharp critique of Greif's historical methodology. They re-analysed in detail five linchpin cases used by Greif to provide empirical grounds for his argument. From this empirical re-analysis, they conclude that "the Maghribi traders combined reputation-based sanctions with legal mechanisms, in ways that resemble the

[7] F. BOLDIZZONI, *The Poverty of Clio. Resurrecting Economic History*, Princeton, 2011, p. 49; see also the highly critical review of Eric Jones on Boldizzoni's *ad hominem* approach in the *American Historical Review* 117, 2012, p. 157-158.

[8] A. GREIF, *Reputation and Coalition in Medieval Trade: Evidence on the Maghribi Traders* in *Journal of Economic History* 49, 1989, p. 857-883; ID., *Institutions and the Path to the Modern Economy. Lessons from Medieval Trade*, Cambridge, 2006.

practices of medieval European merchants."[9] Greif, however, struck back with an equally meticulous re-analysis of the relevant Geniza documents, arguing that he had correctly read and interpreted them by means of a careful traditional historical analysis.[10]

We don't need to concern ourselves here with the merits of this particular case or on who read the sources correctly or not. More important for us is that both Greif and his adversaries agree in principle on the risk of deductive bias and the importance of methodological empiricism in historical research. The lesson is clear enough and hardly controversial: any model or theory, whatever its intrinsic merits, needs reliable input data. The job of historians is always to control the quality of the empirical data on which the analyses rest. Neo-institutional models (or any other economic models) do not in themselves make good economic history if they rest on unreliable or incomplete data. This objection is obviously pertinent, but largely irrelevant to assess the specific validity of NIE as a research approach. The risk of deductive bias is inherent in any model-centred approach. The Finley model provides a classic example of it. While it is beautifully coherent and elegant, it implies rejecting a huge amount of epigraphic, papyrological, and archaeological data along with a good deal of data from literary sources to stand its ground.

Conversely, historians using economic models risk suffering an equally damaging 'inductive bias' when picking and mixing models to fit the sources they happen to have. Moreover, any honest scholar will admit that interpretational disputes and mistaken interpretations of source data are just as frequent among historians who use only 'traditional' methods.

A more fundamental critique, however, is directed against the popular teleological view in NIE that economically relevant institutions develop *in order* to lower transaction costs that obstruct the efficiency of markets. Path dependence may sometimes keep inefficient institutions alive for too long, but in the end market competition ensures that only institutions that lower transaction costs, i.e. increase efficiency, survive. Institutional development would thus be driven by the ingrown tendency of markets to improve Pareto-efficiency.

This efficiency view dominated NIE-inspired research in economic history since the 1970s in virtually every research topic ranging from slavery and serfdom to the role of the guilds. Its theoretical foundations are dubious and flagrantly

[9] J. EDWARDS / S. OGILVIE, *Contract Enforcement, Institutions, and Social Capital: the Maghribi Traders Reappraised* in *Economic History Review* 65, 2012, p. 421-444; for another critique see R. BOYER, *Historiens et économistes face à l'émergence des institutions du marché* in *Ann. (HSS)* 64, 2009, p. 665-693; BOLDIZZONI, *Poverty* [n. 7], 56-60 spends four pages attacking Greif's presumed selective reading and sloppy references.

[10] A. GREIF, *The Maghribi Traders: a Reappraisal?* in *Economic History Review* 65, 2012, p. 445-469; a longer version is available as a SSRN Paper at: http://ssrn.com/abstract=2029327.

ignore developments within neo-institutional economics itself the past 30 odd years (see below). Ogilvie identifies at least three alternative causes of institutional change that are compatible with mainstream economics: (1) stochastic shocks caused by exogenous factors such as natural disasters, epidemics, technological innovation or the decisions of powerful individuals, (2) cultural beliefs that underlie social norms and formal rules, and (3) conflicts over the distribution of resources. The latter in her view provide the best overall explanation for institutional change or stability. An additional problem for the efficiency thesis, according to Ogilvie, is that institutions come in 'bundles'. Inefficient institutions are often impossible to distinguish or isolate from efficient ones.[11]

Ogilvie notes that many supposed efficiencies are only efficient for some players on the market, not for society as a whole. She argues, for instance, that merchant guilds and associations "underpaid employees, overcharged customers, stifled competition, excluded women and Jews, and blocked innovation. ... [They] were so widespread and tenacious not because they efficiently solved economic problems, making everyone better off, but because they efficiently distributed resources to a powerful urban elite, with side-benefits for rulers."[12]

Ogilvie, however, does not reject institutional analysis. On the contrary, she welcomes the "new enthusiasm for delving into the 'humanly devised constraints' on economic life." But "the tendency to explain institutions as an efficient and beneficial response to the needs of the economy" is a dead end. Instead of serving as a 'fashion accessory', institutions should be an "indispensable instrument in the toolkit of every economic historian."[13] Institutions profoundly affect the efficiency of markets, but efficiency is not what drives institutional development.

1.3 Developments in NIE

The efficiency postulate is rooted into the history of New Institutional Economics, which originated as an attempt to expand the applicability of neo-classical theory. This was acknowledged to provide powerful formal mathematical tools to determine the optimal allocation and exchange rate of resources. Unfortunately

[11] S. OGILVIE, *'Whatever Is, Is Right'? Economic Institutions in Pre-Industrial Europe* in *Economic History Review* 60, 2007, p. 649-684.

[12] OGILVIE, *Whatever* [n. 11], p. 663-664; for Ogilvie's views on the guilds see now S. OGILVIE, *Institutions and European Trade: Merchant Guilds, 1000-1800*, Cambridge, 2011; also S. OGILVIE, *Guilds, Efficiency and Social Capital: Evidence from German Proto-Industry* in *Economic History Review* 57, 2004, p. 286-333 contra S. R. EPSTEIN, *Craft Guilds in the Pre-modern Economy: a Discussion* in *Economic History Review* 61, 2008, p. 155-174 and for a counter reply S. OGILVIE, *Rehabilitating the Guilds: a Reply* in *Economic History Review* 61, 2008, p. 175-182.

[13] OGILVIE, *Whatever* [n. 11], p: 650-651.

the model assumes that decision makers are perfectly rational, perfectly informed (including foresight of the results of decisions taken), and are cognitively perfectly able to process this information. Because these conditions rarely if ever occur in the real world, neoclassical theory alone is of limited use for empirical research, either to explain historical developments or to determine policy. By definition, *Homo economicus* is an efficient decision maker, by nature *Homo sapiens* is not.

The theory of transaction costs was developed as an attempt to identify how and why neo-classical price formation operated or failed to operate in the real world. The basis was laid by Ronald Coase in 1937. He explained the origin of the firm as a response to the hidden costs an entrepreneur faced if he relied solely on markets to obtain the resources and services needed for his business. Coase identified search and information costs, bargaining costs and control and enforcement costs. These could be avoided when the entrepreneur himself organized the production of the necessary resources and services to make his final product. Instead of relying on markets, firms integrate various stages of the production cycle.[14] The internal organization of firms is not based on the price-mechanism as a 'co-ordinating instrument' but on the conscious 'co-ordinating function' of the entrepreneur.

The question remained how transaction costs affected the price mechanism of market exchange. Transaction cost theory was further developed in the 1970s and 1980s by Oliver Williamson who identified the underlying problem as one of information asymmetry and uncertainty. He argued that institutions alleviated this problem by establishing a relative certainty regarding what qualifies as relevant information and what the implications and outcomes would be of decisions taken.[15]

Douglas North defined institutions as "humanly devised constraints that shape human interaction."[16] They lay down the rules of the game and define the incentive structure in society. Institutions can be formal or informal. Formal institutions are explicit and subject to public order enforcement. Examples are property and contract law, fiscal regulations, inheritance law and suchlike. Informal institutions are social norms and conventions based on shared beliefs,

[14] R. COASE, *The Nature of the Firm* in *Economica* 4, 1937, p. 386-405.

[15] O. E. WILLIAMSON, *The Economics of Organization: The Transaction Cost Approach* in *American Journal of Sociology* 87, 1981, p. 548-577; for an introduction to TCE see E. G. FURUBOTN / R. RICHTER, *Institutions and Economic Theory. The Contribution of the New Institutional Economics*, 2nd ed., Ann Arbor, 2005, p. 8-11, 39-68; O. E. WILLIAMSON, *Transaction Cost Economics* in C. MÉNARD / M. M. SHIRLEY (eds.), *Handbook of New Institutional Economics*, Heidelberg, 2008, p. 41-65.

[16] D. C. NORTH, *Institutions, Institutional Change and Economic Performance*, Cambridge, 1990, p. 3-4.

subject only to private order enforcement as by social disapproval, reputation damage or exclusion.

The theory of Transaction Cost Economics does not per se imply that markets drive institutional development, but the link was easily made. Almen Alchian argued that economic development was based on a Darwinian selection process with the market acting as the selective environment weeding out inefficiencies.[17] North's neo-institutional economic history as well drew its inspiration from evolutionary biology.[18] This gave rise to the well-known original version of neo-institutional economic history that took shape in the 1970s and inspired economic historians until this day.

Already in the 1980s, however, opposition grew. In a celebrated article, the sociologist Granovetter sharply criticized the idea of market based selection of efficient solutions to transaction costs that only exist with respect to neoclassical theory.[19] North himself, one of the founding fathers of NIE, started to distance himself from market reductionism, looking instead to ideologies, political markets and power strategies to explain why institutions that are patently inefficient from an economic point of view develop and sometimes persist for a very long time.[20]

In the 1990s North turned to culture and psychology ('shared mental models') to explain institutional change.[21] By then it had become painfully clear that institutional reforms imposed on countries by international institutions such as the IMF or the World Bank worked in some countries, but failed miserably in others. North (and others) explained this by reemphasizing the role of informal institutions—social norms, which are much harder to change than formal rules because they are anchored in traditions and cultural habits. Congruence of informal norms and formal institutions increases an organization's efficiency, while discordance weakens it.

Competition remains the driving force for institutional change in the revised NIE model. Efficiency is still a key issue because it determines the survival chance of an organization, but whether the result will be beneficial to society as a whole depends on the incentive structure determined by that society's institutional matrix: "If the highest rate of return in an economy comes from

[17] A. ALCHIAN, 1950, *Uncertainty, Evolution and Economic Theory* in *The Journal of Political Economy* 58, 1950, p. 211-221.

[18] D. C. NORTH, *Institutions and the Performance of Economies over Time* in MÉNARD / SHIRLEY, *Handbook* [n. 16], p. 21 (of p. 21-30).

[19] M. GRANOVETTER, *Economic Action and Social Structure: the Problem of Embeddedness* in *American Journal of Sociology* 91, 1985, p. 481-510.

[20] NORTH, *Structure and change*, [n. 1]; ID., *Institutions* [n. 16].

[21] A. DENZAU / D. C. NORTH, *Shared Mental Models: Ideologies and Institutions* in *Kyklos* 47, 1994, p. 3-31; D. C. NORTH, *Understanding the Process of Economic Change*, Princeton, 2005.

piracy we can expect that the organizations will invest in skills and knowledge that will make them better pirates."[22] Societies can easily get 'locked-in' to an institutional matrix that is utterly inefficient harmful for society as a whole, but is beneficial to the elites that are most influential in determining institutional change.[23] For most of human history states were based on 'closed orders'. Elites formed coalitions to suppress violence and protect their interests. While the outcome sometimes also favoured non-elite groups, the rationale of the state and its institutions was rarely to improve economic efficiency in terms of global production or distribution.[24]

So, while especially in the 1970s NIE remained close to neoclassical theory, in the 1980s it drifted away, an evolution that increased in the 1990s and the 2000s. In the second (2005) edition of their influential handbook on *Institutions and Economic Theory*, Furubotn and Richter call for a radical change because "a proper understanding of institutional phenomena requires the development of a *new paradigm* ... significant progress cannot be made simply by seeking to extend and generalize the neoclassical model."[25]

The debate is far from ended. NIE today hosts various intellectual strands. Some (like North) come close to 'old' institutionalism, looking for institutional change through culture and power structures to explain market developments. Others (like Greif) remain focused on neoclassical choice theory seeing institutions emerge spontaneously as Nash-equilibria from market interactions. Clearly, neoclassical theory remains strong within NIE, but on the whole it has inclined towards other social sciences like sociology or psychology.[26] Whatever economic 'imperialism' it showed in the seventies has abated.

[22] NORTH, *Institutions and Performance* [n. 18], p. 23; the thought culminated in the concept of the 'Natural State', dominated by a coalition of power elites D. C. NORTH / J. J. WALLIS / B. R. WEINGAST, *Violence and Social Orders : a Conceptual Framework for Interpreting Recorded Human History*, Cambridge / New York, 2009; but see already NORTH, *Structure and Change*, [n. 1], p. 62: "Not only is there no implication that economic organization is necessarily 'efficient', but it is stressed that all organization involves dissipation of income because of imperfect measurement and positive enforcement costs. Given both the interests of the rulers of the state and the aforementioned positive transaction costs in economic organization it is not surprising that economic organization that induces economic growth may very well do so by internalizing the benefits and externalizing the costs and hence raising the private rate of return to 'productive' economic activity at the expense of costs imposed on other groups in society."

[23] NORTH, *Institutions* [n. 16], p. 99.

[24] NORTH *et al.*, *Violence* [n. 22]; see also HARRISS, *Institutions* [n. 5], p. 344.

[25] FURUBOTN / RICHTER, *Institutions* [n. 15], p. 3.

[26] V. NEE, *The New Institutionalism in Economics and Sociology* in N. J. SMELSER / R. SWEDBERG (eds.), *The Handbook of Economic Sociology*, 2nd ed., Princeton, 2005, p. 49-74; V. NEE / R. SWEDBERG, *Economic Sociology and New Institutional Economics* in MÉNARD / SHIRLEY, *Handbook* [n. 16], p. 789-817.

2 Other Models

Within mainstream economics, however, other theories and approaches have come to the fore the past few decades. Before taking stock, therefore, of how today's neo-institutional economics—rather than its obsolete seventies version—could help us to explain economic developments in the Roman world, let us consider a few alternatives. The program formulated by *CEHGRW* and the Stanford school behind it, is inspired by North's NIE but is not limited to it. It calls for continuing the engagement with the social sciences initiated by Finley and Hopkins. Besides NIE the editors suggest Development Economics, Human Capital Theory and Economic Sociology as promising frames of analysis. I would suggest adding Behavioural Economics and to distinguish the New Economic Sociology (with its strong emphasis on social networks) from other sociological and anthropological schools of thought like e.g. Bourdieu's theory of fields and habitus.[27]

It would take us too far (and too long) to survey all potentially useful theories and models. For practical reasons, I will limit myself here to Behavioural and Development economics.

2.1 Behavioural Economics

Behavioural Economics has a long prehistory but gained prominence in the 1990s and 2000s, especially after two of its pioneers, Daniel Kahneman and Vernon Smith, won the 2002 Nobel Prize in economics.[28] It is rooted in cognitive psychology and remains strongly connected with it in its conceptual framework and methodology. Besides field work, Behavioural Economics makes extensive use of laboratory experiments common to psychology.

Like NIE, Behavioural Economics recognizes the analytic strength of the formal neo-classical model but finds its descriptive and predictive qualities limited because it is based on the unrealistic assumptions of rational choice theory. Like NIE, the ambition of Behavioural Economics is to salvage the gains

[27] P. Bourdieu, *Les structures sociales de l'économie*, Paris, 2000; P. Bourdieu, *Principles of an Economic Anthropology* in N. J. Smelser / R. Swedberg (eds.), *The Handbook of Economic Sociology*, 2nd ed., Princeton, 2005, p. 75-102.

[28] R. Weber / R. Dawes, *Behavioral Economics* in N. J. Smelser / R. Swedberg (eds.), *The Handbook of Economic Sociology*, 2nd ed., Princeton, 2005, p. 90-107.

of the formal neo-classical model of decision-making in scarcity contexts by expanding it to "make economic analysis more descriptively complete."[29]

While NIE focuses on institutions as rules of the game, Behavioural Economics focuses on the players. It recognizes the importance of rational decision-making in human behaviour, but not in the way textbook economics describes it. Irrationality (beliefs, moral convictions, emotions, superstitions, etc.) is omnipresent in human cognition, including in rational deliberation. The objective of Behavioural Economics is to identify regularities in behaviour and connect these to (rather than explain them by) the rational choice model, thereby substantially modifying the model while retaining its formal (mathematical) strength. Its impact on mainstream economics today is considerable, because it continues to use mathematic concepts and tools familiar to neoclassical theory.

Herbert Simon famously coined the concept of 'bounded rationality' to tackle the problem that rational deliberators face incomplete information, have limited time to process that information and limited psychological capacity to do so. But he went further than that. In his view people do not seek to maximize their utility, but to optimize their satisfaction. Human satisfaction cannot be reduced to utility maximizing. Even in the unreal conditions of perfect rationality and omniscient agents the substantive rationality of economics would not prevail. Norms of fairness, an aversion to inequity, and even pure altruism play a part in rational decision-making, i.e. decisions based on conscious deliberation on what is the most satisfying choice of action.[30]

Simon's work on rationality laid the basis for the development of modern Behavioural Economics. Considerable progress has been made since in identifying and modelling behavioural regularities in decision-making that contradict or complement rational choice theory. Many of these are familiar notions to non-economist social scientists. The contribution from Behavioural Economics, however, lies in modelling their impact on decision-making and exploring their socio-biological (universalist) and socio-cultural (relativist) basis.

Thus, for instance, the exclusive self-interest assumption that underlies neo-classical economics is demonstrably invalid in many situations.[31] Most rational

[29] WEBER / DAWES, *Behavioral Economics* [n. 28], p. 101; note the damning remark by S. BOWLES / H. GINTIS, *A Cooperative Species: Human Reciprocity and Its Evolution*, Princeton, 2011, p. 80 on game-theoretic models of cooperation among self-regarding individuals: "Except under implausible conditions, the cooperative outcomes identified by these models are neither accessible nor persistent. We term them *evolutionarily irrelevant* Nash equilibria", and their conclusion: "Economic theory, favoring parsimony over realism, has sought to explain cooperation without reference to social preferences, and with a minimalist or fictive description of social institutions. This research trajectory, as we have seen, has produced significant insights. But it may have run its course."

[30] H. SIMON, *Reason in Human Affairs*, Stanford, 1983.

[31] WEBER / DAWES, *Behavioral Economics* [n. 28], p. 93-96.

deliberators care about fairness and are prepared to incur costs for the benefit of others even when there are no common interests at stake. However, this preference depends strongly on previous experiences. People are kindly disposed towards those from who have received a kindness in the past even when they cannot expect future kindnesses. They are unkind if they previously experienced unkindness. This disposition to 'reciprocal altruism' is a major example of the role of 'trajectories' in human decision-making. Preferences are not exogenous or stable in the choice model of Behavioural Economics. They change depending on previous choices and future anticipations. Thus an essential characteristic of rational choice theory, viz. consistency, is rejected.[32]

Behavioural Economics have been applied to a wide range of topics, from consumerism to financial markets. For economic historians the work on cooperation may be most relevant, particularly because it includes market exchange as a form of cooperation between unrelated self-regarding individuals. Rational choice theory relies on game-theory to analyse cooperation and agency. Besides incentives from formal contracts the prime mechanism for stable cooperation in game-theoretical models is strategic (instrumental) reciprocity. When seemingly altruistic decisions cannot be explained as a form of direct reciprocity, they are either explained as a form of indirect reciprocity (of the type that A will do B a favour to ingratiate C), or as a reputation building scheme to signal reliability to potential reciprocators. Experiments in Behavioural Economics confirm that such strategic reciprocity stimulates cooperation but also show that it is not sufficient to *maintain* stable cooperation. Most people are conditional co-operators rather than free-riders but strategic reciprocity only very partly explains these conditions. Social proximity, shared identity combined with social symbolic exchange (communication), social (dis)approval, and ability to punish free-riders—in brief membership of a social community—provide much firmer grounds for cooperation. A crucial part is played by altruistic punishment, i.e. costly action to punish norm transgressors even though the victim is unrelated to the punisher. The proximate cause of altruistic punishment is not rational calculation but emotion.[33]

[32] WEBER / DAWES, *Behavioral Economics* [n. 28], p. 96-99.

[33] S. GÄCHTER / B. HERRMANN, *Human Cooperation from an Economic Perspective* in P. M. KAPPELER / C. P. VAN SCHAIK (eds.), *Cooperation in Primates and Humans: Mechanisms and Evolution*, Berlin / Heidelberg, 2006, p. 279-301.

Cultural and social differences appear to have a major effect on how cooperation takes shape. An experiment concerning the willingness to share private resources and contribute to a public good showed significant differences in degrees of sensitivity to norms of fairness in sharing and contributing, between test populations from 15 small-scale non-industrial societies and 2 western university student populations. These appeared to be related to the economic and social organization of the test populations. Both market integration and the dominance of cooperative production stimulate willingness and sensitivity to fair sharing or contributing. Test groups from societies where production is organized at family levels with little cooperation at higher levels share and contribute much less. In two cases (from New Guinea) hyper-fair offers (in which the donor gave more than he kept) were frequently rejected. The researchers related this to the dominance of gift-exchange in these cultures and the wish to avoid being put into moral debt toward the donors.[34]

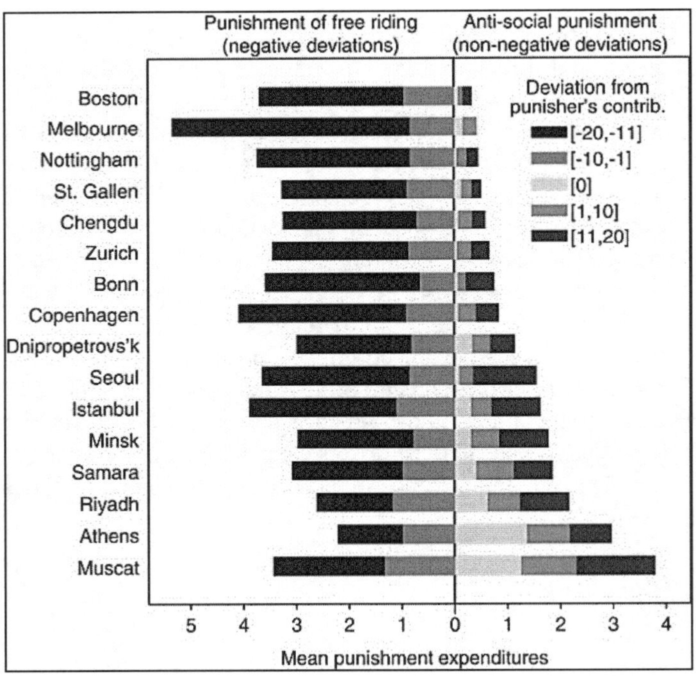

Figure 1. **Herrmann** ***et al., Antisocial Punishment*** **[n. 35], p. 1363**

[34] J. Henrich / R. Boyd / S. Bowles / C. F. Camerer / H. Gintis / R. McElreath / E. Fehr in *Search of Homo Economicus: Experiments in 15 Small-Scale Societies* in *American Economic Review* 91, 2001, p. 73-79.

Another cross-cultural study of 16 populations ranging from rich western societies like Boston to various non-western societies like Chengdu and Riyadh showed that altruistic punishment enhances cooperation, but not always efficiency. In some test-groups altruistic punishment of free-riders triggered altruistic retaliation against the players who inflicted the punishment, resulting in altruistic but anti-social punishment. In two cases (Muscat (Oman) and Athens) anti-social punishment was even more pronounced than free-rider punishment. The researchers found a strong correlation with weakness of civic norms of cooperation and the rule of law. It appears therefore that legitimacy of the punisher is a major requirement for punishments to enhance the efficiency of cooperation.[35] Both experiments point to the importance of (sub-)culture specific social norms and beliefs affecting rational choice in cooperative behaviour.[36]

The past decade has seen contributions coming from behavioural biologists (ethologists) who have successfully applied market models to the analysis of social behaviour among primates. Grooming or offering food in exchange for sex shows signs of relative price formation. Apparently, primates and even lower species of animals have sufficient cognitive skills to makes decisions concerning exchanges based on the relative scarcity of the exchanged goods and services.[37]

While this seems to confirm the innate 'natural' presence of markets among humans, market interactions are far from being the sole or even dominant interaction type among primates. Self-interest is a corner stone in ethology, but only in the sense of 'genetic fitness'. The ultimate aim is not to increase survival of individuals, but to maximize replication of genes. Social insects, like ants or bees are extremely unselfish organisms. Their altruism enhances the reproductive success of the genes driving their behaviour because these are passed on only by the Queen whom they serve. In other words the gene programming for altruistic behaviour is itself extremely 'selfish', but this does not lead to markets becoming a dominant principle of social organization in bee-hives or ant colonies.

The social life of higher animals (such as primates) is much more complex. Altruism stimulates cooperation and thereby strengthens the group, increasing its overall genetic fitness. However, altruistic individuals risk losing out against free-riders in the race for food and sex. So for altruistic traits to survive mechanisms

[35] B. HERRMANN / C. THÖNI / S. GÄCHTER, *Antisocial Punishment Across Societies* in *Science* 319, 2008, p. 1362-1367; cf. BOWLES / GINTIS, *Cooperative Species* [n. 29], p. 26-29; see also GÄCHTER / HERRMANN, *Cooperation* [n. 33].

[36] See also in this sense BOWLES / GINTIS, *Cooperative Species* [n. 29], p. 89.

[37] L. BARRETT / P. S. HENZI, *Monkeys, Markets and Minds: Biological Markets and Primate Sociality* in KAPPELER / SCHAIK, *Cooperation* [n. 33], Berlin / Heidelberg, 2006, p. 209-232; R. NOË, *Digging for the Roots of Trading* in KAPPELER / SCHAIK, *Cooperation* [n. 33], p. 233-262; V. LAKSHMINARAYANAN / L. SANTOS, *Evolved Irrationality* in P. M. KAPPELER / J. B. SILK (eds.), *Mind the Gap. Tracing the Origins of Human Universals*, Berlin / Heidelberg, 2010, p. 245-259, p. 246-247.

are needed to detect and punish free-riders. Reciprocity is the key answer to this problem: individuals are unselfish towards those whom they expect to be unselfish in turn. This is not tit-for-tat mutualism (as in market exchange), but a predisposition to form more and stronger social ties with individuals that have shown themselves to be reliable. Individuals who fail to reciprocate are recognized as being unreliable and will receive less food, sex or help. Hence, even selfishly disposed individuals benefit from engaging in reciprocal altruism.[38]

Cooperation among hominids, however, is problematic from a biological point of view because it is not only more complex than among other primates but also includes non-related individuals. Even our closest relatives, chimpanzees and bonobos, rarely show signs of distress or a willingness to help when unrelated individuals are in serious danger, i.e. when the chance for a return favour is small. High risk cooperation (as in warfare) between unrelated individuals is common in humans but rarely occurs in non-human primates.[39] The deadlock was overcome thanks to culture: behaviour that is socially learned through symbolic interactions, primarily by means of language. This not only enabled more complex cooperation but also gave rise to social institutions: programmed behaviour (through socialisation) that allowed the introduction of social norms to sublimate and expand genetic dispositions. Prime among these is true altruism, which includes the drive to punish individuals that misbehave, even when the victim is unrelated to the punisher and even when this punishment is costly to the individual inflicting it. This behaviour is observed in all human groups, but in no other animal species including primates.[40]

Social behaviour among humans is inevitably institutionalized. This leads us back to institutions, but Behavioural Economics strongly suggests that cooperation between humans, including in firms or principal-agent relations, relies primarily on reciprocity and altruism rather than on market exchange, which

[38] KAPPELER / SCHAIK, *Cooperation* [n. 33], *passim*; particularly J. C. MITANI, *Reciprocal Exchange in Chimpanzees and other Primates* in *ibid.*, p. 107-120.

[39] Although chimps come close; unorganized (i.e. non-cooperative) inter-group and internal aggression and violence is common among chimps, but not among bonobos; A. GAT, *Why War? Motivations for Fighting in the Human State of Nature* in KAPPELER / SCHAIK, *Cooperation* [n. 33], p. 197-222; M. CROFOOT / R. W. WRANGHAM, *Intergroup Aggression in Primates and Humans: The Case for a Unified Theory* in KAPPELER / SCHAIK, *Cooperation* [n. 33], p. 171-195; for the grim link between altruism and organized warfare see BOWLES / GINTIS, *Cooperative Species* [n. 29], p. 102-106, 133-147.

[40] Cf. H. GINTIS, *Strong Reciprocity and Human Sociality* in *Journal of Theoretical Biology* 206, 2000, p. 169-179. Confusingly, ethologists prefer the term 'strong reciprocity' rather than 'true altruism', to distinguish it from 'reciprocal altruism', in fact 'strong reciprocity' is not reciprocal, while 'reciprocal altruism' is not altruistic; there is inconclusive evidence that the cognitive capacity is present in chimpanzees but under natural conditions no primates except hominids have developed such behaviour.

of itself is unable to achieve the social stability it requires to thrive or develop. This insight opens new doors to a study of the economic effects of ancient reciprocity relations and civic ideology.[41]

2.2 Development Economics

Development Economics has a long prehistory. Structural-change paradigms were dominant in the 1970s, neoclassical recipes in the 1980s. Modern Development Economics, however, has been shaped by the work of the Indian economist Amartya Sen, whose entitlement and capabilities approach gained wide acceptance.

Together with Martha Nussbaum and the Pakistani economist Mahbub ul Haq, Sen elaborated a Development Economics Theory that makes the requirements of rational choice (like internal consistency of choice and completeness) subordinate to the constraints posed by external ethical judgments.

Instead of focusing on utility preferences and their maximization, Development Economics starts from entitlements and capabilities.[42] People are endowed with basic entitlements to material and immaterial resources. Different economic systems have different endowment structures. For instance, endowment sets of people in modern market societies include their own labour and whatever resources they own. The endowment set is significantly enlarged by *exchange entitlements*, the bundle of alternatives available in exchange for the resources in a person's endowment set. Central to Sen's Development Economics is the idea that the exchange entitlement set of a person does not depend solely on his endowment set or on the supply of potential exchange entitlements (for instance the supply of food) but is determined by a wide range of factors many of which have little to do with the economic price mechanism. The relation between endowment and exchange entitlement set is defined by 'E-mapping', i.e. the total sum of relevant factors (economic, social, political …) that determine which exchange entitlements a person can obtain.

The entitlement system in a society determines how the exchange entitlement is realized. For instance, a person is the rightful owner of his own labour. Hence

[41] See K. VERBOVEN, *'Like Bait on a Hook'. Ethics, Etics and Emics of Gift-Exchange in the Roman World* in F. CARLÀ / M. GORI (eds.), *Gift Giving and the 'Embedded' Economy in the Ancient World*, Heidelberg, 2014, p. 135-156.

[42] R. GOTOH / P. DUMOUCHEL, *Introduction* in R. GOTOH / P. DUMOUCHEL (eds.), *Against Injustice. The New Economics of Amartya Sen*, Cambridge, 2009, p. 1-35; C. M. NUSSBAUM / A. SEN (eds.), *The Quality of Life*, Oxford, 1993; C. M. NUSSBAUM, *Capabilities as Fundamental Entitlements: Sen and Social Justice* in *Feminist Economics* 9, 2003, p. 33-59; A. SEN, *Poverty and Famines, An Essay on Entitlement and Deprivation*, Oxford, 1981; A. SEN, *On Ethics and Economics*, Oxford, 1987; A. SEN, *Rationality and Freedom*, Cambridge, MA, 2002.

he is entitled to a wage in exchange for this labour, which determines his exchange entitlement. When that person loses his job, he is still the rightful owner of his own labour, but this no longer assures him exchange entitlements. The presence or absence of a social security system will determine whether his exchange entitlement set drops to zero or not. In welfare states, therefore, exchange entitlements are largely based on social rights derived from citizenship or other formal criteria.

Not only exchange entitlements but also endowment sets differ between cultures and societies. In Greco-Roman societies slaves were not rightful owners of their labour nor of any other resource produced or acquired by them. Landownership in Greek poleis was restricted to citizens.

Whereas endowments and entitlements are mostly legally defined, capabilities are much wider. They reflect the actual achievement of human 'functionings', i.e. the 'beings and doings' that constitute human life. They range from being nourished and healthy to having self-respect, participating in community life, and other immaterial states we cherish. A person's 'capability set' consists of all alternative functionings that he *can* choose if he so desires. In Nussbaum and Sen's words: "the freedom that a person has to lead one kind of life or another."[43]

Development Economics provides a framework for approaching economic development that transcends neoclassical economics and factors in social and cultural determinants. It does not, however, provide a single analytical model to explain the interplay of social, economic and cultural determinants or to explain why developments diverge. In general, Sen has a positive stance towards markets as motors of development, but only if they are regulated and socially corrected. Institutions play a major role in Development Economics, but attention is focused on formal institutional change. The object is rarely to understand historical developments, but to achieve modern development goals, particularly those relating to the five basic freedoms that according to Sen create well-being: political, economic, and social freedom, guarantees of transparency and protection.

Sen has been criticized because the entitlements and capabilities that he recognizes are attributes of individuals. In this sense, he remains close to the microeconomic tenet of individual agents making individual choices. Although Sen admits the importance of culture and history in the construction of functionings, their origins and changes are simply not parts of his model.[44]

[43] NUSSBAUM / SEN, *Quality* [n. 42], p. 10; SEN, *Capability and Well-Being* in NUSSBAUM / SEN, *Quality* [n. 42], p. 41-71.

[44] D. O'HEARN, *Amartya Sen's Development as Freedom: Ten Years Later* in *Policy & Practice: A Development Education Review* 8, 2008, p. 9-15 (= http://www.developmenteducationreview.com/issue8-focus1).

While the use of Development Economics to analyse the cause of structural change in historical societies is limited,[45] they have a profound effect on how to express and measure performance. While performance in neoclassical and neo-institutional economics relates to the production and consumption of goods and services, expressed and measured in a common unit of reckoning (usually money), Development Economics sees performance as relating to functionings, capabilities and entitlements that are expressed and measured in various indices.

Instead of focusing on GDP as a single measure for economic performance and growth/decline, Development Economics proposes a composite Human Development Index that combines GDP, life expectancy and education. In its most recent version HDI is adjusted for income inequality. HDI itself is only one criterion used by Development Economics to measure economic performance. In collaboration with the United Nations Development Program Sen and ul Haq started the annual publication of Human Development Reports (HDR) that measure and visualize development using a wide range of alternative indices based on the capabilities and entitlements approach. Using HDI and the other HDR indices, rather than GDP, to measure performance captures characteristics of economic development that neo-classical or neo-institutional economics fail to see.

Development Economics haven't yet been used often in ancient economic history research. Erdkamp used it in his *Grain Market* and Scheidel used it to distinguish between GDP and quality of life.[46] Promising research lines, however, are lying open. For instance, proxy data from the ice core samples, peat bogs, ship wrecks, etc. suggest GDP-growth between c. 100 BCE – 150(?) CE and although contraction seems to have taken place afterwards output remained high until late antiquity. At the same time, however, Nikola Koepke and Joerg Baeten recently argued on the basis of skeletal remains that health status in general declined under Roman occupation while improving significantly after the 'fall of Rome.'[47] If the result is correct, it would be well in line with what HDI shows for contemporary societies: high GDP does not always correlate well with good health.

[45] See also in this sense I. MORRIS, *Social Development*, http://www.ianmorris.org, 2010, p. 23-24.

[46] W. SCHEIDEL, *Stratification, Deprivation and the Quality of Life* in E. M. ATKINS / R. OSBORNE (eds.), *Poverty in the Roman World*, Cambridge, 2006, p. 40-59; W. SCHEIDEL, *Human Development and Quality of Life in the Long Run: The Case of Greece (Version 1.0)*, Stanford-Princeton Working Papers in Classics, 2010, http://www.princeton.edu/~pswpc/pdfs/scheidel/091006.pdf.

[47] N. KOEPKE / J. BAETEN, *The Biological Standard of Living in Europe During the Last Two Millennia* in *European Review of Economic History* 9, 2005, p. 61-95; but note that Geoffrey Kron found opposite results for Italy (G. KRON, *Anthropometry, Physical Anthropology, and the Reconstruction of Ancient Health, Nutrition, and Living Standards* in *Historia* 54, 2005, p. 68-83).

Development Economics also leads us back to culture. The core of Sen's Development Economics is functionings and capabilities. As noted above 'functionings' are culturally bound. A Roman asked to define his 'functionings' is likely to include criteria as being free(born) or being honourable, having citizenship rights, not being hungry, being entertained and other criteria that are either too self-evident or hardly relevant to a modern westerner.

3 Where Does This Leave Us?

Will NIE provide us with the ultimate theoretical frame to explain economic history? Certainly not. But then again: theories never provide ultimate explanations. They are intellectual constructs designed to explain reality, to serve as heuristic devices to search and select relevant information, and to provide analytic toolboxes to generate new information from the data selected. They function as synthetic aids to link data and assemble new models: constructs of the mind that seem to make sense of the world outside.

Successful theories and models tend to have a life cycle of their own. When first formulated they are greeted with enthusiasm because they offer better explanations. Then phenomena are identified which the theory fails to explain and fall outside the accepted models. When this happens, either the theory and its models are refined to cover more ground, or the phenomena are classified as 'exceptions to the rule' and acknowledged to fall outside the theory's scope. When inexplicable phenomena become more numerous the scope of a theory becomes relatively smaller and it becomes an ever more complicated ramshackle building until it is wholly or partly replaced by a new theory. As Copernicus's heliocentrism replaced Ptolemy's geocentrism, Einstein's relativity theory superseded Newtonian physics, and (for sub-atomic phenomena) Quantum Mechanics supplanted Einstain's general relativity theory. Similarly, neo-classical Walrasian market economics were supplemented by New Institutional Economics to explain the conditions under which real markets operate, and Behavioural Economics replaced the rational actor postulate with that of the 'satisficing actor'.

The validity of a theory depends on how much it explains and how robust its explanations are against data it fails to explain, and which consequently must be proven either irrelevant or erroneous. Elegance and logical coherence are basic features of a good theoretical model, but if it fails to explain a good deal of data and is forced to explain away a lot of data, it should be rejected or its scope limited.

If we want to study the role of institutions in economic development, we can now draw some guidelines from the discussion above.

1. If we want to use NIE, we should use its 21st century form, not the 1970s version that economic historians are most familiar with. North's approach is preferable because it allows more links with other promising approaches like Behavioural Economics and Development Economics. Institutions orient and constrain human decision-making in economic and non-economic affairs. Hence to a large extent the institutional setup (locally and globally) of the Roman world determined how much room there was for markets to develop and how efficient they could be. But institutions don't emerge spontaneously from market exchanges. Market efficiency gains/losses feed back into processes of institutional change, but they do not determine these processes. They are powered and directed rather by the interplay of efficiency characteristics with distributional conflicts, cultural beliefs that underlie social norms, and stochastic shocks caused by natural events, technological innovations or human personalities. While we can document the institutional setup and relate this to economic performance, economic performance alone does not explain institutional change or stability. Historians in particular should look out for the role of stochastic shocks on institutional change: epidemics, military conquest, technological innovations ….
2. NIE is not a self-contained model; it should be used together with other models and approaches like Behavioural Economics or Development Economics described above (or Bourdieusian field and habitus theory, New Economic Sociology, Human Capital Theory, Natural Resource Economics …).
3. The relevant question is not whether the ancient Mediterranean economy was a market economy. Insofar as it was, it was only so compared to other preindustrial agrarian economies, not to modern (post-)industrial economies. Neither is the question whether markets existed; they existed since the Stone Age (as even Polanyi emphasized) and are rooted in behaviour that evolved even before hominids entered the scene. The relevant question is whether, to what extent and in what sense (positive or negative) markets affected development, whether (1) economic development as expressed in macro-economics, (2) human development as defined in development economics, or (3) social development as recently defined by Ian Morris.[48]

[48] Measured and expressed by an index based on (i) energy capture, (ii) organization, (iii) war-making capacity, and (iv) information technology. I. MORRIS, *Why the West Rules - For Now: The Patterns of History, and What They Reveal about the Future*, New York, 2010, p. 144: "The bundle of technological, subsistence, organizational, and cultural accomplishments through which people feed, clothe, house, and reproduce themselves, explain the world around them, resolve disputes within their communities, extend their power at the expense of other communities, and defend themselves against others' attempts to extend power." See MORRIS, *Social Development* [n. 45] for details and supporting material.

4. Utility preference and rational choice are human universals, but not in the narrow 'mathematical' sense attributed to them by neoclassical economics. They are not the only universals, moreover. Norms of fairness and a willingness to impose them run just as deep. Because norms and values have to be culturally expressed they show major differences between cultures and sub-cultures. Hence: culture matters as much as (if not more than) institutions. It makes sense therefore not just to look at institutions but also at the culture-specific behavioural norms that affect cooperation and influence the formulation of formal norms.[49]

4 Laying out a Few Tentative Research Lines

I would like to conclude with four hypotheses that I think provide promising research lines based on the considerations above. They will raise objections, no doubt, but I hope that they show the potential of taking an institutional perspective.

1° Institutional Changes in the Roman World from c. 200/100 BCE to c. 100/200 CE Stimulated the Growing Importance of Markets

Institutional change was rampant throughout the Mediterranean and beyond when Rome entered the scene after the second Punic war. These changes grafted onto institutions that had developed in the Greek world of *poleis* and Hellenistic kingdoms but took them further, homogenized them and spread them over the Mediterranean and its hinterlands.

The introduction of coinage and its highly increased supply from the late 3rd century BCE onwards changed the practice of buying and selling. It introduced state-controlled standards and provided instruments for low value transactions. Initially, transaction costs for cash use were high due to its lack of uniformity, vulnerability to counterfeiting and the risks involved in guarding and carrying it. The growing importance of metal currency, however, called for specialists to provide quality controls, exchange facilities and safekeeping. Rome adopted Greek style deposit banking and introduced legislation to protect its clients. Bank loans were low risk and short term, but specialized private moneylenders serves as middlemen and provided reliable gateways for political and landed wealth to finance high risk maritime and other trade. The new financial system crystallized in the late Republic. The introduction and regular supply of a high quality gold currency linked to the medium-value silver *denarius* ensured the empire wide

[49] Cf. K. Verboven, *Cité et réciprocité. Le rôle des croyances culturelles dans l'économie romaine* in *Annales (HSS)* 67, 2012, p. 913-942.

reliability of the currency system. In the second century CE endowments held by cities and voluntary associations increased credit facilities to finance public benefactions expected from political elites (*munera*) and support *collegiati*. The system was flexible and powerful, but continued to rely on a sufficient supply of metal currency and personal networks. Anonymous or easily transferable credit instruments never developed.

Roman law changed profoundly in the second century BCE when *ius honorarium* supplanted *ius civile*. It allowed magistrates to introduce yearly remedies to legal problems based on considerations of equity, rather than formal law. The new, more sophisticated, system of law, driven by considerations of equity, called for a class of specialized jurists. Besides many other innovations, it revolutionized the Roman law of obligations. An important example is the *actiones adiecticiae qualitatis* that set the law of agency on a new footing by making the *pater familias* liable for obligations incurred by his slaves and children *in potestate*. It allowed the *familia* to become the basic unit for commercial enterprises. Characteristically, agency by non-family members was modelled on *amicitia*. The contracts of partnership (*societas*) and commission (*mandatum*) were based on personal trust and loyalty (*fides*). Mandate was valid only if it was unremunerated. It is hard not to relate these changes to the demands of Mediterranean commerce and market participation by elites. However, the strong link between these contractual obligations and social norms derived from the multi-stranded personal relations of *familia* and *amicitia* illustrates the role played by the private order enforcement that underlay legal enforcement. Thus, 'formal' is a very misleading qualification for Roman agency contracts. Rather Roman law provided additional formal sanctions for moral commitments.

The creation of a single political system that superimposed itself on local polities and gradually transformed them not only pacified trade routes, it also linked power structures in a way that lowered uncertainty due to different political interests.

2° Markets Favoured Growth and Development ... But not for All: Entitlement Sets and Capabilities Were Biased Towards Civic Centres.

Although the final word on economic growth, its scale and timing in the Roman World remains to be said, it seems hard not to admit at least aggregate, if not per capita, growth.[50] Even if population growth 'consumed' aggregate growth completely (implying no per capita growth) this would still be significant because it implies that the Roman economy was able to sustain many more people that any of its precursors.

[50] Cf. W. Scheidel, *In Search of Roman Economic Growth* in *JRA* 22, 2009, p. 46-70.

I suggest that the expansion of markets, supported by state intervention to impose social order and facilitate the movement of vital supplies to urban centres and army camps, stimulated growth. Most of this was Smithian growth derived from an increased division, specialization and more efficient organization of labour that increased productivity, but some presumably also was Schumpeterian growth, based on technological innovation and diffusion of new technologies. The former (Smithian growth) was possible because improved connections (more and better roads, port and warehouse facilities), safer roads and a more uniform public enforcement structure, through imperial officials, facilitated trade. Examples of the latter (Schumpeterian growth) are water mills, mining technology, the use of concrete as a building material, and glass technology.

But the link between growth and development is non-linear. Guesstimates of trends in GDP-change based on proxy-data can be supplemented by guesstimates of trends in health status based on skeletal remains. The latter now seem to suggest that the 'average' inhabitants of the empire did not benefit from any rising trend in GDP.

Measuring other variables, like education, gender inequality or political participation is harder. Nevertheless some observations are possible. Medical doctors and teachers (*grammatici* and *rhetorici*) were ubiquitous and were legally privileged. They enjoyed immunities and general freedom of association since Vespasian.[51] The sheer spread of technologically complex operations (buildings, aqueducts, bridges, piston pumps …) and large scale production facilities requiring organizational skills, suppose high levels of long term training and studying. Food supply was a major concern for local notables who faced riots and lynching if grain prices soared.[52] The empire was obviously never a democracy and local polities were predominantly oligarchic. Nevertheless, popular pressure was real in the urban centres, where the *plebs media* succeeded in making sure that its interests were on the political agenda.

These are all indications of real development but there is no point in trying to quantify them. Even if we would achieve agreement on the guesstimates, the chronological and geographical resolution would be extremely 'fuzzy' to say the least. The major point of interest, however, is that real development was mainly related to civic centres and their immediate surroundings. Presumably, in heavily urbanized areas rural populations benefitted as well, but it was primarily political control, not markets per se, that improved real capabilities for non-elite citizens. From an empire-wide perspective and compared to rural populations, urban populations huddled close to social elites—much like todays middle-class

[51] *FIRA* I, no. 73; *Cf. Dig.* XXVII, 1, 6, 8; 50, 4, 18, 30; Cf. SENECA, *Ben.*, VI, 15, 1; 16, 1; 17, 2.

[52] Cf. P. ERDKAMP, *The Grain Market in the Roman Empire: a Social, Political and Economic Study*, Cambridge, 2005, p. 258-316.

Europeans and Americans are stakeholders in the global inequalities imposed by political power structures on most of the earth's population.

3° Civic Ideology (and Interests) Supported Universalist Norms of Fairness and the Rule of Law, but the Ideology (and Interests) of Amicitia and Patronage Counteracted the Development of Civic Institutions

Civic ideology laid the basis for a system of social norms regarding public life that not only stimulated cooperation between unrelated citizens but made the legitimacy of power dependent on service to the citizen community.[53] Perhaps Rome's greatest achievement was that it succeeded in creating an imagined community based on Roman citizenship that transcended local communities and would outlast the empire itself. Membership in this community endowed individuals with basic entitlements to enjoyment of life, physical security, enforceable contract capacities, and so forth.

At the same time however, strong norms of personal trust and reciprocity that determined a person's social reputation, enmeshed agents in webs of expectations that transcended and sometimes conflicted with civic norms. Local elites were in constant competition with each other and depended on patronage networks with neighbourhood and *collegia* leaders to maintain their position. As a result, access to public goods such as justice, protection, water, etc. could be obtained relatively easily through intercession by competing civic leaders. In addition local elites invested private resources to remedy inadequate public goods, partly through voluntary euergetism, largely through liturgies and *munera publica*.

Combined, however, both ideologies tended to favour the status quo and the pre-eminence of the existing political elites. The efforts of *plebs media* leaders went into strengthening private voluntary associations with which they solicited more effective patronage from local and imperial elites. Thus, the *plebs media* never transformed into a 'bourgeoisie' bent on securing influence and power through the development of transparent formal institutions and organizations.

The military (the ultimate basis of imperial power) and bureaucracy (the apparatus through which imperial power was exercised) linked up with the empire-wide patrimonial elite (mostly senators and knights), but never coincided with it. Instead, empire-wide patrimonial elites maintained strong links of patronage and friendship with local elites which gave them bargaining power vis-à-vis the emperor's military and bureaucratic power base. In turn the civic elites derived their bargaining power vis-à-vis the imperial elites from the control they exercised over their citizen communities. In addition, as representatives of their home towns, local elites could directly petition the emperor and his

[53] See VERBOVEN, *Cité* [49].

representatives, which denied patrimonial elites any formal brokerage monopoly they could have hoped for.

The imperial ideology—ritualized through the emperor cult—however, transcended civic ideology. Institutional change at the imperial level favoured the interests of imperial elites and interest groups (including merchants working for the *annona*), rather than local civic communities or elites. Here, in the centre of power, formalization did occur as new administrative functions were created and imperial authority delegated.

The result was an institutional equilibrium in which local elites, imperial patrimonial elites and the emperor's military and bureaucratic apparatus balanced each other. It arose under the Julio-Claudians and expanded as provincial tribes and communities were remodelled into Roman-type citizen communities.

While there were clear legally defined rules to regulate economic action based on equity considerations, and procedures for public enforcement existed, informal rules largely determined how effective these formal constraints could be.

4° Stochastic Shocks Brought the Walls Down

There were already signs of stress well before the middle of the 2nd c. CE in Italy, but elsewhere the best was yet to come. So, there is no reason why the balance could not have been maintained, were it not for a series of events that knocked the breath out of civic communities and induced imperial and local elites to develop new power strategies.

Increased defensive warfare since the 160s—that contrary to previous warfare brought little glory and even less revenue—and epidemics (the Antonine plague for a start), was followed by political unrest. The 3rd century was one of those fascinating times in history when the world seems to gear up. In hindsight it is easy to see where Diocletian's new order came from and how it was rooted in 2nd century structures and institutions,[54] but the political, military and religious chaos could just as easily have produced other outcomes. Like Alexander's empire had fallen apart in smaller kingdoms, the same could have happened with the Roman Empire.

It did not, but what emerged was a polity with a comparatively stronger military and bureaucratic apparatus and weaker local citizen communities. Local elites lost bargaining power; empire-wide patrimonial elites turned to the bureaucracy to transform their huge fortunes into power and glory. The church entered the scene, taking up a middle position between the imperial apparatus and patrimonial elites on the one hand and local communities on the other. Whether

[54] Cf. Eich's 'long third century' (P. Eich, *Zur Metamorphose des politischen Systems in der römischen Kaiserzeit : die Entstehung einer "personalen Bürokratie" im langen dritten Jahrhundert*, Berlin, 2005).

the formal institutional set-up was worse for markets to operate in is not at all certain. The revival in the east seems to suggest that it was not. But the loss of influence of local citizen communities brought down their capability sets and with that also their entitlement sets, redirecting the benefits from market integration to local and imperial elites and leaving the church to comfort the losers.

George GRANTHAM

A Search-Equilibrium Approach to the Roman Economy

There can now no longer be any doubt that the Roman economy—and by extension the Hellenistic and Punic economies the Romans inherited—was a market economy.[1] The evidence of significant specialization and exchange assembled by contributors to the *Cambridge Economic History of the Greco-Roman Economy* effectively puts to rest Finley's claim that the ancient economy was animated by values that promoted economic autarky and discouraged individual enterprise.[2] With the publication of Temin's *Roman Market Economy* the issue would seem to be effectively closed,[3] subject to Andreau's *caveat* that where non-specialists perceive similarities between ancient and modern economies, specialists see differences.[4]

The emerging consensus nevertheless leaves critical questions unresolved. If it was a market economy, what determined its expansion and contraction? When

[1] The bibliography bearing on this question is now massive. Illuminating examples include L. DE LIGT, *Fairs and Markets in the Roman Empire*, Amsterdam, 1993; D. J. MATTINGLY / J. SALMON (eds.), *Economies Beyond Agriculture in the Classical World,* London / New York, 2001; P. ERDKAMP, *The Grain Market in the Roman Empire*, Cambridge, 2005; J. G. MANNING / I. MORRIS, *The Ancient Economy: Evidence and Models*, Stanford, 2005; N. MORLEY, *Trade in Classical Antiquity*, Cambridge, 2007; P. F. BANG, *The Roman Bazaar. A Comparative Study of Trade and Markets in a Tributary Empire*, Cambridge, 2008; J. ANDREAU, *L'Économie du monde romain*, Paris, 2010; J. ANDREAU, *Entretiens avec Jean Andreau* in P. P. FUNARI / A. Pollini (eds.), *Mercato. Le commerce dans les mondes grecs et romains*, Paris, 2012; C. HOLLERAN, *Shopping in Ancient Rome: The Retail Trade in the Late Republic and the Principate*, Oxford, 2012.

[2] W. SCHEIDEL / I. MORRIS / R. P. SALLER (eds.), *The Cambridge Economic History of the Greco-Roman World*, Cambridge, 2007; W. SCHEIDEL (ed.), *The Cambridge Companion to the Roman Economy,* Cambridge, 2012; I reached the same conclusion in 1998 in a paper delivered to the American Economic History Association in 1998 entitled 'The Sherds of Trade.' After the talk, Temin came up to me and said, "George, you scooped me." As occasionally happens, the paper languished on an editor's desk until it was past its expiry date.

[3] P. TEMIN, *The Roman Market Economy*, Oxford, 2013.

[4] ANDREAU, *Entretiens* [n. 1], p. ix.

and where did it originate, and how did it end? The puzzle is not that the Roman economy was a market economy, but that it was part of a market economy that expanded for nearly a thousand years and then imploded. Resolving that conundrum requires more than simple identification of economic type. It requires a different way of thinking about how market economies work.

That the classical economy was a 'market economy' answers a question whose meaning is defined by the taxonomical approach to economic and social phenomena that characterized nineteenth-century historical economics.[5] Opposing the 'timeless' and culture-free affirmations of classical economic theory, which claimed to be true for all times and places on the grounds that men are much the same in all times and places, the historical school proposed a vision—one can hardly dignify it with the term model—of the economy as an ideal type distinguished not only by productivity and social organization, but by social purpose. The notion reflected a common-sense observation that stable societies possess an underlying coherence evidenced by persistence through time, suggesting the presence of a sustaining cause; and as societies evidently differ, so must the sustaining cause. Analytical implementation of this vision rested on the premise that social facts are to be understood in relation to the whole of which they are parts, engendering the conviction that the whole—nation, society, culture, civilization –is a self-sustaining entity ontologically prior to those parts. As an analytical structure, the typological vision was teleological, in which institutions, individual behaviour and sometimes even the means of production were conceived as necessary conditions for existence and temporal persistence of the society as a whole.[6]

Implementation of that vision by economic historians took the form of an account of economic evolution as a succession of stages distinguished by complexity of social and economic organization, including the level of specialization and the extent of market exchange, technological achievement, particularly in industry, and values animating individual actions. This broad structure, which extended the notion of a temporal succession of 'modes of life' proposed by eighteenth-century thinkers like Montesquieu and Adam Smith,[7]

[5] T. RIHA, *German Political Economy: the History of an Alternative Economics*. Bradford, 1985; K. TRIBE, *Strategies of Economic Order. German Economic Discourse, 1750-1950*, Cambridge, 1995; M. PERLMAN / C. MCCANN Jr., *The Pillars of Economic Understanding. Ideas and Traditions*, Ann Arbor, 1998. Though not officially of this school, Marx's dialectical rendering of economic change through a sequence of stages driven by Ricardo's economics and Hegel's logic makes him a family member.

[6] As Teggart pointed out, this vision founders on the problem of identifying efficient causes (F. J. TEGGART, *Theory of History*, New Haven, 1925).

[7] A. S. SKINNER, *Adam Smith: An Economic Interpretation of History* in A. S. SKINNER / T. WILSON (eds.), *The Market and the State: Essays on Adam Smith*. Oxford, 1976, p. 154-178.

provided an ample tent under which historians could shelter research on the economic organization of past societies without worrying too much about formal theory. It was generally assumed that people in earlier times were, if not less selfish than later generations, more constrained by their social milieu. Adam Smith himself noted that men commonly seek wealth not to increase personal consumption, but to better their social condition, implying that their actions are motivated not so much by what they want *ab ovo* but by what they want other people to think of them.[8] The essential insight of the typological approach, then, is that economies differ in space and time because what people desire beyond the necessities reflects social contexts that differ in time and space.[9]

The stages theory seemed to capture changes then taking place in nineteenth-century Europe. Agriculture was becoming more commercialized, markets more geographically extensive and socially intensive, manufacturing more capital-intensive, industrial enterprises larger and more complex and people seemingly more obsessed with gaining wealth at the expense of religious and civic virtue. Ethnological accounts of Stone Age cultures nourished the intuition that European mankind had lifted itself from the stage of family and clan autarky to a capitalist economy transcending national and cultural frontiers. In the canonical sequence of stages, however, the Roman Economy was a troubling anomaly. It seemed to have been economically prosperous—indeed, in the first half of the eighteenth century it was widely believed that Roman agriculture was superior to contemporary English farming practices— and to anyone exposed to a classical education, which meant anyone truly educated, that the Ancients traded, lent funds at interest and remitted them across long distances was common knowledge.[10] But the Roman economy did not evolve into a higher stage of economic development; instead it regressed to 'Naturalwirtschaft'. As the Roman cultural achievement could hardly be denied, preserving the theory required inventing a new economic type to accommodate evidence of large-scale production and extensive trade in the Hellenistic and Roman eras, but lacking elements believed to have inspired European economic development since the turn of the second millennium. The analytical solution to this conundrum proposed a hybrid stage characterized by mass employment of slaves in agriculture and manufacturing as a way of explaining large-scale production using

[8] "An augmentation of fortune is the means by which the greater part of men propose and wish to better their condition. It is the means the most vulgar and the most obvious..." (A. SMITH, *The Wealth of Nations*. 5th ed. New York, 1937 [1791], p. 325).

[9] R. H. FRANK, *Falling Behind. How Rising Inequality Harms the Middle Class*, Berkeley, 2007.

[10] The early eighteenth-century agricultural innovator Jethro Tull castigated such admirers as 'Virgillian'. G. E. FUSSELL, *Jethro Tull: His Influence on Mechanized Agriculture*. Reading, 1973.

primitive technology. Although part of the output of these household economies writ large was commercialized, markets played a minor role in determining the kind and quantity of goods produced, long-distance trade serving mainly to distribute commodities not everywhere available for elite consumption.[11] The missing ingredient was capitalist or, more properly 'bourgeois' enterprise that extended the sphere of commercial activity as its means of existence and primary goal.[12] By contrast, commercial activity in Roman antiquity was geared to maintaining self-sufficiency of elite families on a scale large enough to support their political and social ambitions. That vision is summed up by Finley in his celebrated account of the Roman failure to industrialize:

> Rostovtzeff and others following him have constructed a great theory about economic decentralization, the ruin of the bourgeoisie, the end of emergent capitalism, and the seeds of decline of the Roman Empire. I mean no offence, but this theory is an anachronistic burlesque of the affluent society. All that had happened was that a few minor trades over-reached the market, some hundreds of craftsmen in the western Empire in a few cities were displaced by some hundreds in a few other cities, and nothing else. They were no bourgeoisie to begin with, and imperial society was oblivious to, and unharmed by, the displacements.[13]

1 Neoclassical Economics

Superficially, nothing would seem to differ more from the typological vision of the stages theory than the economy depicted in neoclassical economics. Whereas the stages theory posits a community ontologically prior to the individuals it comprises, neoclassical economics is heir to a philosophical tradition which takes individual experience as the starting point of social construction. Only individuals matter and *de gustibus non est disputandum*. Apart from the anodyne premise that more is better than less, the propositions that proceed from that philosophical

[11] "The Roman economy, in spite of its sophistication in some respects, was predominantly a subsistence economy. The monetary economy constituted a thin veneer of sophistication spread over and tied to the subsistence economy by the liens of taxes." (K. HOPKINS, *Taxes and Trade in the Roman Empire (200 BC - AD 200)* in *JRS* 70, 1980, p. 101-125 (p. 104).

[12] The origins of that mentality were usually dated to the municipal revolutions of the twelfth century, which were thought to have created legal and social space for the capitalist institutions and bourgeois virtues. On the early historiography, see C. CROSSLEY, *French Historiography and Romanticism. Thierry, Guizot, the Saint-Simonians, Quinet, Michelet*, London / New York, 1993.

[13] M. I. FINLEY, *Technical Innovation and Economic Progress in the Ancient World* in *Economic History Review* n.s. 18, 1965, p. 29-45 (p. 42).

foundation claim to be value free.[14] Markets are simply a means of coordinating tastes and talents of individuals in a manner compatible with preferences, resources, and the state of technology. How does one know whether an economy is a market economy? The conventional test is whether observed prices and quantities are consistent with predictions predicated on the assumption that they reflect market supply and demand. Where there is consistency, markets are presumed to be present.[15] This is not the only conceivable test. Where we have archaeological evidence of large-scale specialized production and extensive distribution of the output, even without price data it is reasonable to interpret the data as evidence of market exchange by analogy with similar patterns observed in better documented eras, even though one has no way of observing the individual motivations or the precise institutional mechanisms.

The neoclassical and historical concepts of market economy nevertheless have more in common than meets the eye. One of the deep insights of theoretical economics is that prices and quantities in a closed economy are mutually determined by an accounting identity that makes the seller's income equal to the buyer's expenditure. That interdependence is abstractly captured by a system of simultaneous equations which set supply and demand of every good exchanged equal to each other combined with a 'no-profit' condition stipulating that prices equal the cost of production.[16] Since the number of independent equations equals the number of prices and quantities determined in equilibrium, the system's mathematical solution replicates outcomes a market economy would in principle realize if it were in full equilibrium. The model is called 'Walrasian' after the nineteenth-century economist who invented it.[17] Walras' supreme achievement was to show that (subject to certain qualifications) a general equilibrium logically exists.[18] A loose rendering of this proposition is that market economies tend towards the realization of a general equilibrium of prices and quantities. A corollary is that because the demand equations sum up the utility-maximizing

[14] This premise, though plausible, is not as benign as it seems. Formally it is derived from the logic of revealed preference—i.e., that when people choose, their choice reveals what they prefer, which by definition makes them better off in their own eyes. This is a logical, not an empirical proposition, however, and in practice impossible to verify. Its employment as the foundation of economic reasoning is an act of faith. For trenchant expositions of the problems involved, see I. M. D. LITTLE, *A Critique of Welfare Economics*, 2nd ed., Oxford, 1959 and A. SEN, *Rational Fools: A Critique of the Behavioral Foundations of Economic Theory* in *Philosophy and Public Affairs* 6, 1977, p. 317-344.

[15] TEMIN, *Roman Market Economy* [n. 3] performs several informal tests along these lines.

[16] This condition holds for reproducible goods.

[17] L. WALRAS, *Elements of Pure Economics*. Translated by Willliam Jaffé, Homwood (IL), 1954.

[18] Modern theoretical economics is largely given over to such 'existence proofs', which have much in common with the existence proofs in scholastic philosophy.

choices of individual agents, Walrasian general equilibrium thus maximizes economic welfare.[19] On this reading, a market economy exists to achieve the goal of maximizing welfare. Like the historical economic type, the neoclassical type is strictly functional.[20]

When economists like Temin speak of a 'market economy' this is the economy they are talking about. It is not a real economy; it is a toy economy built to facilitate mental manipulations thought to have a bearing on actual economies.[21] What makes the manipulation possible is a neat distinction between exogenous state variables and the endogenous outcomes generated by the equations. The state variables are the resource endowment (and its distribution among market participants), the technology, and the preferences of individuals with respect to goods, leisure, and saving; the outcomes are the prices and quantities ground out by the equations. Separation of exogenous causes and endogenous effects supports an intellectually simple (though computationally complicated) causal analysis that relates equilibrium prices and quantities change to changes in state variables. Since attitudes and social values can also be considered state variables, the model is similar to the idealization of the stages theory: economic performance is ultimately explained by cultural 'mentalités'.[22] The neoclassical market economy is thus also an ideal type, a static representation: that the Roman economy was a market economy therefore tells us nothing about how it came into being, expanded, and ultimately declined.

Explaining change within the Walrasian system involves identifying changes (and the causes of those changes) in state variables that drive the system. Analytically, the connection between the causes and the effects is secured by the presumption that resources are efficiently and fully employed—i.e., that the economy is operating at capacity given the stock of resources, technology and the

[19] Since individuals are supposed to have independent subjective valuations of their consumption, work, and savings, the maximum condition is expressed as a state in which no one can improve her state (from her own point of view) without worsening the state of someone else (from his point of view).

[20] This functionalist attitude is particularly pronounced in the works of Douglass North, and more generally in the New Institutional Economics. See D. C. NORTH, *Structure and Change in Economic History*, New York, 1981; D. C. NORTH, *Institutions, Institutional Change, and Economic Performance*. Cambridge / New York, 1990.

[21] "The model provides a simplified description of events that can be repeated and discussed, and it allows economists to test *counterfactual* propositions...." (TEMIN, *Roman Market Economy* [n. 3], p. 5).

[22] See Mokyr's remarks on Roman technological stagnation (J. MOKYR, *Technological Inertia in Economic History* in *Journal of Economic History* 52, 1992, p. 325-351); D. S. LANDES, *The Wealth and Poverty of Nations: Why Some are so Rich and Some so Poor*, New York / London, 1998, is a generic example. For a recent exercise of the same type see D. ACEMOGLU / J. A. ROBINSON, *Why Nations Fail: the Origins of Power, Prosperity and Poverty*, London, 2012.

preferences of its population with respect to work and saving. That presumption is commonly defended on the grounds that were the economy not operating efficiently, it would be possible for someone to profit by correcting the deficiencies, and since in the long run significant inefficiencies cannot be hidden, by the calculus of self-interest their persistence is logically impossible: a 50-euro note dropped on the sidewalk has a short half-life. The efficient markets hypothesis thus privileges supply side explanations of economic change.[23] When an economy is 'on its production frontier', the only way to increase output is to increase the input or improve the technology. This proposition is defended on the grounds that changes in state variables in traditional economies occur so slowly that people have sufficient time to discover and eliminate obvious waste, leaving the supply of inputs and technology as the logically sole source of movement.[24] Although the model allows changes in demand to affect outcomes, demand-based explanations are usually dismissed as *ad hoc* on the grounds that unobservable changes in preferences can be adduced to explain anything and are therefore non-scientific.[25] What matters are the factors governing the quantity and quality of inputs, the state of technology and institutional arrangements, to which may be added truly exogenous pandemic, tectonic and climatic events. To explain economic change is to identify when, where, and how these factors changed. For example, the common (and probably true) assertion that the extension of Roman control over the Mediterranean Basin during the late Republic gave a powerful boost to production and exchange identifies economic expansion with institutional change.

Neoclassical economics is especially helpful in interpreting the economic consequences of well-defined exogenous 'shocks' like pandemics,[26] and has been enthusiastically (if not always persuasively) used to interpret institutional arrangements as self-organizing responses to particular circumstances.[27] By

[23] For a vigorous conventional defence of this view, see J. MOKYR, *Demand vs. Supply in the Industrial Revolution* in *Journal of Economic History* 37, 1977, p. 981-1008.

[24] This was the burden of the claim by T. W. SCHULTZ, *Transforming Traditional Agriculture*, New Haven, 1964, that peasant economies are generally efficient.

[25] J. DE VRIES, *The Industrious Revolution. Consumer Behavior and the Household Economy, 1650 to the Present*, Cambridge / New York, 2008, makes an ambitious and in my opinion successful identification of changes in tastes that affected whole economies.

[26] W. SCHEIDEL, *A Model of Demographic and Economic Changes in Roman Egypt after the Antonine Plague* in *JRA* 15, 2002, p. 97-114.

[27] C. HAWKINS, *Manufacturing* in SCHEIDEL *et al.*, *Cambridge Economic History* [n. 2], p. 175-196. See S. OGILVIE, *Institutions and European Trade. Merchant Guilds, 1200-1800*. Cambridge, 2011 for a trenchant criticism of the tendency to over-interpret institutional forms as optimizing adaptations to the structure of transaction cost (see also in this volume the contribution by K. Verboven). It is worth noting that the subtext of adaptation models of self-organization is that government intervention is superfluous, if not positively harmful.

contrast, it is poorly suited to explain developments that endogenously arise in neoclassical equilibrium states in consequence of what Marxists call their 'internal contradictions.'[28] In this regard pre-modern economies pose a special problem for neoclassical explanations of economic change, because the technology and resource base evolved slowly, while population and output experienced wide swings. For lack of alternative explanations, economic historians have resorted to demographic and climatic change as ultimate causal forces. That such explanations withstand criticism is by no means evident.[29]

2 Search-Equilibrium Economics

While the strengths of the Walrasian framework are well-known, understanding its limitations requires exposure to its technical details. As is normally the case with economic models, its limitations are the price of its strengths. The strength is demonstrating the logical connection between factor and product markets in a market economy; the limitation is that a system of simultaneous equations requires everything to happen at the same time, which clearly is not the case in real economies. In particular, the equations tell us that in principle equilibrium exists, but not how it is attained. Walras' response to this difficulty was to imagine the economy as a general stock exchange in which buyers and sellers make bids and offers in response to prices 'cried out' by an auctioneer who raises the going price if demand exceeds supply and vice versa. No exchange takes place until all prices reach market-clearing levels, at which point the auction ceases and participants execute contracts agreed to in the price-making phase of the process. Walras' parable thus supplies a market process that in theory achieves general equilibrium. In fact, it is nothing but a verbal computer algorithm for solving systems of simultaneous equations. Whether it takes a long or a short time for the auction to achieve equilibrium is irrelevant, as no actions are taken until equilibrium is attained; only the solution matters. The auction is hermetically sealed off from acts of production and consumption.[30] Walras claimed the real

[28] See G. GRANTHAM, *The Gaidar Variations*. (The Gaidar Forum on Russian Economic Policy, Moscow. January 15-19, 2013) in *Kritika*, 2013, p. 7-37 for an airing of these issues.

[29] G. GRANTHAM, *Contra Ricardo: On the Macroeconomics of Pre-industrial Economies* in *European Review of Economic History* 2, 1999, p. 199-232.

[30] A particular difficulty is that production takes time, while the contracts for inputs and the sale of output must be simultaneously concluded as a condition of general equilibrium. Walras' solution is to imagine a market consisting of options to buy or sell ('bons'). Unlike real options markets, however, the options are valid only in equilibrium, so there is no speculation on their price as the auction proceeds. This feature further stresses the 'timelessness' of the Walrasian economy.

economy was 'like' his imagined one, but offered no evidence in support of that claim other than that prices tend to adjust to differences in supply and demand. The allegory is sometimes justified by the claim that market economies eventually converge to general equilibrium if you give them enough time, but Walras' great contemporary Alfred Marshall pointed out that the time required is so long as to be practically impossible.[31]

The Problem of Demand

Effective demand for a marketed good consists of market supply of the goods offered in exchange for it; every act of demand is thus simultaneously an act of supply. Where money is employed as a medium of exchange, that connection is loosened in the degree that demand for money fluctuates, as happens when financial crises cause people to hold their money for safe-keeping rather than spend it. In the long run, however, the relation between the stock of money and production of goods and services at a given price level is believed to be stable, which implies that the ultimate source of effective demand is marketed supply. That connection is formalized by an accounting identity known as Say's Law, which states that the market value of goods supplied necessarily equals the market value of goods demanded, a truism expressed by the maxim 'supply creates its own demand.'[32] Increased aggregate demand for goods and services logically must originate in increased capacity to pay for them by means of increased supply. Say's Law restates the Walrasian principle that economic change originates on the supply side.

The problem with that principle is that it is at variance with the facts. As will be discussed below, urban demand for produce was probably the most important factor determining the productivity of Roman agriculture;[33] its importance is well-

[31] "But in fact a theoretically perfect long period must give time enough to enable not only the factors of production of the commodity to be adjusted to the demand, but also the factors of production of those factors of production to be adjusted and so on; and this, when carried to its logical consequences, will be found to involve the supposition of a stationary state of industry, in which the requirements of a future age can be anticipated an indefinite time beforehand ... Thus the uses of the statical method in problems relating to very long periods are dangerous; care and forethought and self-restraint are needed at every step." A. MARSHALL, *Principles of Economics*. 8th ed., London, 1966 [1920], p. 315.

[32] Formally, Say's Law is the aggregate expression of the individual budget constraint that a person's purchasing power cannot exceed the market value of the goods and services he possesses.

[33] See especially ERDKAMP, *Grain Market* [n. 1] and J. J. KRON, *The Much Maligned Peasant. Comparative Perspectives on the Productivity of Agriculture in Classical Antiquity* in L. DE LIGT / S. NORTHWOOD (eds.), *People, Land, and Politics. Demographic Developments and the Transformation of Roman Italy 300 BC – AD 14*. Leiden / Boston, 2008 p. 71-120.

established for medieval and early modern Europe.[34] Similarly, high levels of specialization achieved in the major medieval cloth towns make no sense unless one posits a large (though geographically dispersed) demand for their products.[35] These well-attested facts raise the following question: where did the demand supporting that specialization come from? In the medieval case, demand for urban goods was originally thought to have been stimulated by growing agricultural surpluses made possible by agricultural innovation,[36] but this is now considered unlikely, as the alleged innovations were already present in classical antiquity, reopening the question of what caused them to develop and diffuse in the central period of medieval economic growth.[37] In a somewhat comparable context Allen has proposed that agricultural innovation in early modern England was stimulated by growth in urban demand resulting from the growth of foreign trade.[38] But that plausible argument leaves open the question 'what supported growth in demand for London's commercial services?'

Say's Law has no answer to such questions other than to posit technological change, increase in the resource endowment, or autonomous institutional changes enhancing economic efficiency.[39] It is a logically closed box, a perfect mousetrap: nothing gets out, but by the same token, nothing gets in. When a model ceases to explain significant facts, it is time to look for a new model.

[34] G. GRANTHAM, *Agricultural Supply during the Industrial Revolution: French Evidence and European Implications* in *Journal of Economic History* 49, 1989, p. 43-72; GRANTHAM, *Contra Ricardo* [n. 29]; A. DERVILLE, *L'Agriculture du Nord au Moyen Age. Artois, Cambrésis, Flandre Wallonne*, Lille, 1999.

[35] E. PERROY, *Le travail dans les régions du nord du XIe au début du XIVe siècle*, Paris, 1960. Fourteenth- and fifteenth-century Flemish militia lists reveal levels of specialization exceeding that of the Lancashire cotton towns in the nineteenth century. W. PREVENIER, *La démographie des villes du comté de Flandre aux XIIIe et XIVe siècles* in *RdN* 257, 1983, p. 255-275; A. DERVILLE, *Le nombre d'habitants des villes de l'Artois et et la Flandre Wallonne (1350-1450)* in *RdN* 257, 1983, p. 277-299.

[36] G. DUBY, *Économie rurale et la vie des campagnes dans l'occident médiéval*, Paris, 1962; G. DUBY, *Guerriers et paysans. VIIe - XIIe siècle. Premier essor de l'économie européenne*, Paris, 1973.

[37] G. RAEPSAET, *Les prémices de la mécanisation agricole entre Seine et Rhin de l'Antiquité au 13e siècle* in *Annales HSS* 50, 1995, p. 911-942; G. RAEPSET, *The Development of Farming Implements between the Seine and the Rhine from the Second to the Twelfth Centuries* in G. ASTILL / J. LANGDON (eds.), *Medieval Farming and Technology. The Impact of Agricultural Change in Northwest Europe*, Leiden / New York / Köln 1997, p. 41-68.

[38] R. C. ALLEN, *The British Industrial Revolution in Global Perspective*, Cambridge, 2009.

[39] D. C. NORTH / B. R. WEINGAST, *Constitutions and Commitment: The Evolution of Institutional Governing Choice in Seventeenth-Century England* in *Journal of Economic History* 49, 1989, p. 803-832.

2.1 Search-Equilibrium Economics

Although auctions are found in contexts ranging from highly organized markets for financial instruments and homogeneous commodities to works of art and the sale of fish fresh off the boat,[40] market economies are not general auctions. Most exchange is bilateral: one goes to one's shop to buy bread or fish, one sells one's home to a particular buyer, a company sales rep deals with particular clients. Rather than being simultaneously and continuously coordinated, market transactions are strung out in real time at prices that vary from moment to moment and place to place. Students of retail pricing find that even within relatively confined urban districts, the price of common items like tissue paper varies significantly from shop to shop, presumably because the cost to consumers of seeking out the best price is more than it is worth and because the cost to retailers of calculating optimal prices for everything they sell is also more than it is worth. Individuals in a market economy are therefore more like particles in Brownian motion randomly bumping into each other than participants in a virtual auction. Although people usually shop at the same stores and firms tend to deal with clients they know, the matching parable comes closer to describing what happens in a market economy than the auction parable.

Peter Diamond has developed a formal model that captures this aspect of markets.[41] The model was invented to analyse fluctuations in the 'natural' rate of unemployment, but it is readily adapted to explaining fluctuations in the division of labour and the extent of the market.[42] Rather than conceiving the economy as a general auction in which buyers and sellers continuously interact with each other as they respond to prices called out by the auctioneer, Diamond proposes an exchange economy consisting of a congeries of bilateral transactions matching particular buyers with particular sellers. To put that process in real time, he imagines exchange as a random process described by the probability that a seller achieves a successful match with a buyer within a given interval of time.[43] It is intuitively obvious that the greater the number of agents seeking matches the higher the probability of success. Price plays no role, because lowering the offer price or raising the bid price does not increase the probability of making a successful match. This captures the uncertainty of the market connection. If sales responded to prices, the market connection would already exist, and we would be in a Walrasian world. Diamond's matching model is as much a fiction as Walras' auction. The question is not whether one is nearer the truth than the other, but the

[40] R. S. GOLDFARB, *An Onassis Retrospective: What Products are Auctioned and Why?* In *Journal of Economic Education* 31, 2000, p. 157-167.

[41] P. A. DIAMOND, *A Search-Equilibrium Approach to the Micro Foundations of Macroeconomics*. (*The Wicksell Lectures, 1982*), Cambridge, 1984.

[42] GRANTHAM, *Contra Ricardo* [n. 29].

[43] The probability is the mean of a Poisson distribution. The function of this mathematical construction is to model transactions as occurring in real time.

kind of truth it seeks to uncover. The Walrasian model addresses questions that concern economic efficiency; the search-equilibrium model addresses the relation between the level of specialization and the extent of the market.

The crucial feature of the matching model is that it supports multiple steady states. This is because the probability of a successful market match is positively correlated with the number of agents seeking matches. At high levels of output, more agents are in the market than at low levels. Economies with the same population, technology, and institutional arrangements can therefore have different equilibrium levels of output and productivity depending on whether agents participate to a greater or lesser degree in market production. Because participation takes place continuously in real time, market equilibrium is defined by the condition that the depletion of sellers' inventories by successful matches is exactly replaced by new production.[44] Total output is constant. Unlike in Walrasian equilibrium, however, there can be more than one level of output that satisfies this condition. We now need to consider the decisions determining the level of output.

Decisions to undertake specialized production depend on how much it costs to produce. The costs that matter are irreversible costs that can only be recovered by achieving a successful match. The costs associated with specialization are the cost of acquiring specialized skill (you can't get your time and money back by promising to forget what you learned), investment in special-purpose facilities with no or limited alternative use, and time and money incurred in building up business reputation and knowledge of trading opportunities. For any agent contemplating production for market sale there is a maximum cost he is prepared to incur for the chance of making a sale. That decision depends on the likelihood of making that sale. At low probabilities, the odds are high that the irreversible sunk costs will not be recovered.[45] It follows that the greater the probability of making a sale, the higher the cut-off cost. Since projects with costs below the cut-off are accepted, a higher cut-off cost implies higher levels of aggregate output.[46]

Because individuals who invest in specialized skills and specialized facilities create hostages to fortune, the search-equilibrium approach is well adapted to modelling decisions to specialize. It captures the positive feedback between

[44] In the formal model agents produce to inventory and then attempt to sell that inventory through a random match with a buyer. As in the Walrasian model, theoretical clarity is purchased at the price of unrealistic assumptions. The choice of an appropriate model depends on how the assumptions distort the reality one is attempting to model.

[45] For technical reasons, Diamond represents the schedule of costs as a cumulative probability distribution from which agents contemplating investment make random draws, some projects incurring higher cost than others. The agent makes a draw and then decides whether the project is worth pursuing. This technical apparatus insures that, as in the matching process, decisions to produce occur in real time.

[46] Since projects with costs below the cut-off point are accepted, a rise in the cut-off point increases the total number of projects undertaken.

decisions to produce at higher cost (and thus at higher levels of output here interpreted as higher levels of specialization) and the probability that the sunk costs will be recovered, thus completing and formalizing Adam Smith's maxim that the division of labour depends on the extent of the market. Potential multiplicity of potential equilibrium states is driven by increasing returns in the number of persons engaged in production for the market and in the volume of transactions, but other factors reinforce that relation. In real economies market matching is coordinated by middlemen who invest considerable amounts of fixed capital, such as warehouses and transport facilities, and human capital in building up trade connections, evaluating the reliability of suppliers and customers, and learning how to discern differences in the type and quality of goods.[47] As the volume and profitability of exchange increases, it becomes economically advantageous to invest in roads, bridges, and port facilities. Perhaps the outstanding example from classical antiquity is the port of Ostia, a port only by virtue of its proximity to Rome. Situated on a shallow bay silted up with sediment from the Tiber, the port was an artificial creation of Claudius.[48] When Rome decayed, the port was abandoned.

Diamond's search-equilibrium parable offers a way around the problem of explaining changes in demand without finding a corresponding exogenous shift in supply. Say's Law still holds, as logically it must, but we are not required to seek exogenous causes of change. The search-equilibrium model describes an economy in motion, in which significant elements bearing on productivity and the quantity of goods exchanged interact with each other endogenously to produce varying levels of specialization and aggregate demand without necessarily affecting the resource base or technology. An increase in specialization for whatever reason tends to produce a higher level of aggregate demand, which in turn supports even greater specialization. Supply creates its own demand, but the converse is just as true.

2.2 *Multiple Equilibria*

That market economies with the properties described above can potentially operate at different levels of intensity raises the question of how the actual level is selected. If among the feasible levels only one outcome can be selected, we are back in the conventional world of unique equilibrium that makes economic

[47] These matters comprise the greater part of the material in the older merchant manuals like J. SAVARY / J. SAVARY DES BRUSLONS, *Le Parfait Negociant Ou Instruction Generale Pour Ce Qui Regarde Le Commerce des Marchandises de France, & des Pais Etrangers*, Paris, 1713.

[48] J. ROUGE, *Recherches sur l'organisation du commerce maritime en Méditerranée sous l'empire Romain*, Paris, 1966, p. 124-125.

change a consequence of well-defined causes. Although this can happen, there are reasons to think that it is not generally the case, and that economies with multiple stable equilibria have intermediate unstable points of equilibrium, which means that rather than going back to the initial equilibrium following a modest shock, the economy diverges to a new one that is higher or lower than the starting point depending on whether the shock is positive or negative.

The Malthusian paradigm is an example of stable equilibrium. When living standards diverge from the 'subsistence' target, the demographic response to that divergence forces the productivity of labour to its steady-state value. If the technology is static, population and total production revert to the initial state; if it is improving, population and production grow at a rate that just keeps the standard of living constant. It takes a permanent change in an exogenous variable such as the target subsistence income to change the equilibrium permanently. By contrast, in economies with multiple equilibria generated by economies of scale, a temporary shock can produce a permanent change in equilibrium owing to the positive feedback between changes in the level of output and changes in the level of productivity. If the shock is positive it can expand to a new higher equilibrium point; if it is negative, the economy can implode.[49]

A crucial question is 'what factors set the upper boundary to economic expansion?' There are two logical possibilities: the first is that it is determined by the stock of resources and the state of technology, which is the position held by Malthusianists; the second is that it is set by the institutional capacity to sustain the high volume of trade needed to sustain high levels of specialization. In effect this means maintaining high levels of effective demand. In pre-modern economies, the level of demand needed to sustain significant specialization was achieved through spatial extension of the market because the productivity of the dispersed agricultural population was low. This is the nugget of truth in the claim that the extension of Roman rule and Roman commercial law in the late Republic and the early Empire was a primary engine of economic growth, though one may dispute the claim that the transmission mechanism was the obligation to render tax and tribute to Rome.[50] It also suggests that monetary and fiscal stability, not to mention political stability, were essential to maintaining a market space supporting high levels of trade and specialization.

In brief, economies wherein processes analogous to matching are the primary means of effecting exchange—which would seem to cover all spatially extensive economies—are potentially unstable. Even where the fundamentals of technology, population, tastes, and resources stay the same they may experience wide swings in output and productivity in consequence of the internal dynamics of increasing return. The Great Depression of the 1930s and the current

[49] A graphical exposition of this property is set out in the Appendix.

[50] HOPKINS, *Taxes and Trade* [n. 11]. This original and thought-provoking article is now showing signs of age.

depression in Europe and the United States are modern examples of economies in which output fell without a corresponding regression in technology, population, or institutional structure.

3 Understanding the Classical Market Economy

We now turn from these abstruse matters to the interpretation of the classical economy. The first issue is whether the necessary conditions for a search-equilibrium economy were present in antiquity. One necessary condition is the existence of markets. This is now well-established. That market connections over any significant distance involved high levels of uncertainty concerning not only price but also the possibility of sale is also well-established.[51] The proliferation of regional fairs and the clustering of retail shops selling similar types of goods are naturally explained as evolutionary adaptations to the cost of search, making it advantageous to concentrate transactions in time and space.[52] It has recently been observed that a fruitful way of thinking about the Roman economy is in terms of variations in connectivity, which is better captured by the search-equilibrium parable than the Walrasian one.[53] The other conditions for a powerful positive feedback between the extent of the market and the division of labour are the presence of economies of scale in handicraft production and an agricultural supply function sufficiently elastic to prevent endogenous expansion from being shut down by the rising cost of food and organic raw materials. These two conditions are more problematic, especially the last one. The remainder of this paper is thus devoted to their investigation.

3.1 Economies of Scale

Although the ancients were more successful in harnessing the inanimate power of falling water than was once believed,[54] limited mechanization of industrial processes prior to the Industrial Revolution meant that with a few exceptions involving the harnessing of water power—notably milling grain, crushing ore,

[51] MORLEY, *Trade* [n. 1]; BANG, *Roman Bazaar* [n. 1].

[52] DE LIGT, *Fairs* [n. 1]; HOLLERAN, *Shopping* [n. 1].

[53] "[T]his is not a question of either total disintegration with completely isolated communities or fully correlated markets moving in absolute unison; we are trying to look at differences between a group of highly complex pre-industrial societies with forces working on several levels to tie localities into wider networks." BANG, *Roman Bazaar* [n. 1], p. 172.

[54] A. WILSON, *Machines, Power and the Ancient Economy* in *JRS* 92, 2002, p. 1-32.

and sawing stone slabs—the transformation of raw materials into final goods was done by hand.[55] The limited exploitation of inanimate power has led historians to conclude that the productivity of Roman manufacturing was low, because it was necessarily carried out in households or small workshops.[56] Yet, as Adam Smith pointed out, the gains in productivity through specialization by task in the context of handicraft manufacture were often substantial, as he showed in the celebrated example of the pin factory, which demonstrated the principle at work under a single roof. The common pre-industrial instances involve many roofs.[57] The reasons for the positive correlation between productivity and specialization are well-known: improved motor skills, better control of heterogeneous materials, and higher rates of throughput in industries where different stages of production can be carried out simultaneously.[58] Xenophon's example of the division of labour in shoemaking in fourth-century Athens, some workers cutting the soles, some making the uppers, and still others stitching them together into a finished shoe is a celebrated case in point.[59] Labour productivity can also be increased by reserving difficult tasks for skilled workers and hiving the simpler ones off to less skilled ones.[60] None of this necessitates direction of production under a single management.[61]

[55] See H. SCHNEIDER, *Technology* in SCHEIDEL *et al.*, *Cambridge Economic History* [n. 2], p. 144-171 for a useful brief review of the classical technological achievement.

[56] Commenting on the appearance in the early Empire of mass-produced ceramics on the Roman frontier Fulford writes, "Economy of scale has been suggested as another explanation for the 'marketing' success of these industries, but the labour-intensive nature of both production and distribution in particular argue against this as a significant factor." M. FULFORD, *Territorial Expansion and the Roman Empire* in *World Archaeology* 23, 1992, p. 294-305 (p. 296).

[57] "In those great manufactures, on the contrary, which are destined to supply the great wants of the great body of the people, every different branch of the work employs so great a number of workman, that it is impossible to collect them all into the same workhouse. We seldom see more, at one time, than those employed in one single branch." SMITH, *Wealth of Nations* [n. 8], p. 4.

[58] The impossibility of achieving this division of labour in agriculture, where the sequence of operations is determined by the rotation of the seasons was the main reason why agricultural productivity was less responsive to increases in demand than industrial productivity. This does not mean that there was no responsiveness, but the mechanisms of that response differed. See GRANTHAM, *Agricultural Supply* [n. 34]; G. GRANTHAM, *What's Space Got to Do with It? Distance and Agricultural Productivity Before the Railway Age,* Paper Presented to the Annual Meetings of the Economic History Association. Austin, TX (September, 2007) 2010, for discussion of these issues.

[59] HAWKINS, *Manufacturing* [n. 27], p. 175.

[60] K. L. SOKOLOFF, *Was the Transition from the Artisanal Shop to the Non-Mechanized Factory Associated with Gains in Efficiency? Evidence from the U.S. Manufacturing Censuses of 1820 and 1850* in *Explorations in Economic History* 21, 1984, p. 351-382.

[61] See the discussion of this point and evidence from antiquity in HAWKINS, *Manufacturing* [n. 27].

Ceramics are a good place to start because the ceramic record provides the fullest record of expansion and contraction of specialized production of a non-agricultural commodity.[62] Unlike most manufactured goods pottery does not decompose, nor like glass and iron can it be re-melted or forged into new objects. Pottery sherds thus constitute the most ubiquitous surviving pre-industrial objects. Since pottery is fragile, the need to replace broken pieces implies a potentially huge market. That same fragility made it costly to transport, so that in the absence of significant economies of scale in manufacture or significant reductions in transport cost, production and consumption of common types of pottery known as coarse ware were highly localized.[63] For ceramic articles to be extensively traded in quantities large enough to matter economically, they had to be produced cheaply enough to offset that transport cost.[64] In an age when pottery-making was ubiquitous, the only way to get the cost of commercial production low enough to compete with local producers was by exploiting economies of mass-production, and mass-production required access to thick markets.

The primitive technology of pottery making is simple enough to be part of normal household work, as it still is today in remote parts of Africa and South America. Clay is extracted from local beds, dried in the sun, and broken down and sifted to remove extraneous matter. It is then mixed with water and left to cure for a day or so before being 'tempered' with stones or sand to protect the finished vessel from thermal shock. The fabric is then worked by coiling ribbons of clay into pots, jars, and plates dried and then fired in a depression filled with brushwood.[65] At a slightly higher stage the work is done by part-time village potters who distribute their output locally. The archaeological record of that stage shows geographically scattered distribution of non-overlapping types that an earlier generation of pre-historians used as markers for 'cultures' or

[62] The interpretation of this record as an index of commercialized activity in general is a matter of some delicacy owing to imprecision in dating the material and distinguishing the effect of purely local factors from the general economic context. (K. GREENE, *Roman Pottery: Models, Proxies and Economic Interpretation* in *JRA* 18, 2005, p. 34-56; M. A. CAU / P. REYNOLDS / M. BONIFAY (eds.), *Late Roman Fine Wares. Solving Problems of Typology and Chronology*, Oxford, 2011.

[63] Such localization did not prevent widespread distribution of ceramic wares by persons who cooked with them whilst trading other commodities. Cf. R. TOMBER, *Indo-European Trade: the Ceramic Evidence from Egypt* in *Antiquity* 74, 2000, p. 624-631.

[64] It has been suggested that the fine wares produced in Tunisia might have been transported in ships that carried grain to Rome. A. CARANDINI, *Pottery and the African Economy* in P. GARNSEY / K. HOPKINS / C.R. WHITTAKER, *Trade in the Ancient Economy*, Berkeley / Los Angeles, 1983, p. 145-162; M. BONIFAY, *Ceramic Production in Africa during Late Antiquity: Continuity and Change* in L. LAVAN / E. ZANINI / A. SARANTIS (eds.), *Technology in Transition, AD 300-650,* Leiden / Boston, 2007, p. 143-158.

[65] D. P. S. PEACOCK, *Pottery in the Roman World: an Ethnoarchaeological Approach*, London / New York, 1982, p. 13-14.

'civilizations.' Low entry costs in manufacturing the coarse ware ordinarily used by rural households together with high transport cost constituted a barrier to centralized production that survived into the modern era.[66] The common pottery used as household cooking vessels was inherently non-tradable or at most locally tradable.

In view of these features it is remarkable that mass-produced oil lamps and the dinner ware known as *terra sigillata* were the most widely traded manufactured commodities in Roman classical antiquity of which there is clear evidence.[67] Glossy red slip ware manufactured at Arezzo reached beyond the *limes* to Russia and India, and across the Sahara to the Fezzan.[68] That the trade was well organized can be inferred from a case discovered unopened in the ruins of Pompeii containing 90 red slip vases and 30 pottery lamps shipped from the Gallic pottery at La Graufesenque.[69] The industry that developed in the immediate hinterland of Roman Carthage in the first centuries AD was even more impressive.[70] *Terra sigillata africana* is so omnipresent that it is the principal means of dating late Roman and early medieval strata.

Given the difficulty of transporting ceramics in bulk, it is noteworthy that apart from North African ware, which was produced near enough to the North African coast to be shipped by sea, the principal districts of concentrated ceramic manufacture were in out-of-the-way places. The Arretine industry was situated in the foothills of the Appenines 250 kilometres from Rome and 150 kilometres from the nearest seaport, while the great south Gallic pottery at La Graufesenque emerged in the remote highlands of the Causses and Cevennes. Relative isolation also characterizes the red slip industry in the Argonne, traversed by a single road connecting Metz and Rheims.[71] The location of these centres is not uniquely explained by privileged access to raw materials, for although the type of clay

[66] Shortly before the American Revolution, an attempt to establish a commercial pottery in Philadelphia failed because it could not reproduce wares imported from Britain at the high end of the market and could not compete with the local potteries serving farmers in the back country at the low end. PEACOCK, *Pottery* [n. 65], p. 31.

[67] G. PUCCI, *Pottery and Trade in the Roman Period* in P. GARNSEY / K. HOPKINS / C. R. WHITTAKER, *Trade in the Ancient Economy*, Berkeley / Los Angeles, 1983, p. 105-117; W. V. HARRIS, *Roman Terra Cotta Lamps: the Organization of an Industry* in *JRS* 70, 1980, 126-145.

[68] CARANDINI, *Pottery* [n. 64], p. 146.

[69] G. COULON, *Les Gallo-Romains. Les villes, les campagnes et les échanges*, Paris, 1990, p. 182.

[70] M. BONIFAY, *Etudes sur la céramique romaine tardive d'Afrique,* Oxford, 2004; M. MACKENSEN / G. SCHNEIDER, *Production Centres of African Red Slip Ware (3rd – 7th c) in Northern and Central Tunisia* in *JRA* 15, 2002, p. 121-158; M. MACKENSEN / G. SCHNEIDER, *Production Centres of African Red Slip Ware (2nd – 3rd c) in Northern and Central Tunisia* in *JRA* 19, 2006, p. 163-190.

[71] E. M. WIGHTMAN, *Gallia Belgica*, London, 1985, p. 145-146.

utilized in *terra sigillata* is not ubiquitous, it is widely distributed.[72] The emergence of large-scale production in out-of-the-way places seems therefore to reflect strongly increasing returns to agglomerated production seconded by investments facilitating the transportation and distribution of the final product.

Another indicator is the instability of sites of concentrated production. The spread of *terra sigillata* from Italy to southern Gaul and Tunisia has been long known,[73] but the displacement of primary centres of production within Tunisia over five centuries has only recently come to light[74] and the apparent ease with which a fine ware export industry emerged in the second century AD in northeast Gaul is underappreciated.[75] The instability of fine ware production sites (albeit over significant periods of time) indicates scale economies of agglomeration that could emerge in any number of places, and were held in place by the relative immobility of specialized labour and low transaction cost across short distances.[76] Positive feedback between productivity and volume of production propelling these centres, however, worked against them should they begin to decline. Although archaeological record does not tell us why production shifted from one place to another, the economics explains how it could happen. A further sign is the displacement of locally produced ceramics, which could only happen if there was price advantage for mass-produced pottery.[77] In Pannonia red slip ware produced in the Rhineland and southern Gaul utterly destroyed a local ceramic industry in the second century AD, although the local pottery has been judged by authorities to be technically equal to any contemporary product. The volume of trade was large enough for merchants exporting vessels from La Graufesenque to maintain a warehouse.[78]

[72] PEACOCK, *Pottery* [n. 65], p. 119. This was also true even of fuel. Note the success of the Pantellerian pottery in a context of scarce fuel.

[73] PUCCI, *Pottery* [n. 67].

[74] MACKENSEN / SCHNEIDER, *Production*, 2002 [n. 70]; MACKENSEN / SCHNEIDER, *Production*, 2006 [n. 70]; BONIFAY, *Etudes sur la céramique* [n. 70], BONIFAY, *Ceramic Production* [n. 64].

[75] I. HULD-ZETCHE, *Trierer Reliefsigillata. Werkstatt 1*. Bonn, 1972; WIGHTMAN, *Gallia Belgica* [n. 71]; M. POLFER, *L'Artisan dans l'économie de la Belgique Romaine à partir de la documentation archéologique*, Montagnac, 2005.

[76] On the transactions costs see HAWKINS, *Manufacturing* [n. 27].

[77] M. FULFORD, *Pottery and Britain's Foreign Trade in the Later Roman Period* in D. P. S. PEACOCK, *Pottery and Early Commerce. Characterization and Trade in Roman and Later Ceramics*, London / New York, 1977, p. 35-84. A second-century inscription containing the words *negociatore cretarii Britanniciani* identifies a merchant specialized in importing continental ware to Britain. *Ibid,* 38. In fairness it should be noted that FULFORD, *Territorial expansion* [n. 56] subsequently associated the wide distribution of red slip ware to the Roman military supply system.

[78] E. BONIS, *Pottery* in A. LENGYEL / G. T. B. RADAN (eds.), *The Archaeology of Roman Pannonia*, Lexington / Kentucky / Budapest, 1980.

Production in the main centres was highly standardized.[79] There was a clear effort to identify brands by stamping articles with the name of the pottery and the employee who made them. Moreover, there is clear evidence of attempts to counterfeit the more widely traded wares using false stamps, suggesting that there was a market among consumers who, like buyers of knock-off copies of branded goods today, appreciated but were not prepared to pay the price of the original.[80] The relatively modest quality of Gallic red slip ware, however, suggests it was primarily destined for a mass market spread over a wide area. The same was true of the less widely distributed burnished black ware that dominated the ordinary range of house wares in Britain between the second and the fourth centuries AD. Distribution was widespread, but production was concentrated in a handful of centres.[81]

Most of what we know about sources of increasing returns must unfortunately be inferred from the general characteristics of pottery-making and archaeological vestiges, since the industry has left virtually no literary remains. Nevertheless, with the exception of certain developments in the application of glazes, ceramic technology experienced no fundamental improvement from Roman times to the early eighteenth century, when Europeans successfully copied Chinese porcelain.[82] We thus know enough about ancient ceramic techniques to identify the sources of cost advantages in mass production.[83] The use of specialized equipment was crucial. In contrast to the traditional hand method of building pots from coils of clay, large-scale potters employed a weighted fly-wheel to build the clay rapidly into a cylinder. Used in conjunction with a cylindrical mould with the design cut into the interior wall a skilled potter could execute upwards of two

[79] A. WILSON, *Large-Scale Manufacturing, Standardization and Trade* in J. P. OLESON (ed.), *The Oxford Handbook of Engineering and Technology in the Classical World*, Oxford, 2008, p. 393-417.

[80] Some Gallic red slip vases imitate the Italian form and are stamped *arretinum uerum* or 'genuine Arrezzo'. PUCCI, *Pottery* [n. 67], p. 110; HARRIS, *Roman Terra Cotta Lamps* [n. 67], p. 138-139 documents similar unauthorized use of 'brand names' in copies of terracotta lamps, although he thinks that ceramic historians have exaggerated its extent.

[81] D. F. WILLIAMS, *The Romano-British Black-Burnished Industry: an Essay on Characterizaton by Heavy Mineral Analysis* in D. P. S. PEACOCK (ed.), *Pottery and Early Commerce: Characterization and Trade in Roman and Later Ceramics*, London / New York, 1977, p. 163-220.

[82] M. BERG, *Britain's Asian Century: Porcelain and Global History in the Long Eighteenth Century* in L. CRUZ / J. MOKYR (eds.), *The Birth of Modern Europe. Essays in Honor of Jan de Vries*, Leiden, 2010, p. 133-156.

[83] Fülle's assertion that the evidence does not support large-scale production based on division of labour rests on an undemonstrated assumption that the market for Arretine wares was not extensive enough to support it. This is precisely the question at issue. G. FÜLLE, *The Internal Organization of the Arretine Terra Sigillata Industry: Problems of Evidence and Interpretation* in *JRS* 87, 1997, p. 111-155.

hundred identical vessels per day.[84] There were also economies of scale in the preparatory operations. At Arezzo levigation tanks used to settle out heavier non-clay particles from the clay had a capacity of up to 10,000 gallons.[85] Kilns were built to fire large quantities at a time. Tunisian potters fired up to 2,000 pieces in hermetically sealed boxes.[86] Graffiti inscribed on sherds at La Graufensenque as a means of recording production indicate that as many as 30,000 individual pieces could be fired in a single batch. The same tally records 409,315 pieces produced by 34 workmen employed in a single establishment.[87]

The red ware industry collapsed between the fifth and seventh centuries. While the decline of the Arretine manufacture was probably due to competition from southern Gaul and North Africa (along with an ill-considered attempt to re-site production at a seaside location near Pisa), the Gallic and North African decline surely reflects the general contraction of the late Roman era and the correspondingly greater difficulty of marketing a product that was comparatively costly to distribute. The decline can be clearly seen in the deterioration of the quality of the red slip ware produced at La Graufensenque and other potteries that begins in the later third century and accelerates through the fifth and sixth. Wheel-thrown pottery was displaced by hand turned vessels; pots were made from coarser clays and fired at lower temperatures; slips were less carefully applied and the decoration deteriorated.[88] In Italy the decline is clearly signalled by the abandonment of specialized production in the upper Volturno valley in the early sixth century, although wheel-thrown wares continued to be imported into areas closer to the Adriatic coast, whence manufactured wares from Africa could still be secured at low cost.[89] North of the Alps, centralized production seems to have largely disappeared by the end of the sixth century.[90] The overall pattern is one of reversion to local markets. When the extent of the market contracted, so did large-scale high-quality production.

The ancient iron industry is an example of an industry whose output went mainly into fabricating weapons and agricultural equipment rather than articles

[84] PUCCI, *Pottery* [n. 67], p. 125-26.

[85] PEACOCK, *Pottery* [n. 65], p. 122.

[86] BONIFAY, *Ceramic Production* [n. 64].

[87] PEACOCK, *Pottery* [n. 65], p. 125-26.

[88] P. ARTHUR, *Form, Function and Technology in Pottery Production from Late Antiquity to the Early Middle Ages* in L. LAVAN / E. ZANINI / A. SARANTIS, (eds.), *Technology in Transition, AD 300 – 650,* Leiden, 2007, p. 159-186. The one exception to the general decline was the spread of lead glazed vessels.

[89] R. HODGES / H. PATTERSON, *San Vincenzo al Volturno and the Origins of Medieval Pottery in Italy* in *La ceramica medievale nel Mediterraneo occidentale*. (Congresso Internazionale della Università degli studi di Siena), Firenze, 1986, p. 13-26 (p. 23).

[90] HODGES / PATTERSON, *San Vincenzo* [n. 89], p. 16-17.

of popular consumption.[91] Unlike fine pottery, the techniques of ferrous metallurgy and ironworking were widely diffused through Europe and North Africa well before Roman annexation.[92] The technical mastery of Celtic smiths is well attested. By the end of the seventh century BC they had mastered the art of forging plough shares and by the beginning of the third were fitting iron tires to wooden wheels, more proficiently than their medieval successors who could only nail them.[93] Caesar admits to being impressed by the iron in the ships of the Venetii, noting that cross-pieces were fastened with nails "as thick as a thumb".[94] Iron was worked up in agglomerations like Michelsburg, Manching, and Alesia,[95] but the dispersion of the agricultural clientele that used them produced a sympathetic dispersion of smiths who forged and repaired the tools. That dispersion was re-enforced by the ubiquity of iron ore in quantities sufficient to supply the bowl furnaces used to reduce ore to iron in the first Iron Age. These factors supported widely distributed small-scale production oriented to the needs of local users.

Despite these constraints, archaeological investigations reveal numerous examples of iron smelting on a large scale.[96] Approximately one million nails, c. 10 tons, were discovered in the legionary camp of Inchtuthil in Scotland (occupied only briefly from c. 83-86/90CE). They had been deliberately buried when the camp was abandoned to prevent them from falling in the hands of the

[91] For examples see W. H. MANNING, *Catalogue of the Romano-British Tools, Fittings and Weapons in the British Museum*, London, 1985. Iron cooking vessels are an obvious exception. Perhaps the most sophisticated iron objects of popular consumption were the metal styli used to inscribe wax writing tablets, tweezers, and nail cleaners. A European inventory of these objects might provide useful insight into a metallic consumer industry. On their ubiquity in the Romano-British countryside, see D. MATTINGLY, *An Imperial Possession. Britain in the Roman Empire*, London, 2006, p. 461, 464-465. On their fabrication, see D. N. SIM, *Experiments to Produce Roman Styli by Forging and Machining* in *Antiquity* 71, 1997, p. 1011-1015.

[92] Central Europe 700 to 400 BC. I. BALASSA, *The Earliest Ploughshares in Central Europe* in *Tools and Tillage* 2, 1973, p. 242-255; M. BARANOVA, *The Agricultural Tools of Bohemia at the Beginning of the Iron Age (5th – 3rd Century BC)* in *Tools and Tillage* 6, 1989, p. 107-118.

[93] O. BUCHSENSCHÜTZ, *Les Celtes de l'Âge de Fer*, Paris, 2007, p. 64; S. PIGGOTT, *The Earliest Wheeled Transport. From the Atlantic Coast to the Caspian Sea*, Ithaca, NY, 1983, p. 164-167.

[94] Cited by K. GREENE, *The Archaeology of the Roman Economy*, London, 1986, p. 22.

[95] W. DEHN, *Aperçu sur les Oppida d'Allemagne de la fin de l'époque celtique* in *Celticum* 3, 1962, p. 329-375; G. JACOBI, *Die Ausgrabungen in Manching. Bd 5. Werkzeug und Gerät aus dem Oppidum von Manching*, Wiesbaden, 1974; M. MANGIN, *Un quartier de commerçants et d'artisans d'Alésia*, Paris, 1981.

[96] M. MANGIN, *La production du fer en France avant le haut fourneau* in R. PLEINER (ed.), *Archaeometallurgy of Iron 1967-1987. Symposium Liblica 1987*, Prague, 1989, p. 239-252.

Caledonians.[97] The works at Populonia are the best known,[98] but the list of other centres of production is lengthening as investigators sift through sites where nineteenth-century ironworks exploited and largely destroyed iron-rich slag from Iron Age smelting.[99] The district of Saulieu in the Morvan region of Burgundy is a good example. In the 1980s a systematic survey of 400 km² uncovered more than 200 ancient metal working sites, almost all bloomeries.[100] Iron bars discovered near the bloomeries were flecked with gangue, indicating that the sponge was intended for export to other districts to be worked up into bars and tools.[101] Investigators also found a big increase in the number of smelting sites after the Roman conquest. Specialized industry almost always implied specialized farming,[102] and it is therefore not surprising that the areas producing food for nearby iron-workers were more densely populated in the first centuries AD than 1800 years later.[103] Production fell off sharply in the fifth century AD and the region seems to have abandoned iron-working until the thirteenth century. Even then, production never

[97] W. H. MANNING, *The Iron Objects* in L.F. PITTS, *Inchtuthil : The Roman Legionary Fortress Excavations, 1952-65*, London, 1985, p. 289-299 (p. 289).

[98] O. VOSS, *The Iron Production in Populonia* in G. SPERL (ed.), *The First Iron in the Mediterranean. Proceedings of the Populonia / Piombino 1983 Symposium*, Strasbourg, 1988, p. 91-100. When French mining engineers surveyed the slag at Populonia in the 1850s it extended 600 meters along the strand. The quantity of smelted ore estimated from that pile is 2×10^6 tons over the four to five centuries the works were in operation. The abandoned site was the occasion for an elegiac reflection by Rutilius Namitanius (ca 420 AD) sailing past his way home in Gaul. *Cernimus exemplis oppida posse mori.* (NAMITANIUS, *De reditu suo sive Iter Gallicum* I, 414).

[99] M. RADWAN, *Méthodes appliquées en Pologne dans les recherches sur la sidérurgie ancienne des Monts Sainte Croix* in *Organon* 2, 1965, p. 133-153; M. KUNA, *Die Eisenverhüttungsanlagen der alteren Römischen Zeit in Řičiny* in R. PLEINER (ed.) *Archaeometallurgy of Iron, 1967-1987. Symposium Liblica 1987*, Prague, 1989, p. 109-118; MANGIN, *La production du fer* [n. 99].

[100] M. MANGIN / I. KLEESMAN / W. BIRKE / A. PLOQUIN, *Mines et métallurgie chez les Eduens. Le district sidérurgique et médieval du Morvan-Auxois*, Paris, 1992, p. 219.

[101] MANGIN *et al.*, *Mines et métallurgie* [n. 100], p. 235. Because small bowl furnaces did not reach temperatures high enough to fuse all the material in the ore, the sponge resulting from the smelting process was typically mixed with gangue that had to be removed by hammering.

[102] See in particular the remarkable surveys of central Auvergne. F. TREMENT, *De la Gaule Méditerranée à la Gaule Centrale : Paysages et Peuplements à l'Âge de Fer et à l'époque Romaine*, Mémoire d'habilitation. Aix-en-Provence, 2004; Y. DEBERGE, *Les établissements ruraux fossoyés en Basse Auvergne du IIIe au IIe s.av. n.è.* in C. MENNESSIER-JOUANNET / Y. DEBERGE (eds.) *L'archéologie de l'Age du Fer en Auvergne*. Actes du XXVIIe colloque international de l'AFEAF (Clermont-Ferrand, 29 mai-1er juin 2003), Lattes, 2007, p. 221-241.

[103] MANGIN *et al.*, *Mines et métallurgie* [n. 100], p. 17.

attained Roman levels, which no doubt explains why so many early sites survived to the twentieth century.[104]

Although the bloom produced by individual furnaces increased over time, restriction in the size of furnaces resulting from the use of hand-powered bellows meant that the growth in output was achieved by multiplying the number of furnaces. Archaeological excavation of ancient iron working sites in the Holy Cross mountains of southern Poland reveals batteries of 80 to 200 furnaces, and the remains at Populonia indicate a huge, though as yet undetermined concentration.[105] Concentrating bowl furnaces on a single site afforded economies in preparing and stocking fuel, roasting, crushing, and screening ore prior to smelting. In small works pieces of broken ore were sorted by hand; in large operations the ore was screened.[106] The use of pits to collect molten slag also exhibits local economies of scale. Drawing off slag to an external pit saved fuel and permitted a longer smelt because the slag no longer extinguished the fire in the bowl. To economize the cost of digging pits, furnaces were arranged in circular batteries draining into a common sink. The result was an increase in output per smelt. The size of blooms increased from two to three kilograms in the fourth century BC to 10 kilograms in the early Empire.[107] That the change was induced by increased demand seems certain, as the bloom fell back to around 5 kilograms in the early Middle Ages.[108]

Other industries also afforded significant opportunities to exploit latent economies of scale in the division of labour,[109] but the most interesting case in view of its subsequent importance for European industrialization is the hardest to trace. More than any other pre-industrial manufacture, textiles offered the widest possibility for commercialization because of potentially massive aggregate demand for ordinary products, a high level of product differentiation for signalling status, and low transport costs resulting from their high value relative to weight and bulk. At the same time, the process of production supported high levels of specialization by task, based on a succession of discrete operations transforming raw fibre into finished cloth, all of which could be simultaneously conducted in an on-going operation. In the later Middle Ages and early modern era, the sector supported a vast rural industry carried out in households and

[104] MANGIN *et al.*, *Mines et métallurgie* [n. 100], p. 237.

[105] RADWAN, *Méthodes appliquées* [n. 99]; VOSS, *The Iron Production* [n. 98].

[106] R. M. EHRENREICH, *Trade, Technology and the Iron-Working Community in the Iron Age of Southern Britain*, Oxford, 1985, p. 20-21.

[107] R. F. TYLECOTE, *The Pit-Type Iron-Smelting Shaft Furnace: Its Diffusion and Parallels* in *Early Medieval Studies* 6, 1973, p. 43-47; R. F. TYLECOTE, *Furnaces, Crucibles and Slag* in T. A. WERTIME / J. D. MUHLY (eds.), *The Coming of the Age of Iron*, New Haven, 1980, p. 183-228.

[108] R. F. TYLECOTE, *A History of Metallurgy*, 2nd ed., London 1992.

[109] The most recent survey is by WILSON, *Large-Scale Manufacturing* [n. 79].

organized by merchants who supplied them with raw materials and marketed the output through a 'putting out' system. Unfortunately, the evidence from classical antiquity is hard to come by. Literary references to places known for their textiles and to local breeds of sheep known for the quality of their wool indicate a manufacture resting in some measure on long-distance trade in raw materials and finished goods,[110] but apart from the well-known Igel monument,[111] the archaeological record has proven resistant to generalization derived from physical evidence.[112] The most promising sign of specialized manufacture to be recently recovered is the excavation of a neighbourhood in the Numidian city of Timgad that was given over to fulling (and possibly dying) woollen cloth for export.[113]

There is nevertheless one body of documentary evidence for specialized textile production that comes from inscriptions tax records from Ptolemaic and Roman Egypt that clearly indicate the existence of a local industry with significant division of labour.[114] A third century papyrus from Oxyrynchus records an advance payment to a tapestry weaver for two years' service by the master of a workshop. Another papyrus from the same *fond* mentions the foreman of a workshop said to employ 'scores' of workers.[115] Doss-Krüpe's exhaustive analysis of the tax rolls from the Theban districts of Oxyrynchus and Arsinoites reveals a well-developed industry that drew wool from specialized flocks in the Arsinoites, and a well-developed system of apprenticeship for training wool-

[110] A. M. H. JONES, *The Cloth Industry under the Roman Empire* in *Economic History Review* n.s.13, 1962, p. 183-192; J. P. WILD, *Textile Production* in J. P. OLESON (ed.), *The Oxford Handbook of Engineering and Technology in the Classical World*, Oxford, 2008, p. 465-495.

[111] J. F. DRINKWATER, *The Wool Textile Industry of Gallia Belgica and the Secundinii of Igel: Questions and Hypotheses* in *Textile History* 13, 1982, p. 111-128; J. F. DRINKWATER, *The Gallo-Roman Woollen Industry and the Great Debate: The Igel Column Revisited* in D. J. MATTINGLY / J. SALMON (eds.), *Economies beyond Agriculture in the Classical World*, London / New York, 2001, p. 297-309.

[112] M. GLEBA / U. MANNERING (eds.), *Textiles and Textile Production in Europe from Prehistory to AD 400*, Oxford, 2012: M. GLEBA, *Textile Production in Pre-Roman Italy*, Oxford, 2007.

[113] A. WILSON, *Timgad and Textile Production* in D. J. MATTINGLY / J. SALMON (eds.), *Economies beyond Agriculture in the Classical World*, London / New York, 2001, p. 271-286.

[114] K. RUFFING, *Die berufliche Spezialierung in Handel und Handwerk: Untersuchungen zu ihrer Entwicklung und zu ihren Bedingunen in der römischen Kaiserzeit im östlichen Mittelmeerraum auf der griechischer Inschriften und Papyri.* Rahden, 2008; K. DROSS-KRÜPE, *Wolle - Weber - Wirtschaft. Die Textilproduktion der römischen Kaiserzeit im Spiegel der papyrologischen Überlieferung*, Wiesbaden, 2011.

[115] J.-J. AUBERT, *The Fourth Factor: Managing Non-Agricultural Production in the Roman World* in D. J. MATTINGLY / J. SALMON (eds.), *Economies beyond Agriculture in the Classical World*, London / New York, 2001, p. 90-111 (p. 104-105).

combers, weavers, shearers, and tailors.[116] Although the nomenclature of the specialized occupations is not perfectly clear, there is enough to indicate a high level of specialization by task.[117] The number of persons involved in that manufacture appears to have been substantial, though possibly not so large as implied by an estimate from third-century tax rolls of an output of 100,000 pieces per year, which put Arsinoites "on a par with the greatest textile towns of the Middle Ages."[118] Dross-Krüpe estimates that the workers needed to produce the various kinds of cloaks recorded in the Oxyrynchus documents would have come to 21 percent of the local population.[119]

Across a wide spectrum of activities, then, the market economy of the ancient world possessed latent economies of increasing return. As noted in the first part of this paper, such economies raise the possibility of that economy possessing multiple equilibrium states. Since technologies and resources evolved slowly, rapid growth or decline could well have reflected movement from one state to another.

3.2 Agriculture, Population, and Diminishing Returns

Even if the division of labour and market pooling created a potential for increasing returns in the exchange and processing of raw materials, expansion could always be shut down by diminishing returns in agriculture. That this must have been the case is an article of faith among ancient historians old and new. Summing up the Roman economic experience, Temin writes, "Rome did not have an industrial revolution. Without this momentous change, Rome was subject to Malthusian pressures that limited its economic growth."[120] Commenting on the ancient limits to urbanization, Kehoe observes, "Since the growth of the urban economy was so closely linked to agricultural production, the possibilities for economic growth were limited."[121] Frier sums up the conventional wisdom:

"Simply put, what I wish to observe is that the Roman Empire was clearly exposed to the possibility of excess population growth, and that as a result some

[116] DROSS-KRÜPE, *Wolle* [n. 114], p. 106.

[117] "Diese schiere Vielzahl an Berufen und Spezialisierungenillustriert die Bedeutung dieses Wirtschaftssektors, in dem zweifelsohne eine grosse Zahl an Personnen ihr Auskommen fand." DROSS-KRÜPE, *Wolle* [n. 114], p. 101.

[118] P. VAN MINNEN, *The Volume of the Oxyrhynchite Textile Trade* in *MBAH* 5, 1986, p. 88-95, cited by DROSS-KRÜPE, *Wolle* [n. 114], p. 79.

[119] DROSS-KRÜPE, *Wolle* [n. 114], p. 85.

[120] TEMIN, *Roman Market Economy* [n. 3], p. 193.

[121] D. KEHOE, *The Early Roman Empire: Production* in SCHEIDEL *et al.*, *Cambridge Economic History* [n. 2], p. 543-570 (p. 546).

portions of the population could have approached the "Chinese" situation described by Wrigley and Schofield."[122]

The notion that the ancient economy was effectively constrained by a fixed land supply is a fixed point in reasoning about its expansion, stagnation, and decay. Yet, the proposition rests on its impeccable economic logic more than on empirical evidence—impossible to assemble at scales of aggregation required for effective testing.[123] The correlation between rising wages and large negative population shocks is suggestive, but hardly probative in view of other factors affected by a sharp drop in population unattended by a similar drop in the stock of exchangeable wealth. On the doubtful assumption that they are generated by nationally integrated markets for labour and farm produce, wage and price data provide the best opportunity to demonstrate the presence of Malthusian dynamics, but more than four decades of rigorous work with the extant time series on these data has failed to turn up unambiguous evidence of a Malthusian link between real wages and demographic changes in the pre-modern era.[124] What the data show is that there seems to be a secular ceiling to real wages.[125] It does not explain what imposed that ceiling. There is also little evidence that population pressure in the past depressed living standards to the edge of famine.[126]

The Malthusian paradigm rests on the assumption of diminishing returns for labour in agricultural production.[127] I have elsewhere argued at excruciating

[122] B. W. FRIER, *More is Worse: Some Observations on the Population of the Roman Empire* in W. SCHEIDEL (ed.), *Debating Roman Demography*. Leiden, 2001, p. 139-159 (p. 150).

[123] The Malthusian paradigm models the behaviour of a closed economy subject to diminishing returns, which are plausibly (though as it turns out incorrectly) implied by a fixed land input. Unless one has information on total input and output, individual observations will be contaminated by the possibility of trade in the output, which means nothing can be legitimately inferred from them with respect to the Malthusian hypothesis.

[124] D. R. WEIR, *Perspectives historiques sur les conséquences économiques de la croissance démographique rapide* in G. TAPINOS (ed.), *Conséquences de la croissance démographique dans les pays en développement*, Paris, 1991, p. 31-56; R. LEE, *Accidental and Systematic Change in Population History: Homeostasis in a Stochastic Setting* in *Explorations in Economic History* 30, 1993, p. 1-30.

[125] G. CLARK, *A Farewell to Alms. A Brief Economic History of the World*, Princeton, 2007.

[126] J. COHEN, *How Many People Can the World Support?* New York, 1995; C. Ó GRÁDA, *Famine. A Short History*, Princeton, 2009, but see M. KELLY / C. Ó GRÁDA, *The Preventive Check in Medieval and Preindustrial England* in *Journal of Economic History* 72, 2012, p. 1015-1036.

[127] It also applies to the production of energy, which has recently acquired prominence as the critical limiting factor on pre-industrial economic growth E. A. WRIGLEY, *Energy and the English Industrial Revolution*, Cambridge, 2010; P. MALANIMA, *Energy Crisis and Growth 1650-1850: the European Deviation in a Comparative Perspective* in *Journal of Global History* 1, 2006, p. 101-121.

length why I think that assumption does not necessarily hold for pre-modern economies.[128] The main reason is that traditional husbandry supported significant output in response to changes in market demand. This usually required increasing the input of labour and capital, which for ecological and economic reasons often resulted in rising rather than falling productivity of land and labour.[129] The working out of this effect took extended periods of time, because it was produced by gradual reorganization of the units of production and gradual accumulation of the capital (which assumed many forms, both physical and human) needed for more intensive specialized production. In the short term diminishing returns continued to hold; it was only over longer periods that adjustment market demand led to higher productivity. This process has recently been investigated for the region around Rome, which was particularly well situated owing to the enormous level of consumption of the capital's population. Erdkamp's study of the Roman grain trade at its height in the late Republic and early Empire shows the close connection between large and medium-sized landlords and farmers in the district and the markets they served. He estimates that in well-cultivated districts of Italy—well-cultivated because their farmers had an interest in cultivating them well—yield ratios were probably in the range of 8 to 10 to one, which at sowing rates of 2.5 to 3 hectolitres imply gross yields of 24 to 30 hectolitres per hectare, which is at the top of the range for pre-industrial yields.[130] Kron's review of the Latin agronomical treatises and the emerging picture of the Roman hinterland as a *pays* of prosperous modest farms gives confirming evidence of an agricultural system capable of producing significant surpluses when the occasion offered. The technological reason is that the technology underpinning classical farming was essentially the same as the agricultural technology of early modern and early industrial agriculture, so that, making due allowance for the climatic differences between central Italy and northern Europe, the productive response to local opportunity should have been similar.[131]

Average productivity in the Empire was undoubtedly low. In medieval and early modern Europe, where islands of high productivity are well-attested, everywhere else productivity was abysmal. At the beginning of the fourteenth century, when yields on some manors in southeast England approached 18 to 20 hectolitres per hectare, average yields in the country as a whole were probably

[128] GRANTHAM, *Agricultural Supply* [n. 34]; GRANTHAM, *Space* [n. 58].

[129] The changes also include rearrangements in farm size and lay-out to save labour, and the specialization of traditional tools to specific tasks.

[130] ERDKAMP, *Grain Market* [n. 1].

[131] "[T]he Romans incorporated most of the critical technical advances of seventeenth-century Dutch and nineteenth-century English farming into their already intensive traditional peasant agriculture." KRON, *Much Maligned Peasant* [n 33], p. 73.

around 10.[132] The most plausible explanation for that gap, which is reproduced at higher geographical scales, is that in most places it did not pay farmers to cultivate at levels of intensity producing high yields. The technology was there, but not the incentive.[133] In the pre-industrial era urban demand supplied the strongest and most stable incentives to reorganize agricultural production, which has led historians recently to connect the apparent prosperity of the Roman agricultural hinterland with the market at Rome. The evidence seems to confirm that hypothesis, but one should recall that additional output could sometimes be squeezed out by exploitative means—as apparently happened in Sicily—as well as by the positive intensive responses outlined above.[134] Productive responses to urban growth were not inevitable, as the experience of seventeenth- and eighteenth-century Naples clearly shows.[135] Yet, the balance of evidence suggests that in many parts of the Empire the response was positive. It is reasonable to suppose then, that over large swathes of the territory incorporated by Roman administration or affected by the Roman economy, the agricultural response to non-agricultural specialization (indexed to a large extent, but not entirely, by urbanization), was sufficient to meet the additional demand for food and raw materials it generated. Agricultural elasticity was a permissive, not a causal factor in the elaboration of more specialized economies.

In an argument dealing with agricultural productivity in Roman antiquity, one must inevitably say a few words about the vexed dispute between supporters of 'high' and 'low' counts of the population of Italy under Caesar Augustus. As is well known, Beloch adopted a low count based on his conviction that Italian agricultural productivity in the 1880s could not have been lower than in Roman times (although it might have been lower than during the Renaissance).[136] The finding that Italy's agricultural productivity in the late nineteenth-century was possibly only half what it was in 1300 suggests he was probably mistaken.[137] It is

[132] B. M. S. CAMPBELL, *English Seigniorial Agriculture 1250-1450*, Cambridge, 2000.

[133] G. GRANTHAM, *Searching for an Agricultural Revolution*, Paper Presented to the Stanford Workshop in Economic History, 2007; G. GRANTHAM, *What's Space Got to do with It? Space and Agricultural Productivity Before the Railway Age*, paper presented to the Annual Meeting of the American Economic History Association Meetings. Austin, TX, 2007, revised 2011.

[134] "More significantly, it cannot be automatically assumed that such a rise in the urban population was supported by increased productivity rather than, say, redistribution of the existing surplus production." N. MORLEY, *Cities and Economic Development in the Roman Empire* in A. BOWMAN / A. WILSON (eds.), *Settlement, Urbanization and Population*, Oxford, 2011, p. 143-160 (p. 151).

[135] B. MARIN, *Naples: Capital of the Enlightenment* in P. CLARK / B. LEPETIT (eds.), *Capital Cities and their Hinterlands in Early Modern Europe*, Aldershot, 1986, p. 143-167.

[136] E. LO CASCIO, *The Size of the Roman Population: Beloch and the Meaning of the Augustan Census figures*, *JRS* 84, 1994, p. 23-40.

[137] G. FEDERICO / P. MALANIMA, *Progress, Decline, Growth: Product and Productivity*

clear from the debate, however, that the dispute between the 'high counters' and the 'low counters' is unlikely to be resolved statistically by the kind of evidence that can be brought to bear on it. Deep ploughing of prime farm land in Italy has probably destroyed all possibility of recovering the density of rural settlement at different points of time in antiquity, and without that evidence it is impossible to set narrow bounds on the range of population estimates.[138] Insofar as adherents of the low count base their ultimate defence on the proposition that agricultural productivity was too low to support a high count—as I believe is Scheidel's ultimate line of defence—the claim introduces a premise not in evidence.[139] If anything, the evidence from agricultural productivity discussed above runs the other way. Anthropological evidence bearing on the nutritional status of rural people can potentially throw light on this question, but as yet sample sizes are too small and too dispersed to support broad generalizations about the supply of foodstuffs.[140] My own view is that agriculture was sufficiently responsive to support fairly high levels of non-agricultural specialists, who were not uniquely located in cities. Insofar as that population responded positively to income—or more precisely to opportunities for establishing independent households at customary living standards—low income and endogenous changes in output and specialization could go together. One does not exclude the other.

3.3 Growth and Decay

The Roman economy of the first century BC did not spring fully formed from a subsistence economy like Minerva from the head of Jupiter. The emergence of a spatially integrated economy stretching from the shores of the North Sea to the Euphrates occurred over eight to nine centuries during which trading connections between the eastern and western Mediterranean and between the Mediterranean and northwest Europe were intermittently knitted together.[141] Archaeological

in Italian Agriculture 1000-2000 in *Economic History Review* 57, 2004, p. 437-464.

[138] D. MATTINGLY, *Calculating Plough-Zone Demographics* in A. BOWMAN / A. WILSON, *Settlement, Urbanization, and Population*, Oxford, 2011, p. 76-97.

[139] W. SCHEIDEL, *Roman Population Size: the Logic of the Debate* in L. DE LIGT / S. NORTHWOOD (eds.), *People, Land, and Politics Demographic Developments and the Transformation of Roman Italy 300 BC – AD 14*, Leiden / Boston, 2008, p. 17-70.

[140] Kron gives a possibly over-optimistic assessment of these data (G. KRON, *Anthropometry, Physical Anthropology, and the Reconstruction of Ancient Health and Nutrition* in *Historia* 54, 2005, p. 68-83).

[141] G. GRANTHAM, *The Prehistoric Origins of European Economic Integration*, (Paper Presented to the Copenhagen Conference on Long-Run History. Copenhagen, July, 2003), 2006. This paper, which was submitted to the *Economic History Review* in the summer of 2006, sat on the referee's desk for three years before being rejected on the grounds that it not does cite SCHEIDEL *et al.*, *Cambridge Economic History* [n. 2], published in 2007!

evidence has confirmed and modified references to these developments in the ancient texts, although much remains obscure, particularly events in the fifth and fourth centuries that brought the Celts across the Alps into northern Italy and as far east as Galatia in Asia Minor.[142] One need not exaggerate the intensity of exchange to attest to its existence, which in terms of the search-equilibrium approach sketched out above is all that is needed to set the machine in motion. What seems clear from the record is that by the beginning of the sixth century BC substantial communities with commercial connections to the outside world had established themselves in south-western Iberia, Africa (modern Tunisia), Sicily and southern Italy, and Tuscany. The connecting of the eastern and western Mediterranean seems to have been provoked by rising demand for silver as a means of payment in the Assyrian and Persian empires, that of the Mediterranean and Celtic Europe by the Celts' infatuation with wine and exotic articles of adornment, remarkably including articles made with Chinese silk.[143] The western connection was made possible by the improvements in ship construction and rigging in the late Bronze Age Levant, permitting long voyages involving significant stretches of sailing against the wind;[144] the penetration of the Celtic hinterland probably involved little more than traditional pack animals.[145] One should not exaggerate these early connections. It was not until well into the sixth century BC that signs of quickening development in Iberia, Italy and Tunisia become clearly evident. It is perhaps significant that the Greek colonies in southern Italy adopted coinage almost simultaneously with Greek cities in the homeland.[146]

The real upswing in trade and production between northern Europe and the Mediterranean, however, seems to have begun after the middle of the fourth century BC. By the end of the third century, coins were being minted in Gaul. The following two centuries witnessed accelerated integration with the expanding Roman world. The evident quickening of exchange is associated with alteration in the size distribution of farms and the emergence of nucleated centres of

[142] "Les siècles appelés obscurs dans le monde grec, par lesquels nous allons aborder l'Âge de Fer, ne sont obscurs que pour nous." BUCHSENSCHÜTZ, *Les Celtes* [n. 93], p. 25.

[143] T. CHAMPION / S. CHAMPION, *Peer Polity Interaction in the European Iron Age* in C. RENFREW / J. F. CHERRY (eds.), *Peer Polity and Socio-political Change*, Cambridge, 1986, p. 59-68; F. LAUBENHEIMER, *Le Temps des amphores en Gaule. Vins, huiles et sauces*, Paris, 1991; H. SCHUTZ, *The Prehistory of Germanic Europe*, New Haven / London, 1983, p. 212.

[144] S. WACHSMANN, *Seagoing Ships and Seamanship in the Bronze Age Levant*, College Station, TX, 1998.

[145] LAUBENHEIMER, *Le Temps des amphores* [n. 143].

[146] R. OSBORNE, *Archaic Greece* in SCHEIDEL *et al.*, *Cambridge Economic History* [n. 2], p. 277-301 (p. 278); S. VON REDEN, *Money and Finance* in SCHEIDEL *et al.*, *Cambridge Economic History* [n. 2], p. 266-286.

artisanal production and distribution nodes.[147] In the first century BC these developments reached across the channel into southern Britain. Thus, by the time of the *Pax Romana*, the trading networks that would underpin the Roman economy at its peak were already largely in place. At present it is not yet possible to identify the shocks that set this process into motion, but it is becoming increasingly clear that the western European trading system was moving from a low to high-intensity equilibrium. That movement accelerated after the Roman conquest, likely owing to more rapid transfer of Mediterranean technologies and the imposition of a common law and a common peace.

The decline of the Roman economy was swifter than its rise. Setting aside the survival of a seemingly prosperous economy in North Africa and the eastern Empire through the fifth and into the sixth century, the collapse of the western economy after what now seems to have been a surprisingly prosperous fourth century is nevertheless remarkable for its rapidity.[148] The collapse does not seem to have been caused by a structurally overburdened agriculture or the inefficiencies of a supposedly 'dirigiste' state. The recovery of the fourth century belies the theory that it was triggered by the Antonine Plague. It was not caused by the invasion of 'hordes' of German barbarians, whose numbers we now know were small in relation to the settled Roman populations.[149] But collapse there was. The political chaos in the fifth century no doubt accounts for much of the decline, but its speed suggests that once the contraction began, the positive externalities that had powered growth in the expanding phase went into reverse with a vengeance. Search-equilibrium economics is a two-edged sword. When things are going well, it makes them even better; but when they start going poorly, the fixed costs that underpin increasing returns become more difficult to bear. Trade becomes more difficult and risky; the cost of maintaining connections takes up a higher proportion of the returns. As trade declines, the returns from trade decline. The first signs are the decay of the sites most directly connected with intense exchange: towns, cities, and specialized industrial establishments.

This is the briefest sketch of a possible dynamic of the classical economy. Most of the basic research needed to substantiate the claims made here still needs to be done. I believe that the necessary conditions for a search-equilibrium dynamic are well established. They include market exchange over significant distances, economies of scale in handicraft manufacture, and perhaps more contestably,

[147] BUCHSENSCHÜTZ, *Les Celtes* [n. 93].

[148] On the prosperity of the fourth century, see J.-M. CARRIE, *Les échanges commerciaux et l'État antique tardif* in *Les échanges dans l'Antiquité : le rôle de l'État*, Saint-Bertrand-de-Comminges, 1994, p. 175-211. The Romano-British economy was also at its peak around 350 CE. See MATTINGLY, *An Imperial Possession* [n. 91].

[149] W. GOFFART, *Barbarian Tides. The Migration Age and the Later Roman Empire*, Philadelphia, 2009.

elastic agricultural supply. Getting the chronology right is a more difficult enterprise. I believe a promising avenue is to construct inventories of agglomerated sites at 50-year intervals stretching from the fifth century BC to the sixth to seventh century AD. The growth of trade necessarily involved the creation of small centres that functioned as nodes in the trading network. The continued discovery of small towns from the Roman era whose populations probably ranged from 500 to 1000 persons suggests that this is exactly what happened.[150] Work by Frédérique Trément and his associates along these lines for Celtic and Roman developments in the Limagne in central France shows how this kind of inventory can be constructed over long periods of time.

As to the theoretical perspective, one must keep in mind that because neoclassical and search-equilibrium models address different questions they come up with different answers. The neoclassical model is concerned with the allocation of resources on the assumption that resources are scarce. The search-equilibrium model is concerned with the question of whether and why resources may be underutilized. The claim of this paper is that much (though not all) of the variation in production and productivity in antiquity arose from endogenous variations in the intensity of resource utilization. Resources may always be scarce, but in the presence of increasing returns the resource constraints are conditional on the state of the economy. The search-equilibrium paradigm is a looser, but richer framework for investigating the economic evolution of antiquity.

4 A Non-Mathematical Appendix[151]

Assume a barter economy in which goods are produced to inventory to be sold conditional on the seller finding a buyer. The variable of interest is the probability of meeting a buyer, who is simultaneously a seller of another good from inventory. Matching is a random process described by Poisson distribution the mean of which is the probability of an individual agent making a successful match in a fixed interval of time. It is assumed that this probability rises with the number of agents seeking matches. Equilibrium is defined by the condition of constant inventories—i.e., sales are exactly replaced by new production.

Inventories are produced at costs described by a cumulative frequency distribution.[152] After making a sale, an agent makes a random draw from that

[150] B. C. BURNHAM / J. WACHER, *The Small Towns of Roman Britain*, Berkeley / Los Angeles, 1990. Since the publication of this book, many more such centres have been discovered.

[151] This appendix verbally reproduces the mathematical exposition in DIAMOND, *Search Equilibrium* [n. 41].

[152] A cumulative distribution specifies the probability that a particular outcome has a

distribution. Since individual draws have different costs attached to them, higher levels of production to inventory necessarily involve some draws that incur higher cost, analogous to an upward sloping supply curve. The difference is that in a standard supply function producers compare the marginal cost of additional production with its expected price. Here, agents are presented with a project of predetermined cost, and decide whether to accept it on the basis of whether or not they can find a buyer for the output. There is a maximum cost at which agents will accept the project and produce to inventory.

We can represent the steady states associated with different cut-off costs by a graph with the cost on the vertical axis and inventories on the horizontal one. Following Diamond's notation we designate the inventories by the letter e and the cut-off cost by c^*. The graph sets out the steady state values of e (i.e. where inventories are constant) for different levels of c^*. The graph begins from a point above the origin because the least expensive draw has positive cost. The curve represents the minimum cut-off cost at which a given level of inventory is maintained in the steady state. Alternatively, it is the cost that must be met for production at that level to be sustained. The curve rises with inventories because higher levels of production require the acceptance of more costly projects.

The next step is modelling the cut-off cost for accepting a project to produce to inventory. An agent who sells her inventory makes a new draw from the distribution of possible projects to which there attaches a cost specific to that project. The cut-off cost is that cost at which she is indifferent about accepting or rejecting that project. Given the project's cost, the decision to accept depends on the probability of selling the inventory once it is produced—i.e., the probability of making a successful match within the matching time interval. Sales in that interval cover the cost of production, while failure to sell pushes the matching event forward in time, thereby imposing an additional interest cost. The cut-off cost thus rises with the probability of a successful match. Since that probability is positively correlated with aggregate inventories (i.e., the number of agents seeking matches), the higher the level of production to inventory the higher the cut-off cost. In ordinary language, production increases with the extent of the market, and the extent of the market increases with aggregate production.

probability of less than x, where the maximum value of x is 1. Thus, the probability that an outcome is less than 1 is 100 percent, while the probability of it being less than 0.5 percent will ordinarily be less than 100 percent. How much less depends on the shape of the function.

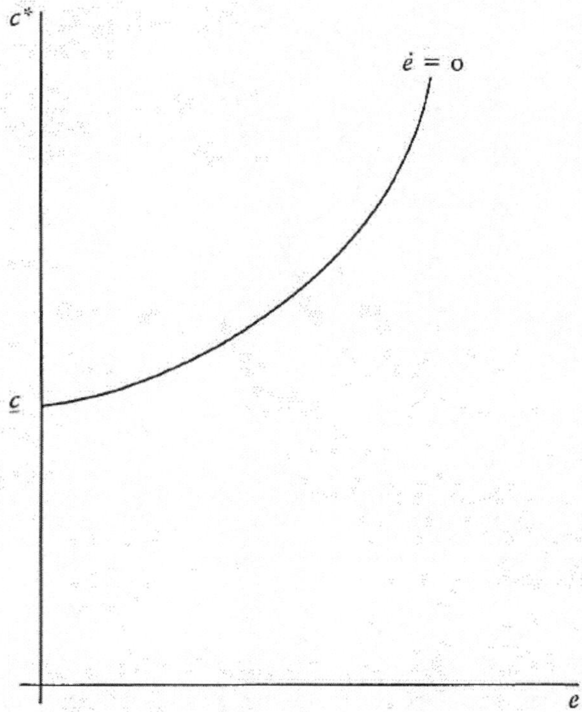

Figure 1

The form of the curve relating the cut-off cost to inventories is thus upward sloping from the origin (if there are no inventories there can be no prospective sales and thus no incentive to produce to inventory). On the assumption that the marginal utility of consumption obtained from the goods purchased with the proceeds from the goods sold from inventory diminishes with the level of output and consumption, the curve has an upper bound, and is therefore concave.

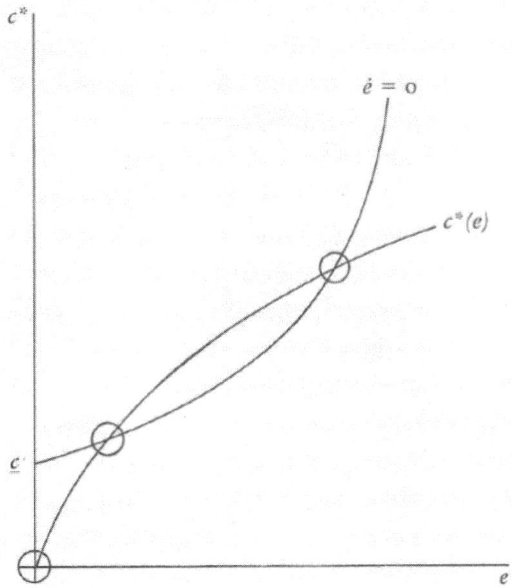

Figure 2

Putting the two functions together yields the steady-state level of aggregate inventories. This is the level at which the maximum acceptable cost associated with that level of production is the same as the minimum cost that must be accepted to sustain it. This equilibrium is illustrated by figure 2.

The concave upward curve is defined by the condition that inventories are constant ($e = 0$). This is the minimum cost that must be accepted to maintain inventories at a given level as denoted by the *e* axis. The concave downward curve is the maximum cost that will be accepted at any given level of inventories. Recall that the level of inventories is positively associated with the probability of a successful match.

Figure 2 shows that under the posited assumptions there is more than one possible equilibrium level of inventories: the origin, where nothing is produced, an intermediate level, where the maximum acceptable cost curve intersects the minimum acceptable curve from below, and a high level where the maximum intersects the minimum from above. The shapes of the curves are merely illustrative. In practice they may both be wavy.

The important equilibrium is the intermediate one. It is unstable. If for any reason inventories fall below that level, the maximum cost which agents will accept at the new level of inventories is below the minimum that must be accepted to maintain that level. As a result production falls. As long as this condition holds it continues to fall. The end point is the origin. This condition characterizes economic implosion. As the extent of the market contracts, the incentive to produce for the market contracts, which further diminishes the extent of the market. Conversely, deviations to the right of the intermediate equilibrium result in the minimum acceptable cost being below the maximum acceptable cost. Projects are accepted, inventories rise, which further increases the acceptable cost, creating a virtuous circle of expansion. That expansion is ultimately cut off by the rising marginal cost of additional projects, which can loosely be interpreted as reflecting the law of diminishing returns. The model thus has two stable equilibria. One in which there is no production, and one at which production is at a maximum.

The moral of the story is that an economy with positive costs of matching buyers and sellers is likely to have more than one stable equilibrium level of activity, which means that it can settle at a low level of output or a high level depending on which side of the unstable equilibrium it happens to land. Note that this account abstracts from feedbacks between the level of production and the menu of costs. Where there are economies of scale in production and distribution, a move to a higher equilibrium will cause the minimum cost of sustaining any given level of inventory to fall and the maximum price of undertaking new projects to rise. These reactions capture much of what Adam Smith had in mind when he asserted that the division of labour is limited by the extent of the market.

Jeroen POBLOME

The Economy of the Roman World as a Complex Adaptive System. Testing the Case in Second to Fifth Century CE Sagalassos

1 May I Introduce Myself?

The website of the research network "Structural Determinants of Economic Performance in the Roman World" claims[1] : "The study of ancient economies entered a new phase in the 1990s. Economic archaeology and natural science research provide new data on economic performance. Neo-institutional and development economics offer new theoretical frameworks. Comparative and 'longue durée' analyses gained central importance." There is a lot that should excite Roman archaeologists in these lines and in the rest of the research network's programme, especially those who, as in my case, have a background in the study of material culture[2] and the fields of artisanal production organization,[3] long-term regional development[4] and interdisciplinary

[1] http://www.rsrc.ugent.be/sdep

[2] J. POBLOME / D. MALFITANA / J. LUND, *Tempus fugit. "FACTA" manent. Editorial Statement* in *FACTA. A Journal of Roman Material Culture Studies* 1, 2007, p. 13-20; J. POBLOME / D. MALFITANA / J. LUND, *Scherben bringen Glück. HEROM's Editorial Statement* in *HEROM. Journal on Hellenistic and Roman Material Culture* 1, 2012, p. 7-22.

[3] J. POBLOME, *The Potters of Sagalassos Revisited* in M. FLOHR / A. WILSON (eds.), *Beyond Marginality. Craftsmen, Traders and the Socioeconomic History of Urban Communities in the Roman World*, Oxford, in press.

[4] J. POBLOME, *Word versus Dirt. History and Archaeology Applied to Proto-Historical Sagalassos* in T. BOIY / J. BRETSCHNEIDER / A. GODDEERIS / H. HAMEEUW / G. JANS / J. TAVERNIER (eds.), *The Ancient Near East, a Life! Festschrift Karel Van Lerberghe* (*Orientalia Lovaniensia Analecta* 220), Leuven, 2012, p. 457-470; J. POBLOME / D. BRAEKMANS / M. WAELKENS / N. FIRAT / H. VANHAVERBEKE / F. MARTENS / E. KAPTIJN / K. VYNCKE / R. WILLET / P. DEGRYSE, *How Did Sagalassos Come to Be? A Ceramological Survey* in M. TEKOCAK (ed.), *Studies in Honour of K. Levent Zoroğlu*, Antalya, 2013, p. 527-540; J. POBLOME, *Shifting Societal Complexity in Byzantine Asia Minor and Dark Age Pottery* in *LRCW4. 4th International Conference on Late Roman Coarse Ware,*

archaeology.[5] However, despite the excitement, the use of archaeology in the reconstruction of past economic patterns, structures and behaviour is not unproblematic or straightforward. In most cases, especially when performing fieldwork, 'ifs' and 'maybes' are an inherent part of archaeological epistemology. An important part of my time on campaign, for instance, is spent in the pottery shed. This is often the place where the gap between the archaeological material and the wider object of study (in this case the Roman economy) becomes very clear and wide. By using pottery templates, functional, typological, chronological, taphonomical and quantified details are gathered from sherds from excavated and surveyed loci, resulting in integrated and systemized information on tens of thousands of fragments of broken pottery.

Over the years, this practice has taught me two things. Firstly, that the use and meaning of numbers and totals of things found by archaeologists is never straightforward. For instance, locus SA-2012-PQ2-00041-0171, excavated in Eastern Suburbia at ancient Sagalassos (SW Turkey) contained 24 sherds of cooking vessels, weighing 659 g in total, and 831 sherds of the local tableware for serving and consuming food and drink, weighing 30,075 g in total. But, what does this actually mean in terms of real life in old Sagalassos? Each archaeological case needs translation to give meaning to 'facts'. Such translation can be provided by theories, concepts and models. One such model will be explored in this paper. The second thing I learned in my pottery shed is that those real people in classical antiquity, particularly the Romans, threw away an awful lot of stuff. So, either these were all very clumsy and dirty people (but I am prepared to positively discriminate against that idea) or a lot of things for day-to-day consumption were available to most citizens in the Roman world. Inevitably, my work with numbers and trying to match ancient production with consumption drove me, eyes wide shut, towards that notorious academic battlefield of the study of the ancient economy.

The first thing to do when in battle is to know your position. This helps to avoid unfortunate events such as, for instance, friendly fire. Considering the position of archaeology in the intellectual battlefield of reconstructing the past, the Cambridge historian and medieval numismatist Philip Grierson expressed his

Cooking Ware and Amphorae in the Mediterranean. Archaeology and Archaeometry. Mediterranean: A Market without Frontiers (Thessaloniki, 7-10 April 2011) (*BAR International Series*), Oxford, Archaeopress, 2014, p. 623-642.

[5] B. Neyt / D. Braekmans / J. Poblome / J. Elsen / M. Waelkens / P. Degryse, *Long-Term Clay Raw Material Selection and Use in the Region of Classical/Hellenistic to Early Byzantine Sagalassos (SW Turkey)* in *Journal of Archaeological Science* 39, 2012, p. 1296-1305; D. Braekmans / P. Degryse / J. Poblome / B. Neyt / K. Vyncke / M. Waelkens, *Understanding Ceramic Variability: An Archaeometrical Interpretation of the Classical and Hellenistic Ceramics at Düzen Tepe and Sagalassos (Southwest Turkey)* in *Journal of Archaeological Science* 38, 2011, p. 2101-2115.

opinion as follows: "It has been said that the spade cannot lie, but it owes this merit to the fact that it cannot even speak."[6] Clearly, it would be uncouth to reduce Philip Grierson's appreciation of archaeology to only one sentence, but as an active participant on the scene of historical archaeology, I sometimes wonder whether there is not some form of truth to this statement. I say this not because I, or any other fellow archaeologist for that matter, believe that we should be ashamed of the empirically driven epistemological trajectories of our archaeological discipline, but because examples of meaningful integration of historical and archaeological lines of thought are hard to come by. The research network "Structural Determinants of Economic Performance in the Roman World" should therefore be considered as a genuine opportunity to find cross-disciplinary synergies. Before the latter are achieved, however, we need to explain some basic points in order to understand each other's scientific rationale. The main aim of this paper, therefore, is to present the archaeological heuristic framework I use in my approach to the ancient economy.

2 Complex Complexity

Admittedly, with its use of machinery labelled "Inductively Coupled Plasma Mass Spectrometer"(to analyse the isotope balance in elements such as Strontium and Neodymium in order to determine geological provenances of raw production materials in antiquity) or of a technique called "Gas Liquid Chromatography"(to determine the presence and nature of chemical residue in archaeological artefacts to determine their function) archaeology—more specifically archaeological science in this case—may sound complicated. The important message to bring across, however, is that archaeology is not complicated, but complex. To most people, an airplane is complicated: it has lots of bits and parts that need to work together for it to operate. Contrary to a complex system, however, each airplane is supposed to function within a relatively narrow and preferably predictable range of possibilities. Archaeology on the other hand, as well as history, is complex, with a wide diversity of subjects, theories, methods, practices and epistemological traditions.[7] Archaeology is characterized by its ability to zoom in and out on an issue, considering its micro-environment as well as its contribution to broader disciplinary currents, giving rise to diverging research questions and paradigms.[8] As a matter of fact, archaeology harbours the fairly unique potential

[6] P. Grierson, *Commerce in the Dark Ages: a Critique of the Evidence* in *Transactions of the Royal Historical Society* 9, 1959, p. 129.

[7] See the arrays discussed in J. Bintliff (ed.), *A Companion to Archaeology*, Oxford, 2004 and I. Hodder (ed.), *Archaeological Theory Today*, Cambridge, 2012.

[8] T. Insoll, *Archaeology. The Conceptual Challenge*, London, 2007.

to explore past societal development by combining the dimensions of materiality and cognition with time and space.[9] What this means in simple terms, is that besides the traditional archaeological 'ifs' and 'maybes', there are also always more sides to an issue that you have not considered yet.

For instance, ground-breaking as the latest historical approaches to the study of the economies of the Greco-Roman world may be,[10] emphasizing how ancient economic structures fostered a potential of moderate growth on a regional scale, their innovative message has not yet been fully embraced in archaeology. More extensive and interdisciplinary archaeological case-studies on long-term regional development are still very much needed in order to map and compare aspects of societal development[11] and improve our understanding of what "moderate growth" could mean. Moreover, although a generation of interdisciplinary archaeological research in the region of ancient Sagalassos has established a pattern of regional growth in the intensity of exploitation of agricultural assets and raw materials, settlement patterning and demographic densities and we deduce from this that societal complexity increased between archaic and Roman Imperial times,[12] how did this affect the life experience of an average citizen in Roman Sagalassos, who did not know he was so-called better off than his archaic predecessor? Also, 'region' is a difficult concept to define, already in antiquity[13] but clearly also in archaeology.[14] For instance, local communities within what is traditionally regarded as a region in antiquity could follow different trajectories.[15] There is an implicit tension in archaeology in approaching regions and places[16] that makes the development of meaningful comparisons of societal and economic

[9] R. W. Preucel / L. Meskell, *Knowledges* in L. Meskell / R.W. Preucel (eds.), *A Companion to Social Archaeology*, Oxford, 2004, p. 3-22.

[10] W. Scheidel / I. Morris / R. Saller (eds.), *The Cambridge Economic History of the Greco-Roman World*, Cambridge, 2007; W. Scheidel (ed.), *The Cambridge Companion to the Roman Economy*, Cambridge, 2012.

[11] E.g. J.-F.Berger / L. Nuninger / S. van der Leeuw, *Modelling the Role of Resilience in Socioenvironmental Co-Evolution. The Middle Rhône Valley between 1000 BC and AD 1000* in T.A. Kohler / S.E. van der Leeuw (eds.), *The Model-Based Archaeology of Socionatural Systems*, Santa Fe NM, 2007, p. 41-59.

[12] Poblome *et al.*, *How Did Sagalassos Come to Be?* [n. 4].

[13] D. Dueck, *Geography in Classical Antiquity*, Cambridge, 2012.

[14] R. Tabor, *Regional Perspectives in Archaeology. From Strategy to Narrative* (*BAR International Series* 1203), Oxford, 2004.

[15] For example, Tanagra, Thespiae and Koroneia in Roman Boeotia as discussed in J. Poblome / P. Bes / R. Willet, *Thoughts on the Archaeological Residue of Networks. A View from the East* in S. Keay (ed.), *Rome, Portus and the Mediterranean* (*Archaeological Monographs of the British School at Rome* 21), London, 2012, p. 393-401.

[16] G. Reger, *Regions Revisited. Identifying Regions in a Greco-Roman Mediterranean Context* in *FACTA. A Journal of Roman Material Culture Studies* 1, 2007, p. 65-74. For a useful, geographical introduction: A. Herod, *Scale*, London, 2011.

development in the past difficult at best. Yet, developing higher level synthesis views on regional trajectories is essential in order to understand the workings of the Roman economy in greater detail, going beyond GDP guesstimates or macro-scale analyses.[17]

Apart from archaeological epistemologies being complex, working in historical archaeology also means that the subject matter is complex. Basically, whereas archaeology in general approaches the analysis of social complexity and its evolution in the long-term, historical archaeology is mostly concerned with specific periods and regions where the functioning of society itself had become complex. Historical archaeologists should consciously avoid aiming to establish a homogeneous, evolutionary account of social and regional development (from chiefdom to polis to state). Instead they should make the particularities and inconsistencies in the archaeological record of their particular study regions or domains contribute to debates in social, economic and regional archaeology. In trying to understand the Roman economy it is important to have an improved understanding of social complexity, and how this is tied to regionally specific pathways.[18] Although, through time, society has become more complex, "complexity should not be conceived as the ultimate goal of social evolution."[19] Rather than evolution, we need to understand social complexity. Different communities in the Roman Empire experienced evolving complexity in different ways, depending on how inequalities were established and contested. Social complexity and its development occurred on many levels, on many scales and in many contexts forming a system that cannot be explained by reducing it to its component parts.[20]

3 Heuristic Frameworks

The more complex things are the clearer the mind-map and intellectual concepts need to be. Combining and contrasting scales of analysis or 'multi-scalarity' is a current buzzword in archaeological circles.[21] In order to approach the issues raised above, we can deploy conceptual triangles as heuristic tools (Fig. 1).

[17] W. SCHEIDEL, *In Search of Roman Economic Growth* in *JRA* 22, 2009, p. 46-70; A. WILSON, *Indicators for Roman Economic Growth: a Response to Walter Scheidel* in *JRA* 22, 2009, p. 71-82.

[18] E.g. P. A. J. ATTEMA / G.-J. BURGERS / P. M. VAN LEUSEN, *Regional Pathways to Complexity. Settlement and Land-Use Dynamics in Early Italy from the Bronze Age to the Republican Period* (*Amsterdam Archaeological Studies* 15), Amsterdam, 2010.

[19] R. CHAPMAN, *Archaeologies of Complexity*, London, 2003, p. 7.

[20] R. BENTLEY / H. MASCHNER, *Complex Systems and Archaeology. Empirical and Theoretical Applications*, Salt Lake City, 2003.

[21] I. HODDER, *Contemporary Theoretical Debate in Archaeology* in HODDER *Archaeological Theory Today* [n. 7], p. 1-14.

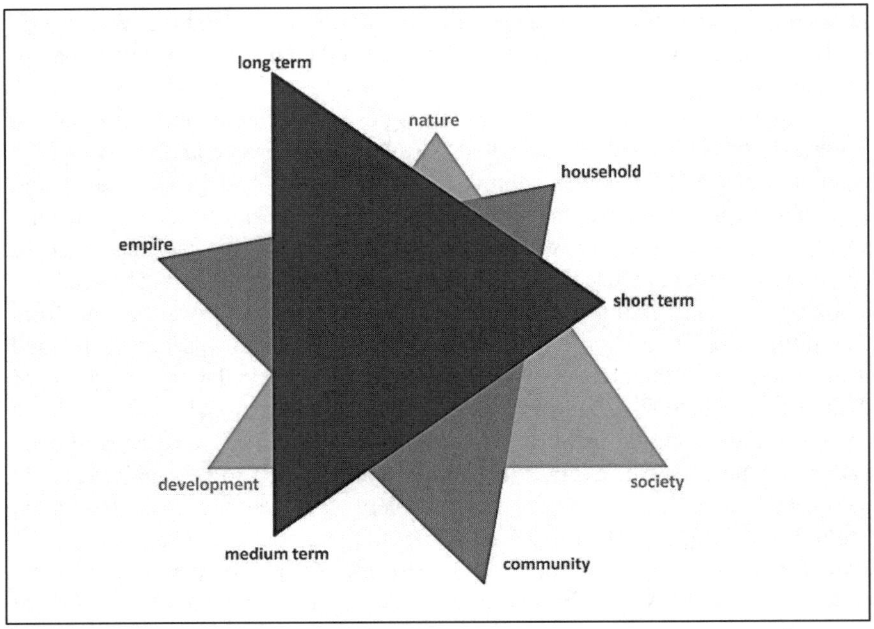

Figure 1. Overlapping heuristic triangles

The first conceptual triangle is focused on the thesis that regions develop in sustainable and economically sound ways (or not), as a result of the interaction over a long time-span between society and the physical environment. The interaction between nature and society constitutes regions socially. Regions are considered not as geographical units but as social constructs reproduced in the particular, localised cultural practices of individuals embedded in social and natural relationships, and these practices are repeated over various spatio-temporal scales.[22] It is the long-term production of the region that provides clues for sustainable social and economic development,[23] possibly resulting in moderate growth.

In order to make this archaeologically operational, a second heuristic triangle distinguishes the various spatial scales at which to unravel the complexity of these

[22] Often the study of material culture provides a useful proxy for approaching regions and regional identities, e.g. S. HALES / T. HODOS (eds.), *Material Culture and Social Identities in the Ancient World*, Cambridge, 2010.

[23] For inspiration, see R. A. DODGSHON, *Society in Time and Space. A Geographical Perspective on Change* (*Cambridge Studies in Historical Geography* 27), Cambridge, 1998; F. BERKES / J. COLDING / C. FOLKE (eds.), *Navigating Social-Ecological Systems. Building Resilience for Complexity and Change*, Cambridge, 2003.

processes: the scale of the household and the individuals composing it,[24] the scale of the community and its vertical interrelations with ecological and regional contexts,[25] and the scale of the horizontal networks that reach beyond communities in context, and connect them to the wider society, in this case the Roman Empire.[26]

Finally, after space, time also needs to be defined. When considering past regional developments, the basic idea developed by the *Annales School* of historiography that different historical processes work at different temporal scales, is often put forward as an alternative to linear interpretations of cultural change and social evolution.[27] The temporal scales of the *Annales School* are: the long-term, describing very slow-moving processes such as environmental changes, the medium-term, referring to social and structural history such as forms of social or economic organization, and the short-term, pertaining to events or individuals, a traditional focus of political history. History is constituted by unique combinations of the short, medium and long-term, whose processes run concurrently but at different wavelengths. It is the task of the historian and archaeologist to present the evidence for processes at the different timescales, and then analyse retrospectively how these interacted to create unique and unpredictable outcomes. Time is not a fixed structure in which changes simply take place, but is as multi-layered as these changes, and is moulded by them as much as it moulds them.[28]

This approach is part of new research programmes that were only recently launched.[29] This paper, therefore, will necessarily remain limited to a preliminary exploration and partial application of these conceptual triangles.

4 Higher Analytical Scales

When considering the *longue durée* as a chronological unit and empires as spatial units and social constructs, one way or the other, higher analytical scales suggest a certain degree of determinism. The homepage of the Orbis website,[30] featuring

[24] E.g. K. BOWES, *Houses and Society in the Later Roman Empire*, London, 2010.

[25] For a non-Roman example, N. MAC SWEENEY, *Community Identity and Archaeology. Dynamic Communities at Aphrodisias and Beycesultan*, Ann Arbor, 2011.

[26] D. J. MATTINGLY, *Imperialism, Power, and Identity. Experiencing the Roman Empire*, Princeton NJ, 2011.

[27] M. PLUCIENNIK, *Social Evolution*, London, 2005.

[28] G. LUCAS, *The Archaeology of Time*, London, 2005.

[29] The CORES network (http://iap-cores.be/): *Comparing Regionality and Sustainability in Pisidia, Boeotia, Picenum and NW Gaul between Iron and Middle Ages (1000 BC - AD 1000)* and BOF/GOA 13/04 on *Approaching Patterns of Nature-Society Interactions in Regional Development. An Interdisciplinary Dialogue between Past and Present in the Region of Sagalassos.*

[30] http://orbis.stanford.edu/

the Stanford Geospatial Network Model of the Roman World states that: "Spanning one-ninth of the earth's circumference across three continents, the Roman Empire ruled a quarter of humanity through complex networks of political power, military domination and economic exchange. These extensive connections were sustained by pre-modern transportation and communication technologies that relied on energy generated by human and animal bodies, winds, and currents. Conventional maps that represent this world as it appears from space signally fail to capture *the severe environmental constraints that governed the flows of people, goods and information*. Cost, rather than distance, is the principal determinant of connectivity" [my stress].

The very title of this book and of the research network 'structural Determinants of Economic Performance in the Roman World' suggests a similar view, for instance, with the ecological component being approached as a structural determinant, although generating both structural constraints and possibilities.

The scope of this research network is limited, however, compared to popular science authors such as Jared Diamond in his study on how societies collapse.[31] Diamond works with a five-point framework of possible contributing factors to collapse. His first factor "involves damage that people inadvertently inflict on their environment", disturbing the balance between the fragility of landscapes and their resilience. Diamond's second consideration is climate change, resulting from "changes in natural forces that drive climate and that have nothing to do with humans", but that provoke huge and sometimes impossible management issues for societies. The third and fourth factors are hostile neighbours, who are always ready to exploit your own weaknesses, and decreased support by friendly neighbouring trading partners. The last set of factors involves the responses of societies to their problems. Diamond's analytical framework tries to balance these factors, but in considering ancient society, he sees one overriding factor: demography. Basically, he takes a Malthusian approach. Population increase pushed up labour input per hectare and levels of land productivity, but also resulted in lower marginal returns per added unit of labour input, leading ultimately to ecological damage, demographic collapse and a reduction or loss of societal complexity. Considering our own global society, ecological problems play a much greater role in Diamond's work. But these too add to a framework that appears to be fairly deterministic, teleological and mostly external to society and human agency. It is as if people are allowed some degree of choice at remedying conditions, but mostly fail to anticipate, perceive, attempt to or manage to solve problems. Of course Jared Diamond cannot change the course of history for the case studies he presents and conjure up a happy ending where there is none, but I would like to come back to the Malthusian appreciation of demographic patterns.

[31] J. DIAMOND, *Collapse. How Societies Choose to Fail or Survive*, London, 2005.

Indeed when considering active, not-yet-collapsing pre-industrial societies, the so-called low-equilibrium trap, as recently discussed in the context of the Roman economy,[32] provokes a similar sentiment. The low-equilibrium trap is a way of expressing how underdeveloped economies cannot generate sufficient turnover, which is a necessary condition to induce investment, innovation and technological progress, from which systematic *per capita* growth can be realized.[33] Economies caught in the low-equilibrium trap cannot grow, as "in the long term, limited increases in output will raise surpluses less than population size and the latter will eventually offset intermittent productivity gains."[34] Somehow, the macro-level of analysis is no source for optimism.

5 Dealing with Change

To be sure, Jared Diamond, Walter Scheidel and the like are rightfully protagonists in this debate as they manage to develop highly original syntheses in interpretative frameworks that give meaning to the particularities and deficiencies of specific case-studies. Even though it is at no point their intention to convey deterministic messages and they basically aim for qualitative historical analysis of past communities as well as provide explanations for change, I wonder whether we cannot allow for more open-endedness in this story. If there is one structural determinant in the archaeological record, for instance, it is its constant change especially at the lower scales of the conceptual triangles, not only in physical terms, but also in how to understand it or to model it so as to better understand the past.[35]

This paper proposes to consider whether aspects of complex systems theory, representing a conglomerate of converging theories from ecology and the social sciences, might be applicable in archaeology, and more specifically in modelling trajectories of regions as dynamic socio-ecologic systems,[36] based on the heuristic framework of the mentioned conceptual triangles. This is done in partial, provisional and preliminary terms, considering the initial stages of the associated research projects and the attested difficulties in reaching meaningful

32 W. SCHEIDEL, *Approaching the Roman Economy* in SCHEIDEL, *Companion* [n. 10], p. 12-16.

33 R. R. NELSON, *A Theory of the Low-Equilibrium Trap* in *The American Economic Review* 46, 1956, p. 894-908.

34 W. SCHEIDEL, *Demography* in SCHEIDEL *et al.*, *Cambridge Economic History* [n. 10], p. 55-56.

35 G. LUCAS, *Understanding the Archaeological Record*, Cambridge, 2012.

36 T. A. KOHLER / S. E. VAN DER LEEUW, *Historical Socionatural Systems and Models* in KOHLER / VAN DER LEEUW [n. 11], p. 1-12.

interdisciplinary comparisons of environmental, climatic and socio-cultural patterns of change.[37] Interestingly, forests and human societies can both be considered good examples of what are called complex self-organizing adaptive systems.[38] In contrast to other (complex) systems, these are open and adapt to new challenges and problems. Complex adaptive systems are non-linear in trajectory, not predictable in behaviour, yet self-organised in the sense that they enhance co-evolution between entities in the system, improving their performance and strengthening complexity. The properties and behaviours of complex systems can only be attributed to the system as a whole, not to any of its particular parts. They are therefore considered as emergent properties. Ecological and social systems are not only complex, they are also integrated as social-ecological systems, as approached in the first conceptual triangle.[39]

The question is whether modelling regions as dynamic and complex adaptive socio-ecologic systems can make a useful contribution to research on the Roman economy. The focus on sustainability and resilience in the study of social-ecological systems seems most compatible with interdisciplinary approaches of past regional development. In this respect, assuming change and explaining stability, rather than the other way round, is a most interesting perspective from an archaeological point of view.[40]

For the social-ecological system of the Roman Empire to develop in sustainable ways, and for its economy to be successful at no matter which analytical scale, energy was needed.[41] Access to energy made the Roman Empire and the development of its regions resilient, adaptive and capable to solve problems, such as (among others) those caused by the level of its societal complexity. These characteristics of social-ecological systems are based on the fact that energy can move and when this happens the resulting flow of energy can sometimes be used to change things in the physical world; energy can produce 'work'. In simple terms, Roman farmers had a healthy breakfast in order to have sufficient energy to work their lands, the produce of which supplied sufficient

[37] M. O. BALDIA / T. K. PERTTULA / D. S. FRINK (eds.), *Comparative Archaeology and Palaeoclimatology. Socio-Cultural Responses to a Changing World* (*BAR International Series* 2456), Oxford, 2013.

[38] C. S. HOLLING, *Understanding the Complexity of Economic, Ecological and Social Systems* in *Ecosystems* 4, 2001, p. 390-405.

[39] F. BERKES / J. COLDING / C. FOLKE, *Introduction* in BERKES *et al.* [n. 32], p. 5-9.

[40] S. VAN DER LEEUW, *Land Degredation as a Socionatural Process* in R. J. MCINTOSH / J. A. TAINTER / S. K. MCINTOSH (eds.), *The Way the Wind Blows. Climate, History and Human Action*, New York, 2000, p. 190-210.

[41] J. A. TAINTER / T. F. H. ALLEN / A. LITTLE / T. W. HOEKSTRA, *Resource Transitions and Energy Gain: Contexts of Organization* in *Conservation Ecology* 7(3), 2003, p. 4: http://www.consecol.org/vol7/iss3/art4; T. HOMER-DIXON, *The Upside of Down. Catastrophe, Creativity and the Renewal of Civilization*, London, 2006, p. 36-42.

energy for landlords or urban councils to capitalize and invest in urban building projects. Mapping flows of energy as well as how much work a given system contains is the province of thermodynamics. In this way, thermodynamics can be considered as very appropriate to capture the global properties of complex systems, such as the Roman economy, without getting lost in details. This paper has no intention to archaeologically emulate thermodynamic laws on energy conservation and increasing entropy, or quantitative measures of the amount of thermal energy not available to do work. But archaeology can learn from this debate.[42]

Despite the fact that energy cannot be created or destroyed, it does inevitable degrade, making it progressively less useful for work. Whereas the thermodynamic laws pertain mostly to closed systems, complex systems such as the Roman economy are open. Such systems interact with other systems within the socio-ecological framework, by requiring high quality energy to maintain its societal complexity and upon work, releasing low quality energy such as waste. The discipline of ecology is currently developing the concept of exergy to apply the Second Law of Thermodynamics to open systems,[43] such as the complex adaptive socio-ecological systems under discussion. By definition, the exergy of a system or resource is the maximum amount of useful work that can be obtained from this system or resource when it is brought to equilibrium with the surroundings through reversible processes. The exergy concept traditionally finds application in technical process analysis, typically employed to find inefficiencies, or in environmental, economic and sustainability analyses of industrial systems. Basically, the flow and loss of exergy through specific parts of a process are mapped, in order to identify opportunities for improving process efficiency by modifying parts of a process that incur maximum loss of energy. For instance, whilst the energy flow diagram of a power plant would identify the large quantity of rejected heat as an opportunity for improving the system, the exergy analysis puts much less stress on this point because of the low temperature of the rejected heat, and thus a low ability to do work. Improving the steam generation system, however, results in much less overall loss of the system, including rejected heat, and much higher exergy generation.

Roman society was an open system receiving external exergy fluxes, mainly as solar radiation. This complex adaptive system used part of that external exergy to increase its internal exergy levels, such as those contained in the institutions

[42] J. BINTLIFF, *The Paradoxes of Late Antiquity: A Thermodynamic Solution* in *Antiquité Tardive* 20, 2012, p. 69-73; J. A. TAINTER, *Energy and Sociopolitical Collapse* in C. J. CLEVELAND (ed.), *Encyclopedia of Energy*, San Diego, 2004, p. 529-543.

[43] J. DEWULF / H. VAN LANGENHOVE / B. MUYS / S. BRUERS / B. BAKSHI / G. F. GRUBB / D. M. PAULUS / E. SCIUBBA, *Exergy: Its Potential and Limitations in Environmental Science and Technology* in *Environmental Science & Technology* 42(7), 2008, p. 2221-2232.

and structure of society, aimed at improving order in the system through selection and learning processes. In general, ecosystems and societies with higher exergy levels are more successful in dissipating external exergy flows; it means that they are better buffered and thus have higher stability, order and complexity.[44] Along these lines, the concept of moderate economic growth in Roman antiquity could be translated into the question of whether some of its communities and regions, and possibly even the Empire itself, were successful in buffering exergy and matching its exergy needs with those of the supporting ecosystems, combining sustainability and resilience. Archaeologists and ancient historians have learned to recognize scenarios of growth and have developed methodologies to analyse and explain these patterns.[45] But knowing the power of numbers in reconstructing the past, I wonder whether we are not sometimes confused by their meaning. Instead of measuring growth in regional systems, should we not be approaching the sustainability and resilience of regions and communities? Indeed, it is only when these manage to increase their exergy levels without substantially reducing that of their ecosystem or connected communities, that the pattern of development can be called sustainable.

A very important notion is that such systems are not in equilibrium—maintaining their operational level requires constant exergy input. Our poor old friend Sisyphos is an ideal metaphor for this condition, forever trying but failing to push his immense boulder up the slopes of Tartaros. But societies are even worse off than Sisyphos. In order to constantly maintain internal exergy levels and head off problems in case they do not, quite often societies increase their levels of complexity, resulting in higher operational costs and, at some point in the balance, in diminishing returns potentially reaching marginal levels.[46] In other words, providing for constant exergy needs implies adaptable strategies and changes in society. In complex adaptive systems, therefore, change is the norm. To an archaeologist, for whom documenting change in material culture or in stratigraphic layers is standard business, the accommodation of change in the concept of complex adaptive systems should sound more attractive than grand

[44] B. MUYS, *Sustainable Development Within Planetary Boundaries: A Functional Revision of the Definition Based on the Thermodynamics of Complex Social-Ecological Systems* in *Challenges in Sustainability* 1, 2013, p. 41-52.

[45] K. HOPKINS, *Taxes and Trade in the Roman Empire* in *JRS* 70, 1980, p. 101-125; R. B. HITCHNER, *Olive Production and the Roman Economy. The Case for Intensive Growth in the Roman Empire* in M.-C. AMOURETTI / J.-P. BRUN (eds.), *La production du vin et de l'huile en Méditerranée* (*Bulletin de Correspondance Héllenique Suppl.* 26) Athens, 1993, p. 499-505; R. SALLER, *Framing the Debate over Growth in the Ancient Economy* in J. G. MANNING / I. MORRIS (eds.), *The Ancient Economy. Evidence and Models*, Stanford CA, 2005, p. 223-238; R. SALLER, *Human Capital and Economic Growth* in SCHEIDEL, *Companion* [n. 10], p. 71-86.

[46] J. A. TAINTER, *The Collapse of Complex Societies*, Cambridge, 1988, p. 91-126.

meta-narratives of social evolution or low-equilibrium traps. Even more so as complex systems literature approaches change in social, economic and ecological systems in the same way, which presents an untapped potential for more integrated interpretation of past phenomena in interdisciplinary archaeology. Moreover, change is configured very close to the human experience. The source and role of change in complex adaptive systems has been conceptualized under the heading of panarchy theory.[47] Coined in contrast to 'hierarchy' in its original meaning of a set of sacred rules, the term 'panarchy' stands for a framework of natural rules, with symbolic reference to the Greek god of nature, Pan. The central conceptual tool in panarchy is the adaptive cycle (Fig. 2). This combines the factors of the rising/declining potential of systems with their degree of connectedness and their rising/declining resilience, and sees complex adaptive systems as typically evolving through variable cycles of growth (r), stability (K), catastrophic shift (α) and reorganization (Ω).[48] During the growth phase, the system's potential and connectedness increase, while its resilience gradually declines. At the top of the curve the system collapses, resulting in diminished connectedness and potential. There is a gradual build-up towards catastrophic shifts as a result of internal or external stress factors, but the exact time and space of regime shift is extremely hard to predict. Constrained breakdown can result in reorganization of the system, leading to a new equilibrium which might be very different from the previous one. In this way "the adaptive cycle embraces two opposites: growth and stability on one hand, change and variety on the other."[49]

Another attractive consideration, which fits in well with archaeology, is that adaptive cycles never exist in isolation but are nested in a hierarchy of slow large and small fast adaptive cycles. This nested hierarchy of adaptive cycles represents a panarchy, potentially spanning a large spatial range, from soil bacteria to the entire planet, and an equally vast temporal range, from seconds to geological epochs.[50] This notion is highly compatible with the concept of multi-scalarity in archaeological analyses,[51] laying out how different archaeological phenomena can be explained at one level but not necessarily pertain to others. Archaeological analysis needs to combine all scales. In survey archaeology, for instance, the *Annales* perspective has become one of the dominant frameworks to explain changes in the surface record (the 'conjoncture'), as this follows from the

[47] L. GUNDERSON / C. S. L. HOLLING (eds.), *Panarchy: Understanding Transformations in Human and Natural Systems*, Washington DC, 2002. See also the website of the Resilience Alliance: http://www.resalliance.org/.

[48] HOLLING, *Understanding* [n. 38], p. 390-405.

[49] HOLLING, *Understanding* [n. 38], p. 395.

[50] C. S. L. HOLLING / G. PETERSON, *Sustainability and Panarchies* in GUNDERSON / HOLLING, *Panarchy* [n. 47], p. 63-102.

[51] I. HODDER, *Contemporary Theoretical Debate in Archaeology* in HODDER [n. 7], p. 9-11.

interplay between the 'histoire événementielle' of historical sources, the more stable background of the landscape ('longue durée') and the 'mentalités' of individuals and societies.[52] History is thus made up of unique combinations of the short-, medium- and long-term, whose processes run at different wavelengths, but concurrently. Going back to panarchy, an interesting observation regarding adaptive cycles working together is that total collapse, in a Malthusian sense, can only happen when the various cycles are at the very same high point in their fore loops or are aligned at the same phase of vulnerability, approaching catastrophic shift. If there is no convergence of cycles, systems change, evolve and adapt. Collapse can happen, but change is more likely. Furthermore, the fact that different adaptive cycles operate at different levels, scales and speeds prevents a situation in which panarchy functions as a single deterministic system with only one outcome scenario.

As a result, adaptive cycles can work as heuristic tools to describe socio-economic complexity, with archaeological phenomena as proxies for the potential, connectedness and resilience of a given society. Archaeological regions, for instance, could be seen as panarchies, with linked adaptive cycles represented by households, communities and empires, and regional development traced according to the *Annales* perspective in order to establish shifting balances in social-ecological systems and the sustainability of regions. Clearly, as a heuristic tool, mapping adaptive cycles allows for breathing life and human agency into complex systems. Not many archaeological studies in this domain have been published, however.[53]

The final reason why concepts of thermodynamics and complex adaptive systems hold potential is that they create a methodological framework for comparison between adaptive cycles. Through the use of proxy data, these become measurable and comparable. The issue of diachronic or inter-regional comparison remains fundamentally unresolved in archaeology. As the concept of exergy revolves around work, both natural and social proxy data can be considered, implying that the full agenda of interdisciplinary archaeology can be

[52] J. Bintliff (ed.), *The Annales School and Archaeology*, Leicester, 1991.

[53] See for instance C. L. Redman / A. P. Kinzig, *Resilience Theory, Society, and the Longue Durée in Conservation Ecology* 7(1), 2003, p. 14: http://www.consecol.org/vol7/iss1/art14. For a comparable perspective applying aspects of thermodynamics, see Bintliff [n. 42], p. 69-73.

brought to bear. More than ever, the successful application of this model depends on sound source criticism and genuine interdisciplinary collaboration.

Touching base again with the Roman economy, recent efforts at higher level synthesis were mostly focused at the higher scale of empire. Notwithstanding the solvability of this research, the integration of other analytical scales remains a

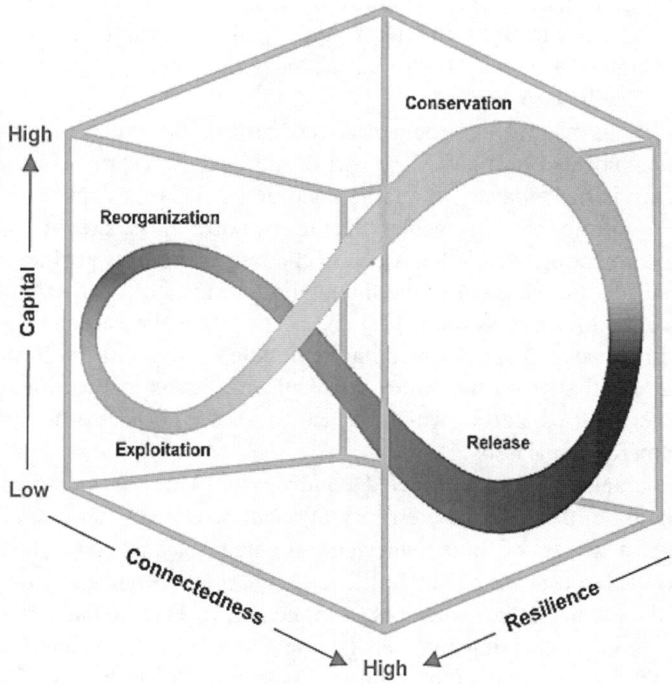

Figure 2. Graphic representation of the adaptive cycle

scholarly requirement. Making the concept of adaptive cycles operational at those lower levels of analysis, such as regional communities and households, could make a contribution to the debate, in order to make variability in development in spatial and chronological terms visible as well as allow for human agency. The Roman economy is not an independent sphere, but intimately connected with nature and its exergy flows and the path dependency, resilience and creativity of its social communities. The economic sphere formed part of a dynamic and dialectic web of relationships with demography, culture, technology, politics, religion and society, in accordance to Heraclitus' adage *panta rhei*.

6 Sagalassos between the Second and Fifth Centuries CE

I will now explore these concepts, building on a range of already published ma terial related to the productive landscape of a case-study with which I grew familiar over the years: the archaeological site and region of Sagalassos (SW Turkey) (ancient Pisidia). Recently, a first attempt was made to approach loss of societal complexity in Byzantine Dark Age Sagalassos within the framework of complex adaptive systems.[54] In this paper, the period between the second to fifth centuries CE will be looked into.[55]

As far as its natural environment is concerned, the archaeological site of Sagalassos is located in the western part of the Turkish Taurus Mountains. The ancient town is tucked away in a large bend of the Ağlasun dağı range (*c.* 1800 m) (Fig. 3), forming the spectacular crest to the north of the site with the Akdağ (2271 m) dominating the northeast end of the range. From its position at the top of a V-shaped valley incised in the mountains, the ancient town (1490-1600 m) overlooked the lower areas to the east and south. The valley acts as a permanent creek, draining several springs feeding the middle course of the Ağlasun Çayı, a permanent small river in the valley south of Sagalassos and a tributary of the ancient river Kestros, part of which formed the eastern border of the territory of Roman imperial Sagalassos.[56]

The mountain landscape directed connectivity. Most of the research area, corresponding to the 1200 km^2 territory of Sagalassos in Roman Imperial times, is actually a series of interconnected mountain basins. The Burdur Plain represents the largest tract of flat, fertile lands within the Roman territory, at *c.* 30 km from the town. Natural corridors from the Bay of Fethiye and Antalya reach the latter plain, connecting into the Isparta Plain. The Augustan *Via Sebaste* followed the east corridor, representing, together with the Kestros Valley, the major lines of communication from the south coast to the interior[57] (Fig. 4).

Pronounced winter precipitation and summer dryness characterize the climate in the vicinity of Sagalassos as Mediterranean, with a shorter dry season and lower temperatures in all seasons compared to coastal zones and significantly cold

54 J. POBLOME, *Shifting Societal Complexity* [n. 4].

55 The terms 'late Roman' and 'early Byzantine' are used as relative chronological indicators of periods, mostly referring to the later 3rd to the first half of the 5th century CE for late Roman and the later 5th to 7th centuries CE for early Byzantine.

56 E. PAULISSEN / J. POESEN / G. GOVERS / J. DE PLOEY, *The Physical Environment at Sagalassos (Western Taurus, Turkey). A Reconnaissance Survey* in M. WAELKENS / J. POBLOME (eds.), *Sagalassos* II. *Report on the Third Excavation Campaign of 1992*, Leuven 1993, p. 229-231.

57 S. MITCHELL, *Anatolia. Land, Men, and Gods in Asia Minor*, 1. *The Celts and the Impact of Roman Rule*, Oxford, 1993, p. 70-79.

winters with a high number of frost-thaw cycles.[58] The environmental and climatic conditions sustained the regional vegetation of the area, forming part of an Oro-Mediterranean vegetation belt with deciduous oak forests found below coniferous forests.

Comparable to what was happening in many other communities in the Roman Empire, the Antonine era was a period of bliss for ancient Sagalassos. The programme of urban monumentalisation peaked with the spectacular Antonine Nymphaeum on the Upper Agora, as well as the completion of the enormous Imperial Baths and the scenic Theatre, worthy of Edward Gibbon's famous praise of the period.[59] Judging mainly from the epigraphic record, the region of Pisidia seems to have escaped the worst effects of the third century CE crisis and even saw "the interests of the Roman state and of their regional subjects in Pisidia ... definitively and consciously aligned, both at the public and private level."[60] The Potters' Quarter of Sagalassos, where Sagalassos red slip ware was produced on a large scale, was also one of the few proficient production centres in the Roman East to continue its production activities throughout this period of crisis.[61] Recently, pollen analysis has picked up contemporary signals of stress of a different nature, however. Also, the second half of the fourth century CE introduction of amphora production in the surroundings of Sagalassos has been considered as part of an agricultural attempt at reconversion,[62] resulting in the local successes during the Theodosian dynasty.[63]

[58] PAULISSEN *et al.* [n. 55], p. 231-233; M. VERMOERE, *Holocene Vegetation History in the Territory of Sagalassos (Southwest Turkey). A Palynological Approach* (*Studies in Eastern Mediterranean Archaeology* 6), Turnhout, 2004, p. 8.

[59] E. GIBBON, *History of the Decline and Fall of the Roman Empire*, London, 1993 [1776-1788], p. 90.

[60] S. MITCHELL, *Greek Epigraphy and Social Change. A Study of the Romanization of South-West Asia Minor in the Third Century AD* in *XI Congresso Internazionale di Epigrafia Greca e Latina*, Rome, 1999, p. 421.

[61] J. POBLOME, *Mixed Feelings on Greece and Asia Minor in the Third Century AD* in D. MALFITANA / J. POBLOME / J. LUND (eds.), *Old Pottery in a New Century. Innovating Perspectives on Roman Pottery Studies*, Catania, 2006, p. 189-212.

[62] J. POBLOME / M. CORREMANS / P. BES / K. ROMANUS / P. DEGRYSE, *It Is Never Too Late... the Late Roman Initiation of Amphora Production in the Territory of Sagalassos* in I. DELEMEN / S. ÇOKAY-KEPÇE / A. ÖZDIZBAY / Ö TURAK (eds.), *Euergetes. Festschrift für Prof. Dr. Haluk Abbasoğlu zum 65. Geburtstag*, Antalya, 2008, p. 1001-1012.

[63] M. WAELKENS / I. JACOBS, *Sagalassos in the Theodosian Period* in I. JACOBS (ed.), *Production and Prosperity in the Theodosian Age,* Leuven, 2014.

Figure 3. View from the Akdağ towards ancient Sagalassos. The town was laid out on the plateaus in the centre of the image

The previous paragraph reads like a traditional historical synthesis of development, albeit with some regional accents. But perhaps this line of thought should allow for a degree of complexity? How do Antonine and Theodosian bliss compare for the community of ancient Sagalassos? I intend to explore the regional complex adaptive system in preliminary ways, considering the interdisciplinary indicators available in publications related to the productive landscape, bearing in mind the heuristic framework discussed above.

The main question is how nature-society interactions sustained and/or limited subsistence strategies and community building from the second to the fifth centuries CE in the study region of the 1200 km^2 territory of Roman Sagalassos. The available indicators are positioned within adaptive cycles, evaluating their rising/declining potential with their degree of connectedness and their rising/declining resilience through time, space and scale in consideration of path dependent assets. Palynological, archaeobotanical, archaeozoological and artisanal data are highly relevant when considering the productive landscape and their analysis provides information on the potential of the regional nature-society interactions, on presence and changes in flora and fauna, and indirectly on environmental and climatological conditions, and human impact and exploitation potentially affecting connectivity and resilience.

7 Pollen, Precipitation and Plants

In this context, some of the published pollen sequences are relevant, collected within the Ağlasun and Çanaklı Valleys, the Gravgaz basin and the Bereket marshes, as the crow flies at respectively 3 and 8 km south, and 15 and 37 km southwest of the town of Sagalassos and within its Roman Imperial territory.[64] The general position of Anatolia, forming a bridge between continents, the rough regional topography of the Taurus Mountains, as well as the long history of human presence in the landscape resulted in a complex history of changes in climate, vegetation and human impact. A traditional focus of palaeo-ecological and palaeo-climatological research is the so-called Beyşehir Occupation Phase,[65] characterized by signs of intense human impact such as revealed by increases in arboriculture, identified at various locations in the Eastern Mediterranean between roughly 1000 BCE and 800 CE. Following the start of the Beyşehir Occupation Phase in the region, the pollen records show an additional increase in anthropogenic indicators during the first century BC. In the Ağlasun Valley oak woodland increased along with secondary anthropogenic indicators, being non-cultivated plants which fare better in association with human activities such as agriculture, while in

[64] VERMOERE *Holocene Vegetation* [n. 58]; J. BAKKER / E. PAULISSEN / D. KANIEWSKI / V. DE LAET / G. VERSTRAETEN / M. WAELKENS, *Man, Vegetation and Climate during the Holocene in the Territory of Sagalassos, Western Taurus Mountains, SW Turkey* in *Vegetation History and Archaeobotany* 21, 2011, p. 249-266; J. BAKKER / E. PAULISSEN / D. KANIEWSKI / J. POBLOME / V. DE LAET / G. VERSTRAETEN / M. WAELKENS, *Climate, People, Fire and Vegetation: New Insights into Vegetation Dynamics in the Eastern Mediterranean since the 1st Century AD* in *Climate of the Past* 9, 2013, p. 57-87; D. KANIEWSKI / E. PAULISSEN / V. DE LAET / K. DOSSCHE / M. WAELKENS, *A High-Resolution Late Holocene Landscape Ecological History Inferred from an Intramontane Basin in the Western Taurus Mountains, Turkey* in *Quaternary Science Review* 26, 2007, p. 2201-2218; D. KANIEWSKI / E. PAULISSEN / V. DE LAET / M. WAELKENS, *Late Holocene Fire Impact and Post-Fire Regeneration from the Bereket Basin, Taurus Mountains, Southwest Turkey* in *Quaternary Research* 70, 2008, p. 228-239.

[65] W. VAN ZEIST / H. WOLDRING / D. STAPERT, *Late Quaternary Vegetation and Climate in Southwestern Turkey* in *Palaeohistoria* 17, 1975, p. 55-143.

Bereket and Gravgaz signals of the increased presence of olive trees and cereals were picked up.[66]

In general, the valleys and the lower hill slopes are considered to have yielded cereals. Bread wheat formed the main part of the diet throughout the study period. Palynological and archaeological evidence allows for postulating that olive cultivation also made a contribution to the regional portfolio, as indicated for the Gravgaz Valley and the slopes surrounding the northern part of the Çanaklı Valley.[67] In addition to the pollen samples, stone weights from lever-and-weight presses are mostly found in the western and central parts of the town's territory.[68] These simple presses could have been used for the processing of olives as well as grapes.[69] Olive trees, however, were not so common in the Ağlasun Valley. Here, walnut cultivation played a role, as did patches of oak woodland and, on the higher slopes, for instance north of Sagalassos, coniferous forests were maintained. M. Vermoere considered the continued presence of both forest types as an indication of "a kind of ecological consciousness"[70] on behalf of the community of Sagalassos. In the wider region, storax was possibly also tapped for its resin while a semi-parasitic insect on kermes oaks produced vermilion dye.[71] Pollen analysis indicated the cultivation of grapes near Gravgaz and also on the southern slopes near Sagalassos.[72]

From the middle of the third century CE onwards, cereal and olive cultivation is proportionally less well represented in the Gravgaz basin, but neither cultivation disappeared before the seventh century CE. At the same time, more pollen linked with pine and moist deciduous trees is picked up, as well as of plants associated with meadows. During the later third century CE, the environment became moister.[73] At Bereket, olive cultivation seems to have come to an end in the first half of the fourth century CE at the latest, while open steppe vegetation became more typical for this valley.[74] In this way, the

[66] VERMOERE, *Holocene Vegetation History* [n. 58], p. 108-111.

[67] VERMOERE, *Holocene Vegetation History* [n. 58], p. 156-164.

[68] VERMOERE, *Holocene Vegetation History* [n. 58], p. 239-276.

[69] R. I. CURTIS, *Food Processing and Preparation* in J.P. OLESON (ed.), *The Oxford Handbook of Engineering and Technology in the Classical World*, Oxford, 2008, p. 381-383.

[70] VERMOERE, *Holocene Vegetation History* [n. 58], p. 114.

[71] VERMOERE, *Holocene Vegetation History* [n. 58], p. 108-114.

[72] VERMOERE, *Holocene Vegetation History* [n. 58], p. 160, 186.

[73] BAKKER *et al.*, *Climate of the Past* [n. 64], p. 70.

[74] BAKKER *et al.*, *Climate of the Past* [n. 64], p. 70; E. KAPTIJN / J. POBLOME / H. VANHAVERBEKE / J. BAKKER / M. WAELKENS, *Societal Changes in the Bereket Valley during the Roman Imperial Period. Results from the Sagalassos Territorial Archaeological*

early end of the Beyşehir Occupation Phase in the Bereket basin more or less coincided with a gradual decrease of human impact on the environment in and around the Gravgaz basin and relatively moister conditions. Although the latter could have been beneficial for intensive agricultural activity, as attested elsewhere in the Roman East,[75] in the cases of Gravgaz and Bereket, and probably also the Ağlasun Valley, expanding marshes and wetlands may have reduced the availability of arable land. It is unclear whether the same was happening in other areas of Sagalassos' territory. Wetlands are actually fairly exceptional landscape phenomena in the study area, but outside of these landscape pockets pollen is insufficiently preserved. Geomorphological analysis, on the other hand, indicates that the Büğdüz river valley accumulated large quantities of fine sediments, mainly from the first century CE onwards. The sediment eroded from the surrounding hill slopes, on which grassland and forests were converted into agricultural land. During the period concerned in this paper, the lack of major disturbances in the river's sedimentation could be indicative of maintained agricultural practices until around 600 CE.[76] In general, the continuity of the pollen signal hints at rational exploitation schemes of the forests, cultivated tree species and cereal cultivation into early Byzantine times, as the relatively moist conditions persisted until the middle of the seventh century CE.[77]

Survey 2008 (Southwest Turkey) in *Anatolian Studies* 63, 2013, 75-95.

[75] Y. HIRSCHFELD, *A Climatic Change in the Early Byzantine Period? Some Archaeological Evidence* in *Palestine Exploration Fund Quarterly Statement* 136, 2004, p. 133-149; M. DECKER, *Tilling the Hateful Earth. Agricultural Production and Trade in the Late Antique East*, Oxford, 2009, p. 8-11.

[76] K. D'HAEN, *Fingerprinting Late Holocene Sediment Fluxes in an Eastern Mediterranean Mountain Catchment*, Unpublished Ph.D. Thesis, University of Leuven, 2012, p. 156; B. DUSAR, *Late Holocene Sediment Dynamics in a Mediterranean Mountain Environment*, Unpublished Ph.D. Thesis, University of Leuven, 2012, p. 170.

[77] VERMOERE [n. 57], p. 171-190; M. VERMOERE / S. SIX / J. POBLOME / P. DEGRYSE / E. PAULISSEN / M. WAELKENS / E. SMETS, *Pollen Sequences from the City of Sagalassos (Pisidia, SW Turkey) in Anatolian Studies* 53, 2003, p. 161-173.

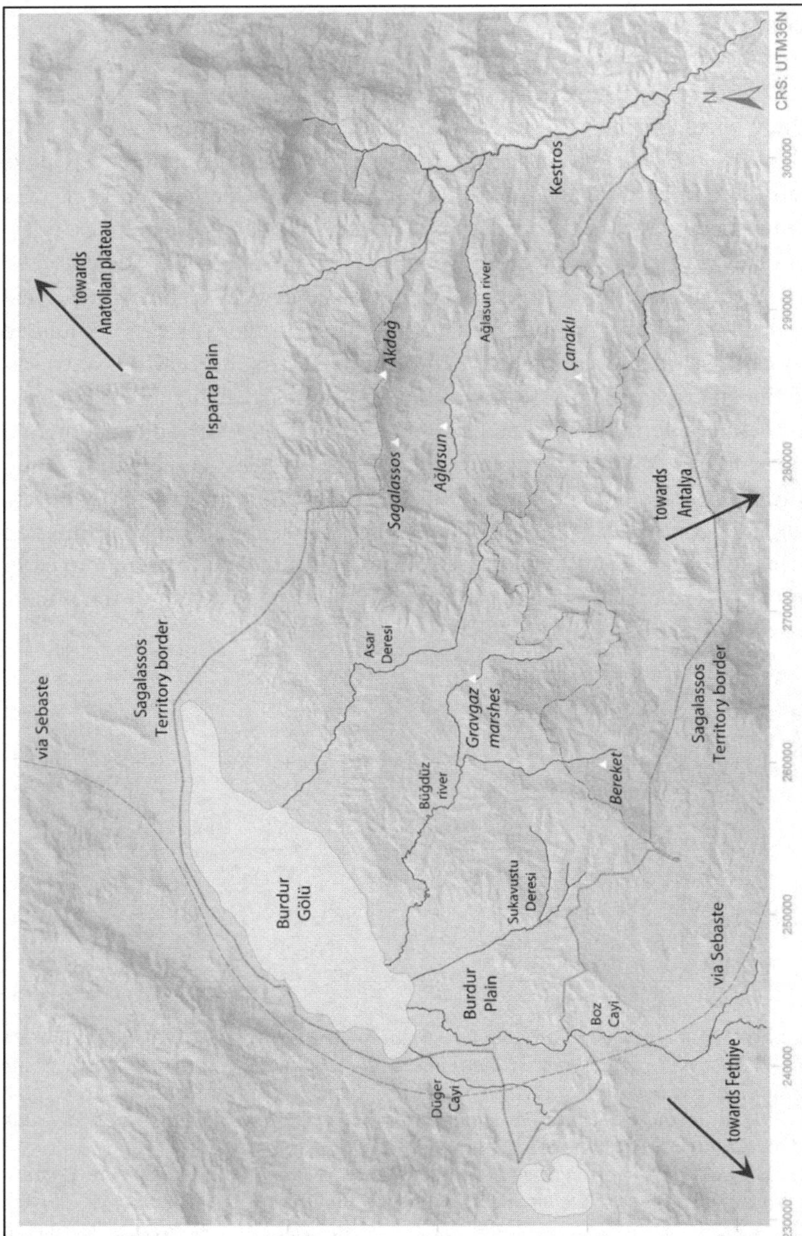

Figure 4. General geographical overview of the study region

In terms of potential, the evolution of the regional vegetation patterns can be considered against a long-term background. In that sense, the discussed centuries clearly form part of the Beyşehir Occupation Phase, with arboriculture and secondary anthropogenic indicators typically represented in the regional pollen profiles. Even if this phase comes to an early end in the Bereket basin, the resulting vegetation pattern in this locality would still be different from how further climatological changes from the middle of the seventh century CE onwards would affect the regional vegetation cover. Moreover, recent analysis of archaeological survey evidence revealed that occupation continued in the Bereket basin but depended on shifts in the local subsistence strategies with a more important role for pastoralism.[78] At the general level, the main difference within the discussed period was an increase in moisture conditions, as indicated from the pollen analysis in the Bereket and Gravgaz basins. In specific areas this may have resulted in an increase in marshes and wetlands, but considering that other landscape elements are also represented in the study region, it is an open question whether and how the regional agricultural potential was affected from the later third century CE onwards, as was the case in other regions of the Roman East.[79] All in all, a heavy human hand is noticeable in the vegetation patterns of managing cereal and olive cultivation. Also the maintenance of oak woodlands and the continued presence of coniferous woods, insofar as these are not over-represented in the pollen diagrams as a result of the long transport of this pollen in open landscapes, could reflect rational measures against soil erosion apart from aiming at harvesting the forest produce. In this respect, the Beyşehir Occupation Phase represented optimal potential for the regional vegetation patterns and resilient human use and maintenance of these in the medium term.

Considering connectivity, since the start of the Beyşehir Occupation Phase different landscape pockets seem to have been characterized to some degree by different vegetation patterns, invoking local exchange. Contemporary agricultural management policies did not erase these differences and if the moister conditions were general in the study region, this basically implied differences shifting. Cereal and olive cultivation stopped in at least part of the Bereket basin, saw a reduction in the Gravgaz basin, while olive cultivation had never been common in the Ağlasun Valley, but possibly continued mainly in the western and central

[78] KAPTIJN *et al.*, *Societal Changes* [n. 73].

[79] A. IZDEBSKI, *Why Did Agriculture Flourish in the Late Antique East? The Role of Climate Fluctuations in the Development and Contraction of Agriculture in Asia Minor and the Middle East from the 4th till the 7th c. AD* in *Millennium. Jahrbuch zu Kultur und Geschichte des ersten Jahrtausends n. Chr.* 8, 2012, p. 291-312; J. BINTLIFF, *The Complete Archaeology of Greece. From Hunter-Gatherers to the 20th Century AD*, Oxford, 2012, p. 351-368; S. MITCHELL, *Olive Cultivation in the Economy of Roman Asia Minor* in S. MITCHELL / C. LATSARI (eds.), *Patterns in the Economy of Roman Asia Minor*, Swansea, 2005, p. 83-113; S. MITCHELL, *A History of the Later Roman Empire*, Oxford, 2007, p. 329-370; DECKER, *Tilling the Hateful Earth* [n. 75].

parts of the territory, insofar as the press weights can be attributed to this period and olive or grape pressing. To be sure, vines and walnut had always been linked to specific localities. In general, the continued management of the vegetation patterns displayed path dependency where possible and rational policies at exploitation throughout.

Archaeological excavation at Sagalassos itself confirms these observations. Upon excavation, occupational deposits are wet-sieved in order to retrieve macro-botanical remains. The botanical analysis revealed the general importance of naked wheat, especially during the Roman Imperial period. From late Roman and especially early Byzantine times onwards, barley, which is more resistant to poor soils, gained in importance, while millet was introduced and some naked wheat was still consumed. In general, through time a larger variety of pulses, vegetables, fruits and nuts were consumed at Sagalassos, with grapes and figs as the most common varieties, as attested in the latrine underneath the Roman Baths.[80] Walnut as well was very abundant in Roman times. Unfortunately, most late Roman deposits were excavated quite early in the excavation history of Sagalassos, when wet-sieving was not yet in operation. In 2012, the remains of a modest house, to the east of the Neon-Library, which had burned down with its original content around 500 CE, were excavated. Wet-sieving resulted in a concentration of well-preserved botanical remains: whole fruits or fragments of almonds, grapes and apple/pear, along with a supply of hulled barley, free threshing wheat, grass pea and lentil. These results confirmed the increasing importance of barley in cereal consumption in these centuries, as already observed in the archaeobotanical studies based on over 800 litres of sediment from different locations at the site. In general, this type of analysis confirms the continuation of arboriculture and the importance of fruits and nuts in the human diet between Roman Imperial and early Byzantine times. In late Roman times, macro-remains related to fruit trees are slightly less attested in the excavated deposits, while pulses and barley seem to increase to some degree. Especially the latter could be an indication of resilience illustrating a shift towards crops with increased resistance to bad conditions, probably grown in more marginal areas. In this respect, the botanical analysis is in correspondence with the pollen analysis, indicating a well-organized anthropogenic landscape in which most pockets were rationally exploited.[81]

[80] J. BAETEN / E. MARINOVA / V. DE LAET / D. DE VOS / M. WAELKENS, *Faecal Biomarker and Archaeobotanical Analyses on Sediments from a Public Latrine Shed New Light on Ruralisation in Sagalassos, Turkey* in *Journal of Archaeological Science* 39, 2012, p. 1143-1159.

[81] I would like to thank Dr. Elena Marinova of the Leuven Centre for Archaeological Sciences for commenting on the botanical analysis, as well as kindly making recent, unpublished results available.

8 Animal Bones, Isotopes and Diachronic Trends

The analysis of faunal remains adds to this picture of potential, connectivity and resilience. Between early Roman Imperial and early Byzantine times, domestic animals or livestock are the most represented category of animal remains found during the excavations in the town of Sagalassos. The combination of the suitability of the different animals to the environment, the work or secondary products the animals could produce and the diet preferences of the local community resulted in goat as the most represented species, closely followed by sheep, cattle and pig. The excavated assemblages of animal bone display some diachronic trends, noting path dependency on ovicaprines, some increase of pig during the first centuries CE and a more marked increase of cattle in late Roman times. Sheep and goat representation would increase again in early Byzantine times.[82]

In terms of exergy, the meat yield is actually a better indicator than counts and proportions of animal bone. Cattle produced proportionally more meat than pig, and pig more meat than sheep and goat. In this way, beef clearly formed the majority of consumed meat between early Roman Imperial and early Byzantine times, varying between 70% and even 90% in the second half of the fourth century CE. Sheep and goat contributed at most 15% of meat on the market, whereas the degree of consumption of pork remained stable throughout the centuries.[83] Recent carbon and nitrogen stable isotope ratio analyses of human bone collagen indicates that the protein portion of the human diet was in general mainly based on C_3 plants, such as wheat and barley, and domesticated animals.[84] Animal protein was not an occasional, but a regular part of the diet at ancient Sagalassos.

The isotope ratio analysis programme also included livestock.[85] As bone collagen mainly reflects the origin of the protein portion of the diet averaged over the animal's lifetime, animal husbandry and feeding practices can be deduced and followed through time. During the study period, after the moderate increase in representation of pig bones in the first centuries CE, their proportion would remain more or less stable into Byzantine times. In contrast to the other livestock, pigs were mainly kept for the production of meat, as indicated by their young

[82] The first half fourth century CE turning point mentioned by B. De Cupere, *Animals at Ancient Sagalassos. Evidence of the Faunal Remains (Studies in Eastern Mediterranean Archaeology* 4) Turnhout, 2001, p. 139, is linked to the fill inside the Neon-Library, which has since been re-dated to the second half of that century Poblome *et al.*, *Old Pottery* [n. 61].

[83] De Cupere, *Animals at Ancient Sagalassos* [n. 82], p. 145-146.

[84] B. T. Fuller / B. De Cupere / E. Marinova / W. Van Neer / M. Waelkens / M. P. Richards, *Isotopic Reconstruction of Human Diet and Animal Husbandry Practices during the Classical-Hellenistic, Imperial, and Byzantine Periods at Sagalassos* in *American Journal of Physical Anthropology* 149, 2012, p. 165.

[85] Fuller *et al.*, *Isotopic Reconstruction* [n. 84], p. 157-171.

slaughter age, and the degree of consumption of pork remained more or less constant throughout the centuries. In this respect, the herding of pigs is an indicator of continued potential for the local economy. Traditionally, these animals are considered to have been pastured in patches of oak, beech and chestnut woodland and also fed with beans and grain.[86] Bea De Cupere linked pig herding with the attested patches of oak woodland, as present for instance in the Ağlasun Valley, representing interlocking interests in maintaining and managing these natural elements in the medium term.[87] Interestingly, the isotope analysis indicates nearly no variation in the pigs' diet through time, confirming aspects of resilience. Their diet was mostly based on C_3 plants and the animal protein portion likely on human refuse.[88] Microwear and hypoplasia analysis of pig teeth, measuring abrasion and development stress, indicates that these animals were most probably free range during most of their lives, and fattened up, possibly in pig sties, prior to slaughter with a soft non-abrasive diet, possibly based on urban waste.[89] Additionally, heavy metal analysis of lead and copper, reflecting pollution resulting from human occupation and industrious activities, contained in soils, sampled throughout the territory of Roman Sagalassos,[90] were matched with a set of pig bones. Anthropological anomalies in soil geochemistry were concentrated in the valleys of Ağlasun and Çanaklı, south of Sagalassos. Not only were high concentrations of the same heavy metals noted in the analysed pig bones, but the analytical results remained high throughout the study period, implying that pigs were herded at Sagalassos and in its polluted environment throughout the study period.[91] From the second half of the fifth century CE onwards, pigs seem to have declined in size possibly indicating less successful breeding and/or keeping strategies,[92] even though the habitat of these pigs did not change. Until then, the pig raising strategies were in balance with environmental strategies, revealing aspects of sustainable practices.

[86] K.D. WHITE, *Roman Farming*, London, 1970, p. 318.

[87] DE CUPERE, *Animals at Ancient Sagalassos* [n. 82], p. 137-144.

[88] FULLER *et al.*, *Isotopic Reconstruction* [n. 84], p. 167.

[89] S. VANPOUCKE / I. MAINLAND / B. DE CUPERE / M. WAELKENS, *Dental Microwear Study of Pigs from the Classical Site of Sagalassos (SW Turkey) as an Aid for the Reconstruction of Husbandry Practices in Ancient times* in *Environmental Archaeology* 14(2), 2009, p. 137-154.

[90] P. DEGRYSE / P. MUCHEZ / B. DE CUPERE / W. VAN NEER / M. WAELKENS, *Statistical Treatment of Trace Element Data and Ancient Animal Bone: Evaluation of Roman Byzantine Environmental Pollution* in *Analytical Letters* 37, 2004, p. 2819-2834.

[91] H. VANHAVERBEKE / P. DEGRYSE / B. DE CUPERE / W. VAN NEER / M. WAELKENS / P. MUCHEZ, *Urban-Rural Integration at Ancient Sagalassos (SW Turkey). Archaeological, Archaeozoological and Geochemical Evidence* in *Archaeofauna* 20, 2011, p. 73-83.

[92] VANPOUCKE *Dental Microwear Study* [n. 89].

For the proportionally largest meat provider, cattle, some more diachronic trends are observable. Fairly large meadows, or the fodder thereof, and sufficient water supply were needed to raise cattle. The first diachronic trend the isotope programme indicates, is that the proportion of C_4 plants became more important in the diet of cattle, while C_3 plants continued to play a part and the protein portion of the diet remained relatively unchanged. Ben Fuller *et al.* consider, therefore, that cattle could have been raised on different farms with different food strategies and environments.[93] In this respect, the identification of the C_4 plants is of interest. As the archaeobotanical analysis of wet-sieved excavation deposits at Sagalassos indicates that millet was only introduced from the early Byzantine period onwards, other such food sources must have played a role in earlier centuries. C_4 plants related to wet conditions are considered a likely candidate by Ben Fuller and his team, linking cattle with a C_4 isotopic signature with pastures near rivers and wetlands or their fodder being collected from such localities. Palynological analysis shows that in specific habitats marshes and wetlands were expanding from the late Roman period onwards. Although the prior use of these lands in agriculture came to an end, reuse of some of these areas for livestock may have been an option and could demonstrate resilient behaviour. C_4 plants also fare relatively better under grazing pressure, so their increased importance in the cattle diet could be seen as an indicator for the general intensification of land use over time, especially in the late Roman period when the cattle bone proportion in the excavated assemblages at Sagalassos was at its height. In general, cattle at Sagalassos were slaughtered at an older age, implying their important prior role as working animals in the field and for transport, and milk providers. This aspect, together with the growing importance of cattle, especially in late Roman times, has been considered to reflect the potential of the regional economy.[94] To be sure, grain and olive cultivation also are important indicators of stability in the productive landscape. The increased proportion of cattle as working animals in the fields also hints at the continued role of agriculture in the region.

Another important diachronic trend derives from the heavy metal analysis of lead and copper pollution in soils and cattle bone.[95] During the High Empire, the cattle consumed at Sagalassos were mainly came from the Ağlasun and Çanaklı Valleys, following the elevated heavy metal content of the bones. In late Roman times, however, the average pollution levels in cattle bones drop, implying that the cattle which were consumed at Sagalassos came from different, less polluted areas. As this is also the period of maximum representation of cattle bone at Sagalassos and cattle reflect intensive agricultural practices and economic

[93] FULLER *et al.*, *Isotopic Reconstruction* [n. 84], p. 167.

[94] DE CUPERE *Animals at Ancient Sagalassos* [n. 82], p. 141.

[95] DEGRYSE *et al.*, *Statistical Treatment* [n. 90]; VANHAVERBEKE *et al.*, *Urban-Rural Integration* [n. 91].

potential, these combined late Roman trends could be read as an indicator for generally successful agricultural practices and management now also in areas beyond the Ağlasun and Çanaklı Valleys. Hannelore Vanhaverbeke *et al.* have considered the late Roman pattern as meaningful to indicate a better integration of parts of the territory into the urban economy.[96] The evolution of the pollution signals in the cattle bone could be read in this way. But in pre-late Roman times Sagalassos was also dependent on other goods which were not sufficiently available in its polluted first degree catchment basin, but are less visible in the archaeological record, such as olive oil and wine,[97] whereas other parts of the territory were clearly doing well also in pre-late Roman times, such as the Bereket basin. Considering the diachronic trend in the palynological evidence that different landscape pockets seem to have been characterized to some degree by different vegetation patterns, invoking local exchange, the shift in provenances of the consumed cattle at Sagalassos could perhaps be understood along similar lines. As a matter of fact, from the middle of the fifth century CE onwards most consumed cattle were again being raised within the most polluted zone.

Also sheep and goats were mostly slaughtered at adult age, implying their initial usefulness in supplying dairy products, wool and hair. Their contribution as urban meat supplier was small in comparison to cattle. Sheep are traditionally considered to require different habitats from goats, preferring pastures or arable land to rough wooded areas.[98] The diet of the goats found at Sagalassos was almost exclusively based on C_3 plants. Before the early Byzantine period a small C_4 component was identified in their diet as well, but less important compared to that of the sheep. Ben Fuller *et al.* consider these isotopic results an indication that goats were allowed to graze more freely, in different areas than the other livestock, possibly on the forested mountain slopes around Sagalassos.[99] As with cattle, during most centuries goats grazed in the polluted zone surrounding Sagalassos, with dropping degrees of heavy metal pollution in their bones and associated different and more distant provenance in the late Roman period.[100] Through time, most sheep were fed on C_3 plants, while some animals' diet contained also C_4 plants or fodder. The isotopic analysis is indicative of subtle diachronic changes in the way sheep were fed, and an interesting association between cattle and sheep on pastures in similar habitats was suggested, especially during High Imperial times. The isotopic signatures are more mixed in late Roman times with sheep possibly shifting throughout the year between cattle and

96 VANHAVERBEKE *et al.*, *Urban-Rural Integration* [n. 91].

97 Considering the fact that in late Hellenistic and Roman Imperial times a range of imported wine amphorae are attested in excavation deposits at Sagalassos, perhaps mostly olive oil was another local product.

98 WHITE *Roman Farming* [n. 86], p. 304-306; 313.

99 FULLER *et al.*, *Isotopic Reconstruction* [n. 84].

100 VANHAVERBEKE *et al.*, *Urban-Rural Integration* [n. 91].

goat grazing areas. In this way, each type of domestic animal had a specific diet in these centuries, reflecting degrees of agricultural specialization and potential. In early Byzantine times, the isotopic analysis indicates that sheep and goats shared the same grazing areas. Although no heavy metal analysis was performed on sheep bones, mostly local provenance is suggested for the High Imperial centuries and the early Byzantine ones, based on the association between sheep and respectively cattle and goats. Considering the mixed late Roman signals shared between sheep on the one hand and cattle and goat on the other, and the fact that the latter two types of animals had low signals of heavy metal pollution in their bones in the same period, a more distant provenance for sheep can also be postulated in those days. This deduction seems to be confirmed by unpublished 2012 survey work on the flanks of the Ağlasun and Akdağ mountains, where shelters for pastoralism datable to the Roman Imperial period fell into disuse. In this way, the diachronic pattern shown in the ovicaprine bones sustained regional potential, connectivity through local exchange and resilience in shifting grazing locations. As mentioned, the proportion of sheep and goat bones would increase again in early Byzantine Sagalassos, but that process seems to be part of a different phase in nature-society interactions.[101]

Considering the long-term perspective, the isotope ratio analysis programme provided evidence for the fact that, during the Classical/Hellenistic period, the values of livestock mostly cluster together indicating that sheep, goats, cattle and pigs were herded together in the same general area or fed on similar foods, most probably providing subsistence to the self-sustaining communities at Düzen Tepe and contemporary Sagalassos. During Roman Imperial times this pattern clearly became more complex, with more specific habitats for each livestock species, albeit still mostly within the general surroundings of the town of Sagalassos. The highest degree of specialization in animal keeping is attributable to late Roman times, while signals of some loss of specialized practices and/or complexity can be associated with early Byzantine times.[102]

9 Other Lines of Production

An earlier study[103] showed that the start of local amphora production during the second half of the fourth century CE was associated with an attempt at intensification of part of the agricultural production. Both reflect a rational decision making process and policy of investment on the part of the landholders.

101 POBLOME, *How Did Sagalassos Come to Be LRCW4* [n. 4].
102 FULLER *et al.*, *Isotopic Reconstruction* [n. 84].
103 POBLOME *et al.*, *It Is Never Too Late* [n. 62].

The ophiolitic/flysch clays of these so-called Fabric 4 amphorae were traced to the central parts of the Ağlasun Valley.[104] Since the amphorae were presumably made on the farming estate(s) where they were to be filled, their contents can be considered to reflect agricultural production choices in the Ağlasun Valley. Initially, because the typology of the local vessels resembles other contemporary and popular amphora series in the late Roman East, an original function as wine containers was suggested. A programme of residue analysis on an early Byzantine collection of Fabric 4 amphorae, however, showed that apart from Dionysos' favourite drink, they had also been used for olive oil and walnut oil.[105] Walnut cultivation is commonly represented in palynological and macrobotanical test results. But, based on pollen analysis, olive cultivation had so far not been attributed an important role in the Ağlasun Valley. In any case, the addition of amphora production in the course of the fourth century CE in a region where pottery manufacturing was endemic is a further sign of specialization in craft production. Possibly the diversity of their contents implies the same for agricultural production.

The application of data distribution techniques on Sagalassos red slip ware, or the locally produced tableware, attested both in urban excavated deposits and survey collections, demonstrated that, in general terms, the High Imperial centuries represented the largest artisanal output, with a declining role for the local tableware during the third and fourth centuries CE and a revival of the industry in the next two centuries.[106] Even though less well represented, the continued production of Sagalassos red slip ware throughout the third century CE in a tableware production landscape where most wares with wide distribution patterns in the Roman East witness a serious reduction or even interruption of production, has been considered important. It seems to indicate that Sagalassos may not have suffered from the contemporary crisis in the empire.[107] During the fourth century CE, a new line of Sagalassos red slip ware was launched, possibly together with the Fabric 4 amphorae and a series of mould-made products, such as oil lamps and figurines as well as so-called *oinophoroi* or wine flasks. The launching of a new design of tableware has recently been considered to depend on general and mixed aspects of regional well-being.[108] What is remarkable in the

[104] NEYT *et al.*, *Long-Term Clay Raw Material Selection* [n. 5].

[105] K. ROMANUS / J. BAETEN / J. POBLOME / S. ACCARDO / P. DEGRYSE / P. JACOBS / D. DE VOS / M. WAELKENS, *Wine and Olive Oil Permeation in Pitched and Non-Pitched Ceramics: Relation with Results from Archaeological Amphorae from Sagalassos, Turkey* in *Journal of Archaeological Science* 36(3), 2009, p. 900-909.

[106] J. POBLOME / R. WILLET / N. FIRAT / F. MARTENS / P. BES, *Tinkering with Urban Survey Data. How Many Sagalassos-es Do We Have?* in P. JOHNSON / M. MILLETT (eds.), *Archaeological Survey and the City*, Oxford, 2013, p. 146-174.

[107] POBLOME, *It Is Never Too Late* [n. 62].

[108] R. WILLET, *Red Slipped Complexity. The Socio-Cultural Context of the Concept and*

case of Sagalassos, is that not only a new typological set of its tableware was introduced on the market, but that the local pottery industry also specialized in further product diversification with the production of mould-made wares in the so-called Coroplast workshop.[109] *Oinophoroi* are an important product within this collection. In contrast to the contemporary tableware, these products saw some supra-regional distribution.[110] Considering that their iconography was mostly based on the wine-god Dionysos and that they are a late representative of a tradition of similar wine flasks in Asia Minor,[111] the start of the production of *oinophoroi* in the Potters' Quarter of Sagalassos could be seen as another indicator for specialization in artisanal production, but possibly also in agricultural produce.

Other craft activities are attested or presumed at Sagalassos, including wool dying, metal production, bone and antler cutting as well as glass blowing. Most evidence for bone cutting has been collected in the second half of the fourth century CE fill inside the destroyed Neon-Library.[112] However, as (fragments of) bone objects are a traditional find in most contexts at Sagalassos, it is unclear whether this specific deposit of bone working refuse has specific chronological importance. The latter does seem to be the case for glass working, however. Whereas in earlier centuries Sagalassos had mostly depended on imported glass vessels, chemical and archaeological analysis confirmed the existence of a local glass workshop working with imported chunks from the second half of the fifth century CE onwards.[113] In this sense, the trend in artisanal production does not necessarily imply increases in output in late Roman times, but the production landscape seems to have become more specialized compared to earlier or later centuries. Part of the increased specialization in craft production seems to have been associated with similar processes in the field of agricultural production.

Use of Tableware in the Roman East, Unpublished Ph.D. thesis, University of Leuven, 2012.

[109] E. MURPHY / J. POBLOME, *Technical and Social Considerations of Tools from Roman-Period Ceramic Workshops at Sagalassos (Southwest Turkey): Not Just Tools of the Trade?* in *JMA* 25, 2012, p. 69-89.

[110] P. TALLOEN / J. POBLOME, *What Were They Thinking Of? Relief Decorated Pottery from Sagalassos: A Cognitive Approach* in *Mélanges de l'École Française de Rome* in *Antiquité* 117, 2005, p. 55-81.

[111] U. MANDEL, *Kleinasiatische Reliefkeramik der mittleren Kaiserzeit. Die 'Oinophoren'-Gruppe und Verwandtes* (*Pergamenische Forschungen* 5), Berlin, 1988.

[112] DE CUPERE, *Animals at Ancient Sagalassos* [n. 82], p. 147-159.

[113] V. LAUWERS, *The Glass of Sagalassos. Towards a Geochemical and Typo-chronological Interpretation*, Unpublished Ph.D. thesis, University of Leuven, 2008, p. 212.

10 Counting Sites and People

In order to give meaning to the attested processes of specialization, these are best projected against the background of the regional settlement pattern and demography, especially considering the mentioned effects of the Malthusian low-equilibrium trap.

Within its territory, ancient Sagalassos remained the most complex and the only urban settlement. During the Severan dynasty the construction of new public monuments came to a halt. Major building activities are not attested afterwards until the end of the fourth century CE, when the Imperial Baths were renovated. Shortly afterwards, a new town wall and a number of churches were built, heralding a new phase in urban development.[114] Surrounded by its necropoleis, the city area measured 37.5 hectares. After an Augustan phase of expansion, this estimated area seems to have remained stable during the study period. Also the extent of the local Potters' Quarter of 3.5-4 hectares seems to have remained the same, following its establishment in Augustan times and subsequent growth until Flavian times. Both in the case of the town and in that of the Potters' Quarter developments cannot be accurately measured, but are extrapolated from the excavated and surveyed parts. Based on the estimated area of 25.22 hectares for the residential quarters and a population density of 100 to 150 people per hectare, the size of the urban population can be estimated as between 2,500 and 3,750 people.[115] Within the study period, unfortunately, the available data do not allow the reconstruction of a pattern of demographic change for the town of Sagalassos. Therefore, the fact that it remained the only urban settlement in the study region is more important than the exact total estimate or its evolution.

It is beyond the scope of this paper to discuss the evolving urban landscape in detail. Instead, we will focus on water provisioning, as its functioning is illustrative of urban potential and its impact on urban-rural connectivity. Considering its long-term potential, at least from the third century BCE onwards, ancient Sagalassos became the most prominent settlement in the wider region.[116] By early Roman Imperial times, Sagalassos had established a territory of approximately 1,200 km², drawing in resources and potential from the wider region. This resulted in spectacular urban building programmes, in which, amongst others, monuments related to water played a prominent role. The late

[114] M. WAELKENS, *Sagalassos. Erste Stadt Pisidiens, Freund und Bundgenosse der Römer* in *Antike Welt: Zeitschrift für Archäologie und Kulturgeschichte* 2011, p. 62-71; M. WAELKENS, *Sagalassos* in R. S. BAGNALL *et al.* (eds.), *The Encyclopedia of Ancient History*, Oxford, 2013, p. 6007-6009.

[115] WILLET, *Red Slipped Complexity* [n. 108], p. 183.

[116] POBLOME, *How Did Sagalassos Come to Be? LRCW4* [n. 4]; WAELKENS, *Sagalassos* [n. 114].

Hellenistic Fountain House, the Flavian, Hadrianic and Severan Nymphaea on the Lower Agora, as well as the Antonine Nymphaeum on the Upper Agora are prime examples. Also the Augusto-Tiberian Bath Building, superseded by the enormous Imperial Bath Complex, testifies to the important role of water in the town of Sagalassos. In antiquity, water-related monuments must have formed some of the more characteristic features of the urban landscape of Sagalassos. They no doubt held great symbolic importance for the local community and became part of their cultural identity.[117] Water was no doubt also an essential commodity in ordinary daily life activities, and served a crucial function in sustaining local craft industries, of which the pottery industry perhaps played the most important role.[118]

Apart from the engineering skills required in antiquity to locate, construct and maintain these water-related monuments, as well as sustain daily life and craft industries, impressive technological knowledge was required to find, capture, tap and guide sufficient amounts of fresh water towards the city of Sagalassos. In addition to the local fresh water springs, such as the one feeding the late Hellenistic Fountain House, remains of various aqueducts were found in the mountains to the west and east of the town.[119] These aqueducts brought water into town, feeding the life and culture that were typical for the splendour of ancient Sagalassos. Fieldwork in 2012, mainly focused on preserved remains on the flanks of the Ağlasun and Akdağ mountains to the east of the town, added in important respects to the earlier studies of the aqueducts of Sagalassos. It resulted in the discovery of the source feeding the eastern aqueducts, the cistern capturing and distributing this resource, as well as many newly discovered preserved sections of the channel, allowing a better understanding of the route of the main eastern aqueduct and its points of bifurcation, feeding different parts of the town (Fig. 5). The source was located on the north-eastern flanks of the Akdağ, near the locality aptly called Başpınar at 1710 m. Clearly, detailed investigation should

[117] J. RICHARD, *In the Elites' Toolkit. Decoding the Initiative and Reference System behind the Investment in the Architecture and Decoration of Roman Nymphaea* in *Facta: A Journal of Roman Material Culture Studies* 5, 2011, p. 65-100; J. RICHARD, *Water for the City, Fountains for the People. Monumental Fountains in the Roman East: an Archaeological Study of Water Management* (*Studies in Eastern Mediterranean Archaeology* 9), Turnhout, 2012; F. MARTENS / J. RICHARD / M. WAELKENS, *The Roman Baths at Sagalassos (SW-Turkey): A Preliminary Study of the Research Potential for a Reconstruction of Its Water Management System* in P. FRICKE / G. SCHMIDT (eds.), *Proceedings of the 'Internationales Frontinus-Symposium zur Technik- und Kulturgeschichte der antiken Thermen'*, Leuven, 2009.

[118] POBLOME, *The Potters of Sagalassos* [n. 3].

[119] E. OWENS, *The Aqueducts of Sagalassos* in M. WAELKENS / J. POBLOME (eds.), *Sagalassos* III. *Report on the Fourth Excavation Campaign of 1993*, Leuven, 1995, p. 91-113.

be continued to map this water provisioning system in more detail, but from the 2012 results the entire length of the eastern aqueducts can be measured at *c.* 24.5 km, completely encircling the higher flanks of the Akdağ, with a difference in height between source and the eastern edge of Sagalassos of around 100 m. Parts of the channel were worked into limestone outcrops on the flanks of the Akdağ and Ağlasun mountains, sometimes to a depth of several meters, with an average width of 0.4 m and watermarks at the average height of 0.5 m. Earlier calculations of the water supply arrived at impressive estimates of 530 litres per second or a total of nearly 45,000 m^3 of water per day.[120] The 2012 discovery should allow reconsideration of these calculations, taking the actual source into account.

Apart from the eastern aqueduct being a testimony to the technical ingenuity of the time, its concept also symbolizes a landscape of power, potential and connectivity, whereby the town of Sagalassos managed to capture and guide one of the more important water sources in the entire region for its civic benefits. Future study is required to accurately date the development of these engineering works, their maintenance and also their moment of abandonment. Considering the water-related monuments that were provided by this system, however, it must have been operational during the entire study period of this paper, providing an important new insight for understanding the wider outreach of the town. More work is also required to understand how, upon taking the eastern aqueduct into use, the lower slopes along its 'tracé' and especially the Ağlasun Valley were still provided with sufficient irrigation water in order to sustain their intensive agricultural use, but clearly the functioning of the aqueduct was an important structural determinant in this respect.

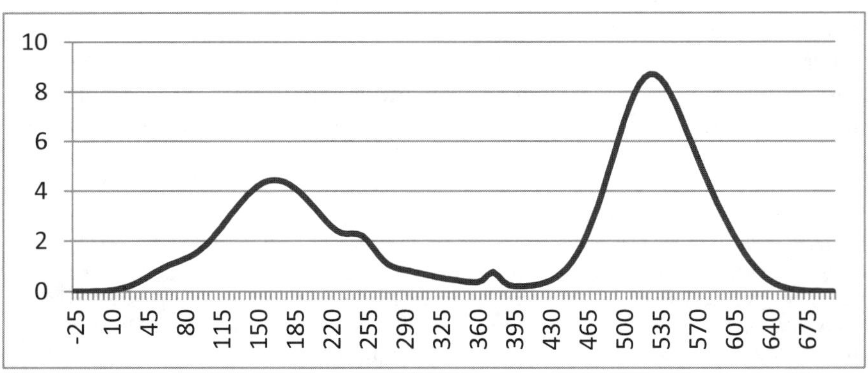

Figure 5. Gaussian distribution graph of datable pottery from the Ağlasun Valley intensive survey campaigns, dated between the end of the first century BCE and the end of the seventh century CE (n=1595 sherds)

120 A. STEEGEN / K. CAUWENBERGHS / G. GOVERS / M. WAELKENS / E. J. OWENS / P. DESMET, *The Water Supply to Sagalassos* in M. WAELKENS / L. LOOTS (eds.), *Sagalassos V. Report on the Survey and Excavation Campaigns of 1996 and 1997*, Leuven, 2000, p. 646.

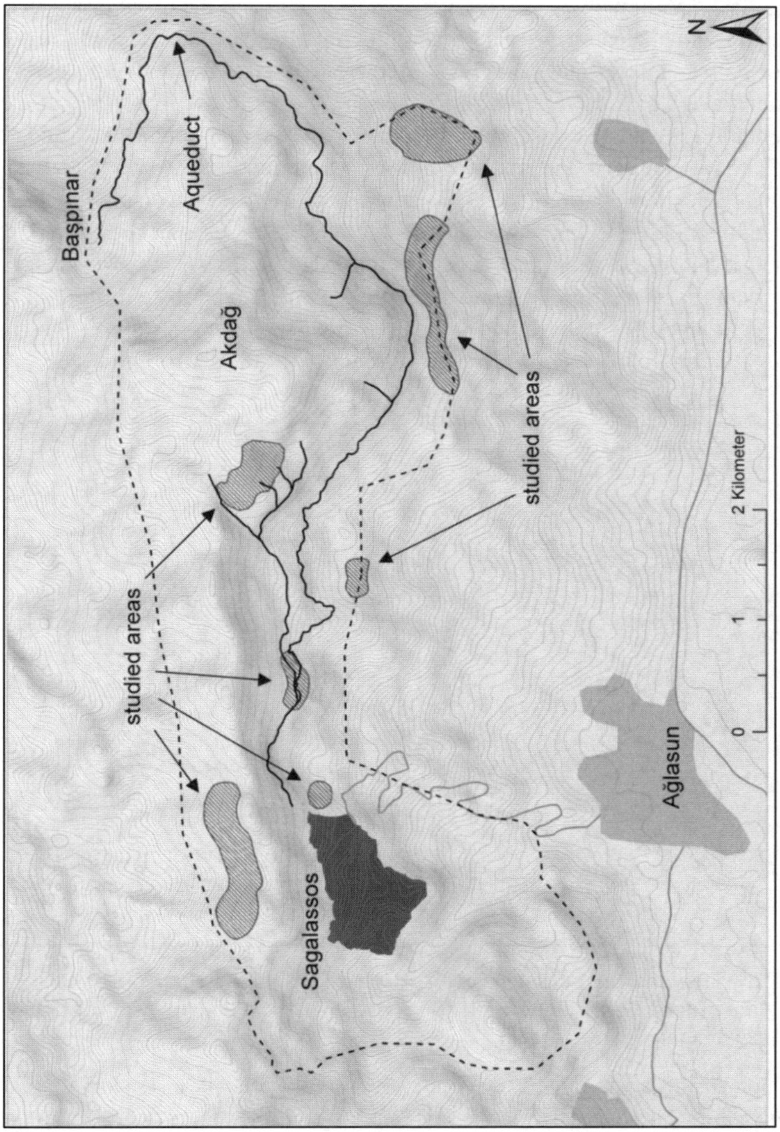

Figure 6. The eastern aqueduct, from the Akdağ mountain into Sagalassos

Considering settlement patterns in the Ağlasun Valley, recent ceramological evaluation of the results of intensive survey campaigns between 1999 and 2004, which mostly covered the central parts of the valley, demonstrated that discrete concentrations of material in the terrain which could be interpreted as farms were fairly easily recognizable for the Classical/Hellenistic and Byzantine periods.[121] Strikingly, late Hellenistic and early Roman Imperial material was mostly missing in the Ağlasun Valley. I would like to propose to see this as the result of a process of demographic nucleation within burgeoning Sagalassos. When considering the totals of pottery fabrics and types recovered from all sites in the central parts of the latter valley datable to the Roman centuries (Fig. 6), a first peak in data representation is situated around the middle of the second century CE and the second and main peak in the first half of the sixth century CE. Although situated in the intermediate period with low data representation, a small peak is recognizable in the second half of the fourth century CE. Compared to the collected urban excavation and survey pottery data (Fig. 7), the two peaks of highest data representation in respectively the second and sixth centuries CE are recognisable in both graphs, albeit in reverse order with a more important signal of occupation in the Ağlasun Valley in the first half of the sixth century CE.

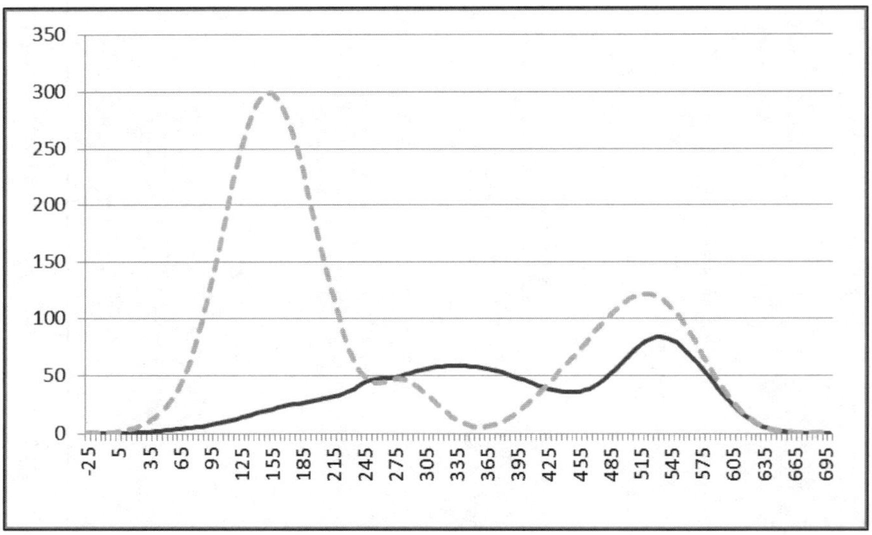

Figure 7. Gaussian distribution graph of selected Sagalassos urban excavation pottery data (dotted grey line; n=53,910 sherds) compared to urban survey data (dark grey line; n=23,464 sherds)

The slope towards the smaller second century CE peak is also slower in the Ağlasun Valley compared to Sagalassos, implying another degree of development of the valley compared to the town, possibly as a result of the process of urban nucleation. Another contrast is that the growth towards the sixth century peak in the Ağlasun Valley is stronger compared to the town, with a fifth century upswing of occupation in the valley. As the residential areas in the town of Sagalassos were considered stable throughout the study period of this paper, with associated

[121] POBLOME *et al.*, *How Did Sagalassos Come to Be? LRCW4* [n. 4].

demographic stability, it does seem to be the case that there were more farms in the Ağlasun Valley in the fifth and first half of the sixth centuries CE. Although the link between sherds and people is never straightforward, the fact that the archaeological material is associated with a slight increase in number of sites and densities of on-site material could be an indirect indication that there were slightly more people in the Ağlasun Valley in these particular centuries. At least in the surveyed, central part of the valley, this period of increased number of farms is more or less contemporary with the period of cattle, goats and by extrapolation also sheep being kept outside of the immediate polluted zone around Sagalassos. As a consequence, the late Roman Ağlasun Valley farms were most probably focusing on other crops, possibly used to fill the local Fabric 4 amphorae, the clays for which were traced to the same landscape pockets.

In addition to the results in the Ağlasun Valley, extensive surveying campaigns in the wider territory of Sagalassos indicated that those lands witnessed the highest overall number of sites ever during the late Roman period.[122] More than double the number of sites could be attributed to these centuries compared to early Imperial times, while site numbers drop considerably in early Byzantine times. Although the available totals are supportive of a contemporary demographic increase, caution is warranted as the total number of sites compared to the extent of the territory is fairly low while also the methodology of extensive surveying cannot sustain fine-grained reconstructions. Settlements were located in the plains, on the lower slopes and for the first time since Hellenistic times again on less accessible, albeit unfortified mountain sites,[123] indicative of intensive exploitation of the landscape. Villages and farms were located at regular intervals in the landscape, functioning as localities for the collection and processing of agricultural produce. In contrast to early Imperial times, little evidence for elite involvement or presence in the countryside is available. Caution is again required, however, since in most cases this can be acceptably demonstrated only by the presence of monumental tombs and sarcophagi. Such markers are no longer common in late Roman times, reducing elite visibility considerably. Another diachronic trend, which is perhaps easier to evaluate based on the available evidence, is that between early Imperial and early Byzantine times the number of villages steadily grew and the number of farms was simultaneously reduced.[124]

[122] VANHAVERBEKE *et al.*, *Urban-Rural Integration* [n. 91], p. 75.

[123] H. VANHAVERBEKE / M. WAELKENS, *The Chora of Sagalassos: The Evolution of the Settlement Pattern from Prehistoric Until Recent Times* (*Studies in Eastern Mediterranean Archaeology* 5), Turnhout, 2003, p. 241-283.

[124] H. VANHAVERBEKE / F. MARTENS / M. WAELKENS / J. POBLOME, *Late Antiquity in the Territory of Sagalassos* in W. BOWDEN / L. LAVAN / C. MACHADO (eds.), *Recent Research on the Late Antique Countryside* (*Late Antique Archaeology* 2), Leiden, 2004, p. 247-279.

Hannelore Vanhaverbeke *et al.*[125] identified farms as sites extending over 2,500 m² on average, while villages were at least four times this size and typically formed a nucleated type of settlement. So although caution is still called for, it seems that we can assume some degree of population increase in parts of the territory of Sagalassos.

In an attempt to compare the demographical potential of the town and territory of Sagalassos with the output of the Sagalassos red slip ware, Rinse Willet recently engaged in the estimation of the regional rural population.[126] Methods to establish rural populations are mostly based on ratios of urban population totals or estimated amounts of people per km². The former traditional methods arrive at very low totals for the territory of Sagalassos, as their premise is in most cases the model of more populated Classical *poleis*. For the latter, recently a ratio of 15 people/km² was proposed for Anatolia,[127] which results in a total population for the territory of Sagalassos of 18,000 people. Considering that the applied ratio is on the low side even for modern countries, this total is possibly an underestimation. Intensive surveying campaigns in parts of the territory as well as the study of agricultural carrying capacities of the territory should shed more light on this issue in future. At the moment, diachronic estimates are not possible given the nature of the evidence, but as the rural settlement pattern was at its densest during late Roman times, we should expect this period to represent the highest diachronic demographic total.

Apart from its palynological record, the high altitude valley of Bereket revealed another important trend related to connectivity within the territory of Sagalassos. This valley is one of the more remote points of the study region, at about 37 km southwest from Sagalassos as the crow flies. In roughly the same period as the mentioned interruption of the intensive cultivation of olives and grain, possibly in favour of increased pastoralism, a change in supply of tableware was noted at the archaeological sites in the Bereket Valley. Before late Roman times, Sagalassos red slip ware was the most common type of tableware represented, which seems acceptable considering the output of the local production centre at Sagalassos and its distance to the Bereket Valley. In late Roman times, the supply of Sagalassos red slip ware is only a trickle of its former self, however, while the valley is provided with red slipped wares from yet unknown production centre(s). Also amphora sherds were discovered at the surface of the sites in the Bereket Valley which are typologically similar to the mentioned Fabric 4 amphorae, but their fabrics were different, suggesting a

[125] VANHAVERBEKE *et al.*, *Late Antiquity* [n. 124], p. 258-259.

[126] WILLET, *Red Slipped Complexity* [n. 108], p. 191-195.

[127] B. FRIER, *Demography* in A. BOWMAN / P. GARNSEY / D. RATHBONE (eds.), *The Cambridge Ancient History*, XI, Cambridge, 2000, p. 812.

different origin for these vessels compared to the ones attested at Sagalassos.[128] While the ceramological evidence seems to indicate a somewhat larger distance between the regional pole of attraction and the Bereket Valley, this is also the period when the cattle and goat bones, and the sheep by association, were supposed to be brought to Sagalassos for consumption from larger distances,[129] when pastoralism is presumed to have become more important at Bereket,[130] and when natural conditions and increased pressure sustained the growth of C_4 plants in wetlands in the general study region.[131] Although there is no precise allocation in time and place nor proof of causality for these suggested changes in connectivity, the archaeological results from the Bereket Valley do indicate that patterns of exchange and relations between Sagalassos and the different parts of its territory need not have stayed constant over time, while changes in subsistence strategies and/or ceramic suppliers most probably reflect rational choices on behalf of the communities involved, trying at all times to make the most from changing situations.

11 General Trends

People, or rather manpower, are everything to a pre-industrial society and economy. Although the available evidence only allows for a crude approximation of numbers, a difference in trends between the second and fifth centuries CE can be cautiously forwarded. Mainly the nature and the distribution of rural sites seem to suggest some demographic increase by late Roman times. The evolution of population totals cannot be reconstructed and the link between the facts of the archaeological record and demographical reconstruction remains a difficult one, but even if future research would prove growth to be minimal, regional population totals seem not to have declined. If growth was realized, this seems to have happened mostly in the rural context. This trend is not dissimilar to the evidence presented by Michael McCormick,[132] with many regions in the Roman East having a stable or slightly increasing population, especially in rural contexts. This rural connection is of importance as: "the countryside was the demographic wellspring of society, since deaths always outstripped births in pre-modern cities … In a pre-modern economy, the extent of land farmed was the first and

[128] KAPTIJN *et al.*, *Societal Changes* [n. 74].
[129] VANHAVERBEKE *et al.*, *Urban-Rural Integration* [n. 91].
[130] BAKKER *et al.*, *Climate of the Past* [n. 64].
[131] FULLER *et al.*, *Isotopic Reconstruction* [n. 84].
[132] M. MCCORMICK, *Origins of the European Economy. Communications and Commerce, AD 300-900*, Cambridge, 2001, p. 30-38.

primordial economic fact determining food production and therefore wealth at its most basic level."[133]

Considering the potential past demographical patterns, pre-industrial societies are typically pulled between two general trends. On the one hand, there is the mentioned low-equilibrium trap,[134] lowering expectations about the possibility of sustained economic growth, with limited resources as a binding constraint for development, income and population growth, especially in non-industrial societies. In this scenario, communities could attempt some reorganization, displaying resilience and creativity, but such attempts mostly resulted in a gradual shift from high-exergy return on investment to low-exergy returns, reflecting or inducing lower social complexity. The decreased role of grain and olive cultivation in the Bereket and Gravgaz basins, whether provoked by changes in the levels of precipitation or resulting from rational decisions to change subsistence strategies, could be read as a move away from high-exergy, export oriented crops such as grain and olive oil, and a contemporaneous shift towards low-exergy livestock cultivation, representing less inherent risk of failure but at the same time less return on investment. In this way, there may have been more people in the Sagalassos countryside, but their average income was dropping resulting from changing subsistence strategies, eventually resulting in the attested regional demographical reduction in early Byzantine times. A sign of the times could be the lower output rates and reduced pattern of distribution of Sagalassos red slip ware reflecting the reduced economic drive towards generating high-exergy income from maintaining distant exchange and export networks. Another indication could be provided by the increasing gap between rich and poor which characterized much of late antiquity, and is best symbolized by the construction of the lavish palatial mansion at Sagalassos in the course of the second half of the fourth century CE.[135] Developments such as these illustrate how economic surplus, in case there was any, could be siphoned off in the hands of the happy few, resulting in outward signs of well-being but masking patterns of social inequality.

Such scenarios, developed from Thomas Malthus' (1766-1834) ideas and work, still inspire economic historians. As we know this is also the case with the Roman Empire. As with most models and theories, when placed in context, aspects and assumptions can be criticized. K.G. Persson in his discussion of the economic history of Europe between 600 CE and the present summarized three

133 McCormick, *Origins* [n. 132], p. 31.

134 Scheidel, *Approaching* [n. 32].

135 I. Uytterhoeven / H. Kökten / M. Corremans / J. Poblome / M. Waelkens, *Late Antique Private Luxury. The Mosaic Floors of the 'Urban Mansion' of Sagalassos (Ağlasun, Burdur – Turkey)* in *JÖAI* 82, 2013, 373-407.

main issues with Malthusian theory.[136] First, Malthusian thinking underestimates permanent effects induced by technological progress, even low-key improvements in agricultural yields, beyond the traditional acknowledgment of short-term influence on income levels and population growth. Secondly, the economy of such communities is traditionally characterized as fairly closed, neglecting potential and connectivity generated from local, regional and wider specialization and resulting exchange. Finally, Malthusian models work with underdeveloped fertility strategies for households, focussed mostly on how increases in income resulted in higher numbers of children, but underestimating how families could be forward-looking in their appreciation that quality of childcare (education, nutrition) mattered too, as well as maintaining given standards of living for the entire family.

Besides Malthusian models, the ideas and work of Adam Smith (1723-1790) have been developed into an alternative analytical framework.[137] According to these views, the conditions for economic growth *per capita* in a pre-industrial economy are the creation of gain from specialization or division of labour, applying knowledge based on experience and trial and error, and from trade based on differences in resource and climate. As a matter of fact, this point of view can be understood along similar lines as the development of optimal exergy buffering strategies by complex adaptive systems. Specialization allows producers to improve their skills, increasing efficiency of practices and labour productivity, creating sufficient margin to increase output and engage in exchange with producers specialized in other goods. The limit for specialization or division of labour is the level of aggregate demand in an economy. As a result, population increase will sustain division of labour as long as this growth is also associated with increasing aggregate income, allowing full-time specialization. The geographical area determining aggregate demand is open and in tandem with the socio-political order of the day, in this case ranging from the scale of the Roman Empire to the regional unit of ancient Sagalassos and its territory. Changes to the socio-political structure of society can reduce demand, making specialization superfluous, and invoking a process of technological regress. K.G. Persson stipulated that: "social order, population growth, transport networks, markets and money are prerequisites for growth based on increased division of labour and trade."[138]

Science rarely produces rich insights by choosing between two so-called rival models. In this case as well the challenge is rather to understand how the study region developed a balance between Malthusian and Smithian forces or between

[136] K. G. Persson, *An Economic History of Europe. Knowledge, Institutions and Growth, 600 to the Present*, Cambridge, 2010, p. 42-59.

[137] Persson, *Economic History* [n. 136], p. 21-41.

[138] Persson, *Economic History* [n. 136], p. 28.

negative and positive demographic effects in order to result in constant above-subsistence income.

It seems to me that the latter condition is met in our case-study, especially in late Roman times. To start with, it is important that the polis of Sagalassos remained functioning, representing a concentration of people which were in most cases not active in food production. Even though farmers may have represented a certain proportion of the urban population, they were not the typical inhabitants. In general, townsfolk are estimated to represent about 10% of the total population in antiquity.[139] Therefore, the very existence of towns proves that the urban dwellers managed to get hold of part of the agricultural surplus. They did not do this occasionally, but year in, year out. In this way, farming produce and surplus entered the towns in a systematic way. As a result, farmers had to create a surplus for their own survival purposes and had a guaranteed market potential in their towns. Surplus agricultural production and its exchange were systematic features of ancient society. Unlike in capitalist societies, however, the farming strategy remained traditional and aimed at minimum risk and maximum options of survival. Having a little of everything was considered better than profit-seeking. Surplus therefore was systematic but also mostly smallish and production was based on small-scale units. We should go one step further, however. Indeed, sometimes harvests went wrong, climatic conditions changed or some cities outgrew their hinterlands. Ancient society and its towns actually had no institutional way of dealing with these problems of distribution. In general, imports reached the market as a result of private initiative. In effect, climate and geography in combination with social and political conditions ensured that there would be a substantial medium-range movement of staple foodstuffs. This medium range exchange of goods is another systematic feature of ancient society. It involved a lot of trade, but also reciprocity between various estates of one owner, as well as with his friends, between imperial estates and between lands owned by churches and monasteries. Redistribution played another major role in supplying institutionally benefiting parties. Also in the case of medium-range exchange the tendency is to restrict risks and loss-on-investment as much as possible. Exchange in antiquity follows a model of delegated, and whenever possible, shared risks. It is very much these tendencies and structural features of ancient society which explain why the comparison of the archaeological record between towns or regions mostly looks like an unintelligible mix. The hotchpotch of distribution and consumption patterns is not dependent on models of direct trade, rather on untraceable models of dependency in exchange and overlap of directions and exchange mechanisms by multiple parties and institutions, fit to be deconstructed as a panarchy.

139 SCHEIDEL, *Demography* [n. 34].

In its own sort of way Roman Imperial Sagalassos was a player in this field, generating potential, resilience and connectivity. This paper did not so much want to dissect the High Imperial conditions, but wanted to engage in diachronic comparisons, applying the mentioned heuristic framework and ideas generated by the debate on complex adaptive systems.

Clearly, there are some similarities between second century CE Sagalassos and its late Roman counterpart, such as the continued tendency of shifting subsistence strategies provoked by nature or man in the different landscape pockets of its ancient territory. This aspect of flexibility and change has been characterized as a feature of complex adaptive systems. There are also differences between High Imperial and late Roman Sagalassos, however, and perhaps more than the similarities, the points of divergence can be considered to be of historical value. Indeed, the two major tendencies of presumed rural population growth and attested increased specialization of the productive landscape may be meaningfully combined, in providing sufficient foundation for recognizing growing aggregate demand as well as increased *per capita* income. The low-equilibrium trap seems not to have worked in case of late Roman Sagalassos. Moreover, the positive demographic evolution and degree of specialization associated with late Roman times can be considered to reflect successful strategies at exergy buffering, resulting in increased stability, order and complexity in society. Finally, a range of indicators have been mentioned which, especially in late Roman times, represented a balance between contemporary exergy needs and the supporting ecosystem. This equilibrium has been defined as a precondition for approaching regional sustainability and developing moderate growth on a regional scale. The heuristic framework of complex adaptive systems has been helpful in unravelling and placing the various aspects of this reconstruction, as well as concluding that there is a degree of increase in the regional potential and connectivity in late Roman Sagalassos and its territory. This conclusion has as a potential consequence, however, that the regional system could have become less resilient over time, as its growing dependency on specialization in the productive landscape made it also more vulnerable to processes of internal and external change. The Justinianic Plague possibly represented such an external shock to the system, amongst others.

It is an open question in which way the so-called third century CE crisis and fourth century CE degree of loss of the role of Sagalassos as regional pole of attraction[140] hampered the gradual build-up of the regional demographical pool as well as the potential, connectivity and resilience of the study area. The notion of panarchy that crisis can be defined when various adaptive cycles converge on the point of collapse does not seem to be compatible with the current understanding of the medium-term development of the region in the third and fourth centuries

[140] POBLOME *et al.*, *Tinkering* [n. 106].

CE, however, at least not when regarded from the particular angle of the productive landscape.

Although I hope to have demonstrated the usefulness of the heuristic framework, including that of complex adaptive systems, in approaching the development of nature-society interaction, regional analysis and diachronic comparison, clearly the exercise is not finished. This paper focused mostly on aspects of production in rural and urban contexts or the generation of means at the regional level, mostly based on material available in publication. Important indicators such as the regional agricultural carrying capacity or forestry yields are still being developed, for instance, and are expected to contribute in important ways to the methodological development as well as to the application of the model. Also, ways need to be examined on how better to measure or define the effects of the different indicators or adaptive cycles onto one another. Future papers should also aim at deeper integration of the indicators and heuristic frameworks, aspiring to investigate regional sustainability from the following formula:

(climate + vegetation + landscape)
+ (agriculture + animal husbandry + artisanate)
+ (society) + (time).

Finally, in order to reconstruct an encompassing socio-ecological system in the past aspects of expenditure of means as well as governance also need to be looked into. In the meantime, however, it should be safe to presume that although it must have been fun to live in Sagalassos during the Antonine period, so much praised by Edward Gibbon, especially if you were rich, the Theodosian age seems to have provided more guarantees at success for every member of society.

Acknowledgements
The research for this paper was supported by the CORES network of the Belgian Programme on Interuniversity Poles of Attraction (http://iap-cores.be/), the Research Fund of the University of Leuven (GOA 13/04), Project G.0562.11 of the Research Foundation Flanders (FWO) and the Hercules Foundation (AKUL/09/16). J. Poblome was appointed Francqui Research Professor for 2011-2014. I should like to thank Wim Van Neer, Bea De Cupere, Elena Marinova, Peter Talloen, Rinse Willet and Patrick Degryse for having commented on earlier drafts of this paper, in the true spirit of academic *camaraderie*.

PART II.
MODELS AND METHODS APPLIED

Wim BROEKAERT

Recycling Networks. The Structure of the Italian Business Community on Delos

1 Introduction

The presence of Italian businessmen on Delos during the Roman Republic has received considerable attention for more than a century now. The local organization of the community and the role of the various associations have puzzled historians from the days of Kornemann and Hatzfeld onwards and still continue to open up new debates on Roman imperialism, associational life and commerce in the Republic. A large part of the discussion is devoted to the nature of the Italian associations on Delos and the function of the *magistreis* in various dedicatory inscriptions. Hatzfeld was the first to attempt to refute earlier hypotheses that the *magistreis* were the leading magistrates of a community of Italians (*conventus*) having settled on the isle and operating as a single organisation.[1] He noticed the similarities between the Delian associations and the ones in Capua and concluded that the three essentially religious *collegia* of the Apolloniastai, Hermaistai and Poseidoniastai simply gathered Italian residents on Delos worshipping a particular deity and that the *magistreis* held the highest functions in these associations. The Competaliastai on the other hand were responsible for the Italian cult of the *Compitalia*, honouring the *Lares* of the crossroads. Exactly 70 years after the publication of this seminal work, Flambard tried to fine-tune Hatzfeld's reconstruction and argued that at least some of the *collegia* must also have been professional associations, the Poseidoniastai being mainly shippers and the Hermaistai merchants.[2] Recently, the old debate was

[1] E. Kornemann, De civibus romanis in provinciis imperii consistentibus, Diss. Berl., 1892; J. HATZFELD, Les Italiens résidant à Délos mentionnés dans les inscriptions de l'île in BCH 36, 1912, p. 10-218, in particular p. 146-176.

2 J.-M. Flambard, Observations sur la nature des magistri italiens de Délos in F. Coarelli / D. Musti / H. Solin (eds.), Delo e Italia. Raccolta di studi, Opuscula Instituti Romani Finlandiae II, 1982, p. 67-77. For the magistreis as officials of associations, see also N. K. Rauh, The Sacred Bonds of Commerce: Religion, Economy, and Trade Society

revived by Hasenohr, who noticed that members of a single Italian family joined several different associations.[3] She claimed that, as business families usually focused on a single profession, the *collegia* could therefore not have been occupational associations. Neither could the *collegia* have been mere religious associations, for a similar reason: in her view, the Italian families would have worshipped a single deity and did not join several religious *collegia*. Hasenohr therefore concluded that the titles 'Apolloniastes', 'Hermaistes' and 'Poseidoniastes' referred to honorary functions bestowed upon powerful and respected individuals by the Italian community. These magistrates were responsible for religious cults similar to the ones encountered in Capua and the negotiations between the Italian community and the Athenian political institutions on Delos. Though not explicitly stated as such, with this hypothesis Hasenohr returned to the old model of a *conventus* of Italian residents and their *magistreis*, "un *conventus* de fait, sinon de droit."[4]

This paper aims to contribute to the debate by reviewing the inscriptional evidence of Delian associations through the lens of a social network analysis (SNA). Instead of focusing on the internal organization of the associations, their mutual relationships or the donations they made, I intend to analyse the composition of the *collegia*, the individuals who had been elected *magistreis* and the personal and familial networks they were embedded in. The purpose of this approach is to detect how the background of the individual *magistreis*, the ties connecting them to each other and their place in the fabric of the Italian community on Delos helped to determine the role, or roles, of the Italian associations. In other words, are the *magistreis* associations of Italian magistrates (the *conventus* hypothesis) or magistrates of Italian associations (the *collegia* hypothesis)?

The following sections will first introduce some general features and limitations of SNA and present a theoretical model of social networks and connectivity within the Italian community. I will then discuss the network structure of the community as a whole and zoom in on the associations. A final section offers some conclusions.

at Hellenistic Roman Delos, Amsterdam, 1993, p. 33-41.

[3] C. HASENOHR, *Les collèges de magistri et la communauté italienne de Délos* in C. MÜLLER / C. HASENOHR (eds.), *Les Italiens dans le monde grec: IIe siècle av. J.-C. -Ier siècle ap. J.-C., Circulation, activités, intégration, Actes de la Table ronde, École Normale Supérieure, Paris, 14-16 mai 1998,* Athens, 2002, p. 67-76.

[4] HASENOHR, *Les collèges* [n. 3], p. 76, approvingly citing P. ROUSSEL, *Délos, colonie athénienne*, Paris, 1987 [1916], p. 80.

2 Social Network Analysis and Ancient History

I have argued elsewhere that SNA may be a promising avenue for ancient historians to evaluate the connectivity and interaction among distinct communities in society and explained which tools are available to start this kind of analysis. I again make use of the freely available computer program Pajek.[5]

As the purpose of this paper is to examine the place of the Italian associations in the Delian community, we first need to reconstruct the network of Italian residents as a whole and to determine its cohesion, limits and opportunities for interaction. The Italian community on Delos provides an excellent occasion for the application of SNA, for the network and the individual nodes can easily be defined. Theoretically, all Italians residing on Delos (so excluding Roman officials and military officers temporarily visiting the island) should be included in the network. However, as the SNA will focus on the level of the family instead of that of the individual for reasons explained below, I excluded all Italians whose name was too fragmentary to yield a *gentilicium* and individuals only known by their *praenomen* or *cognomen*. These criteria reduced the community to a network with 546 nodes. Each was attributed a single node number. I then added the relationships between all nodes. A distinction was made between (possibly) short-term connections as represented in the inscriptions ('ties'), and long-standing relationships, such as marriage, kinship, patronage and slave ownership ('attributes'). Ties were added between all nodes present in an inscription. I assume that the occurrence of two or more nodes in a single inscription identifies at least some kind of connection, however momentary or casual. To contemporary SNA, this may be a rather crude measure, but probably one of the very few available to ancient historians. As we are unable to conduct inquiries into someone's network and have only access to a very limited amount of public sources (instead of personal archives or correspondence), epigraphy provides a suboptimal solution to the restraints of applying SNA to ancient society.[6] Attributes were given to robust, non-coincidental connections, which in itself create stable sub-networks, in this case family networks of individuals sharing the same *gentilicium*. These attributes are, especially for ancient historians, a necessary prerequisite to analyse the features of large networks. As most individuals only occur once in the Delian epigraphy, it is impossible to reconstruct networks for single Italian businessmen. The network analysis must therefore focus on a higher level of shared attributes, viz. belonging to the same

[5] A short introduction to the benefits and limitations of SNA for ancient historians is offered by W. BROEKAERT, *Financial Experts in a Spider Web. A Social Network Analysis of the Archives of Caecilius Iucundus and the Sulpicii* in *Klio* 95, 2013, p. 471-510, with further references. The SNA program Pajek can be downloaded from the developer's website (http://pajek.imfm.si/doku.php or http://vlado.fmf.uni-lj.si/pub/networks/pajek/)

[6] For a more detailed discussion of methodological problems of SNA, see BROEKAERT, *Financial Experts* [n. 5].

family. I assume that individuals of a single family can easily share personal networks, mainly because the majority of the Italian businessmen were residing on Delos during a limited span of time (the final decades of the 2nd century and the first years of the 1st century BC) and for similar reasons (to do business). When an Italian family was present on Delos to make a profit in trade, and no doubt the clear majority of the Italian families had travelled to Delos for this purpose, members had every reason to share individual experience, relationships and knowledge. Personal connections can thus without much difficulty circulate between two or even three generations, in particular within a well-defined framework of a foreign business community as opposed to Greeks and other foreign residents on the one hand, and via the strong ties of family relationships on the other.[7] For this purpose I only take account of individuals who can be connected to an Italian family.

I thus consider the Italians on Delos to be a network with well-defined closure (ethnicity) and frequent internal interaction (within and between families). The structural features of this network shall be analysed below. Yet, this large network consists of several types of sub-networks. The family is an obvious example, but for this paper we focus on associational life. To allow a network analysis of the various associations present on Delos, these will be studied as sub-networks firmly embedded within the Italian network as a whole. Each inscription mentioning *magistreis* of the Competaliastai, Apolloniastai, Hermaistai and Poseidoniastai will be considered a temporary yet complete sub-network, a glimpse of the actual operation of the associations as an institution. The sum of these isolated snapshots will provide a reflection of the role of the associations within the community.

3 The Connectivity of the Italian Community

Before turning to the actual SNA, it is necessary to model the connectivity of the Italian families on Delos, for a better understanding of the subsequent discussion of the associational networks. I argue first that the internal connectivity of the Italian community stimulated the creation of an overarching network and, second, that this large network relied on several smaller, distinct yet mutually supportive sub-networks. As the clear majority of the Italian families had obviously settled on Delos to engage in the lucrative eastern slave trade, I draw on recent findings from the business literature on networks and social capital to model the organization of the Italian community.

[7] Some families, such as the Aemilii, can even be traced through 5 generations. See M.-F. BASLEZ, *La première présence romaine à Délos (vers 250-vers 140)* in A. D. RIZAKIS (ed.), *Roman Onomastics in the Greek East. Social and Political Aspects. Proceedings of the International Colloquium Athens, 7-9 September 1993*, Paris-Athens, 1996, p. 215-224 (especially p. 217).

First, that the Italian business community on Delos functioned as a network requires little proof. The history of pre-modern and modern economies has shown that neither the neo-classical abstract markets nor the institutional model of hierarchies fits the historical evidence very well. Highly centralized firms or free market exchange are atypical forms of organization compared to the dominance in business history of family businesses, guilds, partnerships and trading companies, which operate along completely different lines.[8] The third possible form of organization then is a network, which for the purpose of this paper is defined as "neither a 'hierarchy', i.e. a closed social structure, nor a completely atomized free market, but a constellation 'in between' these, consisting of elements of the institutional and organisational set-up that historically developed in the society in question and structuring the economic transactions that take place within that society."[9] Unlike markets and hierarchies, network forms of organization rely on relational trust, reciprocity, extra-legal sanctions, high commitment among parties and interdependence, precisely the kind of features that appear to have structured most pre-industrial economies.[10] It has now become common knowledge that this kind of network to a large extent determines the levels of social and economic interaction and are often a crucial aspect in deciding between the failure and success of business enterprises. Access to resources such as information and credit, opportunity recognition, decision-making and partnerships largely rely on the networks connecting, or failing to connect, various economic actors, in this case Italian business families.

Second, the large network of resident Italian families was based on two different types of smaller networks, each of which created a different allocation of nodes and a different set of connections. Current research distinguishes between a family's interfamily and intrafamily networks. The first set of networks consists of all external linkages connecting the family and its members to colleagues in trade belonging to different families. Interfamily ties are based on bridging social capital, which allows access to services, information and power outside one's own network.

[8] This is not the place to discuss both economic models in extensive detail. For a comprehensive introduction, see W. W. POWELL, *Neither Market nor Hierarchy: Network Forms of Organization* in *Research in Organizational Behaviour* 12, 1990, p. 295-336 (esp. p. 296-305).

[9] W. BROEKAERT / A. ZUIDERHOEK, *Society, the Market, or Actually Both? Networks and the Allocation of Credit and Capital Goods in the Roman Economy*, forthcoming.

[10] For the pre-modern world, see F. BRAUDEL, *Civilization and Capitalism, 15th-18th Centuries*, London, 1979-1984. For antiquity, see P. F. Bang, *Trade and Empire: In Search of Organising Concepts for the Roman Economy* in *Past and Present* 195, 2007, p. 3-54; N. MORLEY, *Trade in Classical Antiquity*, Cambridge, 2007; W. BROEKAERT, *Partners in Business. Roman Merchants and the Advantages of Being a Collegiatus* in *Ancient Society* 41, 2011, p. 219-254 and ID., *Joining Forces. Commercial Partnerships or* Societates *in the Early Roman Empire* in *Historia* 61, 2012, p. 221-253.

The non-redundant ties to other families provide access to non-overlapping and even unique sources of information. The second set collects all internal linkages between family members, connected by bonding social capital. These particularly strong and lasting relationships promote internal trust, cooperation and cohesiveness. In this case, the interfamily network consists of connections to other competing Italian business families active in the slave trade, while the intrafamily network combines all relationships between persons (freeborn individuals, freedmen and slaves) working within the nuclear business family.[11]

The maintenance of an interfamily network is supported by a shared Italian identity and a number of robust social institutions, including associations, commensality and sporting activities, many of which appear to have been 'exported' from the Italian peninsula and were located in the Italian agora.[12] Despite the fact that all these traditions supported the creation of bridging social capital within a business community actively engaged in trade, there is no clear consensus whether the majority of the Italian institutions were designed or even had the ability to support a network of an essentially economic nature, or whether only a few, such as the professional associations of oil merchants, served this purpose.[13] As will be discussed below, many historians appear to have focused on the social or religious nature of these institutions, thereby seriously downplaying the economic role of bridging social capital. Nevertheless, this economic aspect of Italian institutions on Delos could have been crucial in mitigating the limitations and vagaries of the Roman trading world. If most of the institutions were able to support an economic network, every institution in itself added strength to the business community. Institutions then partially overlapped and became mutually supportive. The major advantage of a network of this kind is that individuals can turn to whichever institution they are most closely affiliated with when facing problems of an

[11] J. WALTER / C. LECHNER / F. W. KELLERMANNS, *Knowledge Transfer between and within Alliance Partners: Private versus Collective Benefits of Social Capital* in *Journal of Business Research* 60, 2007, p. 698-710. For bridging and bonding social capital, see P. S. ADLER / S. W. KWON, *Social Capital: Prospects for a New Concept* in *Academy of Management Review* 27, 2002, p. 17-40.

[12] HATZFELD, *Les Italiens* [n. 1], p. 184-196 on the similarities between the associations in Capua and Delos. For commensality and sporting activities, see N. K. RAUH, *Was the Agora of the Italians an Établissement du Sport?* in *BCH* 116, 1992, p. 293-333, who considers the Agora to be a recreational facility for dining, games, sport etc. A short discussion of the various conflicting interpretations of the role of the Agora is offered by A. MASTINO, *Il Dibattito sull'agorà degli Italici a Delo: un bilancio retrospettivo fra ideologia ed urbanistica* in S. ANGIOLILLO / S. BOLDRINI / P. BRACONI *et al.*, *Le perle e il filo: a Mario Torelli per i suoi settanta anni*, Venosa, Osanna Edizioni, 2008, p. 233-241.

[13] For the association of *elaiopolai*, see *ID* 1713-1714. Other professional associations include those of Alexandrian business agents (*ID* 1528-1529), bankers (*ID* 1715), wine merchants (*ID* 1711) and Italian steersmen (*ID* 2401).

economic nature, hence saving time and effort in finding the right institution. The alternative model presents a more fragmented community, with every group of institutions serving a single purpose (social, religious or economic) and only showing minor overlap. Depending on actual needs, individuals will be forced to turn to a limited amount of institutions and only have access to a small number of supportive sub-networks. In the following sections, I shall use inscriptional evidence and SNA to examine which of the two models fits the Italian associations best.

The intrafamily network on the other hand relies on internalized ties of kinship, patronage through manumission and hierarchical power through slavery. As an isolated unit, the intrafamily network is only able to circulate redundant information among its members, reducing the value and efficiency of the strong family ties.[14] Now, in combination with the interfamily network, the strong ties configure a particularly dense network, capitalizing on goal alignment, quick information flows, the absence of structural holes, undistorted transfer and reduced operational costs. The network requires little support to survive, as kinship and hierarchical ties are created and transmitted in a natural way.

Both networks continuously interact and support each other. First, as has been noted earlier, members of the same family join different associations and hence gain access to different sub-networks. Each membership provides the family with new opportunities, contacts and relationships and benefits the intrafamily network. Second, the intrafamily network guarantees the survival of the interfamily network, because even though the connection between two individuals of different families may be broken, the intrafamily ties of both families are able to assure the stability of the interfamily connection: other members of both families can simply take over and continue the tie.

The two different networks permeating the Italian business community, their supportive institutions and interaction are represented in Figure 1.

The next parts will use a SNA approach to discuss the overarching Italian community and the *magistreis* as a support structure for the interfamily network.

[14] See M. GRANOVETTER, *The Strength of Weak Ties* in *American Journal of Sociology* 78, 1973, p. 1360-1380 and ID., *The Strength of Weak Ties: A Network Theory Revisited* in *Sociological Theory* 1, 1983, p. 201-233.

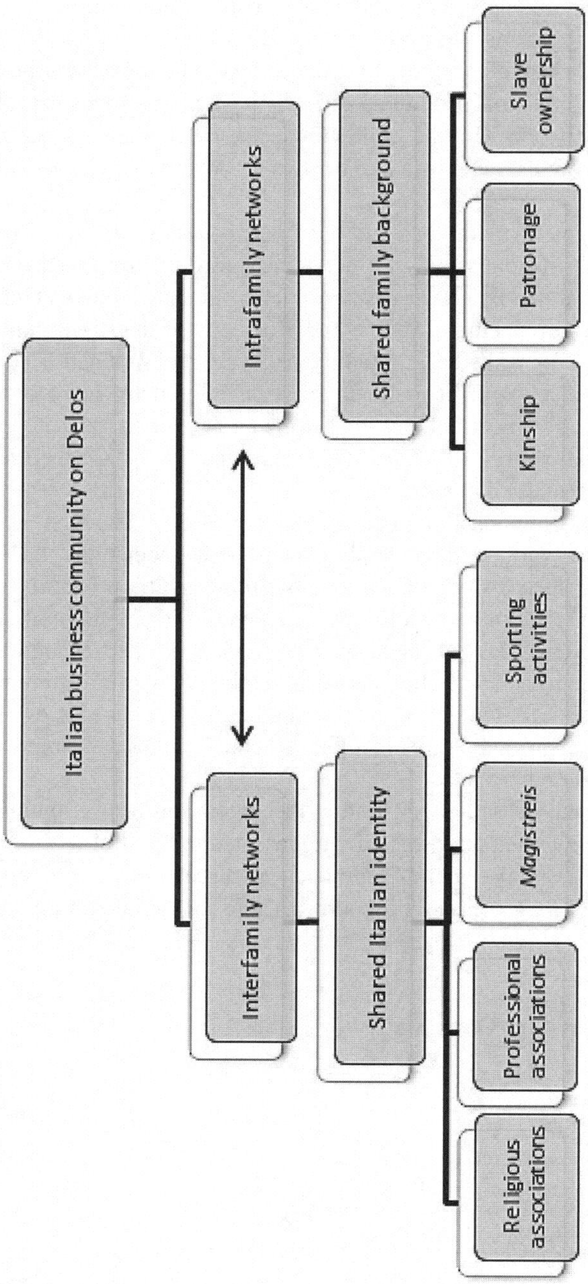

Figure 1. Connectivity of the Italian community

4 A Bird's-Eye View on the Italian Community

This section will shortly analyse the structure and cohesion of the network of all Italian residents on the isle. The visualization of the individual nodes and their personal connections results in a rather dense network, centred around a few 'cliques' or smaller networks in which all ties connect to each other, and with a considerable amount of isolated nodes in the periphery (Figure 2; n=546). This structural feature is to some extent the result of the nature of the evidence. The cliques reflect the activities of associations, joint dedications, contracts, pecuniary contributions etc. As all Italian residents involved feature in the corresponding inscriptions witnessing these events, they form small subgroups with close, personal ties. The isolated nodes surrounding the dense set of subgroups mainly represent residents whose name has only been preserved on a funerary inscription on Rhenia, the nearby cemetery island of Delos.

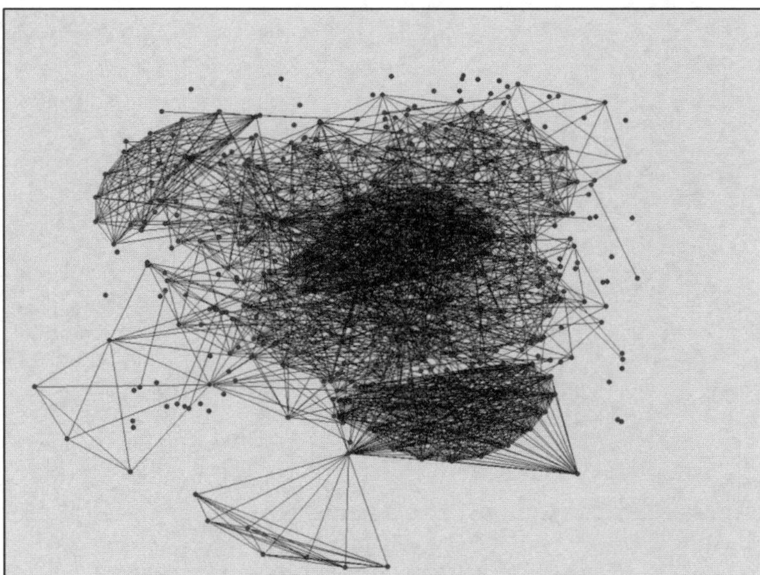

Figure 2. The network of Italian residents on Delos

As most of the inscriptions simply mention a single name or sometimes only a family member, we are unable to reconstruct wider personal networks beyond the intrafamily level. To level out the bias towards either very restrictive, personal networks or isolation as a consequence of the nature of epigraphy, it is more promising to focus on the family level instead and only take into account the ties connecting Italian families. As a family should be considered a dense network in itself (the intrafamily network), where connections can easily be circulated, one can assume that members shared a large part of the ties to other families (the interfamily network). By reducing all individual nodes belonging to a single family to a new node, the 'family node', we will be able to approach the real connectivity of the Italian community. This way many isolated nodes mentioned in the epitaphs from Rhenia, but belonging to families still actively engaged in business on Delos, now become 'reunited' with their family members and are embedded once again in the intrafamily and the shared interfamily networks. This alteration to the first network requires regrouping a large number of nodes and redrawing all interfamily connections. Fortunately, Pajek is programmed to facilitate this kind of modifications and allows us to group all nodes which have been given the same attribute, i.e. membership of the same family (as mentioned earlier). The large network of nearly 550 individual Italians is shrunk to a new network of family connection (Figure 3; n = 187).

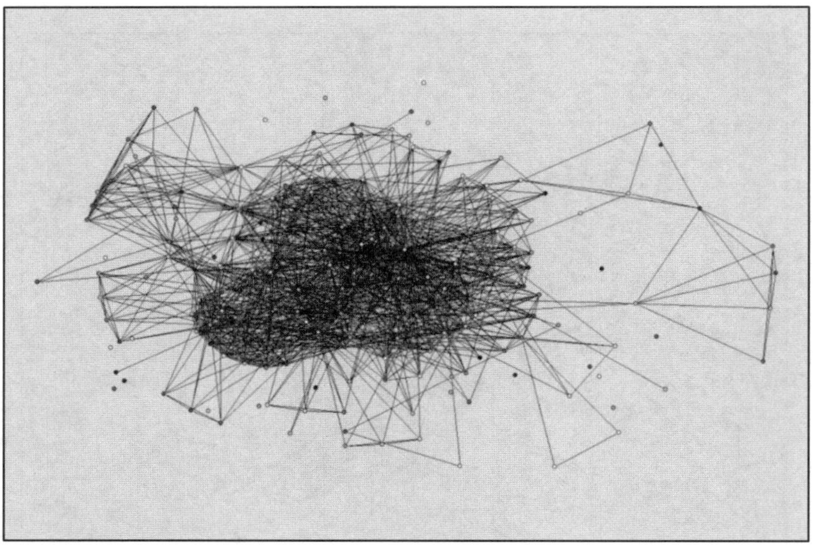

Figure 3. The network of Italian families on Delos

Two conclusions may be drawn. First, as expected, the number of isolated nodes is severely reduced. However, the new network still contains a few isolated family nodes, such as the *gentes* of the Agirii, Filicinii or Ogulnii, who according to the remaining inscriptional evidence and SNA appear to have occupied a rather peripheral place in the Italian community.[15] These families apparently had only minor business interests and must have settled on the isle with a very limited

[15] Agirii: Couilloud 402. Filicinii: Couilloud 91. Ogulnii: *ID* 2354bis.

number of family members. Second, the network retains a fairly densely connected centre. Here we can locate major business families such as the Castricii, Granii and Paconii, residing on Delos with a large number of freed and slave agents and deeply involved in Italian community life.

4.1 Density and Average Degree of the Network

To determine the features of the Italian community network in more detail, we need to assess its level of cohesion: the higher the connectivity of all ties, the tighter the network will be. A dense network facilitates the circulation of information and forging new connections. In SNA, the connectivity of a network is captured by the concept of density or the proportion between the maximum possible number of ties and actual realized ties. The density of the Italian residents' network is 0.01344108, which means that only 1.34% of all possible ties between individuals is present. The density score appears very low at first sight, yet is very common of networks of this large size. Density and network size are inversely related, because large networks have a high amount of possible ties, but the ties an individual can or wishes to maintain are limited. Moreover, the nature of the funerary inscriptions on Rhenia will, for reasons explained above, severely reduce the level of density in the network of Italian residents. When computing the density score for the network shrunk to family level, the bias of the Rhenian inscriptions is largely levelled out, as the score now amounts to 0.07706826. This implies that no less than 7.70% of all possible ties between Italian families is realized. This percentage is to some extent influenced by the lower number of nodes (187 instead of 546), but still confirms the power of the intrafamily network in sustaining the interfamily network. Thus, by moving from the interpersonal to the interfamily level, the Italian community on Delos appears to have been a densely connected network. This result corresponds to the conclusions of migratory studies, confirming the immigrants' shared identity as a major bonding institution which promotes close interaction and connectivity in an essentially foreign environment.[16]

An additional measure of network connectivity is the so-called degree of nodes, or the number of ties in which each separate node is embedded. As we focus on the level of network cohesion instead of individual node connectivity, we can use the average degree of all nodes to capture the network's cohesion. The major advantage of degree scores is that the number does not depend on the size of the network and allows better structural comparison between networks of different size. The average degree of the Italian residents' network is 7.34065934,

[16] H. E. Aldrich / R. Waldinger, *Ethnicity and Entrepreneurship* in *Annual Review of Sociology* 16, 1990, p. 111-135 (esp. p. 127-130).

but for the interfamily network this number increases to 14.55614973. The result thus confirms the importance of the family as a crucial factor in supporting the cohesion in the Italian community.

To increase the explanatory power of these figures, we can compare these against density and average degree scores of other similar networks with the same amount of nodes and ties, randomly created by Pajek. The average degree scores resemble the figures for the Italian community very closely, suggesting that the average amount of ties the individual or family nodes were involved in approaches the numbers predicted by statistical analysis. The density scores on the other hand are significantly higher: random networks present scores of 0.00672222 and 0.03892019 for the individual and family level respectively. This implies that networks of this size and with this amount of ties usually only realize 0.67% and 3.89% of all possible connections, compared to 1.34% and 7.70% for the Italian community. Once again, the conclusion must be that the residents on Delos were living in a close-knit business community.

The remainder of this section will focus on the centrality of individual nodes within the Italian community, to determine which families were crucial for the function and survival of the network.[17] Following previous SNA, I distinguish between 3 measures of centrality:[18]

1. Degree: the connectivity of a single node.
2. Closeness: the reachability of nodes.
3. Betweenness: the node's role in connecting other nodes.

4.2 Degree

As noted above, node degree simply takes into account the number of nodes a singular node is linked to, viz. its direct 'neighbours'. The results can best be presented in a frequency table (Table 1). Degree scores are represented as class numbers, each grouping a number of families sharing the same score.

[17] For the reasons explained, I only take into account the family level. From now on the term 'node' equals 'family node'.

[18] See BROEKAERT, *Financial Experts* [n. 5].

Table 1. Degree frequency table of network of Italian residents on Delos

Degree	Freq	Freq%	CumFreq	CumFreq%	Representative
0	32	17.1123	32	17.1123	Acutius
1	4	2.1390	36	19.2513	Arius
2	9	4.8128	45	24.0642	Annaeus
3	4	2.1390	49	26.2032	Anicius
4	11	5.8824	60	32.0856	Alleius
5	10	5.3476	70	37.4332	Capinius
6	7	3.7433	77	41.1765	Calpurnius
7	5	2.6738	82	43.8503	Allidius
8	5	2.6738	87	46.5241	Alicius
9	6	3.2086	93	49.7326	Aemilius
10	9	4.8128	102	54.5455	Avilius
11	4	2.1390	106	56.6845	Pompilius
12	3	1.6043	109	58.2888	Antonius
13	2	1.0695	111	59.3583	Licinius
14	9	4.8128	120	64.1711	Diobellius
15	3	1.6043	123	65.7754	Aufidius
16	3	1.6043	126	67.3797	Crepereius
17	3	1.6043	129	68.9840	Erucius
18	2	1.0695	131	70.0535	Claudius
20	2	1.0695	133	71.1230	Crassicius
21	1	0.5348	134	71.6578	Clodius
22	3	1.6043	137	73.2620	Carvilius
23	14	7.4866	151	80.7487	Allius
24	2	1.0695	153	81.8182	Felsonius
25	1	0.5348	154	82.3529	Nonius
26	1	0.5348	155	82.8877	Gessius
27	1	0.5348	156	83.4225	Tullius
29	1	0.5348	157	83.9572	Egnatius
31	1	0.5348	158	84.4920	Vicirius
32	1	0.5348	159	85.0267	Rutilius
33	4	2.1390	163	87.1658	Ampius
34	2	1.0695	165	88.2353	Fulvius
35	1	0.5348	166	88.7701	Stlaccius
37	2	1.0695	168	89.8396	Cottius
38	2	1.0695	170	90.9091	Arellius
41	2	1.0695	172	91.9786	Babullius

42	1	0.5348	173	92.5134	Tutorius
44	3	1.6043	176	94.1176	Castricius
45	2	1.0695	178	95.1872	Caecilius
46	1	0.5348	179	95.7219	Seius
48	2	1.0695	181	96.7914	Sextilius
55	1	0.5348	182	97.3262	Gerillanus
61	1	0.5348	183	97.8610	Audius
62	1	0.5348	184	98.3957	Plotius
65	1	0.5348	185	98.9305	Granius
67	1	0.5348	186	99.4652	Maecius
71	1	0.5348	187	100.000	Paconius

A few conclusions can be drawn from the degree frequency table. First, only 17% of all Italian families can be considered isolated. Given the fact that the inscriptions on which this SNA is based evidently represent only a tiny fragment of the real number of interfamily connections on Delos, 17% must be a highly overstated ratio. This figure only reflects the isolation of nodes in a completely arbitrary sample of the Italian network, determined by the survival rate of inscriptions. We can hence only conclude that the families present in this class were probably minor business families with limited interests in the eastern trade, perhaps only temporarily residing on Delos. They failed to gain sufficient wealth and status to join the prestigious associations of *magistreis* and played only a minor role in other aspects of community life. Second, nearly 50% of all Italian families appears to have been involved in close interfamily relationships with at least 10 other families. Nearly 30% maintained relationships with at least 20 different families. Given the nature of the evidence and sample, we can again hypothesize that in reality this number must have been higher. Nevertheless, the figures again present a very dense network with a remarkable level of connectivity. Degree scores for random networks created by Pajek confirm this conclusion, as the 30% of nodes with highest degree scores statistically only realize connections to 15 other nodes instead of 20. Third, the highest degree score in the randomly generated networks is 25, with only 1% of the total population reaching this level of centrality. In the Italian community, nearly 18% of all families managed to control this amount of interfamily connections. The 5 families with the highest scores can even be linked to more than 60 or even 70 other families or some 30% of all Italian families residing on Delos. These numbers confirm previous conclusions on the Italian residents as an extremely close-knit community with an exceptionally dense core (some 15% of the network population or degree 32-71), a relatively well-connected centre (some 35% or degree 10-31) and a more isolated periphery (50% or degree 0-9).

4.3 Closeness

A second measure of centrality, closeness, takes into account the reachability of each node. A node not only interferes with its direct neighbours, but also, through these neighbours, with other nodes. Closeness establishes the minimum distance or number of ties between two nodes, called the shortest path or 'geodesic'. In dense networks, the clear majority of nodes will need few steps to interact and closeness scores will remain low. Sparsely connected networks on the other hand are usually characterized by a small set of nodes in the core with geodesic 1 and rapidly increasing distances for most of the other nodes. For large networks, the variation in distances obviously depends on the central node: with a well-connected node in the centre, geodesics will be low, but the more isolated the central node, the higher the number of steps all nodes will require to connect to the centre. It is therefore important to compute geodesics with different nodes in the centre with varying levels of centrality as determined by their degree scores (Table 2).

When placing the family with the highest degree score, the Paconii, in the centre of the network and excluding all isolated nodes, the highest distance is 3. Only 5 families need 3 steps to interact with a member of the Paconii. The other families are either directly connected to the Paconii (geodesic 1) or only require a single additional step (geodesic 2). With another well-connected family, the Audii, in the middle, the general centrality and the maximum amount of steps of the network remain unaltered: still only 10 Italian families have geodesic 3, 72 geodesic 2 and 61 geodesic 1. When leaving the dense core of extremely connected families and focusing on the centre of nodes with a relatively high degree score, such as the Tullii, Carvilii and Erucii, the ratio of geodesic 2 and 3 slowly start to rise and the maximum geodesic number increases. Still, the number of families now situated at a distance of 4 steps is kept relatively low, mainly because the well-connected core of families such as the Granii, Maecii and Paconii allow more distant families to interact with minimal effort. The clear majority of nodes still only needs 2 steps to reach the central node. Turning to the more isolated families in the periphery, such as the Aemilii, Alleii and Arii, direct connections evidently decrease in favour of longer distances (geodesic 2 to 4), but still none of them is forced to include a 5th step to stay in contact with the central node. Once again, the extremely dense core with connections all over the community prevents a proportional rise in geodesic numbers, even when approaching the network through the lens of the peripheral families.

Table 2. Closeness scores of some Italian families

Family	Degree score	Geodesic 1	Geodesic 2	Geodesic 3	Geodesic 4	Geodesic 5
Paconii	71	47.91%	47.91%	3.47%	/	/
Audii	61	42.36%	50.00%	6.94%	/	/
Tullii	27	17.36%	68.05%	13.88%	/	/
Carvilii	22	15.27%	68.05%	13.19%	2.77%	/
Erucii	17	11.80%	67.36%	15.27%	4.86%	/
Aemilii	9	4.86%	40.27%	48.61%	5.55%	/
Alleii	4	2.77%	54.86%	40.27%	1.38%	/
Arii	1	0.69%	40.97%	51.38%	6.25%	/

These relatively high closeness scores even suggest that we can consider the Italian community on Delos a so-called 'small world', a close-knit network in which all nodes, even though not all directly linked, can be reached with a fairly limited amount of steps. I have argued elsewhere that small worlds rely on strong multiplex connections, i.e. mutually supportive ties of a different nature such as membership of professional associations, religious groups, political elites, friendship, marriage, adoption etc.[19] Multiplex connections severely reduce the costs to create and foster relationships. When the costs are sufficiently low to maximize the benefits of being connected to someone else, nodes will try to incorporate as many ties as possible in their personal networks. The high level of connectivity of the Italian community with an extremely dense core makes the network resistant to rapid dissolution and outside blows. While most of these connections are no longer detectable in the small sample of sources that has come down to us, the general features of the network suggest they lurk in the background and shape the relationships between families. For the Italian community on Delos, obvious candidates for generating strong multiplex ties are the different occupational and religious associations, the *magistreis* and the joint dedications and other acts of munificence as reflected in the inscriptions.

4.4 Betweenness

The final measure of centrality, betweenness, considers the connecting role of a particular node in the network. Does the network suffer from, or even survive, the removal of the node? Moreover, if the node indeed holds a crucial position as intermediary or broker in the connectivity of the network, it has the ability to control the interaction of other nodes, block attempts to connect and isolate other

[19] See BROEKAERT, *Financial Experts* [n. 5].

nodes. Betweenness therefore also indicates the power of single nodes in manipulating, supporting or disrupting the network it is embedded in. Betweenness scores for the Italian families are represented in a frequency table (Table 3). The highest numbers are evidently obtained by the families present in the core of the network, the Granii, Maecii and Paconii. A more important conclusion however is that 60% of the families do not influence the operation of the network nor have the power to manipulate interaction. In a previous SNA of the financial archives of the Sulpicii and Caecilius Iucundus, I concluded that for the control of their personal networks, some 80% of all individuals and 65% of the families were completely irrelevant for the survival of the network.[20] The slightly lower percentage for the Italian community again points to a network with a higher than expected level of connectivity, in which more families were actively engaged in maintaining and supporting interfamily connections.

Table 3. Betweenness frequency table

Vector value	Frequency	Freq%	CumFreq	CumFreq%
0.000	114	60.9626	114	60.9626
0.000-0.007	44	23.5294	158	84.4920
0.007-0.014	12	6.4171	170	90.9091
0.014-0.020	6	3.2086	176	94.1176
0.020-0.027	3	1.6043	179	95.7219
0.027-0.034	2	1.0695	181	96.7914
0.034-0.041	1	0.5348	182	97.3262
0.041-0.047	2	1.0695	184	98.3957
0.047-0.054	2	1.0695	186	99.4652
0.054-0.061	1	0.5348	187	100.0000

5 The Associations of *Magistreis* within the Italian Community

5.1 Data Selection and Methodology

In this section I will examine the role of the associations of *magistreis* as part of the institutions supporting the creation of a shared Italian identity and the maintenance of the interfamily network. The SNA of the associations will test the hypothesis that the sub-networks of the *magistreis* mirrored the structural features of the Italian business community as a whole and hence reinforced the strength of the Italian economic network. If on the other hand the associations as sub-

[20] See BROEKAERT, *Financial Experts* [n. 5].

networks present a structural organization different from the community, a distinct and more exclusive role must be attributed to the *magistreis*. For this purpose, I listed all inscriptions mentioning *magistreis* of the Competaliastai, Poseidoniastai, Hermaistai and Apolloniastai or joint dedications by the *magistreis* of the latter 3 associations. Each provided a combination of individual *magistreis*, which was considered a distinct set of individual nodes or sub-network. For each individual in the sub-network, all interfamily connections have been reconstructed in the same way as for the Italian community as a whole. I also adduced degree scores for the nodes in each sub-network and a visual representation of the network. As the conclusions for all 3 centrality measures (degree, closeness, and betweenness) identified similar features of the network, I only took into account degree scores.[21] For all sub-networks, density scores and average degree scores were computed and for each association averages, medians and modes were added to make comparisons (Table 4). This allows us to assess differences and similarities between sub-networks, their distinctive features and place in the overarching network of Italian residents.

Table 4. Density scores and average degree scores of the Delian Roman associations

Sub-network	Density score and % of realized ties	Average degree score
	Competaliastai	
ID 1760	0.19223140 (19.22%)	21.32727273
ID 1761	0.16834969 (16.83%)	20.21848739
ID 1763	0.19473923 (19.47%)	20.62857143
ID 1764	0.22988628 (22.98%)	22.49484536
ID 1765	0.30537202 (30.53%)	18.30508475
ID 1766	0.19270833 (19.27%)	18.70833333
ID 1768	0.52333991 (52.33%)	20.56410256
ID 1769	0.17513081 (17.51%)	20.14035088
ID 1771	0.23446367 (23.44%)	20.14117647
Average	**24.62%**	**20.27**
Median	**19.47%**	**20.21**
Mode	**19%**	**20**

[21] For reasons of space the associated tables and graphs could not be included here. They are available on request from the author.

	Poseidoniastai	
ID 1751	0.28953693 (28.95%)	23.08860759
ID 1752	0.36532368 (36.53%)	17.44680851
Average	**32.74%**	**20.26**
Median	**32.74%**	**20.26**
Mode	**32%**	**20**
	Hermaistai	
ID 1731	0.35502959 (35.50%)	4.92307692
ID 1732	0.19068715 (19.06%)	19.84466019
ID 1733	0.18974456 (18.97%)	19.72815534
ID 1734	0.46938776 (46.93%)	6.71428571
ID 1735	0.33220604 (33.22%)	20.87096774
ID 1738-1739	0.18980000 (18.98%)	19.18000000
ID 1740	0.47406866 (47.40%)	17.83783784
ID 1741	0.56747405 (56.74%)	9.88235294
ID 1750	0.56000000 (56.00%)	3.20000000
Average	**36.97%**	**13.57%**
Median	**35.50%**	**17.83**
Mode	**18%**	**19**
	Apolloniastai	
ID 1730	0.17135880 (17.13%)	20.38983051
	Joint dedications	
ID 1753	0.15388007 (15.38%)	19.57142857
ID 1754	0.17352854 (17.35%)	20.31034483
ID 1755	0.18992087 (18.99%)	18.83673469
ID 1756	0.68595041 (68.59%)	8.00000000
ID 1758	0.32980600 (32.98%)	21.04761905
Average	**30.65%**	**17.55**
Median	**18.99%**	**19.57**
Mode	**17-18%**	**19-20**

5.2 The Nature of the Delian Roman Associations

Before integrating the results of SNA, I return to the most recent analysis of Hasenohr. As mentioned in the introduction, she asserts that the associations of *magistreis* can have been neither professional nor religious, for members of a single Italian family appear to have joined different associations. Arguing that a family focuses on a single religion and trade, she concluded that the *magistreis* must have held honorary functions and have been responsible for religious festivals and negotiations with the Athenian authorities. The two basic assumptions of her reconstruction can easily be refuted. First, Hasenohr's argument that Italian residents did not join multiple religious associations is contradicted by the epigraphy of Delos itself. A certain Caius C.f. for instance appears to have held priesthoods in the cults of the Dioscuri, Egyptian gods and Syrian deities.[22] Secondly, many business families present on Delos to engage in the slave trade were also involved in exporting Italian wine to the western provinces. A comparison of the names of Republican wine merchants on amphorae stoppers discovered in wrecks along the coast of Spain, France and Italy on the one hand and Italians present in the East on the other, provides a strong argument in favour of business diversification and supply of different areas of the Mediterranean (see appendix). Moreover, given the large number of Italian amphorae on Delos, the same families apparently also supplied the isle with vintages produced in their native region, sailing back with a cargo of slaves and luxury items.[23] Additional evidence for wide-ranging business activities is offered by a comparison of the families on Delos and Republican occupational inscriptions in which several members of the same families occur.[24] Slave trade appears to have been combined with interests in banking, manufacturing, textile industry, iron trade and incense trade. Hence, there is no reason why members of a single family should not have joined different professional associations. Comparative evidence from the Imperial age confirms that Roman businessmen indeed frequently joined several occupational associations with diverging specializations at the same time.[25]

To sum up, inscriptional evidence does not support the conclusion that the Delian associations would have been exclusively occupational, religious or 'political' (as representatives of the Italian *conventus*) groups. The assumption that families would only have focused on a single trade or religion is mistaken. It is certainly difficult to understand why the presence of associations of oil and wine merchants on Delos would prevent other 'religious' associations to function

[22] Dioscuri: *ID* 1900. Egyptian gods: *ID* 2072-2073; 2079 and 2091. Syrian deities: *ID* 2240.

[23] N. L. ZALESSKIJ, *Les Romains à Délos (De l'histoire du capital commercial et du capital usuraire romain)* in F. COARELLI / D. MUSTI / H. SOLIN (eds.) *Delo e l'Italia*, Rome, Bardi, 1982, p. 21-49; RAUH, *The Sacred Bonds* [n. 2], p. 61. The same trade pattern applies to Italian olive oil, which appears to have been consumed in large quantities, probably by the resident Italians.

[24] Inscriptional data are presented by RAUH, *The Sacred Bonds* [n. 2], p. 54-55. See also p. 56-68 for literary and archaeological evidence.

[25] *CIL* VI, 29722 (Sentius Regulianus); XII, 1898 (Rusonius Myron); XII, 4107 (name not preserved); XIII, 1911 and 11179 (Apronius Raptor); XIII, 1954 (Inthatius Vitalis); XIV, 374 (Licinius Privatus); XIV, 409 (Sentius Felix); XIV, 430 (Valerius Threptus).

as an economic trust network, even though this facet of associational life is not indicated in the group's name.[26]

It is indeed remarkable that not a single association, or any occupational inscription for that matter, hints at the major economic role of the isle, viz. the slave trade, particularly in contrast to the abundance of 'religious' associations.[27] Obviously, this lack of evidence can partly be explained by the general moral disapproval of personal engagement in the slave trade. Very few businessmen wished to be remembered for their direct role in the import of slaves to Italy.[28] Moreover, as according to Roman law humans could not be considered proper merchandise (*merces*), slave dealers should not be called *mercatores*, but *mangones* or *venaliciarii* instead.[29] Both factors make it highly unlikely that we will ever discover inscriptional evidence for the involvement of the Italian community in the slave trade. On the other hand, as epigraphy has indicated the existence of professional associations for Italian merchants specializing in the trade of other goods than slaves (wine and oil), one would also expect associations of slave merchant to be present. Here the Delian 'religious' associations, and the Hermaistai in particular, may have provided a solution.

In conclusion, the Delian associations simply incorporated several different social, economic and religious functions, similar to many of the *collegia* of the Imperial age. This is not a particularly earth-shattering conclusion for those familiar with the associational life of the Imperial age, but given Hasenohr's model of the Delian associations, it needs to be stressed that for the *collegia* on Delos as well as for any other place in the ancient world, religion and economic

[26] Or is it, given the fact that the Hermaistai and Poseidoniastai are named after gods of trade and shipping? For a strong negation of the economic role of the *magistreis*-associations, see C. HASENOHR, *Italiens et Phéniciens à Délos: organisation et relations de deux groupes d'étrangers résidents (2e- 1er siècles av. J.-C.)* in R. COMPATANGELO-SOUSSIGNAN / C.-G. SCHWENTZEL (eds.), *Etrangers dans la cité romaine. Actes du colloque de Valenciennes (octobre 2005)*, Rennes, 2006, p. 77-90, in particular p. 86: "A l'inverse, aucune source ne laisse supposer que les Italici se soient réunis dans un but professionnel. En outre, l'existence d'au moins un collège professionnel italien, et sans doute même de deux ou trois, prouve que là n'était pas leur but."

[27] F. COARELLI, *"Magistri Capitolini" e mercanti di schiavi nella Roma repubblicana* in *Index* 15, 1987, p. 175-190.

[28] See W. V. HARRIS, *Towards a Study of the Roman Slave Trade* in J. H. D'ARMS / E. C. KOPFF (eds.), *The Seaborne Commerce of Ancient Rome. Studies in Archaeology and History*, Roma, 1980, p. 117-140 for the epigraphical records of slave dealers.

[29] *Dig.* XIV, 4, 1, 1; XXXII, 73, 4 and L, 16, 207. See also R. ORTU, *"Qui venaliciariam vitam exercebat": ruolo sociale e qualificazione giuridica dei venditori di schiavi* in *Ius Antiquum - Drevnee Pravo* 9, 2002, p. 87-112. Only a single inscription (CIL VI, 9632) mentions the linguistic blend *mercator venaliciarius* as occupational title. The fact that the slave merchant L. Valerius Zabda most likely originated from Judaea might account for his unfamiliarity with Roman practice.

interests were two sides of the same coin.[30] Especially for ethnic business communities, the multifaceted nature of associational life has been stressed time and again. Even for contemporary ethnic economies, it is now generally accepted that "ritualized occasions and large-scale ceremonies also provide opportunities for acquiring information, and some groups have specialized associations and media which disseminate information. (...) Ethnic institutions, such as churches and voluntary associations, are often supported by ethnic entrepreneurs for business reasons as well as a sense of in-group loyalty."[31]

Next, Hasenohr also takes into account the actual titles of the *magistreis*.[32] Only the Latin inscriptions suggest they held some kind of office (usually *magistreis* followed by the deity's name in the dative case), while the Greek equivalents lack any reference to functions or magistracies (Apolloniastai, Hermaistai and Poseidoniastai). This anomaly had already been noticed by Hatzfeld, who argued that Greek society was not familiar with associations governed by multiple magistrates and could not find a Greek alternative for the word *magister*.[33] Hasenohr questions this very economical solution. She first asserts that the Greeks could perfectly have transliterated the word *magister* and refers to De Ruggiero's Dizionario Epigrafico for some examples, but fails to notice that this practice, to the best of my knowledge, never occurs in the epigraphy of the Greek isles. Second, the fact that the Greek terms seemed to refer to associations instead of *magistreis* would, in her view, have been extremely confusing. Given the fact that most members of the associations, including the freedmen and slaves of Greek origin, belonged to prominent Italian families in a no doubt bilingual commercial port city, the phrasing of the Greek inscriptions can only have caused minor confusion.[34] Finally, she remarks that the *magistreis*-inscriptions never mention the name of the association they would have presided over, unlike other Latin inscriptions of Republican associations. Yet, it should be noted that Republican magistrates did not adopt a strict phrasing to indicate their association. For instance, a bilingual joint dedication to Hercules by the Apolloniastai, Hermaistai and Poseidoniastai mentions the *magistreis* as "magistrates of (the cult of) Mercurius, Apollo and Neptune", with the deity's name in the genitive case, somehow suggesting they were governing an

[30] In the same way FLAMBARD, *Observations* [n. 2]; RAUH, *The Sacred Bonds* [n. 2], p. 28-29.

[31] ALDRICH / WALDINGER, *Ethnicity and Entrepreneurship* [n. 16], p. 128-129.

[32] HASENOHR, *Les collèges de magistri* [n. 3], p. 70-72.

[33] HATZFELD, *Les Italiens* [n. 1], p. 177-178.

[34] For the well-entrenched bilingualism on the isle, see J.N. ADAMS, *Bilingualism at Delos* in J. N. ADAMS / M. JANSE / S. SWAIN, *Bilingualism in Ancient Society: Language Contact and the Written Text*, Oxford, Oxford University Press, 2002, p. 103-127.

association.[35] Another inscription calls the Poseidoniastai the "magistrates of Neptune", this time using an adjective (*Neptunales*).[36] This final phrasing closely resembles the name of another association, the *magistri Mercuriales* (the obvious equivalent of the Hermaistai), for which Coarelli has clearly shown that they, together with the *magistri Capitolini*, were operating as a *collegium mercatorum* deeply involved in the slave trade.[37] In conclusion, the actual phrasing of the bilingual inscriptions cannot be used to deny the associational nature of the *magistreis*. On the contrary, the close parallel with the *Mercuriales* and *Capitolini* again suggests the existence of 3 semi-religious, semi-economic associations.[38]

Finally, Hasenohr tries to add strength to her model by comparing the Italian community with the resident Phoenicians, who installed two associations on Delos, viz. the Herakleistai from Tyre and the Poseidoniastai from Beirut.[39] However, the fact that Italians and Phoenicians frequently interacted through marriage or enlisting on the *ephebia* does not provide sufficient grounds to warrant a comparison of the organizational structure of both resident groups. First, Hasenohr rightly remarks that contrary to the Phoenician associations, the Italians never use a word equivalent to *collegium* or *conventus* to indicate their level of organization—striking difference, which she tries to explain rather unconvincingly by stating that Republican associations in Latin inscriptions sometimes fail to mention their status as a *collegium*. Some indeed do omit this indication, which however does not necessarily imply that the *Italici* on Delos consequently (!) decided to leave out any reference to their level of organization. Obviously, an *argumentum ex silentio* cannot inform us about the nature of organization (if any) among the Italian residents. Second, similar phrasing in honorific inscriptions erected by Phoenicians and Italians has more to say on shared local epigraphic habits than on the organization of both communities. The dedication of a statue to a benefactor by "all Italians" (*Italici*) does not prove beyond doubt that they constituted "une entité durable, une véritable association."[40] Similar dedications to Roman magistrates or local powerful businessmen had been jointly erected by Athenians, Italians and other resident groups, without these jointly planned honours suggesting any level of closer

35 *ID* 1753: *magistreis Mirquri Apollini<s> Neptuni.*

36 *ID* 1751: *magistreis Neptunales.*

37 COARELLI, *Magistri Capitolini* [n. 27].

38 In this light Hasenohr's final conclusion (*Les collèges de magistri* [n. 3], p. 72) in particular seems highly unlikely: "Au moment de traduire leurs dédicaces, ils ont cherché un équivalent en grec et, *comme certains d'entre eux vénéraient Poséidon, ils ont trouvé commode d'emprunter le terme Poseidoniastai qu'ils connaissaient par ailleurs, sans se soucier de la réalité qu'il recouvrait."* (emphasis added).

39 HASENOHR, *Italiens et Phéniciens à Délos* [n. 26].

40 HASENOHR, *Italiens et Phéniciens à Délos* [n. 26], p. 81.

organization.[41] Finally, she fails to notice that the Phoenician associations are organized on the level of the city and gather merchants, shippers and other businessmen with a common background. The Italian community on the other hand consists of businessmen from Rome, Campania and southern Italy.[42]

How can SNA contribute to this debate? I start from two basic assumptions, related to the number and place in the community of the families involved. First, if the Apolloniastai, Hermaistai and Poseidoniastai were honorary functions bestowed upon powerful individuals to represent the Italian community during religious feasts and negotiations with the Athenians, one expects a small number of prominent and wealthy families to have held the functions several times. Even if the *magistreis* were selected on a yearly basis and many individuals thus had the opportunity to hold the office, the Italians would have favoured members of families who could exert their wealth and influence to the benefit of the community. Second, given the previously discussed composition of the Italian community as a network with an extremely dense core, one would expect the majority of the *magistreis* to belong to families well established in this core. In order to test these hypotheses, I listed all families whose members were elected Apolloniastes, Hermaistes or Poseidoniastes, the number of family members who had once hold one of these functions and the degree score of the family as criterion for centrality within the community (Table 5).

Table 5. Degree score and number of family members holding the office of Apolloniastes, Hermaistes or Poseidoniastes

Family (n=66)	Degree	Frequency
Ampius	33	1
Anicius	3	1
Arellius	38	3
Audius	61	3
Aufidius	15	1
Caecilius	45	1
Caltius	4	1
Calvius	8	1
Campius	2	1
Castricius	44	3
Cerrinius	6	2
Claudius	18	2
Clodius	21	2

[41] Cf. *ID* 1698; 1726 and 1727.

[42] A.J.N. WILSON, *Emigration from Italy in the Republican Age of Rome*, Manchester-New York, 1966; F. CASSOLA, *Romani e Italici in Oriente* in *DArch* 4-5, 1970-1971, p. 305-329.

Cornelius	4	1
Cossutius	9	1
Cottius	37	3
Crassicius	20	1
Crepereius	16	2
Fulvius	34	2
Gerillanus	55	1
Gessius	26	1
Granius	65	2
Heius	33	1
Laronius	3	1
Licinius	13	1
Lollius	7	1
Lucretius	20	1
Maecius	67	4
Mamilius	5	1
Marcius	7	1
Nimmius	2	1
Nonius	25	1
Novius	24	1
Nummius	10	1
Obellius	4	2
Oppius	15	2
Orbius	2	3
Paconius	71	2
Pactumeius	17	1
Plaetorius	8	1
Plotius	62	1
Pompilius	11	1
Popillius	14	1
Raecius	10	1
Rutilius	32	1
Satricanius	16	1
Saufeius	18	2
Seius	46	3
Servilius	10	1
Sextilius	48	1
Staius	13	2

Stenius	10	1
Stertinius	44	2
Stlaccius	35	1
Sulpicius	10	2
Tullius	27	1
Tuscenius	5	1
Tutorius	42	4
Umbricius	16	3
Venuleius	4	1
Veratius	15	1
Veturius	11	1
Vicirius	31	1
Viseius	4	1
Visellius	2	1
Volusius	6	1

The table clearly indicates that, first, however scanty and biased the inscriptional evidence may be, there is very little evidence that the *magistreis* were predominantly chosen from a selected number of affluent and prominent families. No less than 66 families, or 35.86% of the total number of 187 Italian families residing on Delos, at one time or another counted a *magister* among their members. It is true that this large recruitment pool may have answered to the need of finding sufficient *magistreis* for each year, but at the same time the frequency table suggests that within this group, no families seem to have really dominated membership of the associations. Only two families (1.06%) managed to hold the office 4 times, 7 families (3.74%) had been elected 3 times and 13 (6.95%) family names occur twice on the membership lists. Second, when plotting the degree scores for the *magistreis* against the distribution for the community at large as discussed above, the very core of well-connected business families again does not appear to have totally monopolized the function of *magister* (Table 6).[43]

Table 6. The Apolloniastai, Hermaistai and Poseidoniastai within the community network

Frequency of office-holding	Degree	Place in the community network
4	67	core
	42	core
3	38	core

[43] Consistent with the analysis above, I consider the core to have a degree score of 32-71; the centre 10-31 and the periphery 0-9.

	61	core
	44	core
	37	core
	2	periphery
	46	core
	16	centre
2	6	periphery
	18	centre
	21	centre
	16	centre
	34	core
	65	core
	4	periphery
	15	centre
	71	core
	18	centre
	13	centre
	44	core
	10	centre

Two major tendencies can be drawn from this table. First, the frequency of office-holding is obviously related to the families' place in the community network. Families located in the periphery control fewer resources and relationships relevant for election and will find it more difficult to attain the office multiple times. Nevertheless, some of them clearly did, suggesting that the function of *magister* was not only available for the rich and famous. People from the network centre frequently manage to be elected twice, but struggle to hold the office a 3rd or even a 4th time. This honour is evidently reserved for the network core, the families controlling the largest amount of money and number of agents and maintaining the highest level of connectivity. A predictable outcome, for the most wealthy and prominent families are always the best placed candidates to govern associations of any kind. This conclusion hence certainly does not corroborate the *conventus*-hypothesis: irrespective of the nature of the association, families with the highest status in society will always be elected for offices far more often than families on the periphery. The most important conclusion must be that the function of *magister* was open to a high percentage of the resident Italian families, even if the families with the best connections had a better chance to be elected multiple times. Second, the table also indicates that belonging to the core of the Italian community was no guarantee of becoming a *magister* several times. When comparing the top 5% of the Italian families with the highest degree scores and the families on the lists of *magistreis*, it again appears that the families in the network core did not monopolize office holding (Table 7). They obviously are all present among the families who held the function, but not to the extent that one would have expected them to dominate the lists.

Table 7. Families with highest degree scores and their office-holding

Family	Degree	Frequency of office-holding
Caecilius	45	1
Seius	46	3
Sextilius	48	1
Gerillanus	55	1
Audius	61	3
Plotius	62	1
Granius	65	2
Maecius	67	4
Paconius	71	2

These conclusions again deal a blow to the *conventus*-hypothesis. With the basic assumptions in Hasenohr's model being refuted and SNA suggesting a more open nature of the functions of Apolloniastes, Hermaistes and Poseidoniastes instead of a rather closed office monopolized by the leading families of the community, there is no need to see the *magistreis* as representatives of a general Italian assembly. The parallels with the associations in Capua are therefore somewhat misleading. It is certainly true that the structural features of the inscriptions dedicated by the Delian associations and those in Capua show certain resemblances, but this does not imply that both types of associations had a similar raison d'être. Those in Capua had been established to provide an alternative to the municipal political institutions, forbidden by Rome since 211 BC in the aftermath of the Punic War.[44] The Delian associations on the other hand are more similar to the traditional Roman associations, being partly religious, partly economic, and partly social in nature. They created a framework to facilitate economic cooperation and the celebration of cults.

[44] C. HASENOHR / C. MÜLLER, *Gentilices et circulation des Italiens: quelques réflexions méthodologiques* in C. MÜLLER / C. HASENOHR (eds.), *Les Italiens dans le monde grec, IIe siècle av. J.-C. - Ier siècle ap. J.-C.*, Paris, 2002, p. 11-20 (in particular p. 14).

5.3 The Distinctiveness of the Competaliastai?

In the previous sections, one association has been left out, viz. that of the Competaliastai. It has been argued that a clear distinction needs to be made between the Apolloniastai, Hermaistai and Poseidoniastai on the one hand and the Competaliastai on the other.[45] The first 3 associations were open to freedmen and freeborn and organized in a similar way, viz. with a fixed number of *magistreis* holding office. The Competaliastai however were predominantly recruited among slaves and, to a lesser extent, freedmen. Freeborn Italians appear not to have joined this association. As members hence predominantly originated from the Greek East, the inscriptions of the Competaliastai are only directed in Greek. Other associations frequently erect bilingual inscriptions. Next, they honor different deities than the Apolloniastai, Hermaistai and Poseidoniastai, including the Lares, Hercules, Zeus Eleutherius, Dionysus, Fides and Dea Roma. While the deities revered by the former groups can be linked to a potential economic nature of the associations, this connection is far less straightforward for the Lares, suggesting the Competaliastai were in the first place a religious association.[46] Finally, the number of their magistrates appears to have varied, again in contrast to the other 3 associations.[47]

Yet, as rightly pointed out by Flambard, the organizational dissimilarities do not imply that the nature of the association of Competaliastai was completely different from the other three.[48] It is far more important to highlight the similarities between all 4 associations. All of them forge a name composed of a deity and the suffix -σται. They share a distinctive style of phrasing in the inscriptions. Magistrates are recruited for a single year. The nature of dedications to honor the gods is very similar. There is thus no compelling reason to claim that the Competaliastai were a completely different association, only focused on the celebration of the *Compitalia*. Moreover, it is important to note that despite their Greek origin and language, the Competaliastai had been integrated into Italian business families (the intrafamily network) and defend a cult that is beyond doubt Italian.[49] So even though the members may not have originated from the Italian peninsula, on Delos they contributed in strengthening the Italian identity in a way similar to the other 3 associations. Nevertheless, while Flambard's hypothesis was grounded on formal and structural resemblances in the organizations' names, phrasing of inscriptions and dedicatory practice, SNA can add another shared

[45] HASENOHR, *Les collèges de magistri* [n. 3], p. 69; ID, *Italiens et Phéniciens à Délos* [n. 26], p. 88.

[46] HASENOHR, *Les collèges de magistri* [n. 3], p. 67: "pour vénérer leurs dieux".

[47] HATZFELD, *Les Italiens* [n. 1], p. 154-159; FLAMBARD, *Observations* [n. 2], p. 68-69.

[48] FLAMBARD, *Observations* [n. 2], p. 70.

[49] For the *Compitalia*, see C. HASENOHR, *Les Compitalia à Délos* in *BCH* 127, 2003, p. 167-249 with further references.

characteristic of all 4 associations. Through the lens of connectedness in a network (the Italian community), the embeddedness of the Competaliastai in that community via the intrafamily and interfamily networks exactly matches the level of connectivity of the other associations (Table 3). When comparing the degree scores of the sub-networks, their structure and visual representations as analysed in the Appendix, one can easily conclude that, apart from a few inscriptions too fragmentary to present a complete sub-network, virtually all *magistreis*-inscriptions result in very similar network structures. If the associations had addressed a different audience on Delos or had been established with divergent purposes in mind, no doubt this would have resulted in higher variations in average degree scores, the structure of individual degree scores on family level and the connectivity of the sub-networks. Moreover, their cores, centres and peripheries on the level of interfamily networks coincide with the ones reconstructed for the Italian community as a whole. This suggests that all associations were firmly rooted within the local society in very similar ways. In other words, the social and economic functions of networks, viz. identity building and the creation of a tool to facilitate cooperation and circulation of information, were organized along the same lines. Moreover, the suggestion that this association only engaged in organizing religious feasts without at the same time being involved in supporting an economic network, can easily be refuted. The role of the Competaliastai as economic network is clearly indicated at by the shops lining the Agora of the Competaliastai and three dedicatory inscriptions located on the square and made by commercial groups, viz. the resident bankers, Italian steersmen and wine merchants.[50] Similar to the previous analysis, the conclusion must hence be that neither the inscriptional evidence nor a SNA approach can confirm the single-faceted nature of the association nor the *conventus*-hypothesis. Even Hasenohr herself admits that the claim that the Competaliastai were appointed by the Italian community cannot actually be substantiated: “Il me semble cependant plus probable que les Compétaliastes en étaient officiellement chargés. À cette hypothèse, je ne puis guère apporter de preuves, sinon que ces personnages, dont le nom se trouve n’être attesté qu’en grec, portaient probablement le même titre latin que les Hermaïstes, Apolloniastes et Poséidoniastes : s’ils étaient bien des magistri, ils ressemblent fort à ceux qui présidaient aux ludi compitalicii de Rome.”[51]

The analysis of the frequency of office-holding by Italian families seems to confirm the similarities between all associations (Table 8).

[50] *ID* 1715; 2401 and 1711 respectively. For the Agora of the Competaliastai, see RAUH, *The Sacred Bonds* [n. 2], p. 92-93.

[51] HASENOHR, *Les Compitalia* [n. 49], p. 215.

Table 8. Degree score and number of family members holding the office of Competaliastes

Family (n=40)	Degree	Frequency
Alleius	4	1
Allidius	7	1
Atanius	9	1
Audius	61	3
Aufidius	15	1
Babullius	41	2
Caecilius	45	1
Castricius	44	2
Cispius	5	1
Clodius	21	2
Cluvius	9	1
Corvius	7	1
Crepereius	16	1
Egnatius	29	2
Erucius	17	1
Furius	37	1
Gerillanus	55	1
Graeceius	9	1
Granius	65	6
Laelius	4	1
Lucceius	5	1
Maecius	67	1
Mundicius	38	3
Naevius	23	1
Novius	24	2
Ofellius	23	1
Orarius	7	1
Paconius	71	5
Plotius	62	1
Pomponius	11	2
Raecius	10	1
Rasennius	4	1
Samiarius	17	1
Seius	46	2
Sextilius	48	1

Spedius	5	1
Tullius	27	1
Turpilius	5	1
Veveius	5	1
Vibius	44	1

The fact that 40 Italian families or 21.39% managed to join the Competaliastai again suggests that, similar to the other associations, this group did not only enlist members of the most important families. However, when listing the families who held the office multiple times and making the comparison with the best connected families, an important difference can be noticed (Table 9 and Table 10).

Table 9. The Competaliastai within the community network

Frequency of office-holding	Degree	Place in the community network
6	65	core
5	71	core
3	61	core
	38	core
2	41	core
	44	core
	21	centre
	29	centre
	24	centre
	11	centre
	46	core

Table 10. Families with the highest degree score and their office-holding

Family	Degree	Frequency of office-holding
Caecilius	45	1
Seius	46	2
Sextilius	48	1
Gerillanus	55	1
Audius	61	3
Plotius	62	1
Granius	65	6
Maecius	67	1
Paconius	71	5

Most families who were elected to join the Competaliastai clearly belong to the core of the Italian community. Families located in the centre clearly had difficulties in joining the association several times and those in the periphery only succeed a single time at best. Why the families from the network core are far more prominent among the Competaliastai than among the other 3 associations is not exactly clear. However, a possible explanation can perhaps be found in the interconnectedness of all Delian associations. Members of the most powerful families such as the Granii, Maecii and Paconii joined several associations, be it the Competaliastai for the slaves or the Apolloniastai, Hermaistai and/or Poseidoniastai for the free individuals. For instance, the Apolloniastes D. Fulvius had a son joining the Hermaistai.[52] Even single persons appear to have been members of different associations. Assuming the nomenclature refers to the same individual, L. Mamilius L.f. features on dedications by Hermaistai and Apolloniastai.[53] If these families provided support (through status or monetary donations) to their slaves to join the Competaliastai, one can perhaps understand their dominant position in the association. By encouraging their slaves to join the Competaliastai, these families established and confirmed their leading place in the community and tried to exert control and increase family status on different levels. Moreover, meritorious slave agents could be supported to rise in the associations of Competaliastai, hence receiving some kind of reward and status confirmation unavailable to them via other institutions. One may even assume that several of the freeborn *magistreis* of the Apolloniastai, Hermaistai and Poseidoniastai were in fact the patrons of the slaves joining and presiding the association of Competaliastai, thereby cornering associational life on two different levels. The organization of the Compitalia in Pompeii seems to corroborate this hypothesis, as many shrines for the Lares appear to have been construed in close vicinity of the houses of the most important families of the city district.[54] Apparently, those families tried to promote their slaves to the function of *magister compiti* in order to centre the cult around their houses: they were, very literally, the centre of local power. Additional evidence for this multi-level status model is provided by the case of A. Cerrinius L.l., who held functions among the Competaliastai and the Hermaistai.[55] One can imagine that he first joined the Competaliastai and was later 'promoted' to the Hermaistai.

[52] *ID* 1730 and 1733. See HASENOHR, *Les collèges de magistri* [n. 3], p. 70 for more examples.

[53] *BCH* 87 (1963), 252-253 and *ID* 1730.

[54] W. VAN ANDRINGA, *Autels de carrefour, organisation vicinale et rapports de voisinage à Pompéi* in *RSP* 11, 2000, , p. 47-86; HASENOHR, *Les Compitalia* [n. 49].

[55] *ID* 1734, 1738 and 1739.

6 Concluding Remarks

To sum up, it appears that the Competaliastai on the one hand and the Apolloniastai, Hermaistai and Poseidoniastai on the other only differ for certain in the social status of the groups from which members were recruited (mainly slaves versus freeborn and freedmen). In fact, the association of Competaliastai may have provided the most important families with the opportunity to reward their slave agents and advance their status in society. At the same time all associations were very similar in their role as facilitator in identity construction of the Italian community on Delos as well as in stimulating interaction and creating a trust network for resident businessmen. They all erected shrines close to commercial zones where merchants looking for recourse in commercial conflicts could swear oaths with the honoured deities as prime witnesses.[56] These conclusions bring the Delian associations again closer to the traditional model of Roman *collegia* and at the same time make the hypothesis of an Italian *conventus* represented by *magistreis* again more unlikely.

[56] RAUH, *The Sacred Bonds* [n. 2], p. 129-150. For similar practices in Puteoli, see W. BROEKAERT, *Lucius Lawless. Conflicts, Contract Enforcement and Business Communities in the Archive of the Sulpicii*, forthcoming.

Appendix. Italian Merchant Families on Stoppers and in Greek Epigraphy[57]

1. Afarius[58]:
    a. Western Provinces:
        1. C. Afarius [---] (1st c. BC; H&G B2; Saint-Remy-de-Provence)
    b. Eastern Provinces:
        1. Q. Afarius Matro (Late 1st c. BC–early empire?; *CIL* III, 7094; Pergamum)
2. Alfius:
    a. Western Provinces:
        1. M. Alfius M.f. Vnguentarius (50 BC; H&G B3; Marseille)
    b. Eastern Provinces:
        1. Alfius (1st c. BC; *IGBulg* I² 326; Mesambria)
        2. L. Alfius L.f. (Late 1st c. BC?; *IG* VII, 3123; Lebadeia, Boeotia)
        3. M. Alfius Melilotus (ca. 31 BC; *Ephesos* 241; Ephesus)

[57] Common and wide-spread names such as Claudius, Clodius and Licinius have been excluded, for their distribution has little explanatory power. Abbreviations in the table of amphora stoppers refer to A. HESNARD / P. A. GIANFROTTA, *Les bouchons d'amphore en pouzzolane* in *Amphores romaines et histoire économique - dix ans de recherche : actes du colloque de Sienne (22-24 mai 1986),* Rome, 1989, p. 393-441; P. A. GIANFROTTA, *Note di epigrafia 'marittima'. Aggiornamenti su tappi d'anfora, ceppi d'ancora e altro* in *Epigrafia della produzione e della distribuzione. Actes de la VIe Rencontre franco-italienne sur l'épigraphie du monde romain*, Roma, 1994, p. 591-608; P. A. GIANFROTTA, *Nuovi rinvenimenti subacquei per lo studio di alcuni aspetti del commercio marittimo del vino (I sec.a.C.-I sec.d.C.)* in *El vi a l'Antiguedat, economia, produccio i comerc al Mediterrani occidental, 2e colloqui internacional d'arqueologia romana*, Badalona, 1998, p. 105-112; P. A. GIANFROTTA, *Il commercio marittimo in età tardo-republicana: merci, mercanti, infrastrutture* in J.P. BALLESTER / G. PASCUAL (eds.), *Actas V Jornadas internacionales de arqueologia subacuática (Gandia, 8 a 10 de noviembre de 2006)*, Valencia, 2008, p. 65-78.

[58] The rare name Afarius almost exclusively occurs in the epigraphy of Italy (*CIL* V, 644 [Trieste]; VI, 11194 [Rome]; X, 146 [Potenza]; X, 504 [Regio III, place of discovery unknown]). In the eastern provinces, the name is mentioned only once (*CIL* III, 7094), in a bilingual inscription, found in Zeytindağ, a city on the Turkish coast where in antiquity the harbour of Pergamum may have been located. A certain Q. Afarius Matro, most probably an Italian *negotiator*, there dedicated a funerary inscription to the memory of his late daughter.

3. Arellius:
   a. Western Provinces:
      1. P. Ar[ell]ius L[uci?---] (1st c. BC; H&G B5; La Ciotat)
   b. Eastern Provinces:
      1. N. Arelius M' (f.) (1st c. AD; *IG* II^2, 10145; Attica)
      2. Arellia (1st c. BC–1st c. AD; *IG* II^2, 10736; Attica)
      3. M. Arellius Q.f. (1st c. BC; *IG* VII, 4186; Anthedon, Boeotia)
      4. Q. Arellius M.l. Xenon (1st c. BC; *IG* VII, 4187; Anthedon, Boeotia)
      5. L. Arellius L. et A. l. (125 BC; *ID* 1733; Delos)
      6. P. Arellius Q. (123 BC; *ID* 1753; Delos)
      7. M. Arelius Q. (ca. 100 BC; *ID* 1755; Delos)
      8. P. Arellius Q. (ca. 100 BC; *ID* 1804; Delos)
      9. L. Arellius (125-75 BC; *ID* 2616; Delos)
      10. P. Arellius Q[---] (3rd c. BC; *SEG* XXVI, 919; Lesbos)
      11. M. Arellius (*IG* XII,3, 1643; Thera)
      12. P. Arellius Sp.f. (*IG* XII,5, 39; Naxos)
      13. Q. Arelius Antiochus (*Ephesos* 2005; Ephesus)
      14. App. Arellius Diadochus (*Ephesos* 2173; Ephesus)
4. Cerrinius:
   a. Western Provinces:
      1. T. Cerrinius P.l. (1st c. BC; Gianfrotta 1994, 593; Sentino)
   b. Eastern Provinces:
      1. A. Cerrinius L.f. (125 BC; *ID* 1734, 1738 and 1739; Delos)
5. Furius:
   a. Western Provinces:
      1. M. Furius Vin( ) (60-35 BC; H&G B13; Elba)
   b. Eastern Provinces:
      1. Furius Heliodorus, L. (ca. 100 BC; *ID* 1769; Delos)
      2. Furius Soterichus (125-75 BC; *ID* 2616; Delos)
      3. Furi[---] (108-107 BC; *ID* 2628; Delos)
      4. P. Furius P. (100-75 BC; *ASAtene* 22 (1939/40) 168,21; Rhodos)

6. Gerillanus (?):
    a. Western Provinces:
        1. Q. Ger( )/Gih( ) L( ) (120-100 BC; H&G B14; Spargi)
    b. Eastern Provinces:
        1. A. Gerillanus Mar.f. (*ID* 1687; Delos)
        2. Mar. Gerillanus, Mar.f. (100-75 BC; *ID* 1725-1727; Delos)
        3. Mar. Gerillanus, St.f. (ca. 125 BC; *ID* 1751; Delos)
        4. Alexion Gerillanus, Mar. (93 BC; *ID* 1764; Delos)
        5. Zenon Gerillani Mar. (Couilloud 456; Delos)
        6. C. Gerillanus L. (Herzog, *KFF* 44; Cos)
7. Lucc(e)ius:
    a. Western Provinces:
        1. L. Luccius L.l. (150-50 BC; H&G B17; Carthago)
        2. T. Luccius L.l. (150-50 BC; H&G B17; Carthago)
        3. M. Luccius M.f. (120-110 BC; H&G B18; Var)
    b. Eastern Provinces:
        1. Nicephorus, L. Lucceii s. (94 BC; *ID* 1763.11; Delos[59])
8. Maecius:
    a. Western Provinces:
        1. P. Maecius L.l. (1st c. BC; H&G B21; Marseille)
    b. Eastern Provinces:
        1. L. Maecius Q.l. (*ID* 1686; Delos)
        2. N. Maecius L.l. (*ID* 1687; Delos)
        3. L. Maecius L. (ca. 125 BC; *ID* 1730; Delos)
        4. Maecius ZenodorusQ.f. (*ID* 1738-1739; Delos)
        5. D. Maecius L.l. (113 BC; *ID* 1753; Delos)
        6. Ti. Maecius L.l. (125-100 BC; *ID* 1754; Delos)
        7. Damonicus Q. Maecii s. (100-98 BC; *ID* 1760; Delos)
        8. L. Maecius Q. (*ID* 2401; Delos)
        9. M. Maecius (100-75 BC; *ID* 2619; Delos)
        10. Maecius (100-75 BC; *ID* 2622; Delos)
        11. Maecius Cerdon (108-107 BC; *ID* 2628; Delos)

[59] Cicero also mentions a Q. Lucceius who was active as *argentarius* in Rhegium when Verres was governor in Sicily (*2 Verr.* 5, 165).

12. Q. Maecius Q.l. (130-125 BC; *SEG* XXIII, 514; Delos)
13. L. Maecius Tychius (1st c. BC; Bosnakis, *Epigraphes* 61,II; Cos)
14. Maecius (2nd c. BC-1st c. AD; *SEG* XXXVIII, 1248; Myrina, Aeolis)

9. M(a)evius:
   a. Western Provinces:
      1. P. Maevius C.f. (1st c. BC; Gianfrotta, 1998, 106; Macchiatonda)
   b. Eastern Provinces:
      1. M'. Mevius M. (125-100 BC; *IG* XII,9, 1189; Histiaia, Euboea)
      2. C. Mevius P. (125-75 BC; *ID* 2616; Delos)
      3. L. Mevius (100-75 BC; *ID* 2619; Delos)
10. Orceius:
   a. Western Provinces:
      1. C. Orceius M. [---] (150-50 BC; H&G B25; Ampurias)
   b. Eastern Provinces:
      1. L. Orceius (*ID* 2638; Delos)
11. Pomponius:
   a. Western Provinces:
      1. Cn. Pomponius (1st c. BC; H&G B27; Sainte-Marie-de-la-Mer)
      2. Q. Pomponius (1st c. BC; H&G B27; Sainte-Marie-de-la-Mer)
      3. L. Pomponius M.l. (1st c. BC; H&G B28; Sainte-Marie-de-la-Mer)
   b. Eastern Provinces:
      1. Pomponius Archelaus C. et Cn. l. (98-97 BC; *ID* 1761; Delos)
      2. M. Pomponius M.l. Hieron (ca. 100 BC; *ID* 1766; Delos)
      3. P. Pomponius C. (ca. 112-111 BC; *ID* 2248; Delos)
      4. Pomponia Hilara (1st c. BC; *Iscr. di Cos (Fun.) EF* 403; Cos)

12. Raecius:
    a. Western Provinces:
        1. C. Raecius [---] (Gianfrotta, 2008, 66; Cartagena)
    b. Eastern Provinces:
        1. A. Raecius N.l. Alexander (*ID* 1692; Delos)
        2. N. Raecius M. f. (ca. 100 BC; *ID* 1756; Delos)
        3. Raecius A.l. Damas (ca. 100 BC; *ID* 1769; Delos)
        4. Raecius N.l. Timocrates (125-75 BC; Couilloud 357; Delos)
        5. A. Raecius N.l. Apollonius (125-100 BC; Couilloud 423; Delos)
13. Rubrius:
    a. Western Provinces:
        1. T. Rubrius C.f. (1st c. BC; H&G B29; Ampurias)
    b. Eastern Provinces:
        1. C. Rubrius C.f. (129 BC?; *IMT AdramKolpos* 717; Adramyttenos Kolpos)
14. Saufeius:
    a. Western Provinces:
        1. A. Saufeius (125-75 BC; Gianfrotta, 1994, 594; Isola di Ponza)
        2. P. Saufeius (ca. 100 BC; *CIL* XV, 4922; Praeneste)
    b. Eastern Provinces:
        1. Q. Saufeius P.f. (125-100 BC; *ID* 1754; Delos)
        2. C. Saufeius A.l. Zenodorus (ca. 100 BC; *ID* 1755; Delos)
        3. Callicles A. Saufeii s. (ca. 100 BC; *CIL* I, 3438; Delos)
15. Sornatius:
    a. Western Provinces:
        1. C. Sornatius C.f. (ca. 50 BC?; H&G B33; Giulia Nova)
    b. Eastern Provinces:
        1. C. Sornatius C.f. (ca. 70 BC; *MAMA* VI, 260; Akmonia)
        2. C. Sornatius Epaphras (*Ephesos* 2614; Ephesus)
16. Verginius:
    a. Western Provinces:
        1. Q. Verg( ) L.l. Scae( ) (110-90 BC; H&G B37; Ibiza)

- b. Eastern Provinces:
    1. Theudes Vergini[i/ae s.] (94-93 BC; *ID* 2621; Delos)

17. Vibius:
    - a. Western Provinces:
        1. C. Vibius (125-100 BC; H&G B38; Elba)
    - b. Eastern Provinces:
        1. C. Vibius M.f. (*ID* 1687; Delos)
        2. Alexander P. Vibii s. (ca. 100 BC; *ID* 1766; Delos)

Dennis KEHOE

Poverty, Distribution of Wealth, and Economic Growth in the Roman Empire

My contribution concerns the role that legal and social institutions might play in the performance of the Roman economy, particularly in shaping the distribution of wealth across society in an economy in which the welfare of the vast majority of people was subject to constraints imposed by population. Certainly the capacity for institutions to affect the economy was subject to basic constraints, especially population and technology, as emphasized in the *Cambridge Economic History of the Greco-Roman World* (2007). In the recent debate among ancient economic historians, the major focal point, not to mention the topic of this book, is whether ancient economies, and the Roman economy in particular, were capable of achieving economic growth beyond what can be accounted for by population alone.

To be sure, it is unlikely that, in the Roman Empire, as in any ancient society, workers ever escaped Malthusian constraints and saw their wages increase at the same time that population grew.[1] Rather, even as production of a greater surplus from the countryside made it possible to support the growing urban population, without a substantial increase in the productivity of labor, intensification of agriculture would have come at the expense of per capita income, as farmers competed for dwindling resources of land.[2] At the same time, it seems wrong, as

[1] See W. SCHEIDEL, *Human Development and Quality of Life in the Long Run: the Case of Greece (Version 1.0)*, Stanford-Princeton Working Papers in Classics, 2010 (= http://www.princeton.edu/~pswpc/pdfs/scheidel/091006.pdf; building on R. C. ALLEN, *How Prosperous Were the Romans?: Evidence from Diocletian's Price Edict (AD 301)* in A. BOWMAN / A. WILSON (eds.), *Quantifying the Roman Economy: Methods and Problems*. Oxford, 2009, p. 327-345. See however the contributions above by Erdkamp and Grantham for a critical view on Malthusian constraints.

[2] See W. SCHEIDEL / I. MORRIS / R. SALLER (eds.), *The Cambridge Economic History of the Greco-Roman World*, Cambridge, 2007.

Gregory Clark has done in his book *Farewell to Alms: A Brief Economic History of the World* (Princeton, 2007), to argue that Malthusian constraints overwhelmed any other factors affecting economic performance, making the welfare of workers in pre-industrial economies almost entirely a product of population. In Clark's view, institutions in pre-industrial economies played no significant role in affecting economic performance, and the explanations for major economic changes, notably the industrial revolution, lie in other causes. Such a reductionist perspective, however, essentially makes meaningless the study of different economic arrangements in the pre-modern world. In this paper, I focus on the legal and social institutions in the Roman Empire affecting the welfare of the large class of small farmers and urban workers who comprised the majority of the Roman population. The question for understanding the performance of the Roman economy is whether this group disposed of more than enough wealth to create broad-based demand, or whether consumer products and services, beyond what people needed for subsistence, were largely if not exclusively produced for a minority of relatively wealthy people. Certainly the performance of the Roman economy has to be measured in terms other than simply its per capita GDP, which is likely to have grown only slightly even under the most optimistic assessments. At issue is the quality of life of people across the Roman Empire, whether Roman rule brought material benefits exclusively to a well-connected elite, or whether the wealth that generated the impressive development of cities across the empire was shared more broadly. These benefits would include access to land sufficient to support a family for the rural population, and security from chronic food crises for urban residents.

To consider the economic implications of urbanism, although there is no certainty about the populations of cities in the Roman Empire, the conclusions of Andrew Wilson and other scholars, including those in the Oxford Roman Economy Project, indicate that the Roman Empire achieved a level of urbanization comparable to that of the most urbanized areas of early-modern Europe. Urbanism involved significant economic transformation, and possibly economic growth.[3] Certainly the prosperity of cities across the Roman Empire depended on a transfer of wealth from the countryside, in the form of agricultural income, in accordance with the 'consumer city' model that Paul Erdkamp has

[3] See A. I. Wilson, *Indicators for Roman Economic Growth: a Response to Walter Scheidel* in *JRA* 22, 2009, p. 71-82 and A. I. Wilson, *City Sizes and Urbanization in the Roman Empire* in A. Bowman / A. Wilson (eds.), *Settlement, Urbanization, and Population*, Oxford, 2011, p. 161-195, as well as E. Lo Cascio, *Urbanisation as a Proxy for Economic Growth* in A. Bowman / A. Wilson (eds.), *Quantifying the Roman Economy: Methods and Problems*, Oxford, 2009, p. 87-106; for a more sceptical view on the relationship between urbanism and economic growth, see N. Morley, *Cities and Economic Development in the Roman Empire* in A. Bowman / A. Wilson (eds.), *Settlement, Urbanization, and Population*, Oxford, 2011, p. 143-160.

described persuasively.[4] This transfer of wealth created critical masses of demand concentrated in central locations that made it possible for urban economies to grow and diversify. But the growth of cities in the Roman Empire raises the question of how the process of urbanization affected the welfare of broad sections of the Roman population, whether the profits from the Roman economy were captured largely by a small and increasingly wealthy elite, or whether, rather, the economic processes that led to urbanization also created a more broadly shared prosperity. The possibilities for growth in the Roman economy would be constrained if the economic benefits of Roman rule were captured by a small elite, whereas broad-based demand for goods and services across society seems essential if the Roman Empire achieved any degree of economic growth beyond what can be accounted for by population alone.

It is generally agreed that the distribution of wealth in the Roman Empire was highly stratified, but it makes a great deal of difference for the performance of the economy to what extent this was the case. We can appreciate what was at stake by considering the recent effort of Walter Scheidel and Steven Friesen to estimate the size of the Roman economy and the distribution of wealth within it. In their view, the Roman Empire's GDP was on the order of 20 billion sesterces per year, plus or minus twenty percent, in terms of its per capita income more or less at the ceiling of what pre-industrial societies could achieve.[5] In their assessments of income stratification, Scheidel and Friesen differ from the most pessimistic (i.e., high income stratification) and optimistic (i.e., a more egalitarian distribution of wealth) assessments. In their view an elite, consisting of the senatorial and equestrian orders and members of town councils throughout the empire, represented about 1.5% of the population but accounted for about one-fifth of the empire's income (the range in estimates is between 17% and 26%). A middling group, representing another ten percent of the population, controlled another twenty percent of the income (estimates between 16% and 27%), whereas the vast majority of people, about eighty percent of the empire's population, accounted for a bit more than half of its income (56-58%). The substantial gulf between the

[4] P. ERDKAMP, *Beyond the Limits of the "Consumer City": A Model of the Urban and Rural Economy in the Roman World* in *Historia* 50, 2001, p. 332-356.

[5] W. SCHEIDEL / S. J. FRIESEN, *The Size of the Economy and the Distribution of Income in the Roman Empire* in *JRS* 99, 2009, p. 61-91. See here for a discussion of other efforts to estimate the Roman GDP, including K. HOPKINS, *Rome, Taxes, Rents and Trade* in W. SCHEIDEL / S. VON REDEN (eds.), *The Ancient Economy*, New York, 2002, p. 190-230, first published in *Kodai* 6/7, 1995/1996, p. 41-75; R. W. GOLDSMITH, *An Estimate of the Size and Structure of the National Product of the Early Roman Empire* in *Review of Income and Wealth* 30, 1984, p. 263-288, P. TEMIN, *Estimating the GDP in the Early Roman Empire* in E. LO CASCIO (ed.), *Innovazione tecnica e progresso economico nel mondo romano*, Bari, 2006, p. 31-54 and A. MADDISON, *Contours of the World Economy, 1-2030 AD: Essays in Macro-Economic History*, Oxford / New York, 2007, p. 11-68.

wealthiest and the rest of the population does not mean, however, that membership in these three broad categories was fixed. Certainly demographic factors influenced the distribution of wealth. Thus Rens Tacoma, in his study of the urban elite class of the Egyptian city of Hermopolis, points out that many upper-class families would not produce surviving sons, so that the local town council would consist of an ever changing mix of families.[6] Tacoma's findings are consistent with Keith Hopkins' study of the ability of the Roman Republican aristocracy to reproduce itself.[7] In broader terms, Gregory Clark argues that in many pre-industrial societies, or at the very least in early-modern England, wealthier families tended to produce more surviving children.[8] The reasons for this would seem to be that wealthier men could marry early and that they would be more likely to be able to remarry after divorce or the death of a wife. In Clark's view, this situation would mean that there would be considerable downward mobility among the wealthier classes. Property was divided among multiple heirs. However, medieval and early modern England also experienced considerable upward mobility, as wealthy merchants and others could "buy land and enter the aristocracy."[9]

But our concern here is not primarily with social mobility, but rather with the immense share of the wealth controlled by Scheidel and Friesen's broad third class. It makes a great deal of difference whether this group cumulatively accounted for sufficient wealth to generate considerable demand for consumer products. If the alternative is true, that this group lived on the economic margins of society, then it is likely that whatever economic growth the Roman Empire experienced would have simply exacerbated the distance between the very wealthy and the rest of the population. But as I will argue, the Roman imperial government pursued policies that had consequences for the distribution of income and so to some extent militated against any growing power on the part of the very wealthy. This is not to say that the Roman government pursued any direct policy of poor relief — such policies, as Caroline Humfress and others argue, were more a product of late antiquity and were aimed at mitigating the worst effects of poverty rather than altering economic conditions to the benefit of the poor.[10] Rather, the policies with which I am concerned had two broad effects: 1) to promote the welfare of small farmers in the empire by maintaining the security of

[6] L. E. TACOMA, *Fragile Hierarchies: The Urban Elites of Third-Century Roman Egypt*, Leiden / Boston, 2006.

[7] K. HOPKINS, *Death and Renewal*, Cambridge, 1983.

[8] G. CLARK, *A Farewell to Alms: A Brief Economic History of the World*, Princeton, 2007, p. 112-132. For the demographic pressures on the Roman aristocracy, see also W. SCHEIDEL, *Emperors, Aristocrats, and the Grim Reaper: Towards a Demographic Profile of the Roman Elite* in *CQ* 49, 1999, p. 254-281.

[9] CLARK, *Farewell* [n. 8], p. 162.

[10] C. HUMFRESS, *Poverty and Roman Law* in M. ATKINS / R. OSBORNE (eds.), *Poverty in the Roman World*, Cambridge, 2006, p. 183-203.

their tenure over the land they cultivated and protecting them from threats to their continued ability to cultivate the land; and 2) to increase the spending power of the empire's urban residents, a policy that would have significant consequences for economic conditions in the empire's cities. It was vitally important for the fiscal interests of the Roman imperial government and for the health of the Roman economy to maintain the economic viability of a broad class of people and to maintain broad-based consumer demand, rather than allowing all the wealth generated as a result of population growth to accumulate in the hands of an elite. From another perspective, one possibility is that the third class of people in the Roman Empire enjoyed a standard of living that Dominic Rathbone sees as widespread in the villages of Roman Egypt under the Principate.[11] In Rathbone's view most people in the villages of Egypt had enough work to be able to afford food, clothing, and shelter. On the other side of the coin, William Harris offers a much more dismal assessment of the prevalence of genuine poverty in the Roman Empire.[12] Perhaps the most compelling evidence is the apparently widespread practice of exposure and infanticide, which can reasonably be interpreted as proxy evidence for poverty.[13]

In pre-modern standards, the Roman Empire achieved a remarkable degree of urbanization. The urban population of the empire is quite difficult to estimate, but recently Andrew Wilson's effort to provide reasoned estimates of the populations of individual cities and of the urban population as a whole offers an important perspective.[14] In Wilson's assessment, the empire had a small number of giant cities with populations in the hundreds of thousands, including of course Rome with about one million inhabitants, Alexandria with about 500,000, Carthage with 300,000, and Antioch with about 250,000. In addition, there were a number of regional centres with populations between about 30,000 or 40,000 and 100,000 or so, and numerous smaller cities, defined as ones with populations of at least 5,000. In Wilson's calculation, there were 356 cities with populations of at least 5,000, with a total urban population of over 7 million. In the most conservative estimate of the empire's population at its height in the second century CE, before the onset of the Antonine plague, at 55 million, the urbanization rate would have been 13.4%; if the empire's population was 60 million, the urbanization rate would have been 12.3%, and 9.8% if the population was 75 million.[15] Some areas

[11] D. Rathbone, *Poverty and Population in Roman Egypt* in M. Atkins / R. Osborne (eds.), *Poverty in the Roman World*, Cambridge, 2006, p. 100-114.

[12] W. V. Harris, *Poverty and Destitution in the Roman Empire* in W. V. Harris, *Rome's Imperial Economy: Twelve Essays,* Oxford, 2011, p. 27-54.

[13] Harris discusses fully the relationship between poverty and child exposure and infanticide, see W. V. Harris, *Child-Exposure in the Roman Empire* in *JRS* 84, 1994, p. 1-22.

[14] Wilson, City Sizes [n. 3].

[15] In Scheidel's estimate, the urban population numbered between seven and nine

of the empire had much higher rates of urbanization. Thus Italy's urban population of approximately 1.5 million accounted for about one-fourth of Italy's population, if one accepts a low-count estimate of about 6 million, but about 12% of a high-count population of 12 million. Perhaps the most urbanized area of the empire was Egypt, with an urban population about the same size as Italy's. This urban population represented some 20% of an overall population of 7.5-8 million, and even more if the population is estimated more conservatively at 5 million, as Rathbone has argued.[16] North Africa, with an urban population of perhaps 1 million, Asia Minor, with about 700,000, and Syria, with about 750,000, were also heavily urbanized regions.[17]

Maintaining the empire's urban population required a significant effort to capture resources from the rural economy. Absent major technological advances that substantially increased the productivity of agriculture, the development of cities in the Roman Empire depended on an overall growing population, which allowed a transfer of wealth from the rural economy to the cities. The food supply of cities depended on their ability to capture some portion of the agricultural surplus produced by numerous farm workers, including small owner cultivators, tenants, labourers, and slaves across the Roman Empire. With a growing population, there would be increased competition for land and a tendency for the incomes of farm workers to decline, even as overall production in the rural economy increased. This situation would foster increasing stratification of wealth, at least in terms of the gap between the small farmers in the Roman Empire and the wealthiest landowners.

The changes in the agrarian economy produced by urbanization can be seen most readily in the case of Rome, the pre-eminent consumer city in the ancient world. Sustaining Rome's gigantic population depended not only on the incomes of the Roman elite, the senators and equestrians pursuing political careers in Rome, but also on interventions on the part of the imperial government. These interventions involved the state's maintaining direct control over considerable agricultural resources in the provinces, such as the imperial estates in North Africa and state-owned lands in Egypt, and the extraction of rents and taxes from the provinces to support the *annona* at Rome.[18] The interventions on the part of the imperial government in the empire's agrarian economy to some extent

million, about eleven to twelve percent of the overall population, see W. SCHEIDEL, *Demography* in SCHEIDEL *et al.*, *Cambridge Economic History* [n. 2], p. 79.

[16] D. RATHBONE, *Villages, Land and Population in Graeco-Roman Egypt* in *PCPhS* 36, 1990, p. 103-142.

[17] WILSON, *City Sizes* [n. 3].

[18] I discuss the Roman state's role as an economic actor in the agrarian economy in D. KEHOE, *The State and Production in the Roman Agrarian Economy* in A. BOWMAN / A.WILSON (eds.), *The Roman Agricultural Economy. Organization, Investment, and Production*, Oxford, 2013, p. 33-53.

distorted private markets for foodstuffs and imposed substantial costs on the provinces. It seems likely that some state intervention was required to maintain a stable food supply in Alexandria, although there is not much evidence for how this might have functioned, and perhaps for the other very large cities in the empire. But the effects of urbanism reached far beyond the empire's largest cities. As J. W. Hanson argues in his study of the urban system of Roman Asia Minor, the numerous cities on the coast of Asia Minor were part of a pan-Mediterranean system, and played a role in collecting resources from the interior of Asia Minor and exporting them abroad, particularly to Rome.[19] However, the coastal cities in Asia Minor could not be maintained by their territories alone, but instead depended on food production from the much less urbanized interior of the region. So the empire's urban economy involved exchanges with the rural economy at many levels, and what Hanson has concluded for Asia Minor is suggestive for urban networks in other highly urbanized provinces, such as Africa and Baetica.[20]

In the more urbanized parts of the Roman Empire, it seems likely that most households did not own land. We can gain some perspective on the distribution of land in late Republican Italy by considering Walter Scheidel's analysis of late Roman Republican census categories.[21] As reconstructed by Dominic Rathbone, the late Republican census divided people into five classes, plus the *proletarii*, who had little property.[22] The classes were based on property declarations, in descending order, of 100,000 sesterces, 75,000 sesterces, 50,000 sesterces, 20,000 sesterces, and, finally, 375 sesterces. The top class corresponds to the level of wealth expected, if not formally required, for decurions serving on town councils in Italy under the Principate. But the third and the fourth levels provided sufficient wealth to allow households a degree of economic security. They were generally protected against food uncertainty, and disposed of surplus income that they could use for the purchase of some luxury goods.

It is, of course, very difficult to know how many households had this level of wealth. Scheidel estimates that there were, overall, about 525,000 households in all

[19] J. W. HANSON, *The Urban System of Roman Asia Minor and Wider Urban Connectivity* in A. BOWMAN / A. WILSON (eds.), *Settlement, Urbanization, and Population*, Oxford, 2011, p. 229-275.

[20] For a broad comparative discussion of the changes that Roman rule brought to rural provincial economies, see J. HOFFMANN-SALZ, *Die wirtschaftlichen Auswirkungen der römischen Eroberung: Vergleichende Untersuchungen der Provinzen Hispania Tarraconensis, Africa Proconsularis und Syria*, Stuttgart, 2011.

[21] W. SCHEIDEL, *Stratification, Deprivation and the Quality of Life* in E. M. ATKINS / R. OSBORNE (eds.), *Poverty in the Roman World*, Cambridge, 2006, p. 40-59.

[22] D. RATHBONE, *The Census Qualification of the Assidui and the Prima Classis* in H. SANCISI-WEERDENBURG / R. J. VAN DER SPEK / H. C. TEITLER / H. T. WALLINGA (eds.), *De Agricultura: In Memoriam Pieter Willem de Neeve (1945-1990)*, Amsterdam, 1993, p. 121-152.

five classes together, about one-half of the total number of households in late Republican Italy, with 225,000 of them allocated into the third and fourth classes, spread out among Italy's 400 cities. Scheidel's calculations are based on a low-count estimate of the free population of Italy as on the order of four million. With a larger population, of course, the figures would have to be adjusted, but the point is to confirm both the existence of a substantial group of independent property owners who were not members of the elite but were also not in any meaningful sense poor. At the same time, there was a large class of people who had little property of their own. The pattern that the census categories suggest for Italy seems to have obtained in the provinces as well. For example, to judge by a fourth-century land register from the Egyptian nome capital Hermopolis, landownership in the Hermopolite nome was characterized by substantial stratification.[23] In a city with a population numbering in the tens of thousands,[24] only about one thousand people owned land. And of the 159 landowners recorded in the land registers, twenty–five people owned about three-quarters of the land.[25] These town residents may have owned about twenty-five to thirty percent of the land in the nome, with villagers owning the rest.[26] Among the villagers, landownership was likely to have been more egalitarian, but even so, only a minority of families owned land. In the cities, it is commonly assumed that there were poor people in large numbers, including those who left economic misery in the countryside to seek economic opportunities in cities.

The conditions under which immigrants to the empire's cities lived is a matter of debate. A city as large as Rome depended on a constant influx of immigrants seeking new economic opportunities; as in other large pre-industrial cities, it is likely that life expectancies in Rome were lower than in the countryside, and newcomers to the city would be especially susceptible to diseases for which the native-born population had acquired some immunity.[27] There are differing views about the degree of deprivation that newcomers to Rome faced. Nicholas Purcell

[23] See TACOMA, *Fragile Hierarchies* [n. 6], and earlier A. BOWMAN, *Landholding in the Hermopolite Nome in the Fourth Century AD* in *JRS* 75, 1985, p. 137-163.

[24] According to Wilson (*City sizes* [n. 3], p. 186) 37, 100; TACOMA, *Fragile Hierarchies* [n. 6], p. 93-94 has a higher estimate, about 45,000.

[25] 9,450 out of 12,830 arouras; TACOMA, *Fragile Hierarchies* [n. 6], p. 98, table 1.3.1.

[26] BOWMAN, *Landholding* [n. 23], p. 145-148.

[27] For cities as consumers of people, see CLARK, *Farewell* [n. 8], p. 91-111; for Rome, see N. PURCELL, *The City of Rome and the Plebs Urbana in the Late Republic* in J. A. CROOK / A. LINTOTT / E. RAWSON (eds.), *The Cambridge Ancient History*, IX: *The Last Age of the Roman Republic, 146-43 BC.*, 2nd ed., Cambridge, 1994, p. 644-688 (esp. p. 650); N. MORLEY, *Metropolis and Hinterland: Rome and the Italian Economy, 200 BC-AD*, New York, 1996, p. 39-46, and W. JONGMAN, *Slavery and the Growth of Rome. The Transformation of Italy in the Second and First Centuries BCE* in C. EDWARDS / G. WOOLF (eds.), *Rome the Cosmopolis*, Cambridge, 2003, p. 100-122.

believes that immigrants into Rome were received in social networks that provided some economic security, whereas Neville Morley suggests that this assessment is somewhat optimistic.[28] At any rate, Rome and other large cities surely had large populations of people whose employment was not assured and who were subject to economic insecurity, and food insecurity in particular. The same is likely to have been true in proportion in other cities, and indeed Arjan Zuiderhoek has identified the economic gulf between such economically marginal people and the wealthier citizens as a potentially disruptive force in cities in the eastern Roman Empire.[29]

The Roman imperial government pursued policies with distributional consequences for the economy that, in theory at least, provided greater economic security for the members of Scheidel and Friesen's vast third class whose incomes were close to subsistence. These interventions affected both the rural and urban economies. To consider the rural economy, the most obvious intervention on the part of the imperial government was its policies to maintain direct control over substantial tracts of farmland throughout the empire. Imperial estates in North Africa, as documented in the famous inscriptions from the Bagradas valley, like the various categories of state-owned land in Roman Egypt, produced grain and other foodstuffs and helped to guarantee Rome's food supply, in particular the imperial food distribution programs. When Septimius Severus became emperor and engaged in substantial confiscations of his opponents' properties, new imperial properties in Baetica supplied olive oil and other products to Rome, and also to military markets on the frontiers. The imperial government's reasons for maintaining control of these properties were largely financial—it used them as a way to enhance its revenues and to secure its direct access to vital foodstuffs, a task that would have been more difficult than if it relied on the private market alone. But the role that the imperial government played as the empire's pre-eminently largest landowner had important consequences for the rural economy. In the parts of the empire where we can trace them, including North Africa, Egypt, and Asia Minor, the imperial government provided its tenants with secure and favourable conditions of land tenure, such that land tenure on imperial estates was a desirable privilege that imperial tenants fought hard to protect.[30] At the very least, the imperial government's policies in administering its estates established favourable terms of tenure for a broad class of farmers across the empire. It is difficult to know what percentage of property in the empire was under the control of the imperial Fiscus—in some regions in Egypt, state-owned properties accounted for a quarter of the property or more, and overall

[28] PURCELL, *City* [n. 27]; MORLEY, Cities [n. 3].

[29] A. ZUIDERHOEK, *Feeding the Citizens: Municipal Grain Funds and Civic Benefactions in the Greek East* in R. ALSTON / O. M. VAN NIJF (eds.), *Feeding the Ancient Greek City*, Leuven, 2008, p. 59-80.

[30] D. KEHOE, *Law and the Rural Economy in the Roman Empire*, Ann Arbor, 2007, p. 53-91.

it would seem likely that the state controlled some small multiple of ten percent of the empire's agricultural land.

What this means is that there existed a large class of small farmers who were able to keep some portion of the surplus that they produced. Moreover, since imperial properties were so extensive, the terms of tenure that the imperial government maintained on them also affected what private landowners had to offer.[31] To be sure, this system of agriculture imposed costs on the provinces, since the revenues that the imperial government took as rents were lost to nearby cities, which competed with imperial estates for the resources of tenants.[32] But as the imperial government deprived city governments of resources that would help them to meet their own tax and liturgical obligations, it also helped to keep more resources in the countryside. Imperial tenants were, for the most part, members of the broad third class of people in Scheidel and Friesen's study. But they clearly lived well above a bare subsistence level, and they accumulated resources of their own that helped to create demand.

The imperial government had a continuing interest in maintaining the viability of small farmers in the private agrarian economy, since its ability to exact tax revenues ultimately depended on the production of small farmers. Accordingly, the government sought to provide small farmers protection against any threat to their capacity to cultivate their land. These threats might come in the form of illegal exactions of draft animals and other compulsory services by imperial tax officers or officials from towns, or in creditors' seizing the equipment and draft animals that small farmers needed to cultivate their land.

In broader terms, the Roman government's efforts to define and maintain property rights in the private agricultural economy created legal institutions that provided some protection for small farmers. Thus the imperial government established authoritative legal institutions to allow the adjudication of disputes involving land tenure, and it seems clear that such institutions were available to people beyond the wealthiest residents in the provinces.[33] The contribution of the Roman legal administrative policy in the provinces was to define property rights clearly and to provide authoritative institutions through which disputes, such as between landowners and tenants, could be resolved. Even if only a small proportion of disputes ever came to the attention of the Roman courts, the existence of authoritative legal institutions provided a legal endowment within which parties in a land tenure arrangement could negotiate. Land tenure, in the Roman Empire, was

[31] I address these issues in KEHOE, *State* [n. 18].

[32] T. HAUKEN, *Petition and Response: An Epigraphic Study of Petitions to Roman Emperors 181-249*, Bergen, 1998; KEHOE, *Law* [n. 30], p. 79-89.

[33] See S. CONNOLLY, *Lives Behind the Laws: The World of the Codex Hermogenianus*, Bloomington, IN, 2010 and also B. KELLY, *Petitions, Litigation, and Social Control in Roman Egypt*, Oxford, 2011, p. 243-286.

negotiated "in the shadow of the law."[34] Indeed, one of the aims of the Roman jurists in regulating legal disputes involving farm tenancy, especially those connected with bearing the costs for the risks inherent in Mediterranean agriculture, was to foster, when possible, the continuation of productive lease relationships. In implementing this policy, the Roman legal authorities recognized the importance of the continued occupation of the land for the economic interests of upper-class landowners, but in so doing they recognized as legally valid within Roman law land tenure systems that afforded the tenant security of tenure. To the extent that they protected tenants against the opportunistic behaviour of landowners, say, by prohibiting the latter group from raising customary rents, the Roman legal authorities shifted resources away from landowners to the people actually cultivating the land. This legal policy would tend to raise the purchasing power of Scheidel and Friesen's vast third class.

In its interventions in the urban economy, the Roman imperial government provided more direct subsidies to support the purchasing power of the less wealthy levels of society. The best example, of course, is the *annona* at Rome. Assuming that the free population of Rome was on the order of 600,000, the distribution of free grain to some 150,000-200,000 males would have alleviated the budgets of, at the very least about a third of the population, and possibly of the majority of families.[35] The amount of grain distributed each month, five *modii*, was much more than any one individual would be likely to consume, and it is best interpreted as a subsidy for a family. Over the course of the Principate, food subsidies increased, with Septimius Severus offering distributions of olive oil and Aurelian pork. When one considers that procuring food can consume the majority of the budget for pre-industrial households, these subsidies worked to raise the purchasing power and standards of living of hundreds of thousands of people, and surely had a profound effect on Rome's economy by freeing up funds that people would otherwise have spent on food for other goods and services. These considerations are consistent with what Keith Hopkins has maintained about the economy of the city of Rome, that the cumulative demand of its population was an important stimulus to commerce and manufacturing.[36] In comparison to modern societies in which poor people depend on uncertain subsidies for food and fuel, the Roman population lived in relative security, and this security had positive economic consequences.

[34] R. H. MNOOKIN / L. KORNHAUSER, *Bargaining in the Shadow of the Law: the Case of Divorce* in *Yale Law Journal* 88, 1979, p. 950-997.

[35] P. ERDKAMP, *The Grain Market in the Roman Empire: a Social, Political and Economic Study*, Cambridge, 2005, p. 242-243.

[36] For discussion of Hopkins' view on the purchasing power of the Roman poor, see R. OSBORNE, *Introduction: Roman Poverty in Context* in M. ATKINS / R. OSBORNE (eds.), *Poverty in the Roman World*, Cambridge, 2006, p. 1-20 (esp. 7); for the demand generated in pre-industrial cities, see also MORLEY, *Metropolis* [n. 27], p. 13-32.

No other city in the empire benefited from subsidies on the scale that Rome enjoyed, but there still were some subsidies that enhanced the purchasing power of common people. One example would be the imperial alimentary foundations, which established funds in numerous Italian cities to defray some of the costs involved in raising children. Private individuals also established alimentary foundations in Italy and in the provinces. In the best known of the imperial foundations, from Veleia in the early second century,[37] patrons of the program received loans from the imperial government representing approximately eight percent of the value of the properties pledged. These patrons made annual interest payments of five percent on the capital they had received, which generated 52,000 sesterces to support food purchases for some 281 children of various classes.[38] Pliny the Younger, in the same period, established a private program at his hometown of Comum, funded by an impost imposed on one of his properties valued at 500,000 sesterces that was to yield 30,000 sesterces each year.[39] In the largest private foundation known, the equestrian P. Licinius Papirianus set aside a fund to feed six hundred boys and girls each month at the town of Sicca Veneria in Africa in the mid second century.[40] The fund was to yield 65,000 sesterces, a five percent return on a capital fund of 1,300,000 sesterces. The amounts yielded by these funds would have varied considerably from one town to the next, depending on the number of subscribers or patrons in the imperial alimentary foundations, and the resources of the donors in the case of private ones. But the economic significance lies in the fact that these funds would represent a substantial boost to the budgets of potentially hundreds of families in many towns. Like the imperial *annona* at Rome, the imperial and private alimentary foundations increased the purchasing power of many people of modest means. In addition, as Elio Lo Cascio has suggested,[41] the initial provision of capital in the imperial foundations can be viewed as a subsidy that potentially would have helped landowners improve their farms, although the recipients of such capital infusions were the wealthier landowners in the communities affected. Private alimentary foundations represent a clear-cut redistribution of resources away from the wealthiest classes in Roman cities to people of much more humble means. They were not designed to serve as poor relief, but they increased the food security and the spending power of the recipient households.

[37] *CIL* XI, 1147; *ILS* 6675.

[38] For a clear discussion of how the imperial alimentary programs worked, see R. P. DUNCAN-JONES, *The Economy of the Roman Empire: Quantitative Studies*, 2nd ed., Cambridge, 1982, p. 288-319.

[39] PLINY, *Ep.* I, 8, 5; 7, 18.

[40] *CIL* VIII, 1641; *ILS* 6818.

[41] E. LO CASCIO, *Alimenta Italiae* in E. LO CASCIO, *Il princeps e il suo impero: Studi di storia amminitrativa e finanziaria romana*, Bari, 2000, p. 265-291.

Certainly one form of public spending in Rome with distributional consequences was public building. As P. A. Brunt argued, the vast majority of construction workers in imperial Rome are likely to have been free.[42] Although the amount of construction work varied from one reign to another and depended on the resources available to a given emperor, the building of public monuments could employ thousands of workers. Janet DeLaine has illustrated the likely economic impact for Rome of a massive construction project like the Baths of Caracalla.[43] This project employed thousands of people, injecting a significant amount of money into Rome's economy. It seems likely, moreover, that Rome's working population, as in many cities in the modern world, was dynamic, with people moving in and out of the city to seek work depending on the season. So workers may have taken some of the wages they earned in construction with them into the towns from which they came, while also bringing into Rome wages that they had earned elsewhere, say by working in the harvest. Construction and seasonal agricultural labour added to the food subsidies in creating demand in Rome, and it seems likely that the large urban market in Rome fostered craft industries in Rome's *suburbium* and exchanges between the capital city and the surrounding countryside.[44] Certainly the food subsidies and construction programs in Rome did not come free, since they imposed substantial costs on the provinces, which received little in return in this exchange.

In provincial cities, monument building would also have provided employment to numerous people, albeit on a more modest scale than in Rome, and with much less frequency. In addition, such construction programs, since they were largely paid for by members of the local elites, ultimately depended on a transfer of wealth from the countryside. Thus they served to boost the prosperity of urban residents at the expense of the countryside. Local civic euergetism also had potentially pernicious side effects, if members of the local elites engaged in wasteful competition and spent money recklessly on entertainments and buildings that provided little public utility. Indeed, the Roman government recognized the potential pitfalls of this type of competition and sought to exercise some control over it.[45]

But one form of local spending that the imperial government consistently supported was the establishment of funds for the purchase of grain, *sitoneiai*, as recently discussed in an important article by Zuiderhoek, and earlier by Erdkamp.[46]

42 P. A. BRUNT, *Free Labour and Public Works at Rome* in *JRS* 70, 1980, p. 81-100.

43 J. DELAINE, *The Baths of Caracalla : a Study in the Design, Construction, and Economics of Large-Scale Building Projects in Imperial Rome*, Portsmouth, R.I., 1997, p. 175-205.

44 See R. WITCHER, *The Extended Metropolis: Urbs, Suburbium and Population* in *JRA* 18, 2005, p. 120-138. For discussion of the importance of construction, see PURCELL, *City* [n. 27], p. 670-71.

45 KEHOE, *State* [n. 18].

46 ZUIDERHOEK, *Feeding* [n. 29]; ERDKAMP, *Grain Market* [n. 35], p. 258-268.

As Zuiderhoek and other scholars have argued,[47] urban populations faced considerable risk for volatility in food prices, and, in contrast to farmers, they had to view options, other than simply saving money, to protect against the risk of harvest failures. To address this issue, city governments in the Greek East established funds for the purchase of grain, with the support of the Roman imperial administration. Just how these funds worked is not altogether clear; ideally they would have allowed city authorities to purchase and stockpile grain, so as to stabilize prices by purchasing when grain was plentiful and releasing supplies onto the market at times of scarcity. However they worked, such funds are likely to have had the same effect, although on a much more modest scale, as the food distributions at Rome, in that they would protect urban residents against the hazards posed by food uncertainty. This protection would make living in the city a more economically viable option for people of modest means, and would mean that they would have to divert less of their incomes into the purchase of food, leaving more for discretionary purchases.

In this survey I have sought to bring attention to the potential purchasing power of the large class of people in the Roman Empire whose incomes were likely to have been close to subsistence, and its importance for the Roman economy as a whole. The gulf between the wealthiest members of society and those in Scheidel and Friesen's third class was substantial, and the policies of the Roman imperial government to define and protect private property rights certainly benefited the wealthiest members of society. But this survey suggests that the Roman Empire also maintained institutions, some resulting from the fiscal policies of the imperial government, and others from the social values to which members of the elite subscribed, that redistributed wealth, or at the very least checked the seemingly inexorable process by which the fortunes of the wealthier landowners grew at the expense of the rural workforce. These institutions created subsidies that imposed substantial costs on some elements of society: maintaining Rome's immense population depended on the imperial government's ability to direct resources there away from the provinces. The empire struggled to balance the interests of Rome and the provinces, cities and the countryside, and the rich and the poor. But the Roman imperial government did address these competing interests by creating institutions that played a significant role in the economy. The Malthusian constraints on the Roman and other ancient economies do not tell the whole story about economic performance, and I would argue that legal and social institutions could have an important effect on the distribution of wealth and the overall performance of the economy of the Roman Empire.

[47] E.g. N. MORLEY, *The Poor in the City of Rome* in M. ATKINS / R. OSBORNE (eds.), *Poverty in the Roman World*, Cambridge, 2006, p. 21-39 (esp. 33).

Annalisa MARZANO

Villas as Instigators and Indicators of Economic Growth

There is no doubt that villas and farms were a key element of the rural landscape of the Roman Empire. The villa was the typical unit of land exploitation and agricultural production and such a role can be seen in the spread of farms and villas that occurred in Italy in the Republican period, when the degree of land occupation increased sharply, and in the progressive appearance of rural buildings employing typically Roman architectural forms in the provinces. The appearance of villas in newly annexed territories, together with the introduction, in some regions, of new crops such as grapes and olives, is so much linked with Rome's territorial and political annexation, that scholars have used villas as an indicator of the degree of Romanization of a given region. In this chapter, the term 'villa' is used to refer to rural building(s) equipped with residential quarters and agricultural processing and storage facilities at the centre of an estate devoted to either agriculture, animal husbandry, or both. This chapter does not address the debate on the 'origin of the villa-system'—whether, both from an architectural and organizational point of view, it originated from Greek, Punic, or Etrusco-Italic antecedents[1] —but rather focuses on the appearance and diffusion of villas in given provincial territories. The underlining question at the basis of this paper is whether villas can be considered as instigators of economic growth[2] in a given region or whether they were simply indicators of the presence of pre-existing favourable economic conditions. The chapter will argue that villas were both.

[1] X. LAFON, Villa maritima*: recherches sur les villas littorales de l'Italie romaine (IIIe siècle av. J.-C. / IIe siècle ap. J.-C.)*, Rome, 2001, p. 15-40; E. FENTRESS, *Villas, Wine, and Kilns: The Landscape of Jerba in the Late Hellenistic Period* in *JRA* 14, 2001, p. 149-168; N. TERRENATO, *The Auditorium Site and the Origins of the Roman Villa* in *JRA* 14, 2001, p. 5-32.

[2] Economic growth in the context of the ancient world is a very difficult phenomenon to prove since we do not have precise data on population and cannot calculate the real GDP, which is used to measure economic growth in modern societies; see the conclusions below.

1 Provincial Villa Development

The installation and diffusion of villas in the provinces generally followed two basic paths. In one case, the appearance of villas was connected to colonization and distribution of provincial land to colonists, normally military veterans. Farms were built on the allocated land and, within one or two generations, most of these farms became, in scale and décor, proper villas. In the second case, the appearance of villas was linked to purchases of land (or politically-based gifts of land) by the landowning elite. Whatever the scenario, the new proprietors had some important advantages over the indigenous population. Even though at first glance it may appear that there was not much difference between—say—an ex-centurion settling in a new colony and a native farmer, in fact their conditions differed in two important respects: social connections and know-how. Let us imagine the case of a hypothetical ex-centurion receiving a land allotment in Gaul. He is a Roman citizen and, through his former army affiliation, family ties and patronage, has a network of social connections outside the province in which he is settling; these are connections the native farmer does not have. In addition, he also knows how to plant and grow new crops that are more profitable, particularly vineyards. This hypothetical veteran colonist probably also has another advantage: a share of the booty from the wars or some discharge bounty, received in addition to the land allotment. Even if not amounting to much, this money can be sufficient to help in sustaining the veteran and his family for a time, giving him a competitive edge against the natives and, possibly, also against his neighbours, while the crops on the estate reach fruit-bearing maturity. Instead of tilling the earth for cereals and vegetables (which he can purchase from the locals) to feed his family, the colonist can focus on cultivating cash crops. After a few years, if everything is proceeding well, he might be able to purchase the land of another veteran who started some commercial or artisanal activity in town and does not have the interest to work his land, or he might purchase the land of a colonist who is not doing as well because he does not have very good connections. In other words, the hypothetical colonist expands his holdings, his estate grows bigger, he exports his wine, and is in a position to make improvements to his farm, to the storage and production facilities, and to the residential quarters too, where now some amenities typical of Roman houses and villas on Italic soil appear.

The hypothetical scenario I just sketched above is supported by the archaeological evidence pertaining to rural settlements that has been collected in the past decades and by the pattern in type and quantity of foodstuffs exported from a given region that emerges from the evidence offered by amphorae. In the provinces, the appearance of villas and of given cultivars as cash crops, particularly vine and olive trees, is clearly linked with Rome's territorial conquest, the foundation of colonies, and the process of Romanization. This pattern can be discerned especially well through the archaeological evidence collected for ancient Gaul(s) and the Iberian Peninsula, although in recent years a shift in focus to investigating and recording Roman era evidence, neglected in the past, is revealing similar trends in areas traditionally considered 'untouched' by the villa-phenomenon, such as mainland Greece.[3]

2 Villas in the Iberian Peninsula and Gaul: the Archaeological Evidence

During the second and first centuries BC, when villas and viticulture for the export market grew greatly in central Italy and Campania, imports of Italian wines completely dominated in Iberia and Gaul. The territorial conquest and arrival of Italic colonists in the south-western part of the Iberian Peninsula occurred some decades earlier than the colonization of Gaul. Most colonies in the territories that would become the provinces of Tarraconensis and Baetica were created right after the end of the Sertorian war in 72 BC. Many settlements sprang up in the valley of the Baetis, which, with its important mines, was the main drive for Rome's interest in the territory. However, the region was also very fertile, and soon acquired a reputation for abundant agricultural production in wheat, wine, and oil.[4] Baetica became an important producer of predominantly olive oil, whereas Tarraconensis produced large quantities of wine. The diffusion of intensive oleiculture and viticulture in these two regions was achieved through the establishment of many farms and villas in the territory. Initial installations were small and medium-sized farms. It was after the arrival of the Italian colonists that the typical large terracotta vessels sunken in the ground (the *dolia defossa*) in which the must fermented into wine appeared.[5] By the mid-first century BC, lever presses were installed and *cellae vinariae* with *dolia defossa* were built at many farms/villas.[6] These machines and processing methods had already been in use in

[3] In the past, scholars working on Greece have considered the 'villa' as a 'western' phenomenon that did not apply to Greece and Asia Minor; cf. e.g. R. M. ROTHAUS, *Urban Space, Agricultural Space and Villas in Late Roman Corinth* in P. N. DOUKELLIS / L. G. MENDONI (eds.), *Structures rurales et sociétés antique. Actes du colloque de Corfou 14-16 mai 1992*, Paris, 1994, p. 391-396 (esp. p. 391-392).

[4] STRABO III, 2, 6, dependent on Posidonius of Apamea; Y. PEÑA CERVANTES, Torcularia: *La producción de vino y aceite en Hispania*, Tarragona, 2010, p. 158-162 for an outline of available archaeological data on wine production in Tarraconensis in the second century BC.

[5] The use of *dolia defossa* for the wine fermentation process is typical of Campania and the central Italian regions; the must could also ferment directly in the amphorae, a vinification process of Phoenicio-Punic tradition, but Italian tradition preferred to use courtyards or storerooms equipped with the sunken *dolia* as can be seen at Villa Regina excavated at Boscoreale, near Pompeii.

[6] PEÑA CERVANTES, *Torcularia* [n. 4], p. 161-162.

central Italy and Campania for some time.[7] By the Augustan period, Tarraconensis, especially the area corresponding to modern Catalonia, was exporting surplus wine (the Laietanian wine). Large quantities were sent to Narbonensis and Aquitania,[8] where viticulture had started only some decade earlier and had not reached full maturity and production capacity yet (see discussion below).

In the Julio-Claudian period, villa sites in the Iberian Peninsula underwent architectural interventions aimed at improving the residential quarters and the production facilities. In some cases, multiple wine (or oil) presses were installed, an indication not only of the availability of capital for such ameliorations, but also of the increased size of the estates. However, judging from data on amphorae,[9] excavations of some villa sites, and field surveys,[10] it seems that intensive wine production, particularly of Laietanian wine, came to a halt towards the end of the first century AD. In this period various wine production centres were abandoned, and there was a sharp decline in the volume of wine exports; also the sites that continued to be occupied show a reduction in the amount of wine production.[11] This phenomenon might have been related to the development of intensive viticulture that had occurred in the meantime in Gaul, one of the first export markets for Tarraconensis wine. Although, in comparison to the large number of rural settlements that existed in the Iberian peninsula, only a few villa sites have been excavated,[12] the development of successful intensive viticulture and oleiculture in these two provinces is clearly linked to the arrival of colonists and the construction of many farms, employing technology (the lever press)[13] and

[7] K. D. WHITE, *Farm Equipment of the Roman World*, Cambridge, 1975, p. 229-232 for a synthetic overview of press types (these types are the same for oil and wine); the lever press, which used ropes, pulleys and a capstan to lower the long beam, is also known as the Catonian press since this is the type described by Cato (*Agr.* 18).

[8] R. ÉTIENNE / F. MAYET, *Le vin hispanique*, Paris, 2000, p. 236.

[9] It has to be noted that some scholars have proposed that the disappearance of certain wine amphorae from the region does not indicate a drastic contraction of wine production in general but a shift to barrels: PEÑA CERVANTES, *Torcularia* [n. 4], p. 167.

[10] Overall in the *Ager Tarraconensis* the most recent survey work has identified that by the third century AD 58% of rural settlements had been abandoned (O. Olesti, pers. comm.); only larger villas continued to be occupied and produce wine.

[11] e.g. Torrent de les Voltes or Mafumet villas near Tarraco; at these villas the *cella vinaria*, in use from the first to the fifth century AD, was downsized in the late second century.

[12] The great hiatus between number of villas and farms existing in the territory in Roman times and those archaeologically investigated is most notable in the case of the oil-producing villas of the Guadalquivir Valley, which supplied Rome and the army: it has been estimated that more than 1,000 presses must have been in use in order to produce the amount of oil that reached Rome every year, but only six oil-producing centres have been excavated in the region, see PEÑA CERVANTES, *Torcularia* [n. 4], p. 177.

[13] The lever and screw press (first mentioned by PLINY, *N.H.* XVIII, 8, 317 as a Greek

practices (fermentation of the must in sunken *dolia)* typical of Italic soil. Some of these farms grew larger in the Julio-Claudian period, becoming proper villas, and these larger sites generally continued to be occupied until late antiquity.

Gaul followed a somewhat similar development. The dominant presence in the region of Italic wine imports started to diminish after the capitulation of Massilia in 49 BC. Caesar, and later Augustus, established several colonies; as at this time enrolment into the legions was still based on recruitment in Italy, settlers for the new colonies originated chiefly from central Italy. They brought with them their knowledge and experience of Italian agriculture, especially viticulture, which had been at the core of Italy's great growth in central Italian villas in the Republican period.[14] The introduction of viticulture in these provincial territories in connection with Roman colonization emerges clearly from the archaeological record. Trenches for vineyards associated with colonial foundations have been identified in different areas of Gaul and dated to the early first century AD.[15] The most notable examples are the trenches for vineyards identified in the context of Roman land centuriation in the territories of Orange, Lapalud, and Girardes or the trenches identified in the Oise and Aisne, around ancient Lutetia. Here, more than 5,000 drainage trenches associated with viticulture and dated to the mid-first/early second century AD were found near a villa occupied from the first to the fourth century AD.[16] As already mentioned in the case of the Iberian Peninsula, also in Gaul the colonists brought with them specific technical knowledge and very distinctive techniques used in the processing of crops: the *cellae vinariae* with *dolia defossa* and the use of the lever press.[17] The development revealed by the

invention dating back to *c.* 100 years before his own time and which spread from the mid-first century AD onwards) is thought not to have spread in Hispania before the late second / early third centuries AD; however, Peña Cervantes in her study including recent archaeological data for presses in Spain (PEÑA CERVANTES, *Torcularia* [n. 4], p. 214) concludes that Baetica was actually the birthplace of this technology.

[14] N. PURCELL, *Wine and Wealth in Ancient Italy* in *JRS* 75, 1985, p. 1-19.

[15] J.-P. BRUN, *L'oléiculture et la viticulture antiques en Gaule d'après les vestiges d'installations de production* in M.-C. AMOURETTI / J.-P. BRUN (eds.), *La production du vin et de l'huile en Méditerranée: Actes du symposium international organisé par le Centre Camille Jullian (Université de Provence-C.N.R.S.) et le Centre archéologique du Var (Ministère de la Culture et Conseil Général du Var), (Aix-en-Provence et Toulon, 20-22 novembre 1991)*, Athens / Paris, 1993, p. 307-341; J.-P. BRUN, *Carte archéologique de la Gaule, 83 Var*, Paris, 1999; J.-P. BRUN, *Archéologie du vin et de l'huile en Gaule romaine.* Paris, 2005.

[16] BRUN, *Archéologie du vin et de l'huile* [n. 15], p. 126-127.

[17] The adoption of the lever press, and later, of the lever and screw press, was not equal throughout the Gallic provinces; in Aquitania, for instance, the central screw press, with all its elements made of wood, seems to have been predominant (BRUN, *Archéologie du vin et de l'huile* [n. 15], p. 116). This type of press, used in wine making, remains largely archaeologically invisible because wood is rarely preserved; it was much smaller than the large lever press and in late antiquity started to be used more widely.

archaeological evidence for farms and villas in Gaul is exemplificative of such patterns. Even outside the temperate, Mediterranean region of southern France, viticulture spread considerably starting in the early first century AD. In fact, viticulture in non-Mediterranean Gaul spread earlier and more widely than previously thought or imagined on the basis of the literary texts alone. In particular, in the Tres Galliae (comprising the area of Lyon, Aquitania, and Belgica) and Germania new evidence for viticulture has been collected in archaeological investigations in recent years: pits for the planting of vineyards, palaeobotanical data, remains of installations for wine presses, amphora kilns, and agricultural tools connected to vine growing.[18] It is now clear that the planting of vineyards in the Tres Galliae and in Germania started as early as the arrival of colonists in the region, wherever soil conditions were favourable. Viticulture expanded very rapidly, providing largely for local and regional markets, and continued to be practised at least until late antiquity. Viticulture worked in this region as a vehicle for the spread of Roman culture in the same way as the spread of Roman religious cults or the use of town planning of Mediterranean classical tradition did.

3 From Farm to Villa

Although these initial installations built in Gaul and Iberia were, in size and décor, just modest farms, the colonists brought with them not only their technical knowledge about the cultivations and how to best process it, but also their contacts and networks. Even if modest in size when compared to the social network of an upper class member, still most of the colonists originated from Italy and had served in the army: they had connections outside the province in which they settled. Once their estates started producing wine, part of the surplus was exported to Rome and to military forts along the German *limes*. Within one or two generations, these modest farms took up the appearance of villas: the residential quarters became larger and more elegantly decorated, while the storage and processing facilities increased in size. In southern France (Gallia Narbonensis), Roman farms excavated in Provence, Languedoc, and the Rhône valley feature the addition of improved production facilities and of a larger and more elegant *pars urbana* during the Flavian period.[19] An example is the villa of Pardigon 2 in the Bay of Cavalaire. The Augustan period farm[20] was razed to the ground in the

[18] M. POUX / J.-P. BRUN / M.-L. HERVE-MONTEIL (eds.), *La vigne et le vin dans les trois Gaules*, Paris, 2011 (Gallia 68.1).

[19] BRUN, *Archéologie du vin et de l'huile* [n. 15], p. 25.

[20] Only a kiln of Dressel 2-4 amphorae remained from this phase.

reign of Nero in order to build a luxury villa provided with residential and service quarters, including a wine-producing area and *cella vinaria*. The site was occupied until the fifth century AD.[21] Improvements made to farms and larger agricultural production facilities in the Flavian period are phenomena not limited to large sites, but occur also in small and medium-sized farms.[22] The inferences to be drawn from these data are that the owners were in this period in a position to invest more capital in the improvement of their production facilities and in the beautification of their residences. It is a reasonable assumption that this capital came from the successful wine production begun in the late Republican/Augustan periods. Increased size of production facilities may also reflect the enlargement of the portion of land under cultivation.[23]

In the Tres Galliae, the general pattern is similar to the trend identified for Narbonensis, as exemplified by the villa at Saint-Laurent d'Agny, located in what was the territory of ancient Lugdunum (Lyon), a colony founded in 43 BC. A small Roman colonist farm was built on the site previously occupied by a Gallic rural settlement; during the reigns of Augustus and Tiberius the farm was transformed into a peristyle villa.[24] Investigators of the site suggested that Lyon was a bridgehead in the introduction of viticulture techniques in non-Mediterranean Gaul. Destroyed by fire in the reign of Nero or in the Flavian period, the villa was rebuilt on larger scale, and this time the service area was equipped with a least two wine presses. This pattern is attested elsewhere in the region: wine producing centres started as modest farms, but then, within a few generations, were enlarged considerably, both in respect to the residential quarters and production facilities. Presumably these changes attest a successful wine production for the commercial market that generated capital that could be invested in the amelioration of the villa and estate.

In the second century AD, installations for the processing of agricultural produce increased in number and at times the residential part was reduced to a

[21] BRUN, *Archéologie du vin et de l'huile* [n. 15], p. 37-39.

[22] BRUN, *Archéologie du vin et de l'huile* [n. 15], p. 71; he also wondered whether one could see in this the effect of the *lex Manciana* known in the context of North Africa that stimulated the cultivation of unoccupied land.

[23] BRUN, *Archéologie du vin et de l'huile* [n. 15], p. 68-70; V. REVILLA, *Agrarian Systems in Roman Spain: Archaeological Approaches* in P. P. A. FUNARI / R. S. GARRAFFONI / B. LETALIEN (eds.), *New Perspectives on the Ancient World: Modern Perceptions, Ancient Representations*, Oxford, 2008, p. 117-129, esp. 122 for methodological considerations about arbitrarily relating production capacity and size of an estate.

[24] M. POUX, with the collaboration of T. DEBIZE / B. CLEMENT / A. COLLET *et al.*, *Le «vin du Triumvir» à Lyon: témoignages archéologiques et littéraires d'une production de vin sur le territoire colonial de Lugdunum* in M. POUX / J.-P. BRUN / M.-L. HERVE-MONTEIL (eds.), *La vigne et le vin dans les trois Gaules*, Paris, 2011 (Gallia 68.1), p. 13-92.

minimum, as can be seen in the villa excavated at Saint Martin, Taradeau.[25] This additional development, observable at several villas in Gaul, indicates that only minimal residential facilities were needed, evidently for occasional visits on the part of absentee landlords, prioritizing the use of space for production and storage facilities. In this villa, rooms that had been part of the residential quarter in the first-century AD phase housed four treading vats, presses, and a *cella vinaria*.[26] These transformations, in addition to pointing to an owner no longer in residence, indicate also that the size of the properties had been growing, as now more presses were needed to press a larger amount of grapes more efficiently as was more space to store the wine produced. The ownership of these properties in the second century consisted either of descendants of the original colonists, who with time had purchased more land, or of new owners to the area, such as the landed upper classes, who had arrived in the region and acquired several estates. Such an evolution, from small-sized farms to sizable villas producing for the regional and export markets, indicates also that the social and commercial network available to the landlords had grown.

4 The Non-Colonial Path

The second possible path in the development of rural occupation in the provinces did not start with colonial assignation of land, but with purchases by the landed elite. It is important, in these cases, to ask why the wealthy invested in land and why they chose one area versus another. Land and landowning were important in antiquity; traditionally, one's place in Roman society and to which social class one belonged were defined by land— the minimum property qualification of one million *sestertii* for senators referred to the value of land owned, not to cash money. Landownership, and in particular agricultural activities, were the proper occupation for the elite and were the type of investment someone who had made money with other ventures, especially trade, should turn to. Commerce is not too vile an activity if, once satisfied with the riches made, one leaves "the port and turns to the country estate", wrote Cicero in the *De Officiis*.[27] But how did the

[25] In some parts of Gaul viticulture contracted and was possibly replaced by animal rearing in the second half of the second century AD. For instance, in the Tricastin region near the Rhône, an area developed for intensive viticulture with the Roman conquest, drainage channels associated with vine cultivation were filled in (BRUN, *Archéologie du vin et de l'huile* [n. 15], p. 46-47). Pollen analysis indicates a move from vineyards to meadows in the same period, which might point to cattle and horse breeding replacing viticulture: see BRUN, *Archéologie du vin et de l'huile* [n. 15], p. 72-73.

[26] BRUN, *Archéologie du vin et de l'huile* [n. 15], p. 42-45.

[27] CICERO, *Off.* I, 151.

elite see landownership? Was it just what a person of standing should do, because it guaranteed an income and was a respectable activity or was it seen as a proper economic opportunity? Was all good land, regardless of geographic location, equal? Were the reasons behind the buying of landed property what, in modern terms, can be called a 'real economic decision'?

For Finley, "investment in land...was never in antiquity a matter of systematic, calculated policy, of what Weber called economic rationality."[28] A well-known and oft-quoted passage from Pliny the Younger's letters is illuminating in this sense.[29] The letter, addressed to Cornelius Nepos, deals with Trajan's decision to have provincial senators running for office in Rome invest at least 1/3 of their wealth in lands in Italy, so that a stronger bond with Rome and Italic soil could be established. Pliny rightly wrote that such a conjuncture was very favourable to those owning properties in Italy, particularly in the vicinity of Rome; these properties could now be sold for a high price, because of the sudden increase in demand, while, on the other hand, it would be possible to buy estates in the provinces at good prices:[30]

> Do you know that the price of lands has gone up, especially of suburban properties?... he (i.e. Trajan) has also forced them (i.e. the provincial candidates for office) to concentrate one third of their patrimony in real estate, thinking it improper—and indeed it was so—that those who run for office should treat Rome and Italy not as their homeland but as a lodging house or inn on their visits. Therefore, the candidates out-bid one another everywhere, and buy up whatever they hear is on sale; and by doing so increase the amount available for sale. If you are weary therefore of your estates in Italy, this is certainly the time to sell them off, as well as of buying in the provinces, while the candidates are selling there to purchase here. (PLINY, *Ep*. VI, 19, 1-6)

The implication of such statements is that provincial senators, having to sell and buy in a short time to comply with the emperor's decision, were not in a position to negotiate for high prices for their provincial estates and would be at the mercy of the buyer, a reversal of a situation that normally sees the seller in a stronger position; ultimately, it was a question of supply and demand. In the letter, Pliny is very explicit in considering the buying and selling of property as an economic opportunity. However, to turn the opportunity into a feasible investment requires the capability to access information on the situation in a given region, particularly information on the potential and characteristics of a given property/land. If the

[28] M.I. FINLEY, *The Ancient Economy. Updated with a new foreword by Ian Morris*. Berkeley, 1999, p. 117.

[29] PLINY, *Ep*. VI, 19.

[30] Alföldi suggested that the contraction in Hispanic wine production was the effect of this imperial decision (G. ALFÖLDI, *Hispania bajo los Flavios y los Antoninos: Consideraciones históricas sobre una época* in M. MAYER / J. M. NOLLA / J. PARDO (eds.), *De les estructures indígenes a l'organització provincial romana de la Hispània Citerior*, Barcelona, 1998, p. 11-32).

area was already known, as in the case of someone already owning properties in the region, one would know whether the land could potentially increase in value and whether production would generate sufficient income. But if the area was not well known, then obtaining reliable information was crucial. To draw on modern parallels, an investor would not buy land in a faraway country even if he were told that prices were excellent and he could make a good investment, unless he had some kind of link with that area already and/or had a trusted contact that could pass on all the needed information. Nowadays, personal connections with someone based locally, or sending an agent to explore and evaluate the investment opportunity, is the determining factor in making the decision to invest or not in a foreign country. By drawing this parallel, I do not intend to propose that economic decision making in the modern world can be used as a simple template to understand ancient phenomena, which were rooted in a very different socio-political context. But in the case of the decision to buy estates elsewhere I believe that access to key information through personal contacts (and the elite had many opportunities to establish such ties, especially with local notables, during posting in their political and military career) was crucial in reaching the final decision on what and where to buy, even though Finley thought that most land purchases in antiquity were windfall purchases and that therefore there was no incentive to speculate in order to maximize gain.[31] Ownership of land in faraway provinces was a common scenario for the wealthy; Columella refers to "men who purchase lands at a distance, not to mention estates across the seas",[32] warning that, not being able to visit the property regularly and check on its management, this would leave one's slaves to enjoy the fruits of the property. These comments touch on an additional problem always experienced by absentee landlords: the necessity to have a trusted overseer on site.

5 The Villa and the Local Economy

Once a villa was established, the decisions on the management of the property had an obvious economic and social impact on its surroundings. It is thought that the 'villa system' was indissolubly linked to slavery, and obviously the type of labour used on the estate had a series of consequences. Historians generally believe that using tenants did not offer the opportunity to maximize the possible profit from the estate, but rather guaranteed a steady income while ensuring that the land and property maintained their value.[33] On the contrary slaves, if directly

[31] FINLEY, *Ancient Economy* [n. 28], p. 119.
[32] COLUMELLA, *Rust.* I, 3, 20.
[33] D. KEHOE, *Law and the Rural Economy in the Roman Empire*, Ann Arbor, 2007,

managed, attentively selected on the basis of their capabilities, and assigned specialized tasks—this is what Columella believed—could generate higher income from the estate.[34] But the range of possibilities in terms of labour and management, of course, was not just black or white; there were various grey areas in between, such as the case of the *servus quasi colonus*, that is to say a slave-tenant.[35] This legal category dates as early as the first century BC at least, since one of the excerpts from Alfenus Varus' *Digesta* mentions the rental of an estate by a landowner to his own slave,[36] and another quotation in the *Digest* from the Augustan jurist M. Antistius Labeo mentions that a "*seruus quasi colonus in agro erat*".[37] Such slaves were put in charge of a farm as tenants, paid the rent out of the *peculium* (normally in cash, sometime in kind), and performed other obligations pertaining to the maintenance of the estate. Furthermore, these slave tenants might not simply have a 'quasi-lease', but also be entrusted to act as *vilici* or overseers of the estate as a whole.[38]

The decision of whether to use slaves or free labour on agricultural estates had also an impact on the social fabric of the surrounding territory. What to cultivate, what kind of labour and what kind of management to use, how much capital to invest in new technology must all have been important factors taken into consideration, as was the initial decision to purchase the land. The successful

p. 176-177.

[34] COLUMELLA, *Rust.* I, especially 8-9.

[35] On *servi quasi coloni* see G. GILIBERTI, Servus quasi colonus: *forme non tradizionali di organizzazione del lavoro nella società romana*, Napoli, 1988; W. SCHEIDEL, *Sklaven und Freigelassene als Pächter und ihre ökonomische Funktion in der römischen Landwirtschaft (Colonus-Studien III)* in H. SANCISI-WEERDENBURG *et al.* (eds.), *De Agricultura: In memoriam Pieter Willem de Neeve (1945-1990)*, Amsterdam, 1993, p. 182-196. The legal sources have numerous references to *servi quasi coloni*, in particular in the context of discussing legacies of estates *cum instrumentum* (the apparatus which included slaves and equipment that was included as part of a farm/villa), as one of the problem was whether to regard the *servus quasi colonus* as part of the *instrumentum* or not, since he performed two different functions at the same time: legally he was a slave, usually acting as overseer, but from an economic point of view was a proper tenant making a profit from the revenues generated by the farm to the advantage of the *peculium*; he could also employ slaves of his own like a free *colonus* (*Dig.* XX, 1, 32): D. KEHOE, *Investment, Profit, and Tenancy. The Jurists and the Roman Agrarian Economy*, Ann Arbor, 1998, p. 166-172. On villa managerial practices, especially for Italy see P. ROSAFIO, *Slaves and Coloni in the Villa System* in J. CARLSEN / P. ØRSTED / E. SKYDSGAARD (eds.), *Land Use in the Roman Empire*, Rome, 1994 (Analecta Romana Instituti Danici, Supp. 22), p. 145-158; J.-J. AUBERT, *Productive Investments in Agriculture:* Instrumentum Fundi *and* Peculium *in the Later Roman Republic* in J. CARLSEN / E. CASCIO (eds.), *Agricoltura e scambi nell'Italia tardo-repubblicana,* Bari, 2009, p. 167-185.

[36] 2 *Dig.* = *Dig.* XV, 3, 16; Alfenus Varus was consul in 39 BC.

[37] *Dig.* XXXIII, 7, 12, 3.

[38] KEHOE, *Investment* [n. 35], p. 167-168.

establishment of villas in a region had an effect not simply in respect to surplus agricultural produce that was directed to regional or extra-regional consumption. Villas acted also as stimuli to the local economy by creating a new demand for certain goods such as tools, fuel, and amphorae that were regularly needed on an agricultural estate. Although the agronomists, especially Cato, indicate that, ideally, the estate manager should be a seller rather than a buyer, meaning that all that was needed on the estate should be produced internally, there are many examples even in Cato's treatise of suggestions for the best places to buy agricultural tools, ropes, and even an olive rotary crusher. These were objects that were too difficult to produce on a villa, or not worth the effort of setting up the needed equipment to produce only a few tools easily purchasable at town markets.[39] The idea of villas' self-sufficiency is largely a myth, and the appearance of villas in a region meant that craftsmen were needed as well. To give a banal example, because of the needs of the villas and farms in the town's territory, a local shopkeeper might start to stock goods he did not used to stock before, such as nails and ropes, because there had not been a constant demand for them. In other words, the establishment of villas put in motion a series of economic transactions that ranged from the very small-scale and localized ones, to larger-scale in the case of the export of wine, which required the existence of a good social, commercial, and transport network.

6 Villas and Subsidiary Activities

As examples of stimuli in sectors other than the growing of crops, but clearly intended for the agricultural needs of the villa and kindled by the appearance of villas, one can take the case of amphora manufacturing. In the same period when villas and farms appeared in the provinces, various amphora production centres also started to operate in the region. For instance, in Baetica production of Haltern 70 amphorae, used to transport *defrutum*[40] and olives preserved in *defrutum,* as indicated by the *tituli picti*, started as early as the mid-first century BC.[41] In Gaul,

[39] CATO, *Agr.* 135, e.g., for iron tools, Cales and Capua are mentioned; Capua is also given as the centre for the manufacture of ropes; Nola and Pompeii as the best places where to buy an olive mill (*trapetum,* but Cato's discussion of the transport cost for such an heavy item mentions Pompeii and Suessa: *Agr.* 22); WHITE, *Farm Equipment* [n. 7], p. 213-214.

[40] *Tituli picti* give *defrutum* also as the content of the Dressel 28 amphorae on the wreck of Port-Vendres, dated to the reign of Claudius: D. COLLS / R. ÉTIENNE / R. LEQUÉMENT / B. LIOU / F. MAYET, *L'Épave Port Vendres II et le commerce de la Bétique a l'époque de Claude* in *Archeonautica* 1, 1977, 1-144.

[41] On the basis of their appearance on wrecks e.g. on the Madrague de Giens shipwreck of 60-50 BC: A. HESNARD / P. POMEY / A. TCHERNIA / M. COUVERTN *L'épave romaine de la Madrague de Giens (Var) (Campagnes 1972-1975). Fouilles de l'Institut d'archéologie*

various amphora production centres started to operate right after the colonial foundations and distributions of land to veterans. The workshops of the area of Orange, where trenches for vineyards were identified, produced imitations of Italian amphorae such as Dressel 1 and Dressel 2–4, and also Pascual 1 (originally a Spanish type) and Gauloise 2. The typical flat-bottomed Gallic wine amphorae, suitable for transport on riverine barges, were also an innovation of this period; the kilns to the west of Port d'Aix produced the Gauloise 2, the Gauloise 1, and later the 4 and 5 types, which became the standard wine amphorae for the whole province during the second and third centuries AD. Because of the need for containers for the transport of wine (and oil), natural resources present in the region (clay-beds and fuel) started to be exploited to new ends.

However, even when estates had their own clay-beds and easy access to fuel and water, often owners preferred to lease these out, guaranteeing themselves a steady income, and at the same time asking for part of the rent to be paid in produce, in this case in amphorae or *dolia* needed on the estate. This type of arrangements is best attested in documents surviving from Roman Egypt, but such leases were not confined to Egypt. The preference for renting clay beds and potteries on one's rural estate, while asking for a rent 'in kind' is exemplified in one papyrus from Oxyrynchus recording a lease for a potting establishment dated to AD 243.[42] The pottery with storeroom and kiln was located in the large farmstead on the estate of the lessor and the annual rent stipulated by the terms of the lease consisted of some 15,300 wine jars, to be delivered pitched and ready to be used by the owner of the property, who evidently produced wine on his estate. It could be argued that leasing the use of such natural resources while guarantying the sufficient supply of items needed on the estate was a risk-adverse attitude, but it could equally be argued that it was a rational decision that eliminated unnecessary managerial costs associated with running a *figlina* directly. In other instances, suppliers of amphorae were completely separated from the villa estates and the oil- or wine-producing business, as in the case of the Guadalquivir Valley, where intensive olive oil production took place starting from the early first century AD.[43] It has been estimated, on the basis of the evidence provided by

méditerranéenne. in *Gallia Suppl. XXXIV*, Paris, 1978; J.-P. BRUN, *Archéologie du vin et de l'huile dans l'Empire romain*, Paris, 2004, p. 261-264. Initially, the wine from Baetica was commercialized in amphorae imitating the Italian Dressel 1, and probably also in the flat-bottomed Dressel 28. Towards the end of the first century AD, Haltern 70 and Dressel 28 amphorae were substituted by imitations of the Gallic Gauloise 4 produced in various ateliers of Baetica.

42 *P. Oxy*. 3595.

43 The majority of archaeological data on the region come from the field surveys carried out by Ponsich: M. PONSICH, *Implantation rurale antique sur le Bas Guadalquivir: Séville-Alcalá del Río-Lora del Río-Carmona*, Paris, 1974; ID., *Implantation rurale antique sur le Bas Guadalquivir: La Campana-Palma del Río-Posadas*, Paris, 1979; ID., *Implantation*

Monte Testaccio in Rome, that the Guadalquivir Valley exported every year millions of litres of olive oil to Rome;[44] considerable quantities of oil were also sent to the army on the Rhine-Danube frontier. The many kilns identified archaeologically in the valley, located along the river course, were not located on the olive-growing estates, and thanks to the stamps and *tituli picti* on the amphorae it is clear that in some cases the same *figlina* was providing amphorae for several oil producers. Therefore, to use modern economic terminology, in this region the case of the amphora manufacture is a clear example of spin-off commercial activities connected to the production of agricultural surplus. The economic impact the establishment of villas had in the region was far-reaching.

7 Networks

An existing social network, that is to say, the ability to access information, was not only at the core of much decision-making in relation to buying estates or accessing markets and realizing higher profits, but also at the base of connections between different players—be it merchants, producers, buyers, or consumers. Since such a network was built around the villa-owner (or the estate manager) the loss of such a person also meant the loss, at least temporarily, of the connections between individuals and/or communities. The complexity of the networks involving urban local elite of Italic descent, slaves and freedmen on rural properties, and traders is becoming clearer for areas such as Tarraconensis.[45] The villas themselves, in connection with urban centres, played an important role in the circulation of goods and the creation of aggregate demand from the point of view of the peasantry. Villas, in fact, were also the centres of periodical markets

rurale antique sur le Bas Guadalquivir. Bujalance, Montoro, Andújar, Madrid, 1987; ID., *Implantation rurale antique sur le Bas-Guadalquivir, IV : Écija, Dos Hermanas, Los Palacios y Villafranca, Lebrija, Sanlúcar de Barrameda*, Madrid, 1991.

[44] Monte Testaccio is a hill entirely made up of discarded oil amphorae; the excavations carried out here and the study of the *tituli picti* has shed light on the complex organization behind the supply of state-subsidized oil for the capital: J. M. BLÁZQUEZ MARTÍNEZ / J. REMESAL RODRÍGUEZ (eds.), *Estudios sobre el monte Testaccio (Roma)*, Barcelona, 1999–2010; J. T. PEÑA, *The Mobilization of State Olive Oil in Roman Africa: The Evidence of Late 4th c. Ostraca from Carthage* in J. T. PEÑA *et al.*, *Carthage Papers: The Early Colony's Economy, Water Supply, a Public Bath, and the Mobilization of State Olive Oil* in *JRA* Suppl. 28, Portsmouth, RI, 1998, p. 116-238; J. REMESAL RODRÍGUEZ, *Baetica and Germania: Notes on the Concept of 'Provincial Interdependence' in the Roman Empire* in P. ERDKAMP (ed.), *The Roman Army and the Economy*, Amsterdam, 2002, p. 293-308.

[45] O. OLESTI / C. CARRERAS, *New Methods for the Study of the Social Landscape from Laietania Wine Production Region (NE Spain)* in P. P. A. FUNARI / R. S. GARRAFFONI / B. LETALIEN (eds.), *New Perspectives on the Ancient World: Modern Perceptions, Ancient Representations,* Oxford, 2008, p. 131-144.

(*nundinae*) organized on the estates, and these were an important medium for distributing goods in the countryside, especially in the absence of nearby urban centres. There are some references to *nundinae* organized on villa estates in the literary and epigraphic sources, but I believe this practice was much more widespread than the scattered references we have suggest.[46] The attestations in the sources include Pliny the Younger's letters about the ex-praetor Bellicius Sollers, who had asked for the senate's permission to hold *nundinae* on his estate in Northern Italy.[47] This Sollers was probably T. Lucius Bellicius Sollers, epigraphically known at Verona and Rome and its environs.[48] He and his wife Claudia Marcellina are known to have owned *figlinae* in their *praedia* near Rome.[49] In this case, the market-fair was a large one, probably regional, if not inter-regional, to the point that a delegation from the nearby town of Vicentia, where Sollers' estate was probably located, opposed his request in the senate, evidently because the town wanted to keep control over the organization of the local *nundinae* for financial reasons, including the collection of taxes and fees connected with commercial transactions in the market.[50] Although the *nundinae* were to be organized on one's private estates, nonetheless the senate had to grant permission. The emperor Claudius himself asked to be authorized to have a

[46] The North African corpus on markets and rural estates is particularly rich: H. PAVIS D'ESCURAC, *Nundinae et vie rurale dans l'Afrique du Nord romaine* in *BCTH* 17, 1981, p. 251-258; B. SHAW, *Rural Markets in North Africa and the Political Economy of the Roman Empire* in *AntAfr* 17, 1981, p. 37-83; L. MELONI, *Le nundinae nel Nord Africa: produzione, merci e scambi nell'economia dei vici* in J. GONZÁLEZ / P. RUGGERI / C. VISMARA / R. ZUCCA (eds.), *L'Africa romana. Le ricchezze dell'Africa. Risorse, produzioni, scambi. Atti del XVII convegno di studio, Sevilla, 14-17 dicembre 2006*, Rome, 2008, p. 2533-2546 ; for periodic markets and sanctuaries in this region see E. FENTRESS, *Where Were North African Nundinae Held?* in C. GOSDEN *et al.* (eds.), *Communities and Connections: Essays in Honour of Barry Cunliffe*, Oxford, 2009, p. 125-141. Two cases of *nundinae* are known for Gaul from literary evidence (*Paneg. Lat.* IV, 8, 9; SIDONIUS APOLLINARIS, *Ep.* V, 7) and one from third-century Asia Minor (*TAM* V, 1, 230): MELONI, *ibid.*, p. 2533, note 3. Varro, *Rust.* I, 16, 3 recommends to purchase goods directly on villa-estates; see also N. MORLEY, *Markets, Marketing and the Roman Elite* in E. LO CASCIO (ed.), *Mercati permanenti e mercati periodici nel mondo romano. Atti degli Incontri capresi di storia dell'economia antica (Capri 13-15 ottobre 1997)*, Bari, 2000, p. 211-221 (esp. 218-219).

[47] PLINY, *Ep.* V, 4; 13.

[48] *CIL* V, 3337; 3338; VI, 37071; XIV, 3609; for stamps on *instrumentum* see e.g., *CIL* XV, 887, 2: *ex f(iglinis) L(uci) Bellici Sollerti(s)*.

[49] L. CRACCO RUGGINI, *Plinio il Giovane a proposito di nundinae private inter-cittadine: dispositivi giuridici e collusioni di fatto tra centro e periferia* in E. LO CASCIO (ed.), *Mercati permanenti e mercati periodici nel mondo romano. Atti degli Incontri capresi di storia dell'economia antica (Capri 13-15 ottobre 1997)*, Bari, 2000, p. 161-175.

[50] L. DE LIGT, *Fairs and Markets in the Roman Empire: Economic and Social Aspects of Periodic Trade in a Pre-Industrial Society*, Amsterdam, 1993, p. 155-198; 202-224.

market on his *praedia*.[51] Epigraphic evidence supports the literary record on this. For instance, a *senatus consultum* dated to AD 138 granted to the senator Lucilius Africanus the right to hold *nundinae* twice a month on his African estate, in the region '*Beguensis, territorio Musulumianorum*' in Byzacena, the modern el-Bejar.[52] El-Bejar is in the Kasserine area, where many rural sites equipped with multiple presses are known.[53] The settlement pattern in this region, with no towns but many 'agro-villages' and rural buildings for the large-scale processing of olives into oil,[54] suggests that estates were large and that production was centralized; in such a scenario characterized by a low level of urbanization (towns and cities were located on the coast), periodic markets held in the villages located on these estates played the role that in other regions town markets had.[55] By the third century AD, it was only the emperor who deliberated about *nundinae* rights, as declared by the jurist Modestinus and confirmed by an inscription from Numidia, reporting an edict of the emperor Probus giving Munatius Flavianus the right to organize a market, exempt from *vectigalia* and *portoria*, in a *vicus* of his property, the *vicus Emadaucapensis*, near Cirta.[56]

8 The Display

Many villas had very luxurious and opulent residential quarters and such establishments have been seen as an expression of conspicuous consumption on the part of the Roman elite. As I have argued in the past,[57] displaying one's social standing and achievements in public life was very important also in the case of villas, not simply that of the family urban house. This holds particularly true for the imperial period. Whereas in the Republic the various villas the elite owned in different geographic locations were foremost, ideologically, the place for learned *otium*, with the town-house in Rome having the main role in representing the

[51] SUETONIUS, *Claud.* 12.

[52] *CIL* VIII, 270.

[53] R. B. HITCHNER, *The Organisation of Rural Settlement in the Cilium-Thelepte Region (Kasserine, Central Tunisia). L'Africa Romana* 6, 1989, p. 387-402; R. B. HITCHNER, with contributions by S. ELLIS / A. GRAHAM / D. MATTINGLY / L. NEURU, *The Kasserine Archaeological Survey. 1987* in *AntAfr* 26, 1990, p. 231-259.

[54] e.g., the site at Henchir et Touil, equipped with four oil presses: HITCHNER, *Kasserine Survey* [n. 53], site KS 225.

[55] See also Festus 502-8 L. remarking that in territories with no villas, but organized only in *pagi* and *vici*, the *vici* offered the venues for basic forms of commercial exchanges and markets.

[56] *Dig.* L, 11, 1; *AÉ* 1903, 243; CRACCO RUGGINI, *Plinio* [n. 49], p. 64.

[57] A. MARZANO, *Roman Villas in Central Italy. A Social and Economic History*. Leiden / Boston, 2007, p. 176-198.

public persona of the owner and his *gens,* this situation started to change already in the Augustan period. With the progressively curtailed opportunities open to members of the upper class in respect to financing public buildings in Rome and the drastic changes in the traditional form of political career available to them, members of the elite became more involved in local euergetism, especially in areas where they already owned properties. Thus, the villas assumed a more prominent 'public function', since they needed to reflect and celebrate the social standing of the owner for the local audience of clients, notables, etc. The inscriptions, copies of public decrees of the senate or of the decurial order granting honours to various individuals for their merits, which were placed in villas in the imperial period, reflect this shift. The honorific inscriptions on statue bases from the villa of the Neratii at Saepinum (copies of those placed by the decurions in the forum of the town),[58] the two identical dedicatory inscriptions to L. Iulius Marinus Caecilius Simplex found at a villa near Cures and in modern Canneto Sabino[59] (where the ancient town must have been), or of the long inscription from the villa of the Volusii at Lucus Feroniae[60] (which reproduced the senatorial decree granting extraordinary honours to the deceased L. Volusius Saturninus), illustrate the importance of villas located near communities where the proprietors had social connections, as a venue to affirm, through the architecture and the décor, the standing of the owner.

Furthermore, there was also another feature that one can include when considering villas as 'institutions': the importance of reaching high visibility in the landscape. This was not simply to reflect one's social standing, but also, clearly, to impress people. The maritime Roman villas that flourished in Istria starting in the first and second centuries AD were monumental and impressive. They were places for production, largely of olive oil and at some sites—it seems—purple dye, but these were also lavish residences, built on a truly grand scale. The maritime façade of these villas, unfolding on several terraces, featuring long colonnaded porticoes and temple-like structures, was meant to be seen from the sea by whoever passed by on a boat or ship. The villa on the island of Brijuni or, a few km away, the one at Valbandon, or the imposing villa built on multiple terraces at Stari Trogir (some 40 km west of Salona) are fine examples of this kind of impressive architectural display.[61] It is plausible to say that such a view had some effects on the person's reputation and, by extension, on his networks: such a display of one's power and wealth must have made people hope to establish

[58] M. GAGGIOTTI, *La villa dei Neratii nel territorio di Saepinum* in *AnnPerugia* 8, 1984-1985, p. 113-124.

[59] *AÉ* 1947, 156; *ILS* 1026.

[60] *AÉ* 1972, 174.

[61] V. BEGOVIC DVORZAK / I. DVORZAK SCHRUNK, *Roman Villas in Istria and Dalmatia, Part III: Maritime Villas. Rimske vile u Istri i Dalmaciji III - Maritimne vile* in *Prilozi Instituta za arheologijo u Zagrebu* 21, 2004, p. 65-90.

a connection with this person. In other words, the display element was not useless; it ultimately reinforced the network structure and social power on which the villa system was based. Once a proprietor owned sufficient land to be included among the notables, whether local notable (to be part of the decurial class a minimum landed property qualification worth 100,000 *sestertii* was needed) or higher up the social scale, he also acquired political power. From membership of the city council some may have later risen to provincial offices and even entered the senate in Rome. To the extent allowed by Roman imperial political and governmental structure, such proprietors had the capability of directing decision making and policies.

9 Villas and Capital Investment

As it has been pointed out, in the last decade a key issue in the debate about villas and the ancient economy has been the extent to which Roman landowners invested in improvements on their estates in order to maximize returns.[62] The issue of degree of capital investment in improving the efficiency of agricultural production goes hand in hand with the debate on the degree of the use of technology in the ancient world and on whether, as Finley thought, the availability of slave labour was a disincentive to practical applications of technical advances. To put it in Wilson's words:

> The debate on investment and economic rationality seems to have been under-pinned by the assumption that technological investment was unimportant, either because little significant advance was made in technology and therefore its application would have had little return, or because elite economic culture worked against investment and so any technological advances that were made were not widely applied.[63]

To this one has to add an additional assumption present in studies on the ancient economy, the fact that because ancient landowners did not measure profit and loss according to modern economic methods, they would have tended not to make capital investments, because they could not predict the return with precision.[64]

More recent archaeological data on villas, collected in excavations that have not focused exclusively on the elegant residential quarters but that have investigated the production facilities as well, offer some indication about attitudes to, and trends about, capital investment to ameliorate and maximise production on rural estates. In particular, the installation of wine presses is a

[62] A. I. WILSON, *Machines, Power and the Ancient Economy* in *JRS* 92, 2002, p. 1-32.
[63] WILSON, *Machines* [n. 62], p. 5-6.
[64] WILSON, *Machines* [n. 62], p. 6.

first important indicator of the willingness to invest capital in improving production. Unlike oil making,[65] a press is not necessary to make wine; it is possible to simply tread the grapes. However, adding a wine press increases efficiency in the extraction of the juice and when dealing with surplus production for the market outside the estate's needs, we always find one or more wine presses. Even though we do not know the exact cost of such installations, I would like to stress that the lever press (and later the lever and screw press), which was in common use in the late republican and early imperial period, was a bulky installation, that often occupied two entire rooms, housing the press-bed, the long wooden beam, and the counterweights used to bring down the beam. It was often the case that these rooms were purpose-built in the villa in order to install the press. Therefore, the installation of a wine press was an investment that required not simply the cost of the press itself, with its various components, but also the construction and commitment of a dedicated space, not to mention the regular maintenance needed for the apparatus. As mentioned above, many of the wine-producing villas identified in Gaul and Iberia, when they became larger and more opulent by the late first century / early second century AD, also notably increased the production facilities by installing multiple presses.[66] In Gaul, the chronology of all known multiple presses indicates that the peak in their installation occurred in the first and the first half of second century AD, in conjunction with the villa expansion (Fig. 1). In the Iberian Peninsula, where a higher number of sites with multiple presses is known, the available chronological data show a peak in installations in the Julio-Claudian period, followed by a smaller peak in the second half of the first century (Fig. 2). In the case of both wine and oil, the installation of multiple presses is concentrated in the first century AD.

[65] Rudimentary extraction methods in oil making that do not use presses are very inefficient, being able to extract only a small portion of the oil present in the fruit.

[66] For capital investment in multi-press facilities see: A. MARZANO, *Capital Investment and Agriculture: Multi-Press Facilities from Gaul, the Iberian Peninsula, and the Black Sea Region* in A. K. BOWMAN / A. WILSON (eds.), *The Roman Agricultural Economy: Organisation, Investment and Production*, Oxford, 2013, p. 107-142.

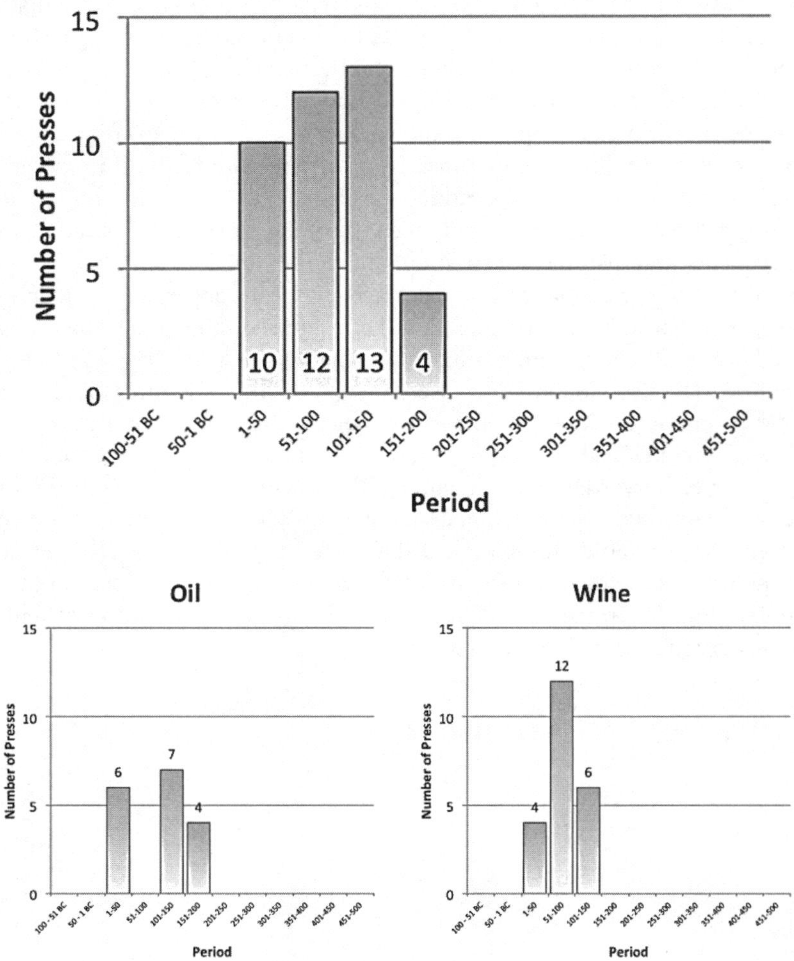

Figure 1. Gaul: installation date of all presses at multi-press sites, and according to type of production (n=39; n_{oil}=17; n_{wine}=22) (graphs by A. Marzano).

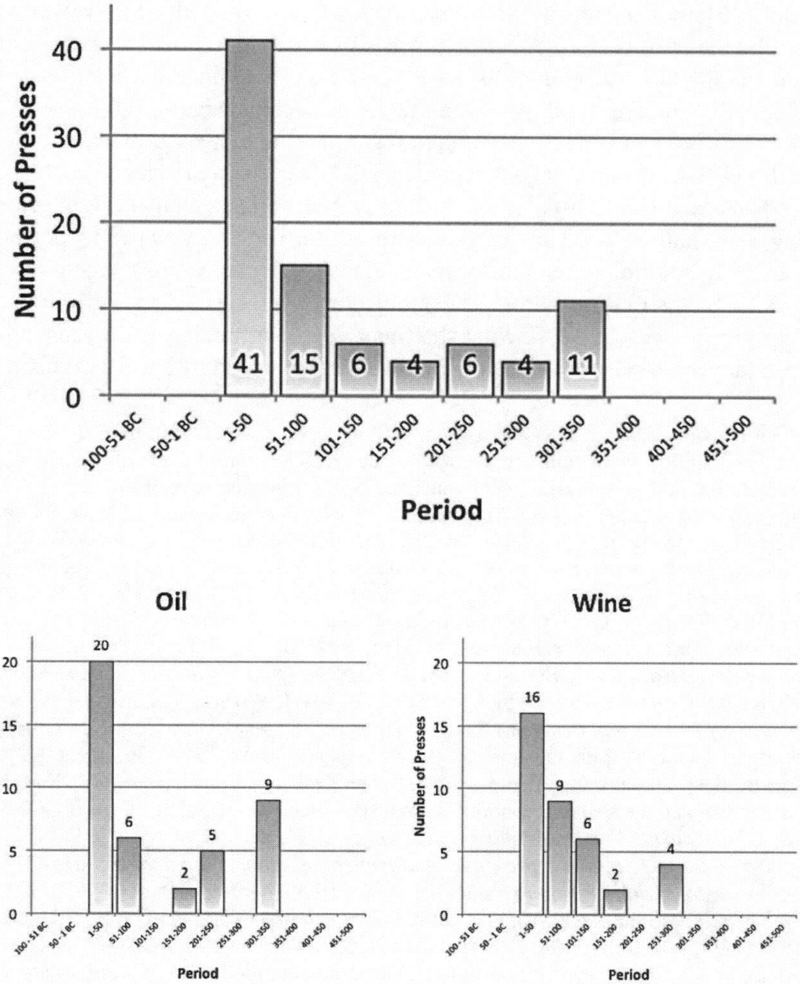

Figure 2. Iberian Peninsula: installation date of all presses and according to type of production (n=87; n_{oil}=42; n_{wine}=37) (graphs by A. Marzano).

That villas were indeed the place for investment in the rationalization of production and not simply in ostentatious display of wealth can be seen, in addition to the case of the presses, also in the case of the water-mills. Unlike decades ago, when it was believed that the water-mill had become common only in the Middle Ages and that water-mills were the foremost example of antiquity's missed opportunity in practically applying known technological advances to production,[67] we now know that, on the contrary, this technology spread rather rapidly. Many Roman water-mills are currently known, and we now even know that, by the third century AD, water-wheels were used to power stone saws.[68] In Gaul particularly several mills have been excavated in the context of villas equipped with other food processing facilities such as wine or oil presses.[69] The villa at St. Martin I mentioned above regarding the increased of the production facilities to the disadvantage of the residential quarters in the second century AD, also had a water-mill installed in the same period, taking advantage of the existing long and shallow pool in the garden to access necessary water to power the wheel.[70] In addition to remains of mills identified in excavations, recent research work by Samuel Longepierre has examined ancient millstones known in various local French museums, showing that many of them belonged to water-mills,[71] since they are too large and heavy to have been powered by animals. This points

[67] Vitruvius describes the geared water-mill at *Arch.* X, 5, 1-2, but until the late 1970s very few mills were known archaeologically. The refinement of archaeological investigation and preservation techniques and better understanding of the remains left by mills when the organic material (the wood of the wheel) is not preserved, have completely reversed this position: Wikander listed 23 water-mill sites known in 1984 (Ö. WIKANDER, *Exploitation of Water-Power or Technological Stagnation? A Reappraisal of the Productive Forces in the Roman Empire*, Lund, 1984), in 2000 he listed 56 (Ö. WIKANDER, *The Water-Mill* in Ö. WIKANDER (ed.), *Handbook of Ancient Water Technology. Technology and Change in History* 2, Leiden, 2000, p. 371-400); in 2006 just above 70 mills were known (A. K.BOWMAN / A. I. WILSON, *Quantifying the Roman Economy: Integration, Growth, Decline?* in A. K. BOWMAN / A. I. WILSON, *Quantifying the Roman Economy. Methods and Problems*, Oxford, 2009, p. 3-84 (esp. 34 and Fig. 1.2). Other early literary attestations of the existence of water-mills are Strabo XII, 3, 30, about the palace of Mithridates Eupator at Cabeira, and Antipater of Thessalonica, *Anth. Gr.* IX, 418. On water power and the ancient economy see WILSON, *Machines* [n. 62]; J.-P. BRUN, *L'energie hydraulique durant l'empire romain: quel impact sur l'economie agricole* in E. LO CASCIO (ed.*), Innovazione tecnica e progresso economico nel mondo romano: atti degli incontri capresi di storia dell'economia antica (Capri 13-16 Aprile 2003)*. Bari, 2006, p. 101-130.

[68] The relief on the sarcophagus of M. Aurelius Ammianos from Hierapolis, dated to the second half of the third century AD, depicts a stone saw mill with crank and connecting rod system; another funerary inscription from the same necropolis and of similar date attests the existence in Hierapolis of an association of water-millers (*syntechnia ton hydraleton*): T.RITTI / K.GREWE / P. KESSENER, *A Relief of a Water-Powered Stone Saw Mill at Hierapolis and Its Implications* in *JRA* 20, 2007, p. 138-163. Physical remains of stone-saw mills are known at Ephesus (water-powered marble saw located in a room of *Hanghaus* 2, at the end of at least five water-mills along the slope of the Bülbül Dağ, dated to the sixth century AD) and at Gerasa (stone saw-mill identified in the cryptoporticus of the Artemis Temple, also dated to the sixth century) (*ibid.*, p. 149-153).

[69] see e.g. J.-P. BRUN / M. BORREANI, *Deux moulins hydrauliques du Haut Empire romain en Narbonnaise. Villae des Mesclans à La Crau et de Saint-Pierre / Les Laurons aux Arcs (Var)* in *Gallia* 55, 1998, p. 279-326.

[70] BRUN, *Archéologie du vin et de l'huile* [n. 15], p. 43 for a plan and 45.

[71] S. LONGEPIERRE, *Meules, moulins et meulières en Gaule méridionale du IIe s.av. J.-C. au VIIe s. ap. J.-C*, Montagnac, 2012.

to the fact that the diffusion of water-mills in the rural context was much higher than what one can infer from the excavated mills alone.

It has to be stressed that these mills installed on the villa estate do not seem to have been used to process surplus grain in order to make flour for an external market; on the contrary, they were mills for the internal needs of the estate and its inhabitants/workers. The mills, usually operated by water coming from an aqueduct already servicing the villa, were in many cases located next to the kitchen and a bread oven. It is interesting that even in the case of the internal needs of the villa, capital was invested in order to expedite recurrent tasks, such as grinding wheat to make bread. This shows that there was a general interest in investing capital in technological advances and in rationalizing the use of the available resources. A water-mill had a higher output than an animal mill or one propelled by human force. It could work continuously and would thus free manpower and/or animals for other tasks. It is the larger villa sites that display the introduction of this technology, the same sites where we find the installation of multiple presses. These are the villas whose owners had more capital at their disposal, and who had larger networks and better connections, and could thus increase production. The appearance of villas in a region, then, could also be a tool in the diffusion of technology. As the arrival of colonists in a province introduced certain practices and technical knowledge, the large villa estates of the wealthy with available capital could also act as an instrument in the diffusion and application of new technologies.

10 Conclusions

The appearance of villas in an area is a recognisable sign of the growth potential in a given region—we have seen, for instance, that viticulture was introduced where before it was absent— so in this respect villas can be seen as indicators of regional growth. However, villas also put into motion a long series of decisions that had an impact on the economic and social fabric of the region, and even on trans-regional trade patterns, and can therefore be seen as instigators of growth. The regional economy was affected, as was labour and the degree of transfer of technology that took place. However, whether and how much the effects that the establishment of villas had on a region, which I discussed above, translated into proper economic growth (in macroeconomic terms) at the empire level remains an open question. Recently, the attempts of ancient historians to use deductive methods and proxy data in order to prove economic growth in antiquity have been heavily criticized.[72] These observations I offer on villas are meant to stimulate us to think of villas outside the rigid paradigm of the 'villa system'.

When using this expression, modern studies refer to estates producing predominantly cash crops for the market and employing slave labour. However, 'villa system' does not necessarily imply the use of slave labour; tenants in combination with slaves and seasonal workers often co-existed in the realm of the villa. In my opinion, more important features of the 'villa system' were the networks the owner had, which allowed for the wide distribution of the produce: access to labour, whether this consisted of tenants, hired seasonal labour, slaves, or a combination of all of these, and access to capital, to transportation means, and marketing networks. The decision to invest capital in the amelioration of productivity on an estate, a phenomenon which can be clearly seen in provinces such as Gaul, Baetica and Tarraconensis by the late first century and the second century AD, had repercussion for the whole region.

The owner's social network and the ability to access information were crucial. Without personal relations between, for example, a Roman senator and a local notable or without a Roman notable acquiring knowledge of an area perhaps through his service in the provincial administration, we would probably not see the willingness on the part of the upper class to own land in different parts of the empire. Even in the case of the establishment of farms and villas in the context of colonial foundations—therefore of land that was assigned to someone without the receiver's input into where he would end up owning the land—the later transformations of these farms into larger estates and well-equipped villas indicates that someone with purchasing power had increased the estate size, seeing these lands as an opportunity for growth, and made specific decisions about its management. The difference between a farm and a villa rests not simply in the total area they covered, in the volume of production, and in the cultivation of cash-crops versus polyculture aimed at self-sufficiency. Villas represent also access to information, social networks, organization, and management practices with social, political, and economic impact.

Archaeology also shows that large estate-owners were not, in principle, hostile to, or disinterested in, the practical application of technological advances that improved the efficiency of production. Capital was invested in ameliorating wine production by installing multiple presses (a technology that Italian colonists had brought with them when settling in the provinces), and man and animal power were freed from the laborious but necessary task of grinding grain for the internal needs of the villa by installing water-mills. Thanks to archaeological work carried out especially in the last ten years in France, it is now clear that the use of water-mills spread very quickly in the Roman world. Most large villas extensively

[72] F. Boldizzoni, *The Poverty of Clio. Resurrecting Economic History*, Princeton, 2011, p. 83-86.

excavated in France had water-mills, dating to between the mid-first century and the second century AD. Once, with the changed socio-political structure, these villas were abandoned in the fifth and sixth centuries and villages sprang up around the ruined villa structures, these water-mills were no longer used and people went back to use the basic and inefficient hand quern.

Anne KOLB

Epigraphy as a Source on Ancient Technology*

Economic productivity in antiquity was already substantially based on highly sophisticated procedures in the fields of agriculture, crafts, trade, building, transport as well as finance. With respect to technological progress, the thesis of stagnation caused by a lack of rationalisation or empirical orientation, postulated by Finley and others, is outdated.[1] Studies in the history of technology have shown that important technical achievements were not only used for military purposes, or in building or for water lifting[2] but also in many other areas, as, for instance, in power engineering.[3]

*This article is a revised version of my paper *Technik und Innovation des Imperium Romanum im Spiegel der epigraphischen Denkmäler* in B. ONKEN / D. RHODE (eds.), *In omni historia curiosus. Studien zur Geschichte von der Antike bis zur Neuzeit. Festschrift für Helmuth Schneider zum 65. Geburtstag*, Wiesbaden, 2011, p. 31-42, I thank Benjamin Hartmann (Zürich) for the translation.

[1] M.I. FINLEY, *The Ancient Economy. Updated with a New Foreword by Ian Morris*. Berkeley, 1999; lately on the broader discussion and the role of epigraphy J. EDMONDSON, *Economic Life in the Roman Empire* in C. BRUUN / J. EDMONDSON (eds.), *Oxford Handbook of Roman Epigraphy*, Oxford, 2014, p. 671-695; on ancient technology and its research B. MEISSNER, *Die antike Technik in der althistorischen Forschung* in W. KÖNIG / H. SCHNEIDER (eds.), *Die technikhistorische Forschung in Deutschland von 1800 bis zur Gegenwart*, Kassel, 2007, p. 163-188; H. SCHNEIDER, *Die antike Technik in der deutschen Archäologie nach 1945* in *ibid.*, p. 191-205; J. P. OLESON, (ed.), *The Oxford Handbook of Engineering and Technology in the Classical World*, Oxford, 2008.

[2] This limitation is still in J. P. OLESON, *Greek and Roman Water-lifting Devices*, Dordrecht, 1984.

[3] For the dissemination of watermills see W. PLEKET, *Greek Epigraphy and Comparative Ancient History: Two Case Studies* in *EA* 12, 1988, p. 25-38 (esp. p. 26-28); on the same topic and on further technologies see A. WILSON, *Machines, Power and the Ancient Economy* in *JRS* 92, 2002, p. 1-32; Ö. WIKANDER, *Sources of Energy and Exploitation of Power* in J. P. OLESON (ed.), *The Oxford Handbook of Engineering and Technology in the Classical World*, Oxford, 2008, p. 136-157; M. MALOUTA / A. WILSON, *Mechanical Irrigation. Water-Lifting Devices in the Archaeological Evidence and in the Egyptian Papyri* in A. BOWMAN / A. WILSON (eds.), *The Roman Agricultural Economy. Organization, Investment, and Production*, Oxford, 2013, p. 273-305. See also above the

Roman technologies and innovations are documented in various literary and material sources. The archaeological record and specialist literature are of special importance as they illustrate or—in the case of archaeological artefacts—even directly hand down the ancient state of knowledge and the practices associated with it, helping us to understand and reconstruct them.[4]

Inscriptions, however, have only rarely been studied in this context. This may be due to the fact that at first sight they either seem to be completely missing or provide only scarce and rudimentary information. By and large, scholars have only taken into consideration three longer inscriptions.[5] Two of these—the *lex metallis dicta* and the *lex territorio metalli Vipascensis dicta* (end of 1st / beginning of 2nd c.)—concern operating regulations of the mining district of Vipasca in modern southern Portugal.[6] A third and singular inscription, found in the North African city of Lambaesis, gives a detailed account of the problematic tunnel construction of an aqueduct that was undertaken around the middle of the 2nd century in Saldae (modern Bejaia in Algeria).[7]

This very limited yield of inscriptions containing references to technological achievements and innovations inevitably leads to the question of the representativity of the epigraphic evidence. The aim of this paper, therefore, is to analyse specific texts that provide information about techniques and technologies

contribution by Marzano.

4 For the sources see S. CUOMO, *Ancient Written Sources* in J. P. OLESON (ed.), *The Oxford Handbook of Engineering and Technology in the Classical World*, Oxford, 2008, p. 15-34 (esp. p. 28); B. CECH, *Technik in der Antike*, Darmstadt, 2010, p. 17.

5 See especially H. SCHNEIDER, *Die Gaben des Prometheus. Technik im antiken Mittelmeerraum zwischen 750 v. Chr. und 500 n. Chr.* in W. KÖNIG (ed.), *Propyläen Technikgeschichte*, Berlin, 1990, p. 19-313 (esp. 226, 228, 288); H. SCHNEIDER, *Einführung in die antike Technikgeschichte*, Darmstadt, 1992, p. 76-77, 87, 192; H. SCHNEIDER, *Geschichte der antiken Technik,* München, 2007, p. 93, 116; cf. the literature in notes 6 and 7.

6 *CIL* II, 5181 (*Metallum Vipascense*, Lusitania) = C. DOMERGUE, *La mine antique d'Aljustrel (Portugal) et les tables de bronze de Vipasca*, Paris, 1983, p. 114-121; edited individually: a) *Lex metallis dicta:* FIRA I² 104 = D. FLACH, *Die Bergwerksordnungen von Vipasca* in *Chiron* 9, 1979, p. 399-448 (esp. p. 399-407); b) *Lex metalli Vipascensis:* FIRA I² 105 = FLACH, *ibid.*, p. 407-413; cf. S. LAZZARINI, Lex metallis dicta. *Studi sulla seconda tavola di Vipasca*, Roma, 2001; for questions about the administration and the scope of the regulations found in the two inscriptions see P. EICH, *Zur Metamorphose des politischen Systems in der römischen Kaiserzeit: die Entstehung einer "personalen Bürokratie" im langen dritten Jahrhundert*, Berlin, 2005, p 315, 322-323, concerning the dating of the inscriptions 322 note 2; A. M. HIRT, *Imperial Mines and Quarries in the Roman World. Organizational Aspects 27 BC-AD 235*, Oxford, 2010, p. 2-4, 261-269 and *passim*.

7 *CIL* VIII, 2728 = 18122 = *ILS* 5795 (Lambaesis, Numidia); thereto most recently K. GREWE, *Tunnels and Canals* in J. P. OLESON (ed.), *The Oxford Handbook of Engineering and Technology in the Classical World*, Oxford, 2008, p. 319-336 (esp. 329-333); S. CUOMO, *A Roman Engineer's Tales* in *JRS* 101, 2011, p. 1-23.

of any kind and that refer to details about technological methods. We will question the intention and context of these sources. The documents will be presented according to the conventional generic classification of epigraphic sources. Finally, we will briefly ask whether these and other sources provide information about the economic purposes and consequences of technological achievements and innovations.

1 Public records

As already mentioned, the two texts from Vipasca (end of 1st / beginning of 2nd c.) provide information about the operating regulations of the local silver mines. They describe various aspects of mining technology and regulations, particularly regarding security measures. In the Roman west such *leges* were, just like other important and long-standing rulings, recorded on bronze tablets (cf. particularly the town statutes). They were intended to communicate provisions of the Roman administration, primarily trying to guarantee a smooth organisation (including the social conditions of the local population) and an efficient management.

Two further extraordinary public records explicitly focus on technology in the Roman building trade. These inscriptions cannot be compared to any other document, as they not only record specifics regarding building projects but also technically explain the organisation of the construction works in question. An epigraphic legal document of republican times from Puteoli, the so-called *lex parieti faciundo Puteolana* (105 BC), contains a request to tenders.[8] Besides legal and organisational aspects of the work—such as deadlines, magistrates in charge, salary and the name of the contractor—the document accurately lists the particulars on how to erect the enclosure and the monumental gateway to a sacred precinct, complete with information about measurements, building materials and timber construction technique. Because the initial invitation to bid was issued by the community of Puteoli, the epigraphic publication announcing the completion of the construction works took the form of a deed of foundation. In this way, every single citizen was able to assess the works financed by the community.

The second document describes organisational and technical problems related to the construction of a theatre in Miletus (AD 120) that were solved by the

[8] *CIL* I², 698 = *ILS* 5317; for text, translation, and comprehensive commentary see Th. WIEGAND, *Die puteolanische Bauinschrift sachlich erläutert* in *Jahrbücher für classische Philologie* Supp. 20, 1894, p. 660-778; most recently with text and a translation J.-M. LASSÈRE, *Manuel d'épigraphie romaine*, Paris, 2005, p. 402-405, nr. 249; cf. for legal aspects J.-J. AUBERT, *En guise d'introduction: contrats publics et cahiers des charges* in J.-J. AUBERT (ed.), *Tâches publiques et entreprise privée dans le monde romain*, Neuchâtel / Genève, 2003, p. 1-25.

consultation of the oracle of Apollo of Didyma. The answer of the god, who was questioned by workers on how to proceed after a change in construction management, is recorded on a limestone block in the theatre.[9] The builders had discontinued work on the arches and cross vaults of the upper ambulatory, possibly because these operations turned out to be more difficult, complex, or dangerous than expected. The oracle resolved the uncertainties and the disputes that had sprung from them. Thus, with the god's assistance, the complex construction works were brought to a successful conclusion. By eventually incorporating the inscription into the building, this fact was made clearly visible to all visitors.

Irrigation techniques are illustrated by a series of other epigraphic documents. These texts record the regulations necessary to define the conditions under which the water could be received, or more specifically used, by residents and others for economic (usually agrarian) purposes. Most commonly, the landowner guaranteed the irrigation by limiting the times at which water could be tapped. The corresponding public documents on stone or bronze were intended to set up the modalities and disclose these to the public.[10]

An official record from Greece contains particularly interesting evidence, revealing objectives of construction engineering as well as economic policy. In a letter dating from AD 125, the emperor Hadrian informed the citizens of the west Boeotian community of Koroneia about his plans to protect the cropland of the Kopais valley from flooding: at his order, the estuarial areas of the rivers were to be regulated while the Kopais valley was to be drained by erecting dams at the banks of the Kephisos, the Herkynna, and other rivers.[11] Furthermore, the

[9] *I. Milet* VI 2, 935 = *SGO* 01/20/01; cf. M. DONDERER, *Die Architekten der späten römischen Republik und der Kaiserzeit: epigraphische Zeugnisse*, Erlangen, 1996, p. 91-93, 156-158. On the circumstances of the find Th. WIEGAND, *Dritter vorläufiger Bericht über die Ausgrabungen der Königl. Museen zu Milet* in *Archäologischer Anzeiger* 19, 1904, p. 2-10 states: "beim Eingang in den oberen Umgang auf einem Kalksteinblock an der Südseite des obersten Treppenabsatzes des Westflügels in situ" (p. 8).

[10] *CIL* VI, 1261; XIV, 3676; VIII, 4440 = 18587 = *ILS* 5793; *AÉ* 2006, 676; thereto F. BELTRÁN LLORIS, *An Irrigation Decree from Roman Spain: The Lex Rivi Hiberiensis* in *JRS* 96, 2006, p. 147-197 and ID., *La lex rivi Hiberiensis nel suo contesto. I pagi e l'organizzazione dell'irrigazione in Caesar Augusta* in L. MAGANZANI / C. BUZZACCHI (ed.), *Lex Rivi Hiberiensis. Diritto e tecnica in una comunità di irrigazione della Spagna Romana. Giornate di studio in ricordo di Giorgio Luraschi, Milano 2-3 luglio 2012*, Napolina, 2014, p. 55-73; cf. C. J. BANNON, *Gardens and Neighbors; Private Water Rights in Roman Italy*, Ann Arbor, 2009, p. 76-81, 111-113.

[11] *AÉ* 1986, 636a = *SEG* 32, 460 (Koroneia, Achaia): Ἀγαθὴ τύχῃ / Αὐτοκράτωρ Καῖσαρ, θεοῦ Τραϊανοῦ Παρθικοῦ υἱός, θεοῦ Νέρουα υἱωνός, / Τραϊανός Ἁδριανὸς Σεβαστός, ἀρχιερεὺς μέγιστος, δημαρχικῆς ἐξουσίας / τὸ θʹ, ὕπατος τὸ γʹ, Κορωνέων τοῖς ἄρχουσι καὶ τῇ βουλῇ καὶ τῶι / / δήμωι vac. Χαίρειν vac. / Ἐκέλευσα γενέσθαι χώματα τῷ Κηφεισῷ καὶ τῇ Ἑρκύννῃ καὶ τοῖς ἄλ/λοις ποταμοῖς καθὸ ἤδη μετ'ἀλλήλων ῥέοντες εἰς τὴν

emperor announced he would deal with the water supply of the city at his own expenses. This imperial letter, announcing new building projects, was designed to warrant flood control as well as to ensure agrarian production, as these measures were vital not only to the population's food supply but ultimately also to the area's tax revenues. While the epigraphic document attests technological achievements, its primary concern nonetheless was of a fiscal and economic nature.

2 Funerary, Honorific, and Votive Inscriptions

The already mentioned inscription from the North African city of Lambaesis gives an elaborate account of the cutting of an aqueduct tunnel through a mountain from both ends.[12] The construction works in Saldae (modern Bejaia in Algeria, middle of 2nd c.) were confronted with several problems, described in detail by the leading engineer Lucius Nonius Datus. He describes how the two work units that according to his plans were ordered to channel through the mountain from both ends simultaneously had missed each other at the centre. It was only after his return and through renewed efforts of measurement that the error was corrected and the work could be finished. The inscription seems originally to have belonged to the funerary monument of Lucius Nonius Datus (in the form of an octagonal *cippus*, partly ornamented with images in bas-relief), erected by himself during his lifetime. The inscription served as a medium of self-representation, visualising the accomplishments of the proud architect in the field of surveying engineering.[13]

No other documents describing technological methods in a similarly exhaustive way are known today. However, such testimonia must have been much more frequent than the small number of surviving monuments suggests.[14] Several funerary inscriptions of engineers and craftsmen, especially in the sectors of water

Κωπαΐδα / λίμνην ἐμβάλλουσιν· καὶ γενήσεται τὴν ταχίστην ὡς κατὰ τὰς / ὄχθας ῥέοντες μὴ ἐκτρέποιντο τοῦ πόρου μήδε, ὥσπερ νῦν, // ἐπικλυζοῖεν τὴν πολλὴν τῆς χώρας τῆς ἐργασίμου· Κατάξω / δὲὑμεῖνκαὶὕδωρ· Καὶ τὸ μὲν ἀργύριον δοθήσεται παρ'ἐμοῦ / ἕξ καὶ ἥμισυ μυριάδες ὅσου δεήσειν ἔφασκον οἱ τῶν τοιού/των ἐπιστήμονες, ὑμεῖς δὲ ἑλέσθε τοὺς ἐπιμελησομέ/νους.

[12] *CIL* VIII, 2728 = 18122 = *ILS* 5795 (Lambaesis, Numidia); see further note 7.

[13] Note the wording in *CIL* VIII, 2728, ll. 54-60: … *ego qui pri/mus libram feceram / ductum atsignaueram(!) / fieri institueram se/cundum formam quam Petronio Celeri pro(curatori) / dederam opus (!) effectum….*

[14] Cf. the glassmaker in *CIL* XIII, 2000 = *ILS* 7648 (Lugdunum, Gallia Lugdunensis): *D(is) M(anibus) / et memoriae aetern(a)e Iul/i Alexsa(n)dri(!) natione Afri ciui / Carthagine(n)si (h)omini optimo opif/ici artis uitriae ....*

engineering[15] and the building trade,[16] display a comparable self-confident demeanour. Nevertheless, they mention only a few details concerning the technical realisation of the projects involved.

Such displays of praise for and pride in extraordinary technological achievements are also found in other types of epigraphic texts that were used to represent their authors or other protagonists, such as honorific, panegyric, and votive inscriptions.

A special honorary inscription is found on a well-known monument at the centre of the empire; the inscription on Trajan's column in Rome:

> *Romanus / Imp(eratori) ... Neruae / Traiano ... pontif(ici) / maximo ... p(atriae) / ad ... altitudinis / mons et locus tant[is oper]ibus sit egestus.*[17]

The text on the base of Trajan's column, inaugurated on the 13th of May AD 113 as the showpiece of the emperor Trajan's (AD 98-117) *Forum Traiani*, refers to the building operations conducted during the years AD 107 to 112 that prepared the construction of this massive triumphal site—still admired by the emperor Constantius II during his visit to Rome in AD 354 as "a construction unique under the heavens […] and admirable even in the unanimous opinion of the gods".[18] Trajan had this imperial forum, which was the last and grandest of the imperial fora of Rome, built from the spoils of his Dacian wars (AD 101-102 and 105-106). The senate and the people of Rome honoured their emperor by donating this honorary monument consisting of a column and a mounted effigy of Trajan. Thus, they not only acknowledged him as a victorious general and extraordinary ruler, but also as a magnificent architect, who had achieved exceptional building feats at the heart of the empire's capital. Indeed, in order to make room for the huge building complex consisting of a square (lined by two galleries with exedrae and a monumental gateway), the Basilica Ulpia as well as two libraries, the ridge between the Quirinal and the Capitol was removed. Huge amounts of soil were

[15] *CIL* XII, 722 = *ILS* 7715 (Arelate, Gallia Narbonensis) *D(is) M(anibus) / Q(uinti) Candi[di] Benigni fab(ri) tig(narii) c/orp(oris) Ar(elatis) ars cui summa fuit / fabricae, studium doctrin(ae) / pudorque, quem magni / artifices semper dix{s}ere / magistrum. doctior hoc ne/mo fuit, potuit quem uinc/ere nemo, organa qui nosse/t facere aquarum aut duce/re cursum hic couuiua (!) fui/t dulcis, nosset qui pasce/re amicos, ingenio studio / docilis animoque benig/nus. Candidia Quintina / patri dulcissimo et Val(eria) / Maxsimina(!) coniugi kar(issimo).*

[16] See the two funerary poems for builders in *IK* XXXIV, 468 (Mylasa, Asia) and in E. BERNAND, *Inscriptions métriques de l'Egypte gréco-romaine; Recherches sur la poésie épigrammatique des Grecs en Egypte*, Paris, 1969, p. 128-133, no. 23; cf. DONDERER, *Architekten* [n. 9], p. 91-93, 110-112.

[17] *CIL* VI, 960 = *ILS* 294; further A. KOLB / F. FUGMANN, *Tod in Rom. Grabinschriften als Spiegel römischen Lebens*, Mainz 2008, p. 36-40.

[18] Ammianus XVI, 10, 15: *(...) singularem sub omni caelo structuram, ut opinamur, etiam numinum assensione mirabilem (...)* (Transl. J. C. Rolfe).

moved, according to the inscription amounting to the height of the column of 100 Roman feet (29.78 m). Thus, this honorary inscription for the emperor Trajan constitutes important evidence of Roman engineering as the monument explicitly documents the technological effort needed to build the forum and at the same time commemorates this extraordinary achievement of Roman engineering.

An inscription from Lycia (AD 134) is quite remarkable too. It contains the self-praise of two woodworkers who apparently were the first to transport cedar wood of the highest quality, presumably for use as building material, out of a deep and inaccessible ravine.[19] Apart from solving the logistical problems, the innovation of the two specialists primarily consisted of cutting up the logs already at the felling site, i.e. in the ravine itself, making it easier to transport the timber to the collecting point, which must have been situated near the road. The inscription is recorded on a plain limestone block (in a *tabula ansata*). Unfortunately, its original architectural context is lost. As the inscription was found close to the Claudian road from Neisa to Choma, the original location of the monument might have to be sought in its proximity, e.g. in a possible terminal or storage location. It is unusual that the inscription is not formulated as an honorary or votive inscription but as outright evidence for the achievement of the woodworkers. One could perhaps assume that the woodworkers ascribed their success to divine help and subsequently erected a votive monument. Accordingly, the block, if it did not serve as a basis for a statue of a deity, might originally have belonged to such a monument, for example as an element of a small cultic building.

While donors usually offered such votive gifts in recognition of the divine help they experienced, other votive inscriptions display the additional purpose to reveal the labours and expenditures that were needed to accomplish the donation. Information about technology is usually either wholly absent or only mentioned briefly and summarily.[20] The texts only offered more technological detail if

[19] *SEG* 57, 1667 = S. ŞAHIN, *Zwei Holzfäller und der Wald in der Kartapis bei Neisa* in *Gephyra* 4, 2007, p. 37-45: Ἐπὶ ἀρχι(ερέως) Κιλόρτου / ἀπὸ τῆς ἐν Καρταπίδι ὕ/λης οὐδέποτε οὐδεὶς πρί/ωμα ἔξήγαγε<ν> ἴκρι<α>, ἀλλὰ / μόνοι Ἀρτεμῆς Ἑρμαίου / τοῦ Ἀπολλωνίου *(vac.)* καὶ / Ἑρμαῖος δὶς τοῦ Θεοδότο/υ Νεισεῖς ἐπεχείρησαν. / οἱ ἀναγεινώσκοντες / εὐτυχεῖτε.

[20] *CIL* V, 1863 = *ILS* 5886 (Iulium Carnicum, Italia): *[I(oui) O(ptimo)] M(aximo) / [Triuiis Quadri]uiis ceterisque dib(us) / aram o[b solutum merit]o sollemne uotum d[ed(it)] / Hermias succeptor operis aeterni, / titulum immanem, montem Alpinum / ingentem litteris inscripsit, quot saepe / inuium, commiantium (!) periclitante / popu[l]o, ad pontem transitum non / placuit, curiae et Attio Braetiano / q(uaestore) eorum, uiro ornato, uiam nou(am) / demonstrante Hermia. Multa ni/mis fides operisque paratus una/nimes omnes hanc uiam explicuit*; *CIL* III, *259 = *AÉ* 1955, 119 (Cetium, Noricum): *D(eo) Neptuno / [aq]uarum / [po]tenti / [ob i]nductum / [in] Tragisa(mum) / [riu]um / [---] Aur(elius) / [---]lius / [u(ir) p(erfectissimus)] a(gens) u(ices) p(raesidis) / [u(otum) s(oluit)] l(ibens) l(aetus) m(erito).*

special circumstances warranted such, as one inscription from North Africa shows: *Caelesti Aug(ustae) Granianae sacr[um] / Voltius Senecio templum ui fluminis ereptum transtulit et a solo fecit idemque dedica[uit].*[21] The sanctuary of a popular local sky goddess had been carried away by the rising flood waters of a river. Voltius Senecio, an euergetist, took care of disassembling the cult building and re-erecting it at another site. Such actions may have been common in ancient times, although they are not mentioned otherwise.[22]

Further references to difficult or interesting building techniques and facilities can be found in epigraphic epigrams that celebrated especially successful, important, or useful buildings.[23] Some of these texts also focus on the architect or the builder by publicly stating his achievements so that his name might be remembered. A late antique epigram from Adana (first half of 4th c. AD) describes the massively solid reinforcement of a river bank and the related building of a bridge by an architect called Auxentius, whose execution of the construction work is specified by technical details. The quays, which were built on a foundation reinforced by iron dowels and were spanned by an extremely sturdy and wide bridge, were designed to hold back the mostly wintry rip tides of the Saros and prevent it from flooding the surroundings.[24] Whether this poem for the glory of the architect, written on a

[21] *ILAfr.* 345 (Haut Mornag, Africa Proconsularis).

[22] This inscription once again shows how the genres of votive and building inscriptions overlap if a votive inscription at the same time documents a building measure.

[23] *CIL* VIII, 21081 = *CLE* 276 = S. BUSCH, *Versus Balnearum. Die antike Dichtung über Bäder und Baden im römischen Reich*, Stuttgart, 1999, p. 229-230 (Caesarea, Mauretania): *Vit<r>ea quot longis sunt / tecta excepta columnis / ac docili libra teretem q/uot flexus in arcum est, / marmore quot Pareo uiuunt / spirantia signa aequo[ris] / [e]t uario quot p[rofluit unda meatu ---]*; *SEG* 36, 1343 (Gadara, Syria): Μηκέτι τάρβος ἔχοιτε λοετροφόρου ἀσαμίνθου / οὐλομένης ἣ μύρια πολλοῖς ἄλγε' ἔθηκεν / [ἄ]νδρας σινομένη κτείνουσά τε πολλάκι παῖδας / [---]ς γὰρ ὕπερθεν ὅλην κατεχώσατο γαίη· / [χώματ]α δὲ στορέσας φιλοπαίγμονα θήκατο χῶρον / [πηγάς τ'ἔκτο]θι δοὺς τερψίμβροτον ἑλκέμεν ὕδωρ; *Fouilles des Xanthos* I, 1958, 110 (Xanthos, Lycia): Ὀνάσανδρος Ὀνασάν[δρου τοῦ] / Ὀνασά[ν]δρου Ξάνθιος ἀρχιτ[εκτονή]σας / τὸν κα[---]α σὺν τῇ[β]άσει [καὶ τῷ] / ἐπικε[ιμένῳ] κόσμ[ῳ ---] / ἐπ΄αὐτῷ [---]ιστεμ[---] / εντωμ[---]νρ[---]υθ[---] / μι[--- ἀπ]οκαθελὼν ἑλκύσας / μετέθηκεν; *SEG* 32, 1502 = *SGO* 21/22/01 (Gadara, Syria): Εὐδοκίας Αὐγούστης / Πολλά μὲν ἐν βιότῳ κ(αὶ) ἀπίρονα θαύματ'ὄπωπα / τίς δέ μεν ἐξερέοι, πόσα δὲ στόματ', ὦ κλίβαν' ἐσθλέ / σὸν μένος, οὐτιδανὸς γεγαὼς βροτός; Ἀλλά σε μᾶλλο(ν) / ὠκεανὸν πυρόεντα νέον θέμις ἐστὶ καλεῖσθαι. / Παιάνα καὶ γενέτην γλυκερῶν δοτῆρα ῥεέθρων. / Ἐκ σέο τίκτεται οἶδμα τὸ μυρίον, ἄλλυδις ἄλλῃ, / ὅππῃ μὲν ζεῖον, πῇ δ'αὖ κρυερόν τε μέσον τε. / Τετράδας ἐς πίσυρας κρηνῶν προχέεις σέο κάλλος. / / ... / ἀλλὰ θεὸν κλυτόμητιν ἀείσο[μαι ---] / εἰς εὐεργεσείην μερόπων τε χρ[---].

[24] *CIG* III, 4440 = *IGR* III, 887 = *SGO* 19/14/01 (Adana, Cilica): ὄντως σῆς ἀρετῆς, Αὐξέντιε, καὶ τόδε θαῦμα / δείμασθαι ποταμοῦ χειμερίοισι δρόμοι[ς] / ἄῤῥηκτον (?) κρηπῖδα σιδηροθέτοισι θεμείλοις /ὧν ὕπερ εὐρείην ἐξετάνυσσας ὁδόν, / ἣν πολλοὶ καὶ πρόσθεν ἀπειρείῃσι νό[οι]ο / Κυδναίων ῥείθρων τεῦξαν ἀφαυροτέρην. /σοὶ δ' ὑπὲρ ἀψίδων αἰώνιος ἐῤῥίζωθαι / καὶ ποταμὸς πλήθω[ν] πρηΰτερος τε[λ]έθει, / αὐτὸς τήνδ[ε] γέφυραν ἀνασχόμενος τελέσ[α]σθ[αι / ἡγεμόνος π[ε]ιθο[ῖ] τοῦ διασημοτάτο[υ, / ὄφρα

block of stone, originally belonged to an honorary monument, a consecration for a god, or rather to a building inscription cannot be ascertained.

3 Building Inscriptions

The mention or description of technological feats of craftsmanship is most common in building inscriptions when difficulties had been encountered with very complex and elaborate constructions. In general, inscriptions that attest the construction of highly engineered facilities such as aqueducts, tunnels, roads, or canals only rarely specify the procedure, working methods, difficult working conditions, or other interesting features. Most inscriptions merely attest the conclusion of the works by adding *f(aciendum) c(urauit)* or similar formulations.[25] Inscriptions with technological details were set up—as is usual for building inscriptions—at the instigation of private builders,[26] municipal magistrates,[27] governors or other representatives of the Roman

σε καὶ μετόπισθεν ἔχοι κλέος ἶσον ἐκείνοις / οἳ Νείλου προχοὰς ζεῦξαν ἀπειρεσίους; cf. DONDERER, *Architekten* [n. 9], p. 94-96.

[25] See e.g. the brief inscription of the formidable tunnel construction by Vespasian and Titus in Cevlik/Seleukia Pieria in modern Turkey: *CIL* III, 6702 = *IGLS* 3/2, 1131: *Diuus Vespasianus / et diuus Titus f(aciendum) c(urauerunt).*

[26] *CIL* IX, 3018 = *ILS* 5761 (Teate Marrucinorum, Italia): *In honorem domus / Augustae / Dusmia M(arci) f(ilia) Numisilla / nomine suo et L(uci) Trebi Secundi / uiri sui aquam quae a C(aio) Asinio / Gallo perducta interciderat / repetitam a capite adiecta structura / specus et puteorum nouis bracchis / ampliatam s(ua) p(ecunia) reduxit; CIL* XII, 2494 = *ILS* 5768 (Marigny-Saint-Marcel, Gallia Narbonensis): *C(aius) Sennius C(ai) f(ilius) Vol(tinia) Sabinus praef(ctus) fabr(um) / balineum campum porticus aquas iusque / earum aquarum tubo ducendarum ita ut recte / perfluere possint uicanis Albinnensibus d(e) s(uo) d(edit).*

[27] *CIL* X, 6526 = *ILS* 5772 (Cora, Italia): *C(aius) Oppius Verus L(ucius) Turpilius / Priscus f(ilius) IIIIuir(i) i(ure) d(icundo) / ex aquam caelestem dilabentem mon/tibus collectam interciso aggere / per formam cur(a) sua factam in pisci/nis repurgatis longo tempore ces/santibus p(ecunia) p(ublica) perduxerunt / et PE[---]AO[---]; CIL* X, 4654 = *ILS* 5779 (Cales, Italia): *Ex s(enatus) c(onsulto) honoris Q(uinti) Paconii Q(uinti) f(ilii) / Lepta[e] ergo / lacus fistulaeque con/stitutae substructae quo / commodius in eius domum / aqua pura duceretur quod / is de r(e) p(ublica) saepe numero bene / meritus esset mereretur q(ue) / Q(uintus) Paconius Q(uinti) f(ilius) Lept[a] IIIIuir / quinquennalis ex s(enatus) c(onsulto) / locauit idemqu[e] probauit.*

administration,[28] or the emperor himself.[29]

A very interesting example in this category is an inscription from the Lycian city of Patara, which attests the construction of an aqueduct commissioned by Vespasian and the innovation triggered by these works:[30]

> After the wall of the aqueduct had been destroyed by an earthquake, Imperator Caesar Flavius Vespasianus Augustus had it rebuilt together with the aqueduct made of stone blocks on top of it. In addition, he ordered earthenware pipes of a hand's width for water under pressure to be laid in three rows along the wall. As a result, the flow of the

[28] *CIL* VIII, 2661 (p. 1739) = *ILS* 5788 (Lambaesis, Numidia): *Aquam Titulensem quam ante annos / plurimos Lambaesitana ciuitas in/teruerso ductu ui torrentis amiserat / perforato monte instituto etiam a / solo nouo ductu Seuerinius Apronianus u(ir) p(erfectissimus) p(raeses) p(rouinciae) N(umidiae) / pat(ronus) col(oniae) restituit cur(ante) Aelio Rufo u(iro) e(gregio) fl(amine) p(er)p(etuo) cur(atore) r(ei) p(ublicae); ILAlg* II, 3596 (Castellum Tidditanorum, Numidia): *Ex i[ndu]lgentia prouidentiaq(ue) / diuina dd. nn. (i.e. dominorum nostrorum duorum) / Impp. (i.e. imperatorum duorum) <<Galli>> et <<Vol{l}usiani>> Augg. (i.e. Augustorum duorum) / M(arcus) Cocceius Anicius Faustus Flauianus / consular(is) et XVuir curator / et patronus coloniar(um) Cirt(ensium) / egestis per populum quae uicina / superauerant ruderibus / caesoque ad planitiem qui / nudatus extiterat monte / ad salutem populi aquam / excipi prouidit*; cf. the building of a pier and a basin in the harbour of Smyrna commissioned by the governor Venetios, *Anthologia Palatina* IX, 670 = *SOG* 05/01/19 (Smyrna, Asia).

[29] *CIL* VI, 1245 (p. 3125, 3797, 4363) = *ILS* 98b (Roma): *Imp(erator) Caes(ar) M(arcus) Aurellius(!) Antoninus Pius Felix Aug(ustus) Parth(icus) maxim(us) / Brit(annicus) maximus pontifex maximus / aquam Marciam uariis kasibus impeditam purgato fonte excisis et perforatis / montibus restituta forma adquisito etiam fonte nouo Antoniniano / in sacram urbem suam perducendam curauit*; *CIL* X, 6811 = *ILS* 489 (Ardea, Italia): *Imp(erator) Caes(ar) [[C(aius) Iulius]] / [[Verus Maximinus]] / Pius Felix Aug(ustus) / pontif(ex) max(imus) Germ(anicus) max(imus) / Dacicus max(imus) Sarm(aticus) max(imus) / trib(unicia) potest(ate) IIII imp(erator) V / co(n)s(ul) proco(n)s(ul) p(ater) p(atriae) et / [[C(aius) Iulius Verus Ma]]/[[ximus nob(ilissimus) Caesar]] / Germ(anicus) max(imus) Dacicus max(imus) / Sarmaticus max(imus) / princeps iuuentutis / litus uicinum uiae Seuerianae / adsiduis maris adluentibus / fluctibus ad labem ruinae / labefactatum aggeribus / marini operis a fundamentis / ut periculum commeantibus / abesset extrui curarunt.*

[30] *SEG* 57, 1673; S. ŞAHIN, *Die Bauinschrift auf dem Druckrohraquädukt von Delikkemer bei Patara* in Ch. SCHULER (ed.), *Griechische Epigraphik in Lykien; Eine Zwischenbilanz*, Wien, 2007, p. 99-109; now also H. IŞKAN-IŞIK / W. ECK / H. ENGELMANN, *Der Leuchtturm von Patara* in *ZPE* 164, 2008, p. 91-121 (esp. p. 116) (with German translation): Αὐτοκράτωρ Καῖσαρ Φλάουιος Οὐεσπασιανὸς Σεβαστὸς / τὸ τοῦ ὑδραγωγίου ἀνάλημμα συμπεσὸν σεισμοῖς ἐκ θεμελίων ἀποκατέστησε σὺν / τοῖς ἐπ' αὐτῷ λιθίνοις ἐκ τετραπέδου λίθου σωλῆσι προστεθέντος καὶ ἑτέρου παρὰ τὸ / ἀνάλημμα θλειμματικοῦ ὑδραγωγίου διὰ τριστίχων σωλήνων ὀστρακινῶν παλαιστι/αίων ὥστε δυεῖν ὄντων εἰ θάτερον ἐπισκευῆς δεηθείῃ, μὴ ἐνποδίζεσθαι τὸν δρόμον / ἀδιαλείπτου μενούσης τῆς χρήσεως...; relevance and context discussed by Ch. SCHULER, *Fernwasserleitungen und römische Administration im griechischen Osten* in KOLB, *Infrastruktur* [n. 9], p. 103-120.

watercourse is not hindered when the pipes need maintenance and the usage is not interrupted because there now are two channels.

This text not only documents the completion of the building or repair work, but points also to a technological achievement of the new construction: next to the stone aqueduct a second supply channel was constructed out of earthenware pipes in order to ensure the water supply of the population of Patara during the frequent cleaning and overhaul periods. By recording the precise technical execution and the design of the water supply in Patara as well as its novelties, the inscription constitutes an important document in the history of technology. Yet, this inscription with its extensive account and mention of innovation makes a singular appearance in its genre, as building inscriptions are usually only interested in the builder, the building as such and the completion of it, while information about building methods is either completely lacking or is only given briefly and summarily.

The biggest group of building inscriptions that provide information on building techniques consists of documents about road building. This is not surprising as questions of transportation infrastructure were a domain of particular interest to the emperors. Indeed, good transport connections between cities and the dense network of roads and waterways throughout the empire—made possible by the *Pax Romana* due to imperial protection—were not only important to imperial policy but above all to the administration and the economy. In order to travel and conduct transport efficiently—primarily on behalf of the state—the main links had to be open to traffic. Difficult terrain often demanded technically complex operations, which, if successful, were documented by inscriptions. Particular works consisted of the removal and the intersection of mountains and rocks, often expressed in inscriptions with established phraseology like *montibus caesis*.[31] The

[31] *CIL* III, 227 = 12118 = 14177, 11 = *IK* LV, 135 (Gülek Bogazi, Cilicia): *Imp(erator) Ca(e)sar Marcus Au/relius [[Antoninus pi]]us / felix inuictus Augu/stus montibus caesi[s] / uiam latiorem fecit.* ὅροι Κιλί/κων; *CIL* III, 206 (p. 973) = *ILS* 5865 (Berytus, Syria): *Imp(erator) Caes(ar) M(arcus) Aurelius / Antoninus Pius Felix Augustus / Part(hicus) max(imus) Brit(annicus) max(imus) Germ(anicus) maximus / pontifex maximus / montibus inminentibus / Lyco flumini caesis uiam delatauit / per [[leg(ionem) III Gallicam]] / Antoninianam suam; CIL* III, 199 (p. 1228) = *ILS* 5864 (Suq Wadi Barada, Syria): *Imp(erator) Caes(ar) M(arcus) Aurel(ius) Antoninus / Aug(ustus) Armeniacus et / Imp(erator) Caes(ar) L(ucius) Aurel(ius) Verus Aug(ustus) Ar/meniacus uiam fluminis / ui abruptam interciso / monte restituerunt per / Iul(ium) Verum leg(atum) pr(o) pr(aetore) prouinc(iae) / Syr(iae) et amicum suum / inpendiis Abilenorum*; *CIL* III, 6983 = *ILS* 5883 = *IGR* III, 83 = Ch. Marek, *Stadt, Ära und Territorium*, Tübingen, 1993, p. 158, no. 1c (Amastris, Pontus et Bithynia): *Pro pace Au[gusti] in honorem Ti(beri) Claudi / Germanici [Caesaris Aug(usti)] Diui Aug(usti) perpetuus sacer/dos C(aius) Iulius [Aquila pr]aef(ectus) fabr(um) bis in aerar(ium) delatus / a co(n)s(ule) A(ulo) Gabin[i]o [Secundo Ta]uro Statilio Coruino mon/tem cecidit e[t uiam ---]essionem d(e) s(ua) p(ecuni) f(ecit) / /* Ὑπὲρ τῆς Σεβα[στῆς εἰρήνης εἰς] τὴν τειμὴν Τιβερίου Κλαυ/δίου Γερμαν[ικοῦ Σεβαστοῦ],

crossing of great rivers by bridges was also important—a technological achievement that was also commemorated by epigraphic monuments.[32]

Epigraphic documents of this type are often inscribed on milestones. These are to be counted among the genre of building inscriptions, as in many cases they attest the construction of new roads.[33] As indicators of distance, put up at every mile along the *viae publicae*, they are a mass phenomenon. Besides indicating places and distances, the texts on milestones first and foremost served the representation or reverence of the emperor, which found expression in the detailed forms of address and honorific titles. By adding information on the particularities of important technological achievements of road, bridge, or tunnel construction, the epigraphic monuments increased their praise for the emperor.[34] Overcoming the forces of nature emphasised the encompassing authority and expertise of the emperor, which is repeatedly underlined by the wording and rhetoric of such inscriptions.[35]

τοῦ ἐποθρανίου θεοῦ / Σεβαστοῦ ἀρχ[ιερεὺς Γάιος] Ἰούλιος Ἀκυίλας, ἔπαρχος / δὶς εἰς τὸ αἰρ[άριον φερόμεν]ος ὑπὸ ὑπάτων Ὤλου Γα/βεινίου Σεκο[ύνδου, Ταύρου Στα]τειλίου Κορουίνου τὸν λόφον / κόψας τὴν ὁδ[ὸν καὶ τὸ βάθρον?] ἐκ τῶν ἰδίων ὑπαρχόντων / ἐποίησεν; *CIL* III, 1699 = 8267 = *ILS* 5863 = *ILJug* I, 63 (Ogradina, Moesia superior): *Imp(erator) Caesar diui Neruae f(ilius) / Nerua Traianus Aug(ustus) Germ(anicus) / pontif(ex) maximus trib(unicia) pot(estate) IIII / pater patriae co(n)s(ul) III / montibus excisi[s] anco[ni]bus / sublat[i]s uia[m r]e[fecit].*

[32] *CIL* III, 467 = *IK* LIII, 56 (Ilium, Asia): *Imperator Caesar / Mar(cus) Aur(elius) Antoninus / Pius Felix Part(h)icus / maximus Germanicus maximus / trib(unicia) p(otestate) I imp(erator) XV(!) co(n)s(ul) III / prouinciam Asiam / per uiam et flumina / pontibus subiugauit / / Imp(eratore) Caesar(e) Aug(usto) / Diocletiano regnante.* For late antiquity see the building of the Sangarios bridge by Justinian, attested in the *Anthologia Graeca* IX, 641 = *SGO* 09/06/04 (Nikomedia, Pontus et Bithynia): Καὶ σὺ μεθ' Ἑσπερίην ὑψαύχενα καὶ μετὰ Μήδων / ἔθνεα καὶ πᾶσαν βαρβαρικὴν ἀγέλην, / Σαγγάριε, κρατερα ᾗσι ῥοὰς ἀψῖσι πεδηθεὶς / οὕτω ἐδουλώθης κοιρανικῇ παλάμῃ. / ὁ πρὶν δὲ σκαφέεσσιν ἀνέμβατος, ὁ πρὶν ἀτειρὴς / κεῖσαι λαϊνέῃ σφιγκτὸς ἀλυκτοπέδῃ.

[33] For the topic see A. Kolb, *Communications and Mobility in the Roman Empire* in Bruun / Edmondson, *Oxford Handbook Epigraphy* [n. 1], p. 649-670, esp. 654-660.

[34] *IK* LV, 132 (Tyana, Cappadocia): *[Imp(erator) Caes(ar)] / [M(arcus) Aurelius Seuerus Antoninus] / [Pius Feli]x {C} A[ugustus Parth(icus) max(imus)] / [Brit(annicus) m]ax(imus) Ger[m(anicus) max(imus)] pontif(ex) / [max(imus) tr]ib(unicia) potest(ate) XX imp(erator) III co(n)sul IIII / [proco(n)]s(ul) p(ater) p(atriae) uiam Tauri uetustate / [conl]apsam conplanatis monti/[bus e]t c[a]esis rupibus ac dilata/[tis i]tineribus cum pontibus / institutis restituit / a Pylas (!) m(ilia) p(assuum) XV* ...; *CIL* II, 4911 = J. Lostal Pros, *Los miliarios de la provincia Tarraconense*, Zaragoza, 1992, p. 225-226, no. 277 (Siresa, Hispania citerior): *Iussu domini et princip[is nostri] / Magni Maximi uicto[riosissimi] / semper Augusti / Antonius Maximinu[s --- -] / noua[e] prouinciae Ma[ximae] / primus consularis e[t antea] / praeses uiam ad fa[uces] / rupibus famosam ia[m fluui]/alibus aquis peruiam [---] / conplanaui solo paca[to] / perdomito auerso fl[umine] / inundationes soliti[s ---].*

[35] See e.g. *CIL* III, 467 = *IK* LIII, 56 (Ilium, Asia) above note 32: *prouinciam Asiam / per uiam et flumina / pontibus subiugauit*; *SGO* 09/06/04 (Nikomedia, Bithynia) above n. 32.

Moreover, an important part of Roman transportation infrastructure consisted of canals. These were dug in order to ease the use of specific routes or to shorten certain routes and thus to improve the accessibility of important centres.[36] However, only very few inscriptions testify to their construction or maintenance.[37] Information about the technical design or the characteristics of building measures are even rarer. An exception in this respect is the inscription found at the southern end of the canal built by Trajan at the Danube near the 'Iron Gates' (Djerdap).[38] Trajan's artificial waterway allowed ships to bypass the barely navigable rapids (*cataractae*) at present-day Sip. Further documents stem from the Egyptian Nile delta, attesting technically difficult works on canals. According to these records, the waterways—of which at least one connected the Nile harbour Schedia with Alexandria—had to be cleaned down to the bedrock at both banks on a regular basis in order to prevent them from silting up and becoming muddy:[39] *foditu(m) est ... at tria soldu(m) usque ad petras*. Such work of grand proportions was—as the example of Trajan's column also illustrates—a technological achievement par excellence, which visualised the glory and the authority of the emperor and was thus recorded for posterity in the form of inscriptions. By documenting construction projects to improve public safety in

[36] cf. GREWE, *Tunnels* [n. 7], p. 333-336.

[37] *AÉ* 1983, 927 (Küçük Dalyan Köyü, Syria); *AÉ* 1986, 694 = *SEG* 35, 1483 (Antiocheia, Syria); *CIL* III, 12046 (Alexandria, Aegyptus).

[38] *AÉ* 1973, 475 = *ILJug* II, 468 (Karatas bei Sip, Moesia superior): *Imp(erator) Caesar diui Neruae f(ilius) / Nerua Traianus Aug(ustus) Germ(anicus) / pont(ifex) max(imus) trib(unicia) pot(estate) V p(ater) p(atriae) co(n)s(ul) IIII / ob periculum cataractarum / deriuato flumine tutam Da/nuui nauigationem fecit.*

[39] *OGIS* 672 = *I Delta*, 332, 3 = 412, 10 = *IGR* I, 1098 = *SB* V, 8902 (Schedia, Aegyptus): ἔτους τρίτου / Αὐτοκράτορος Τίτου / Καίσαρος Οὐεσπασιανοῦ / Σεβαστοῦ ἐπὶ Γαΐου / Τεττίου Ἀφρικανοῦ /Κασσιανοῦ Πρίσκου ἡγεμόνος /ὠρύγη Ἀγαθὸς Δαίμων / ποταμὸς ἐπὶ τὰ τρία στερεὰ / καὶ ἐπὶ τὸ ἀρχαῖον ἀπεκατε/στάθη ἕως τῆς πέτρας καὶ / ἐτέθησαν παρ' ἑκάτερα τῶν τοί/χων πλάκες ἐπιγεγραμμέ/ναι δεκατέσσαρες; *OGIS* 673 = *I Delta* 334, 4 = 412, 11 = *IGR* I, 1099 = *SB* V, 8903 (Schedia, Aegyptus): *Anno VI Imp(eratoris) [[Domitiani]] / Caesar(is) Aug(usti) Germanic(i) / sub C(aio) Septimio Vegeto praef(ecto) Aeg(ypti) / foditu(m) est flumen Philagrianu(m) / at tria soldu(m) usque ad petras.* / Ἔτους ς´ Αὐτοκράτ[ορος] / Καίσαρος [[Δ̣ο̣μ̣ι̣τ̣ι̣α̣(νοῦ)]] / Σεβαστοῦ Γερμανικοῦ / ἐπὶ Γαΐου Σεπτιμίου / Οὐεγέτου ἡγεμόνος / ὠρύγη ποταμὸς / Φιλαγριανὸς ἐπὶ τὰ / γ´ στερεὰ ἕως τῆς πέτρας.

the event of natural disasters such as floods[40] or on dangerous terrain[41] the emperors could at the same time emphasise their role as saviours.

4 The Significance of Inscriptions

Considered together, Roman epigraphic documents indeed provide information about technology and innovation in the Roman Empire. Yet, funerary, honorific, or votive inscriptions as well as public records mostly offer only individual bits of information or summary formulations. The reference to expert knowledge and specialised terminology was of no interest to the broad public and was thus only rarely included in inscriptions. According to their function, these monuments rather served as testimonials to the renown of their creators, honorands, or donors. Self-confidence and pride in technological skills or achievements were thereby publicly presented and recorded for posterity. By attesting regulations and measures, public epigraphic documents primarily immortalised the concern of the Roman administration and especially of the emperor for the inhabitants of the empire. The commissioners of such inscriptions on the one hand intended to present their actions to the public, while on the other hand they sought to emphasise their good relations with the emperor as well as underline the ruler's benevolence.

The largest group of inscriptions referring to technological achievements are building inscriptions. They mainly served to document the spending and the commitment of the builders, such as members of the municipal elite or the emperor himself, who presented themselves as generous euergetists. Building inscriptions are thus most likely to mention interesting technological or organisational details as well as innovative approaches. By doing so, the commissioner or financier visualised and perpetuated his honour and fame in a prestigious way. Among these building inscriptions, evidence for road construction under the direction of the emperors is most prominent. This fact may be due not only to the government's effort concerning the traffic system, but also to the omnipresence of milestones. The rhetoric of these texts presents the

[40] *CIL* XIV, 85 = *ILS* 207 (Ostia, Italia): *Ti(berius) Claudius Drusi f(ilius) Caesar / Aug(ustus) Germanicus pontif(ex) max(imus) / trib(unicia) potest(ate) VI co(n)sul design(atus) IIII imp(erator) XII p(ater) p(atriae) / fossis ductis a Tiberi operis portu[s] / caussa(!) emissisque in mare urbem / inundationis periculo liberauit*; cf. P. ARNAUD, *Maritime Infrastructure. Between Public and Private Initiative* in KOLB, *Infrastruktur* [n. 9], p. 170-172.

[41] *CIL* IX, 5947 = *ILS* 5856 (Paterno, Italia): *Imp(erator) Caes(ar) diui / Neruae f(ilius) Ner/ua Traianus / Aug(ustus) German(icus) / Dacicus pontif(ex) / maximus trib(unicia) / p[ote]state XV imp(erator) / VI co(n)s(ul) V p(ater) [p(atriae) s]ub/structionem con/t[ra l]abem montis / fecit;* further on the topic CH. P. JONES, *Earthquakes and Emperors* in KOLB, *Infrastruktur* [n. 9], p. 52-65.

technological achievements as a conquest of nature by the emperor and hence perpetuates his extraordinary authority and quality.

5 Economic Goals?

To what extent can these sources provide information about economic goals and consequences of technological achievements and innovations? Although the inscriptions we discussed often correlate technological achievements and building projects, they only rarely make reference to economic aspects. Only Hadrian's letter to the community of Koroneia and the self-praise of the woodworkers from Lycia reveal an obvious economic background, besides mentioning technological methods. Only relatively few other inscriptions, which relate to various significant or prominent technological measures in the proper sense, may be associated with economic policy matters. Among these, surely Hadrian's regulation of the river Kaystros, for which he was thanked in AD129 by the city council and the people of Ephesos, and the edict of the proconsul Lucius Antonius Albus that laid down measures to keep the harbour of the same city clear, are to be mentioned.[42]

When looking at literary sources of the Roman imperial period in search of statements on economic goals and consequences of technological innovations, we find only few and isolated cases. Suetonius reports the anecdote that Vespasian rejected a cost-effective invention for the transport of columns, which is interpreted as an economic or socio-political venture.[43] Cassius Dio's information about Tiberius, who had a glassmaker killed because he had devised unbreakable glass, can be interpreted along the same lines, although Dio primarily concentrates on the motive of the emperor's jealousy.[44] Only the governor Pliny explicitly shows a rational interest in fostering the economy of his province by improving its transportation infrastructure. Thus he suggested to the emperor building a new canal from Nicomedia to the Lake of Sapanka.[45]

[42] *IK* XI, 23 and *IK* XII, 274; cf. *IK* XVII, 3071 (all Ephesos, Asia); for evidence of further, comparable measures see E. WINTER, *Staatliche Baupolitik und Baufürsorge in den römischen Provinzen des kaiserzeitlichen Kleinasien*, Bonn, 1996, p. 185-187; on this dossier see now Ch. KOKKINIA, *Rome, Ephesos, and the Ephesian Harbor: a Case Study in Official Rhetoric* in KOLB, *Infrastruktur* [n. 9], p. 180-196.

[43] SUETONIUS, *Vesp.* 18, 2; cf. otherwise the emperors' building initiatives as measures of employment-creation, e.g. the example of Herodes II in Josephus, *Bell. Iud.* I, 12, 11; on this see WINTER, *Staatliche Baupolitik* [n. 42], p. 129-131; M. HORSTER, *Bauinschriften römischer Kaiser; Untersuchungen zu Inschriftenpraxis und Bautätigkeit in Städten des westlichen Imperium Romanum in der Zeit des Prinzipats*, Stuttgart, 2001, p. 241-246.

[44] DIO LVII, 21, 6; PETRONIUS, *Sat.* 50-51.

[45] PLINY, *Ep.* X, 41 and 61; cf. H. SCHNEIDER, *Infrastruktur und politische Legitimation*

Altogether, the few inscriptions and literary sources that reveal a specific interest in technology with respect to fostering economic procedures without doubt attest the purposeful utilisation and planning of technological methods and innovations in order to boost economic potential. The fact that these matters are only inadequately handed down by literary and epigraphic sources might stem from their predominantly aristocratic viewpoints. Pursuit of profit and economic performance did not belong to the aristocratic ideals and values. [46]

im frühen Principat in KOLB, *Infrastruktur* [n. 9], p. 36.

[46] For the discussion about economic mentality see K. RUFFING, *Die Selbstdarstellung von Händlern und Handwerkern in den griechischen Inschriften* in *MBAH* 33, 2004, p. 85-101; G. VIVENZA, *Roman Economic Thought* in W. SCHEIDEL (ed.), *The Cambridge Companion to the Roman Economy*, Cambridge, 2012, p. 25-44.

COLLECTION LATOMUS

OUVRAGES DISPONIBLES

21. **Deonna W.**, *De Télésphore au "moine bourru". Dieux, génies et démons encapuchonnés*, 1955, 168 p. + 50 pl. 30 €
23. *Hommages à Max Niedermann*, 1956, 352 p. 50 €
27. **Van Weddingen R.**, *Favonii Eulogii Disputatio de Somnio Scipionis*, 1957, 72 p. 30 €
28. *Hommages à Waldemar Deonna*, 1957, 548 p. + 69 pl. 50 €
30. **Bolaffi E.**, *La critica filosofica e letteraria in Quintiliano*, 1958, 64 p. 30 €
32. **Astin A.E.**, *The Lex Annalis before Sulla*, 1958, 47 p. 30 €
33. **Favez C.**, *Saint Jérôme paint par lui-même*, 1958, 56 p. 30 €
35. **Paladini M.L.**, *A proposito della tradizione poetica sulla battaglia di Azio*, 1958, 48 p. 30 €
36. **Richter G.M.A.**, *Greek Portraits II. To what extent where they faithful likenesses?*, 1959, 49 p. + 16 pl. 30 €
39. **Tsontchev D.**, *Monuments de la sculpture romaine en Bulgarie méridionale*, 1959, 44 p. + 24 pl. 30 €
40. **Deonna W.**, *Un divertissement de table. "À cloche-pied"*, 1959, 40 p. 30 €
41. **Stengers J.**, *La formation de la frontière linguistique en Belgique ou de la légitimité de l'hypothèse historique*, 1959, 56 p. 30 €
42. **Van Essen C.-C.**, *Précis d'histoire de l'art antique en Italie*, 1960, 152 p. + 71 pl. 30 €
43. **Bodnar E.W.**, *Cyriacus of Ancona and Athens*, 1960, 256 p. 40 €
44. *Hommages à Léon Herrmann*, 1960, 815 p. + 52 pl. 60 €
47. **Balty J.C.**, *Études sur la Maison Carrée de Nîmes*, 1960, 204 p. + 27 pl. 40 €
51. **Harmand J.**, *Les origines des recherches françaises sur l'habitat rural gallo-romain*, 1961, 52 p. + 6 pl. 30 €
52. **Cambier G.**, *Embricon de Mayence. La vie de Mahomet*, 1961, 94 p. 30 €
53. **Chevallier R.**, *Rome et la Germanie au Ier siècle de notre ère*, 1961, 49 p. 30 €
55. **Vandersleyen C.**, *Chronologie des préfets d'Égypte de 284 à 395*, 1962, 202 p. 40 €
56. **Le Glay M.**, *Les Gaulois en Afrique*, 1962, 43 p. + 1 carte 30 €
58. **Renard M. (ed.)**, *Hommages à Albert Grenier*, 1962, 1679 p. + 338 pl. (3 vol.) 90 €
59. **Herrmann L.**, *Perse: Satires*, 1962, 55 p. 30 €
61. **Joly R.**, *Le Tableau de Cébès et la philosophie religieuse*, 1963, 92 p. 30 €
62. **Deonna W.**, *La Niké de Paeonios de Mendé et le triangle sacré des monuments figurés*, 1968, 220 p. 40 €
63. **Brown E.L.**, *Numeri Vergiliani. Studies in "Eclogues" and "Georgics"*, 1963, 146 p. 30 €
64. **Detsicas A.P.**, *The Anonymous Central Gaulish Potter known as X-3 and his Connections*, 1963, 73 p. + 16 pl. 30 €
65. **Bardon H.**, *Le génie latin*, 1963, 264 p. 40 €
67. **Herrmann L.**, *Le rôle judiciaire et politique des femmes sous la République romaine*, 1964, 128 p. 30 €
69. **Herrmann L.**, *Les fables antiques de la broderie de Bayeux*, 1964, 62 p. + 42 pl. 30 €

71. **Fletcher G.B.A.,** *Annotations on Tacitus*, 1964, 108 p. 30 €
72. **Decouflé P.,** *La notion d'ex-voto anatomique chez les Étrusco-Romains. Analyse et synthèse*, 1964, 44 p. + 19 pl. 30 €
73. **Fenik B.,** *"Iliad X" and the "Rhesus". The Myth*, 1964, 64 p. 30 €
75. **Pascal C.B.,** *The Cults of Cisalpine Gaul*, 1964, 122 p. 30 €
76. **Croisille J.-M.,** *Les natures mortes campaniennes. Répertoire descriptif des peintures de nature morte du Musée National de Naples, de Pompéi, Herculanum et Stabies*, 1965, 134 p. + 127 pl. 30 €
77. **Zehnacker H.,** *Les statues du sanctuaire de Kamart (Tunisie)*, 1965, 86 p. + 17 pl. 30 €
78. **Herrmann L.,** *La vision de Patmos*, 1965, 150 p. 30 €
79. **Pestalozza U.,** *L'éternel féminin dans la religion méditerranéenne*, 1965, 83 p. 30 €
80. **Tudor D.,** *Sucidava. Une cité daco-romaine et byzantine en Dacie*, 1965, 140 p. + 30 pl. 30 €
81. **Fitz J.,** *Ingenuus et Régalien*, 1966, 72 p. 30 €
82. **Colin J.,** *Les villes libres de l'Orient gréco-romain et l'envoi au supplice par acclamations populaires*, 1965, 176 p. + 5 pl. 30 €
84. **des Abbayes H.,** *Virgile: Les Bucoliques*, 1966, 92 p. 30 €
85. **Balty J.C.,** *Essai d'iconographie de l'empereur Clodius Albinus*, 1966, 70 p. + 10 pl. 30 €
86. **Delcourt M.,** *Hermaphroditea. Recherches sur l'être double promoteur de la fertilité dans le monde classique*, 1966, 76 p. + 10 pl. 30 €
87. **Loicq-Berger M.-P.,** *Syracuse. Histoire culturelle d'une cité grecque*, 1967, 320 p. + 21 pl. 50 €
89. **Newman J.K.,** *The Concept of Vates in Augustan Poetry*, 1967, 132 p. 30 €
92. **Cambier G. (ed.),** *Conférences de la Société d'Études Latines de Bruxelles. 1965-1966*, 1968, 132 p. 30 €
93. **Balil A.,** *Lucernae singulares*, 1968, 98 p. 30 €
97. **Cambier G.,** *La vie et les œuvres de Gislain Bulteel d'Ypres 1555-1611. Contribution à l'histoire de l'humanisme dans les Pays-Bas*, 1951, 490 p. + 1 pl. 50 €
101. **Bibauw J. (ed.),** *Hommages à Marcel Renard I. Langues, littératures, droit*, 1969, 840 p. + 14 pl. 75 €
102. **Bibauw J. (ed.),** *Hommages à Marcel Renard II. Histoire, histoire des religions, épigraphie*, 1969, 896 p. + 41 pl. 78 €
104. **Veremans J.,** *Éléments symboliques dans la IIIe Bucolique de Virgile. Essai d'interprétation*, 1969, 76 p. 30 €
105. **Benoit F.,** *Le symbolisme dans les sanctuaires de la Gaule*, 1970, 109 p. 30 €
106. **Liou B.,** *Praetores Etruriae XV populorum. Étude d'épigraphie*, 1969, 118 p. + 16 pl. 30 €
107. **Van den Bruwaene M.,** *Cicéron: De Natura Deorum. Livre I*, 1970, 191 p. 30 €
111. **Mansuelli G.A.,** *Urbanistica e architettura della Cisalpina romana fino al III sec. e.n.*, 1971, 228 p. + 105 pl. 40 €
113. **Thevenot E.,** *Le Beaunois gallo-romain*, 1971, 292 p. 40 €
114. *Hommages à Marie Delcourt*, 1970, 454 p. + 17 pl. 50 €
115. **Meslin M.,** *La fête des kalendes de janvier dans l'empire romain. Étude d'un rituel de Nouvel An*, 1970, 138 p. 30 €
117. **Dulière W.L.,** *La haute terminologie de la rédaction johannique. Les vocables qu'elle a introduits chez les Gréco-Romains: Le Logos-Verbe, le Paraclet-Esprit-Saint et le Messias-Messie*, 1970, 83 p. 30 €

118. **Bardon H.**, *Propositions sur Catulle*, 1970, 160 p. 30 €
119. **Righini V.**, *Lineamenti di storia economica della Gallia Cisalpina. La produttività fittile in età repubblicana*, 1970, 102 p. 30 €
120. **Green R.P.H.**, *The Poetry of Paulinus of Nola. A Study of his Latinity*, 1971, 148 p. 30 €
122. **Fitz J.**, *Les Syriens à Intercisa*, 1972, 264 p. 40 €
123. **Stoian L.**, *Études Histriennes*, 1972, 176 p. 30 €
124. **Jully J.J.**, *La céramique attique de La Monédière, Bessan, Hérault. Ancienne collection J. Coulouma, Béziers*, 1973, 362 p. 50 €
125. **De Ley H.**, *Macrobius and Numenius. A Study of Macrobius, In Somn., I, c. 12*, 1972, 76 p. 30 €
126. **Tordeur P.**, *Concordance de Paulin de Pella*, 1973, 122 p. 30 €
128. **Mortureux B.**, *Recherches sur le "De clementia" de Sénèque. Vocabulaire et composition*, 1973, 88 p. 30 €
129. **Broise P.**, *Genève et son territoire dans l'Antiquité. De la conquête romaine à l'occupation burgonde*, 1974, 370 p. 50 €
131. **Piganiol A.**, *Scripta Varia I – Généralités. Éditées par R. Bloch, A. Chastagnol, R. Chevalier et M. Renard*, 1973, 564 p. 57 €
132. **Piganiol A.**, *Scripta Varia II – Les origines de Rome et la République. Éditées par R. Bloch, A. Chastagnol, R. Chevalier et M. Renard*, 1973, 384 p. 50 €
133. **Piganiol A.**, *Scripta Varia III – L'Empire. Éditées par R. Bloch, A. Chastagnol, R. Chevalier et M. Renard*, 1973, 388 p. 50 €
134. **Amit M.**, *Great and Small Poleis. A Study in the Relations between the Great Powers and the Small Cities in Ancient Greece*, 1973, 194 p. 30 €
136. **Hierche H.**, *Les Épodes d'Horace. Art et signification*, 1974, 212 p. 40 €
138. **Gramatopol M.**, *Les pierres gravées du Cabinet numismatique de l'Académie Roumaine*, 1974, 131 p. 30 €
139. **Hus A.**, *Les bronzes étrusques*, 1975, 164 p. 30 €
140. **Priuli S.**, *Ascyltus. Note di onomastica petroniana*, 1975, 67 p. 30 €
143. **Sauvage A.**, *Étude de thèmes animaliers dans la poésie latine. Le cheval – les oiseaux*, 1975, 293 p. 40 €
144. **Defosse P.**, *Bibliographie étrusque. Tome II (1927-1950)*, 1967, 345 p. 50 €
145. **Cambier G. (ed.)**, *Hommages à André Boutemy*, 1976, 452 p. 50 €
146. **Hus A.**, *Les siècles d'or de l'histoire étrusque (675-475 avant J.-C.)*, 1976, 288 p. 40 €
147. **Cody J.V.**, *Horace and Callimachean Aesthetics*, 1976, 130 p. 30 €
148. **Fitz J.**, *La Pannonie sous Gallien*, 1976, 88 p. 30 €
150. **Desmouliez A.**, *Cicéron et son goût. Essai sur une définition d'une esthétique romaine à la fin de la République*, 1976, 937 p., ISBN: 978-2-87031-000-7 63 €
154. **Van den Bruwaene M.**, *Cicéron: De Natura Deorum. Livre II*, 1978, 224 p., ISBN: 978-2-87031-004-5 40 €
158. **Cambier G., Deroux C., Préaux J. (eds)**, *Lettres latines du Moyen Âge et de la Renaissance*, 1978, 249 p., ISBN: 978-2-87031-008-3 40 €
160. *Le bucchero nero étrusque et sa diffusion en Gaule Méridionale. Actes de la Table-Ronde d'Aix-en-Provence (21-23 mai 1975)*, 1979, 170 p. 30 €
161. **Develin R.**, *Patterns in Office-Holding, 366-49 B.C.*, 1979, 109 p., ISBN: 978-2-87031-101-1 30 €
162. **Olmsted G.S.**, *The Gundestrup Cauldron. Its Archaeological Context, the Style and Iconography of its Portrayed Motifs, and their Narration of a Gaulish Version of Táin Bó Cúailnge*, 1979, 306 p., ISBN: 978-2-87031-102-8 50 €

163. **Bonelli G.,** *Aporie etiche in Epicuro*, 1979, 135 p., ISBN: 978-2-87031-103-5 30 €

164. **Deroux C. (ed.),** *Studies in Latin Literature and Roman History I*, 1979, 542 p., ISBN: 978-2-87031-104-2 55 €

165. **Austin N.J.E.,** *Ammianus on Warfare. An investigation into Ammianus' Military Knowledge*, 1979, 171 p., ISBN: 978-2-87031-105-9 30 €

167. **Herrmann L.,** *Sénèque et les premiers chrétiens*, 1979, 92 p., ISBN: 978-2-87031-107-3 30 €

168. **Deroux C. (ed.),** *Studies in Latin Literature and Roman History II*, 1980, 532 p., ISBN: 978-2-87031-108-0 53 €

169. **Shochat Y.,** *Recruitment and the Programme of Tiberius Gracchus*, 1980, 98 p., ISBN: 978-2-87031-109-7 30 €

171. **Grondona M.,** *La religione e la superstizione nella Cena Trimalchionis*, 1980, 104 p. + 10 pl., ISBN: 978-2-87031-111-0 30 €

172. **Catlow L.,** *Pervigilium Veneris*, 1980, 105 p., ISBN: 978-2-87031-112-7 30 €

173. **Rubin Z.,** *Civil-War Propaganda and Historiography*, 247 p., ISBN: 978-2-87031-113-4 40 €

174. **Dury-Moyaers G.,** *Énée et Lavinium. À propos des découvertes archéologiques récentes*, 1981, 252 p. + 37 pl., ISBN: 978-2-87031-114-1 40 €

175. **Van den Bruwaene M.,** *Cicéron: De Natura Deorum. Livre III*, 1981, 212 p., ISBN: 978-2-87031-115-8 40 €

177. **MacBain B.,** *Prodigy and Expiation. A Study in Religion and Politics in Republican Rome*, 1982, 140 p., ISBN: 978-2-87031-117-2 30 €

178. **Sartre M.,** *Trois études sur l'Arabie romaine et byzantine*, 1982, 226 p., ISBN: 978-2-87031-118-9 40 €

179. **Croisille J.-M.,** *Poésie et art figuré de Néron aux Flaviens. Recherches sur l'iconographie et la corrrespondance des arts à l'époque impériale*, 1982, 742 p. + 167 pl. (2 vol.), ISBN: 978-2-87031-119-6 122 €

180. **Deroux C. (ed.),** *Studies in Latin Literature and Roman History III*, 1983, 440 p., ISBN: 978-2-87031-120-2 50 €

181. **Fitz J.,** *L'administration des provinces pannoniennes sous le Bas-Empire romain*, 1983, 113 p., ISBN: 978-2-87031-121-9 30 €

182. **Anderson J.J.C.,** *The Historical Topography of the Imperial Fora*, 1984, 201 p. + 30 pl., ISBN: 978-2-87031-122-6 40 €

183. **Green M.,** *The Wheel as a Cult-Symbol in the Romano-Celtic World. With Special Reference to Gaul and Britain*, 1984, 408 p. + 85 pl., ISBN: 978-2-87031-123-3 60 €

184. **Guillaumont F.,** *Philosophe et augure. Recherches sur la théorie cicéronienne de la divination*, 1984, 214 p., ISBN: 978-2-87031-124-0 40 €

185. **Bradley K.R.,** *Slaves and Masters in the Roman Empire. A Study in Social Control*, 1984, 164 p., ISBN: 978-2-87031-125-7 30 €

186. **Bonelli G.,** *I motivi profondi della poesia lucreziana*, 1984, 337 p., ISBN: 978-2-87031-126-4 50 €

187. **Renard M., Laurens P. (eds),** *Hommages à Henry Bardon*, 1985, 400 p. + 20 pl., ISBN: 978-2-87031-127-1 51 €

188. **Develin R.,** *The Practice of Politics at Rome 366-167 B.C.*, 1985, 354 p., ISBN: 978-2-87031-128-8 50 €

189. **Frécaut J.-M., Porte D. (eds),** *Journées Ovidiennes de Parménie. Actes du Colloque sur Ovide (24-26 juin 1983)*, 1985, 289 p. + 8 pl., ISBN: 978-2-87031-129-5 40 €

190. **Audin A.,** *Gens de Lugdunum*, 1986, 192 p. + 28 pl., ISBN: 978-2-87031-130-1 30 €

191. **Heurgon J.,** *Scripta Varia*, 1986, 500 p. + 41 pl., ISBN: 978-2-87031-131-8 65 €
192. **Van den Bruwaene M.,** *Cicéron: De Natura Deorum. Tables*, 1986, 175 p., ISBN: 978-2-87031-132-5 30 €
193. **Deroux C., Decreus F. (eds),** *Hommages à Jozef Veremans*, 1986, 407 p. + 2 pl., ISBN: 978-2-87031-133-2 51 €
194. **Pack E.,** *Städte und Steuern in der Politik Julians. Untersuchungen zu den Quellen eines Kaiserbildes*, 1986, 420 p., ISBN: 978-2-87031-134-9 51 €
195. **Reichler-Béguelin M.-J.,** *Les noms latins du type mens. Étude morphologique*, 1986, 271 p., ISBN: 978-2-87031-135-6 40 €
196. **Deroux C. (ed.),** *Studies in Latin Literature and Roman History IV*, 1986, 550 p., ISBN: 978-2-87031-136-3 68 €
197. **Goar R.J.,** *The Legend of Cato Uticensis from the First Century B.C. to the Fifth Century A.D. With an Appendix on Dante and Cato*, 1987, 115 p., ISBN: 978-2-87031-137-0 30 €
198. **Mrozek S.,** *Les distributions d'argent et de nourriture dans les villes italiennes du Haut-Empire romain*, 1987, 115 p. + 14 pl., ISBN: 978-2-87031-138-7 30 €
199. **Pomathios J.-L.,** *Le pouvoir politique et sa représentation dans l'Énéide de Virgile*, 1987, 421 p., ISBN: 978-2-87031-139-4 51 €
200. **Ferguson J.,** *A Prosopography to the Poems of Juvenal*, 1987, 250 p., ISBN: 978-2-87031-140-0 40 €
201. **Porte D., Néradeau J.P. (eds),** *Res Sacrae. Hommages à Henri Le Bonniec*, 1988, 466 p. + 12 pl., ISBN: 978-2-87031-141-7 59 €
202. **Joulia J.-C.,** *Les frises doriques de Narbonne*, 1988, 289 p. + 117 pl., ISBN: 978-2-87031-142-4 55 €
203. **Delmaire R.,** *Les responsables des finances impériales au Bas-Empire romain (IVe-VIe s.). Études prosopographiques*, 1989, 321 p., ISBN: 978-2-87031-143-1 50 €
204. **Martin S.D.,** *The Roman Jurists and the Organization of Private Building in the Late Republic and Early Empire*, 1989, 57 p., ISBN: 978-2-87031-144-8 30 €
205. **Roques D.,** *Études sur la Correspondance de Synésios de Cyrène*, 1989, 274 p. + 3 pl., ISBN: 978-2-87031-145-5 40 €
206. **Deroux C. (ed.),** *Studies in Latin Literature and Roman History V*, 1989, 516 p. + 1 pl., ISBN: 978-2-87031-146-2 60 €
207. **Moscati Castelnuovo L.,** *Siris. Tradizione storiografica e momenti della storia di una città della Magna Grecia*, 1989, 175 p. + 3 pl., ISBN: 978-2-87031-147-9 30 €
208. **Bertrand-Dagenbach C.,** *Alexandre Sévère et l'Histoire Auguste*, 1990, 216 p., ISBN: 978-2-87031-148-6 40 €
209. **Croisille J.-M. (ed.),** *Neronia IV. Alejandro Magno, modelo de los emperadores romanos. Actes du IVe Colloque International de la SIEN*, 1990, 398 p. + 6 pl., ISBN: 978-2-87031-149-3 58 €
210. **Mellinghoff-Bourgerie V.,** *Les incertitudes de Virgile. Contributions épicuriennes à la théologie de l'Énéide*, 1990, 275 p., ISBN: 978-2-87031-150-9 40 €
211. **Montero Herrero S.,** *Política y adivinación en el Bajo Imperio Romano. Emperadores y harúspices (193 D.C. - 408 D.C.)*, 1991, 195 p., ISBN: 978-2-87031-151-6 30 €
212. **Paltiel E.,** *Vassals and Rebels in the Roman Empire. Julio-Claudian Policies in Judaea and the Kingdoms of the East*, 1991, 352 p. + 19 pl., ISBN: 978-2-87031-152-3 50 €

213. **Ginestet P.,** *Les organisations de la jeunesse dans l'Occident Romain*, 1991, 336 p. + 11 pl., ISBN: 978-2-87031-153-0 50 €
214. **Wulff Alonso F.,** *Romanos e Itálicos en la Baja República. Estudios sobre sus relaciones entre la Segunda Guerra Púnica y la Guerra Social (201-91 a.C.)*, 1991, 389 p., ISBN: 978-2-87031-154-7 55 €
215. **Schettino M.T.,** *Tradizione annalistica e tradizione ellenistica su Pirro in Dionigi (A.R. XIX-XX)*, 1991, 120 p., ISBN: 978-2-87031-155-4 30 €
216. **Keller M.,** *Les verbes latins à infectum en -sc-. Étude morphologique à partir des informations attestées dès l'époque préclassique*, 1992, XI-564 p., ISBN: 978-2-87031-156-1 75 €
217. **Deroux C. (ed.),** *Studies in Latin Literature and Roman History VI*, 1992, 516 p., ISBN: 978-2-87031-157-8 68 €
218. **Verdière R.,** *Le secret du voltigeur d'amour ou le mystère de la relégation d'Ovide*, 1992, 168 p., ISBN: 978-2-87031-158-5 30 €
219. **Dehon P.-J.,** *Hiems Latina. Études sur l'hiver dans la poésie latine, des origines à l'époque de Néron*, 1993, 385 p., ISBN: 978-2-87031-159-2 54 €
220. **Simelon P.,** *La propriété en Lucanie depuis les Gracques jusqu'à l'avènement des Sévères. Étude épigraphique*, 1993, 215 p. + 6 pl., ISBN: 978-2-87031-160-8 40 €
221. **Desy P.,** *Recherches sur l'économie apulienne au IIe et au Ier siècle avant notre ère*, 1993, 346 p. + 4 pl., ISBN: 978-2-87031-161-5 50 €
222. **Ulrich R.B.,** *The Roman Orator and the Sacred Stage. The Roman Templum Rostratum*, 1994, 345 p. + 81 pl., ISBN: 978-2-87031-162-2 52 €
223. **Devillers O.,** *L'art de la persuasion dans les Annales de Tacite*, 1994, 390 p., ISBN: 978-2-87031-163-9 53 €
224. **Loutsch C.,** *L'exorde dans les discours de Cicéron*, 1994, 583 p., ISBN: 978-2-87031-164-6 75 €
225. **Wardle D.,** *Suetonius' Life of Caligula. A Commentary*, 1994, 395 p., ISBN: 978-2-87031-165-3 55 €
226. **Le Bohec Y. (ed.),** *L'Afrique, la Gaule, la Religion à l'époque romaine. Mélanges à la mémoire de Marcel Le Glay*, 1994, 876 p. + 134 pl., ISBN: 978-2-87031-166-0 125 €
227. **Deroux C. (ed.),** *Studies in Latin Literature and Roman History VII*, 1994, 596 p. + 6 pl., ISBN: 978-2-87031-167-7 77 €
228. **Poignault R.,** *L'Antiquité dans l'œuvre de Marguerite Yourcenar. Littérature, mythe et histoire*, 1995, 1096 p. (2 vol.), ISBN: 978-2-87031-168-4 120 €
229. **Leclercq R.,** *Le divin loisir. Essai sur les Bucoliques de Virgile*, 1996, 712 p. 95 €
230. **André J.-M., Dangel J., Demont P. (eds),** *Les loisirs et l'héritage de la culture classique. Actes du XIIIe Congrès de l'Association Guillaume Budé (Dijon, 27-31 août 1993)*, 1996, 712 p., ISBN: 978-2-87031-170-7 88 €
231. **Darwall-Smith R.H.,** *Emperors and Architecture. A Study of Flavian Rome*, 1996, 342 p. + 75 pl., ISBN: 978-2-87031-171-4 60 €
232. **Lolli M.,** *D.M. Ausonius: Parentalia*, 1997, 281 p., ISBN: 978-2-87031-172-1 40 €
233. **Rochette B.,** *Le latin dans le monde grec. Recherches sur la diffusion de la langue et des lettres latines dans les provinces hellénophones de l'Empire romain*, 1997, 423 p. + 3 pl., ISBN: 978-2-87031-173-8 60 €
234. **Rambaux C.,** *Tibulle ou la répétition*, 2000, 117 p., ISBN: 978-2-87031-174-5 30 €
235. **Dillemann L.,** *La Cosmographie du Ravennate. Ouvrage édité avec préface et notes additionnelles par Y. Janvier*, 1997, 262 p., ISBN: 978-2-87031-175-2 40 €

236. **Pansiéri C.**, *Plaute et Rome ou les ambiguïtés d'un marginal*, 1997, 807 p., ISBN: 978-2-87031-176-9 98 €
237. **Lehmann Y.**, *Varron théologien et philosophe romain*, 1997, 391 p., ISBN: 978-2-87031-177-6 55 €
238. **Vössing K.**, *Schule und Bildung im Nordafrika der Römischen Kaiserzeit*, 1997, 690 p., ISBN: 978-2-87031-178-3 80 €
239. **Deroux C. (ed.)**, *Studies in Latin Literature and Roman History VIII*, 1997, 506 p., ISBN: 978-2-87031-179-0 68 €
240. **Viré G.**, *Synthèses romaines. Langue latine, Droit romain, Institutions comparées. Études publiées en hommage au professeur J.-H. Michel*, 1998, XXIV-458 p. + 1 pl., ISBN: 978-2-87031-180-6 64 €
241. **Loupiac A.**, *La poétique des éléments dans La Pharsale de Lucain*, 1998, 235 p., ISBN: 978-2-87031-181-8 40 €
242. **Deroux C.**, *Maladie et maladies dans les textes latins antiques et médiévaux. Actes du Ve Colloque International "Textes médicaux latins" (Bruxelles, 4-6 septembre 1995)*, 1998, VI-458 p. + 3 pl., ISBN: 978-2-87031-182-0 68 €
243. *Liberalitas. Scripta varia. Rassemblés et présentés en hommage à M.J. Hellegouarc'h*, 1998, XXIII-767 p. + 1 pl., ISBN: 978-2-87031-183-7 100 €
244. **Deroux C. (ed.)**, *Studies in Latin Literature and Roman History IX*, 1998, 504 p., ISBN: 978-2-87031-184-4 68 €
245. **Martini M.C.**, *Due studi sulla riscrittura annalistica dell'età monarchica a Roma*, 1998, 153 p., ISBN: 978-2-87031-185-1 30 €
246. **Maggi S.**, *Le sistemazioni forensi nelle città della Cisalpina romana, dalla tarda repubblica al principato augusteo (e oltre)*, 1999, 186 p., ISBN: 978-2-87031-186-8 30 €
247. **Croisille J.-M., Martin R., Perrin Y. (eds)**, *Neronia V. Néron: histoire et légende. Actes du Ve Colloque International de la SIEN (Clermont-Ferrand et Saint-Étienne, 2-6 novembre 1994)*, 1999, 493 p. + 26 pl., ISBN: 978-2-87031-187-5 63 €
248. **Benoist S.**, *La Fête à Rome au premier siècle de l'Empire. Recherches sur l'univers festif sous les règnes d'Auguste et des Julio-Claudiens*, 1999, 407 p., ISBN: 978-2-87031-188-2 55 €
249. **Laigneau S.**, *La femme et l'amour chez Catulle et les Élégiaques augustéens*, 1999, 420 p., ISBN: 978-2-87031-190-5 55 €
250. **Salmon P.**, *La limitation des naissances dans la société romaine*, 1999, 103 p., ISBN: 978-2-87031-191-2 30 €
251. **Texier Y.**, *La question de Gergovie. Essai sur un problème de localisation*, 1999, 417 p., ISBN: 978-2-87031-192-9 55 €
252. **Billault A.**, *L'univers de Philostrate*, 2000, 145 p., ISBN: 978-2-87031-193-6 30 €
253. **Bernard J.-E.**, *Le portrait chez Tite-Live. Essai sur une écriture de l'histoire romaine*, 2000, 482 p., ISBN: 978-2-87031-194-3 65 €
254. **Deroux C. (ed.)**, *Studies in Latin Literature and Roman History X*, 2000, 501 p. + 8 pl., ISBN: 978-2-87031-195-0 65 €
255. **Foucher A.**, *Historia proxima poetis. L'influence de la poésie épique sur le style des historiens latins de Salluste à Ammien Marcellin*, 2000, 487 p., ISBN: 978-2-87031-196-7 65 €
256. **Vons J.**, *L'image de la femme dans l'œuvre de Pline l'Ancien*, 2000, 480 p., ISBN: 978-2-87031-197-4 67 €
257. **Haan E.**, *Thomas Gray's Latin Poetry. Some Classical, Neo-Latin and Vernacular Contexts*, 2000, 198 p., ISBN: 978-2-87031-198-1 39 €

258. **Brachet J.-P.,** *Recherches sur les préverbes de- et ex- du latin*, 2000, 400 p., ISBN: 978-2-87031-199-8 55 €
259. **Renucci P.,** *Les idées politiques et le gouvernement de l'empereur Julien*, 2000, 537 p. + 2 pl., ISBN: 978-2-87031-200-1 70 €
260. **Bouquet J.,** *Le songe dans l'épopée latine d'Ennius à Claudien*, 2001, 204 p., ISBN: 978-2-87031-201-8 40 €
261. **Rambaux C.,** *Properce ou les difficultés de l'émancipation féminine*, 2001, 347 p., ISBN: 978-2-87031-202-5 50 €
262. **Lehmann A.,** *Varron critique littéraire. Regard sur les poètes latins archaïques*, 2002, 299 p., ISBN: 978-2-87031-203-2 45 €
263. **Wulff Alonso F.,** *Roma e Italia de la Guerra Social a la retirada de Sila (90-79 a.C.)*, 2002, 341 p., ISBN: 978-2-87031-204-9 50 €
264. **Deman A., Raepsaet-Charlier M.-T.,** *Nouveau recueil des inscriptions latines de Belgique (ILB2)*, 2002, 288 p. + 65 pl., ISBN: 978-2-87031-205-6 48 €
265. **Spaltenstein F.,** *Commentaire des Argonautica de Valérius Flaccus (livres 1 et 2)*, 2002, 491 p., ISBN: 978-2-87031-206-3 62 €
266. **Defosse P. (ed.),** *Hommages à Carl Deroux I. Poésie*, 2002, XXIII-546 p. + 2 pl., ISBN: 978-2-87031-207-0 93 €
267. **Defosse P. (ed.),** *Hommages à Carl Deroux II. Prose et linguistique, Médecine*, 2002, XXIII-577 p. + 1 pl., ISBN: 978-2-87031-208-7 90 €
268. **Croisille J.-M., Perrin Y. (eds),** *Neronia VI. Rome à l'époque néronienne. Institutions et vie politique, économie et société, vie intellectuelle, artistique et spirituelle. Actes du VIe Colloque International de la SIEN (Rome, 19-23 mai 1999)*, 2002, 604 p. + 28 pl., ISBN: 978-2-87031-209-4 96 €
269. **Verboven K.,** *The Economy of Friends. Economic Aspects of Amicitia and Patronage in the Late Republic*, 2002, 399 p., ISBN: 978-2-87031-210-0 54 €
270. **Defosse P. (eds),** *Hommages à Carl Deroux III. Histoire et épigraphie, Droit*, 2003, XXIII-488 p. + 7 pl., ISBN: 978-2-87031-211-7 80 €
271. **Goguey D.,** *Les animaux dans la mentalité romaine*, 2003, 138 p., ISBN: 978-2-87031-212-4 30 €
272. **Deroux C. (ed.),** *Studies in Latin Literature and Roman History XI*, 2003, 504 p., ISBN: 978-2-87031-213-1 71 €
273. **Lévy C., Besnier B., Gigandet A. (eds),** *Ars et Ratio. Sciences, arts et métiers dans la philosophie hellénistique et romaine. Actes du Colloque international organisé à Créteil, Fontenay et Paris du 16 au 18 octobre 1997*, 2003, 274 p., ISBN: 978-2-87031-214-8 40 €
274. **Puccini-Delbey G.,** *Amour et désir dans les Métamorphoses d'Apulée*, 2003, 317 p., ISBN: 978-2-87031-215-5 50 €
275. **Haan E.,** *Andrew Marvell's Latin Poetry: From Text to Context*, 2003, 536 p., ISBN: 978-2-87031-216-2 52 €
276. **Turcan-Verkerk A.-M.,** *Un poète latin redécouvert: Latinius Pacatus Drepanius, panégyriste de Théodose*, 2003, 194 p. + 3 pl., ISBN: 978-2-87031-217-9 30 €
277. **Defosse P. (ed.),** *Hommages à Carl Deroux IV. Archéologie et Histoire de l'Art, Religion*, 2003, XXIII-567 p. + 72 pl., ISBN: 978-2-87031-218-6 107 €
278. **Peurière Y.,** *La pêche et les poissons dans la littérature latine. I. Des origines à la fin de la période augustéenne*, 2003, 268 p., ISBN: 978-2-87031-219-3 40 €
279. **Defosse P. (ed.),** *Hommages à Carl Deroux V. Christianisme et Moyen Âge, Néo-latin et survivance de la latinité*, 2003, XXIII-619 p. + 13 pl., ISBN: 978-2-87031-220-9 95 €

280. **Aygon J.-P.,** *Pictor in fabula. L'ecphrasis-descriptio dans les tragédies de Sénèque*, 2004, 534 p., ISBN: 978-2-87031-221-6 73 €
281. **Spaltenstein F.,** *Commentaire des Argonautica de Valérius Flaccus (livres 3, 4 et 5)*, 2004, 564 p., ISBN: 978-2-87031-222-3 78 €
282. **Martini M.C.,** *Le vestali. Un sacerdozio funzionale al "cosmo" romano*, 2004, 264 p., ISBN: 978-2-87031-223-0 40 €
283. **Fontanille M.-T.,** *Vieillir à Rome. Approche démographique*, 2004, 94 p. + 8 pl., ISBN: 978-2-87031-224-7 30 €
284. **Chappuis Sandoz L.,** *Terres d'abondance. Paysages et images poétiques de la fertilité et du don dans la littérature latine*, 2004, 478 p., ISBN: 978-2-87031-225-4 62 €
285. **Nadeau Y.,** *Safe and Subsidized. Vergil and Horace sing Augustus*, 2004, 327 p., ISBN: 978-2-87031-226-1 50 €
286. **Colton R.E.,** *Régnier and Horace*, 2004, 81 p., ISBN: 978-2-87031-227-8 30 €
287. **Deroux C. (ed.),** *Studies in Latin Literature and Roman History XII*, 2005, 496 p., ISBN: 978-2-87031-228-5 71 €
288. **Chambert R.,** *Rome: le mouvement et l'ancrage. Morale et philosophie du voyage au début du Principat*, 2005, 411 p., ISBN: 978-2-87031-229-2 57 €
289. **Georgacopoulou S.,** *Aux frontières du récit épique: l'emploi de l'apostrophe du narrateur dans la Thébaïde de Stace*, 2005, 296 p., ISBN: 978-2-87031-230-8 42 €
290. **Burnand Y.,** *Primores Galliarum. Sénateurs et chevaliers romains originaires de Gaule de la fin de la République au IIIe siècle. I. Méthodologie*, 2005, 450 p. + 41 pl., ISBN: 978-2-87031-231-5 60 €
291. **Spaltenstein F.,** *Commentaire des Argonautica de Valérius Flaccus (livres 6, 7 et 8)*, 2005, 575 p., ISBN: 978-2-87031-232-2 80 €
292. **Benferhat Y.,** *Ciues Epicurei. Les épicuriens et l'idée de monarchie à Rome et en Italie de Sylla à Octave*, 2005, 369 p., ISBN: 978-2-87031-233-9 54 €
293. **Rambaux C.,** *L'accès à la vérité chez Tertullien*, 2005, 264 p., ISBN: 978-2-87031-234-6 41 €
294. **Spevak O.,** *La concession en latin*, 2005, 260 p., ISBN: 978-2-87031-235-3 40 €
295. **Scafoglio G.,** *L'Astyanax di Accio. Saggio sul background mitografico, testo critico e commento dei frammenti*, 2006, 157 p., ISBN: 978-2-87031-236-0 30 €
296. **Amato E., Roduit A., Steinrück M. (eds),** *Approches de la Troisième Sophistique. Hommages à Jacques Schamp*, 2006, XXVIII-614 p. + 1 pl., ISBN: 978-2-87031-237-7 89 €
297. **Pedroni L.,** *Crisi finanziaria e monetazione durante le Guerra Sociale*, 2006, 224 p., ISBN: 978-2-87031-238-4 40 €
298. **Guillaumont F.,** *Le "De diuinatione" de Cicéron et les théories antiques de la divination*, 2006, 396 p., ISBN: 978-2-87031-239-1 57 €
299. **Thomas J.,** *L'imaginaire de l'homme romain. Dualité et complexité*, 2006, 246 p. + 3 pl. + 8 fig., ISBN: 978-2-87031-240-7 40 €
300. **Merriam C.U.,** *Love and Propaganda. Augustan Venus and the Latin Love Elegists*, 2006, 121 p., ISBN: 978-2-87031-241-4 30 €
301. **Deroux C. (ed.),** *Studies in Latin Literature and Roman History XIII*, 2006, 496 p. + 1 pl., ISBN: 978-2-87031-242-1 71 €
302. **Burnand Y.,** *Primores Galliarum. Sénateurs et chevaliers romains originaires de Gaule de la fin de la République au IIIe siècle. II. Prosopographie*, 2006, 630 p. + 24 pl., ISBN: 978-2-87031-243-8 80 €

303. **Roman D., Roman Y.,** *Aux miroirs de la Ville. Images et discours identitaires romains (IIIe s. avant J.-C. - IIIe s. après J.-C.)*, 2007, 442 p., ISBN: 978-2-87031-244-5 63 €
304. **Garambois-Vazquez F.,** *Les invectives de Claudien. Une poétique de la violence*, 2007, 315 p. + 6 pl., ISBN: 978-2-87031-245-2 50 €
305. **Perrin Y. (ed.),** *Neronia VII. Rome, l'Italie et la Grèce. Hellénisme et philhellénisme au premier siècle après J.-C. Actes du VIIe Colloque International de la SIEN (Athènes, 21-23 octobre 2004)*, 2007, 510 p. + 27 pl., ISBN: 978-2-87031-246-9 78 €
306. **Burnand Y.,** *Primores Galliarum. Sénateurs et chevaliers romains originaires de Gaule de la fin de la République au IIIe siècle. III. Étude sociale. 1. Les racines*, 2007, 301 p. + 30 pl., ISBN: 978-2-87031-247-6 50 €
307. **Garcia Quintela M.V.,** *Le Pendu et le Noyé des Monts Albains. Recherches comparatives autour des rites et des mythes des Monts Albains*, 2007, 222 p., ISBN: 978-2-87031-248-3 40 €
308. **Briquel D.,** *Mythe et Révolution. La fabrication d'un récit: la naissance de la république à Rome*, 2007, 354 p., ISBN: 978-2-87031-249-0 53 €
309. **Tordeur P.,** *Deux études de métrique verbale*, 2007, 325 p., ISBN: 978-2-87031-250-6 50 €
310. **Nadeau Y.,** *Erotica for Caesar Augustus. A Study of the Love-poetry of Horace, Carmina, Books I to III*, 2008, 532 p., ISBN: 978-2-87031-251-3 75 €
311. **Lyasse E.,** *Le Principat et son fondateur. L'utilisation de la référence à Auguste de Tibère à Trajan*, 2008, 388 p., ISBN: 978-2-87031-252-0 57 €
312. **Fain G.L.,** *Writing Epigrams. The Art of Composition in Catullus, Callimachus and Martial*, 2008, 238 p., ISBN: 978-2-87031-253-7 57 €
313. **Vallat D.,** *Onomastique, culture et société dans les Épigrammes de Martial*, 2008, 673 p., ISBN: 978-2-87031-254-4 95 €
314. **Roussel D.,** *Ovide épistolier*, 2008, 348 p., ISBN: 978-2-87031-255-1 52 €
315. **Deroux C. (ed.),** *Studies in Latin Literature and Roman History XIV*, 2008, 529 p., ISBN: 978-2-87031-256-8 76 €
316. **Viré G. (ed.),** *Autour du lexique latin. Communications faites lors du XIIIe Colloque international de Linguistique latine, Bruxelles, 4 au 9 avril 2005*, 2008, 294 p., ISBN: 978-2-87031-257-5 45 €
317. **Casali S., Stok F.,** *Servio: stratificazioni esegetiche e modelli culturali. Servius: Exegetical Stratifications and Cultural Models*, 2008, 280 p., ISBN: 978-2-87031-258-2 42 €
318. **Spaltenstein F.,** *Commentaire des fragments dramatiques de Livius Andronicus*, 2008, 232 p., ISBN: 978-2-87031-259-9 42 €
319. **Burnand Y.,** *Primores Galliarum. Sénateurs et chevaliers romains originaires de Gaule de la fin de la République au IIIe siècle. III. Étude sociale. 2. Les horizons de la vie*, 2009, 382 p., ISBN: 978-2-87031-260-5 55 €
320. **Fratantuono L.,** *A Commentary on Virgil, Aeneid XI*, 2009, 340 p., ISBN: 978-2-87031-261-2 50 €
321. **Loutsch C., Melchior M.,** *Humanistica Luxemburgensia: la Bombarda de Barthélemy Latomus, les Opuscula de Conrad Vecerius. Textes édités, traduits et annotés par Myriam Melchior et Claude Loutsch*, 2009, 238 p., ISBN: 978-2-87031-262-9 40 €
322. **Morzadec F.,** *Les Images du Monde. Structure, écriture et esthétique du paysage dans les œuvres de Stace et Silius Italicus*, 2009, 461 p., ISBN: 978-2-87031-263-6 63 €
323. **Deroux C. (ed.),** *Studies in Latin Literature and Roman History XV*, 2010, 528 p., ISBN: 978-2-87031-264-3 76 €

324. **Louis N.,** *Commentaire historique et traduction du Diuus Augustus de Suétone*, 2010, 761 p., ISBN: 978-2-87031-265-0 106 €
325. **Van Laer S.,** *La préverbation en latin: étude des préverbes ad-, in-, ob- et per- dans la poésie républicaine et augustéenne*, 2010, 501 p., ISBN: 978-2-87031-266-7 70 €
326. **Vannesse M.,** *La défense de l'Occident romain pendant l'Antiquité tardive. Recherches géostratégiques sur l'Italie de 284 à 410 ap. J.-C.*, 2010, 583 p., ISBN: 978-2-87031-267-4 87 €
327. **Perrin Y. (ed.),** *Neronia VIII. Bibliothèques, livres et culture écrite dans l'empire romain de César à Hadrien*, 2010, 399 p., ISBN: 978-2-87031-268-9 60 €
328. **Burnand Y.,** *Primores Galliarum. IV. Indices*, 2010, 200 p., ISBN: 978-2-87031-269-8 32 €
329. **Nadeau Y.,** *A Commentary on the Sixth Satire of Juvenal*, 2011, 473 p., ISBN: 978-2-87031-270-4 68 €
330. **Hamdoune C., Echalier L., Meyers J., Michaud J.-N.,** *Vie, mort et poésie dans l'Afrique romaine. D'après un choix de Carmina Latina Epigraphica*, 2011, 379 p., ISBN: 978-2-87031-271-1 80 €
331. **Deroux C. (ed.),** *Corolla Epigraphica. Hommages au professeur Yves Burnand*, 2011, 743 p., ISBN: 978-2-87031-272-8 115 €
332. **Rambaux C.,** *La genèse du judaïsme et du christianisme. Les faits et les problèmes dans leur contexte historique*, 2011, 450 p., ISBN: 978-2-87031-273-5 72 €
333. **Galtier F.,** *L'image tragique de l'Histoire chez Tacite. Étude des schèmes tragiques dans les Histoires et les Annales*, 2011, 344 p., ISBN: 978-2-87031-274-2 53 €
334. **Ratkowitsch C.,** *Von der Manipulierbarkeit des Mythos. Der Paris/Helena-Mythos bei Ovid (her. 16/17) und Baudri von Borgueil (carm. 7/8)*, 2012, 105 p., ISBN: 978-2-87031-275-9 30 €
335. **Cavalieri M.,** *Nullus locus sine genio. Il ruolo aggregativo e religioso dei santuari extraurbani della Cisalpina tra protostoria, romanizzazione e piena romanità*, 2012, 221 p., ISBN: 978-2-87031-276-6 44 €
336. **Albertson F.C.,** *Mars and Rhea Silvia in Roman Art*, 2012, 241 p., ISBN: 978-2-87031-277-3 45 €
337. **Thomson M.,** *Studies in the Historia Augusta*, 2012, 155 p., ISBN: 978-2-87031-278-0 30 €
338. **Deroux C. (ed.),** *Studies in Latin Literature and Roman History XVI*, 2012, 670 p., ISBN: 978-2-87031-284-1 92 €
339. **Grillone A.,** *Gromatica militare: lo ps. Igino. Prefazione, testo, traduzione e commento*, 2012, 269 p., ISBN: 978-2-87031-285-8 49 €
340. **Napoli J.,** *Évolution de la poliorcétique romaine sous la République jusqu'au milieu du IIe siècle avant J.-C.*, 2013, 239 p., ISBN: 978-2-87031-287-2 45 €
341. **Foucher A.,** *Lecture ad metrum, lecture ad sensum: études de métrique stylistique*, 2013, 274 p., ISBN: 978-2-87031-288-9 49 €
342. **Nadeau Y.,** *Dog Bites Caesar! A Reading of Juvenal's Satire 5 (with Horace's Satires I.5; II.5; II.6; Epistles I.1; I.16; I.17)*, 2013, 100 p., ISBN: 978-2-87031-289-6 30 €
343. **Engels D., Van Nuffelen P. (eds),** *Religion and Competition in Antiquity*, 2014, 307 p., ISBN: 978-2-87031-290-2 51 €
344. **Spaltenstein F.,** *Commentaire des fragments dramatiques de Naevius*, 2014, 708 p., ISBN: 978-2-87031-291-9 99 €

345. **Lusnia S.,** *Creating Severan Rome. The Architecture and Self-Image of L. Septimius Severus (A.D. 193-211)*, 2014, 293 p., ISBN: 978-2-87031-292-6 59 €

346. **Bonet V.,** *La pharmacopée végétale d'Occident dans l'œuvre de Pline l'Ancien*, 2014, 513 p., ISBN: 978-2-87031-293-3 73 €

347. **De Giorgio J.P.,** *L'écriture de soi à Rome. Autour de la correspondance de Cicéron*, 2015, 305 p., ISBN: 978-90-429-3238-8 51 €

348. **Coutelle É.,** *Properce, Élégies, livre IV. Texte établi, traduit et commenté*, 2015, VI-1021 p., ISBN: 978-90-429-3241-8 125 €

349. **Engels D. (ed.),** *Von Platon bis Fukuyama. Biologistische und zyklische Konzepte in der Geschichtsphilosophie der Antike und des Abendlandes*, 2015, 336 p., ISBN: 978-90-429-3274-6 52 €

350. **Erdkamp P., Verboven K. (eds),** *Structure and Performance in the Roman Economy. Models, Methods and Case Studies*, 2015, 238 p., ISBN: 978-90-429-3280-7 45 €

351. **Courtil J.-C.,** *Sapientia contemptrix doloris : Le corps souffrant dans l'œuvre philosophique de Sénèque*, 2015, 620 p., ISBN: 978-90-429-3281-4 90 €